Modern Perspectives on
B. F. Skinner and
Contemporary Behaviorism

Recent Titles in
Contributions in Psychology

Modern Perspectives on B. F. Skinner and Contemporary Behaviorism

Edited by

James T. Todd
&
Edward K. Morris

Foreword by ERNEST R. HILGARD

Contributions in Psychology
Number 28

GREENWOOD PRESS
Westport, Connecticut • London

Library of Congress Cataloging-in-Publication Data

Modern perspectives on B. F. Skinner and contemporary behaviorism /
edited by James T. Todd and Edward K. Morris.
     p.   cm.—(Contributions in psychology, ISSN 0736–2714 ; no.
28)
   Includes bibliographical references and index.
   ISBN 0–313–29601–4 (alk. paper)
   1. Skinner, B. F. (Burrhus Frederic).   2. Behaviorism
(Psychology)   I. Todd, James T.   II. Morris, Edward K.
III.   Series.
BF109.S55.M63   1995
150.19'434'092—dc20   94–42729

British Library Cataloguing in Publication Data is available.

Library of Congress Catalog Card Number: 94–42729
ISBN: 0–313–29601–4
ISSN: 0736–2714

First published in 1995

Greenwood Press, 88 Post Road West, Westport, CT   06881
An imprint of Greenwood Publishing Group, Inc.

Printed in the United States of America

∞™

The paper used in this book complies with the
Permanent Paper Standard issued by the National
Information Standards Organization (Z39.48—1984).

10 9 8 7 6 5 4 3 2

To the Memory of B. F. Skinner

Contents

Illustrations

FIGURES

Foreword

As everyone familiar with the history of psychology in America must know, in 1913 John B. Watson initiated the influential movement now known as *classical behaviorism* and, in 1938, 25 years later, B. F. Skinner proposed a different version, now often known as *radical behaviorism*. As usual, such turning points are never without some antecedents and, in the meantime, other psychologists with differing viewpoints called themselves behaviorists. But as "movements" within scientific psychology, these two men—Watson and Skinner—initiated points of view affecting the beliefs and conduct of numerous other psychologists enlisted as followers or disciples and had wide influence on nonpsychologists. In recording the history of behaviorism, the authors of the chapters in this book and its companion volume, *Modern Perspectives on John B. Watson and Classical Behaviorism* (Todd & Morris, 1994), have historical justification for selecting these two as the primary foci of their review.

This does not mean, of course, that the other antecedents of behaviorism are to be ignored, for mentions of the Russians, Sechenov (1829–1905), Bekhterev (1857–1927), and Pavlov (1849–1936) are unavoidable—if for nothing else than because of the persistence of their emphases on objectivity and the vocabulary of conditioned reflexes they introduced: *reinforcement, extinction, generalization,* and *discrimination.* In a letter I received from Watson in 1937, he attributed his interest in the conditioned reflexes as the unit of habit to his study of the French edition of Bekhterev's objective psychology, entitled *La Psychologie Objective* (1913), but later gave Pavlov his due.

We owe to Watson the popularization of classical behaviorism that enlisted wide public interest in behaviorism as a "new" psychology to displace the older "introspective" psychology. While many psychologists began, sooner or later, to call themselves behaviorists, it remained for Skinner to enlist the committed support for his novel form of behaviorism as an essentially closed or completed system of method, procedures, equipment, and common vocabulary so that eventually hundreds of psychologists sufficiently identified themselves as Skinnerians to make this the most visible second "movement" within behaviorism. In asserting this, I am agreeing with the editors in their decision to focus primarily on Watson and Skinner.

This does not mean, of course, that others who influenced behaviorism are to be ignored. Some were contemporaries with Watson and others were active when Skinner entered the field. It may be noted that Pavlov recognized that some of his ideas resembled Edward L. Thorndike's experimentation and theorizing. Others influential in American behaviorism included Max F. Meyer (1873–1967) and his student, A. P. Weiss (1879–1931), whose book entitled *A Theoretical Basis of Human Behavior* (1925) was a defense of his variety of behaviorism from a biosocial standpoint. Another variety of behaviorism had been announced by Stevenson Smith and Edwin Guthrie in their *General Psychology in Terms of Behavior* (1921) and was defended later in Guthrie's *The Psychology of Learning* (1935).

Edward Tolman's *Purposive Behavior in Animals and Men* (1932) gave expression to his form of behaviorism which he thought of as non-Watsonian because it was "molar" rather than "molecular." He was more sympathetic toward Skinner's position than to Watson's. Clark L. Hull considered himself to be an arch-behaviorist as he presented his systematic position in a series of articles in the *Psychological Review*, beginning in 1929, and eventually in his book *Principles of Behavior* (1943), with others to follow.

A mention must also be made of J. R. Kantor, whose two large volumes *Principles of Psychology* (1924) presented his variety of behaviorism, later summarized briefly in his "Preface to Interbehavioral Psychology" (1942).

This is enough to indicate the existence of considerable turmoil within the ranks of those who considered themselves behaviorists. At the same time, many psychologists did not go along at all, and the criticisms of behaviorism are ably discussed in the chapters of this book. As is well pointed out, the criticisms of behaviorism were often misleading. For example, Watson's aim was not to narrow the focus of psychology but instead to broaden it—to permit more objective studies in comparative psychology, child psychology, abnormal psychology, and applied psychology—without making unnecessary reference to unobservables.

The influence of behaviorism went far beyond the creation of a body of devoted behaviorists. The term *behavioral sciences* became applied not only to psychology but also to the other social sciences, as shown, for example, in the creation of a division in Behavioral Sciences in the Ford Foundation and the establishing by the Ford Foundation of the Center for Advanced Studies in the Behavioral Sciences on the lands of Stanford University.

Any development as widespread as this, very much alive after more than seventy-five years, deserves a careful reappraisal based on a critical understanding of its history. That is what these two volumes seek to provide and, as such, they should prove to be landmarks as a record of one of the remarkable developments within twentieth-century psychology.

Ernest R. Hilgard

Acknowledgments

Many people have contributed to this book. We are indebted first, of course, to the chapter authors for their fine contributions and for their gracious tolerance of our editorial blue pens. We thank James T. Sabin, George Butler, Mildred Vasan, Maureen Melino, and the staff at Greenwood Press for their patience and assistance as we assembled a collection of manuscripts into a finished book. We are grateful to Shelley Marcotte and the staff at the Department of Human Development and Family Life at the University of Kansas and the staff of the Department of Psychology at Eastern Michigan University for technical support and clerical assistance. Gina E. Truesdell-Todd, Erin K. Ward, Suzanne McKinley, and Zarina-Razia Aftab ably checked hundreds of last-minute details as we prepared the completed manuscript for mailing to the publisher. Last, Noël A. Dryden deserves special thanks for her tireless work reading, typing, proofing, photocopying, and mailing all the manuscripts.

Our efforts were partially supported by funds from the University of Kansas Small Grants fund (#3835), a Public Health Service Predoctoral Training Grant to James Todd (#HD07173-10 0111), and sabbatical facilities provided to Edward K. Morris by the Department of Psychology at Harvard University and the May Institute (Chatham, Mass.). Additional sources of support for individual chapters are described in the notes accompanying each contribution. In no case, however, are any of the departments, agencies, individuals, or entities responsible for the conclusions or interpretations described within.

Individually, James T. Todd is grateful to Edward K. Morris for encouraging and shaping his initial interest in Skinner's radical behaviorism, allowing him to explore far beyond the standard curriculum, and treating him as a professional long before he deserved the honor; to the faculty and students of the Department of Human Development who provided a stimulating atmosphere for all his varied interests; to the members of the Association for Behavior Analysis who, over sixteen consecutive annual meetings, provided a yearly dose of reinforcement for his interest in behaviorism as a scientific, intellectual, professional, and social enterprise; and last, to many friends and colleagues, in the United States and abroad, who contributed in a variety of ways.

Edward K. Morris would like to thank Parker Lichtenstein and Irv Wolf (Denison University) for introducing him to the scientific evolution of psychology; Don Dulany (University of Illinois) who, perhaps inadvertently, sent him seeking important distinctions among behaviorisms; Shep White (Harvard University) who shared with him a delight and an intimacy with the history of psychology and encouraged his seeking the same; the Cherion Society members at the 1990 meetings (Westfield, Mass.) who could not have cared less that he was a "behaviorist," as long as he was a "historian"; and the Department of Human Development at the University of Kansas which encouraged (or allowed) his teaching a variety of courses on "The History, Philosophy, and Systems of Psychology and Behaviorism," as well as the students who bravely enrolled in those courses.

For ourselves, the preparation of this book brought many enjoyable and gratifying opportunities to learn from one another and our contributors and has contributed to our professional relationship and friendships in countless important ways.

Introduction

James T. Todd and Edward K. Morris

The beginning of behaviorism as a distinct viewpoint within psychology is usually traced to the publication of John B. Watson's 1913 "manifesto," "Psychology as the Behaviorist Views It." Here, Watson argued that psychology's status as an "undisputed natural science" was threatened by the narrowness and subjectivity of structuralism on one side and the aimlessness of functionalism on the other. According to Watson, the only solution to the dilemma he described was to redefine psychology as an "objective natural science" with behavior (rather than consciousness) as its primary subject matter.

The beginning of radical or *contemporary* behaviorism, the focus of the present volume, may be traced to the publication in 1938 of B. F. Skinner's *The Behavior of Organisms: An Experimental Analysis. The Behavior of Organisms* and Skinner's philosophy of science were clearly based on the behaviorist tradition established by Watson. The correspondences between Skinner's views and Watson's behaviorism, as expressed in the first paragraph of "Psychology as the Behaviorist Views It," are obvious and fundamental (see Todd, 1994a). Skinner's social views as expressed in *Walden Two* (1948), *Beyond Freedom and Dignity* (1971), and *Enjoy Old Age* (Skinner & Vaughan, 1983) seem to be deliberate extensions of Watson's own progressive pragmatic philosophy, as taken by Watson from his teachers at the University of Chicago: John Dewey, Henry Donaldson, and Jacques Loeb (see Samelson, 1994).

Skinner's intellectual family tree (Figure I.1) depicts the interlocking influences responsible for these correspondences (see also Michael, 1993). Skinner was not simply a modern Watson, however. Watson's manifesto, especially its first paragraph, which accurately describes the fundamental aspects of both Watson and Skinner's philosophies, should be taken as a point of divergence. Skinner went far beyond Watson's mechanistic stimulus–response conception

Figure I.1
Intellectual "Family Tree" of B. F. Skinner

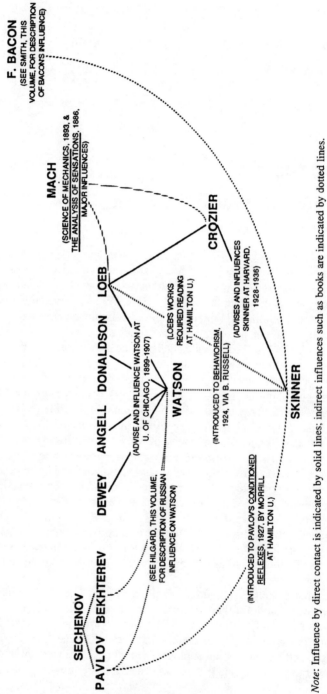

Note: Influence by direct contact is indicated by solid lines; indirect influences such as books are indicated by dotted lines.

of behavior to establish a sophisticated theoretical and experimental approach to the study of behavior that today is a major influence throughout psychology (Norcross & Tomcho, 1994).

Given behaviorism's continued and sometimes unrecognized (see Todd & Morris, 1992) vigor after more than seventy-five years, the serendipitous dual anniversary of its two seminal works was an auspicious occasion for the scholarly consideration of Watson and Skinner's contributions to the development of behaviorism, psychology as a discipline and profession, and twentieth-century culture. Anniversary events at the 1988 meetings of the Association for Behavior Analysis (ABA) and the American Psychological Association (APA) provided the setting for many interesting and provocative analyses of the past and present significance of Watson and Skinner's many and varied contributions. A special issue of the *Journal of the Experimental Analysis of Behavior* (Catania, 1988a) featured a reprint of Ernest Hilgard's 1939 review of *The Behavior of Organisms* (Hilgard, 1939), as well as original analyses of the significance of Skinner's book after fifty years (Catania, 1988a; Dinsmoor, 1988; Donahoe & Palmer, 1988; Galbicka, 1988; Killeen, 1988; McDowell, 1988; Timberlake, 1988). *Contemporary Psychology* marked the anniversary in a similar fashion with a retrospective review of *The Behavior of Organisms* (Thompson, 1988). The dual anniversary was also an inspiration for this volume and its companion, *Modern Perspectives on John B. Watson and Classical Behaviorism* (Todd & Morris, 1994).

The anniversary was not, however, the only inspiration. Behaviorism's continued influence in psychology after more than seventy-five years raises important questions for analysis: What are contemporary behaviorism's philosophical, scientific, and cultural antecedents and how have they contributed to its survival? How did contemporary behaviorism's early proponents, such as Fred Keller, contribute to the "culture" of behavior analysis as well as the science of the experimental analysis of behavior? What aspects of behavior-analytic descriptions have proven difficult for nonbehaviorists to understand? In other words, an important inspiration of this book was our desire to promote the serious consideration of behaviorism's history, philosophy, and place within psychology after three-quarters of a century.

The answers to the questions posed above and others might help promote a more scholarly and productive analysis of behaviorism than has sometimes been the case. It is clear that despite contemporary behaviorism's continued influence throughout psychology, behaviorism per se is not well understood. Much misunderstanding relates directly to behaviorism's historical background and philosophical assumptions. Skinner (1974) has stated; "Behaviorism is not the science of human behavior; it is the philosophy of that science" (p. 3). For many psychologists, however, whose views seem to correspond to textbook accounts (Todd, 1987; Todd & Morris, 1983), contemporary behaviorism is seen as a particular brand of learning theory devoted primarily to the analysis of the effects of reinforcement on the lever pressing and key pecking of rats and pigeons under controlled laboratory conditions. As a result of psychology's reliance on textbook descriptions of the science of *behavior analysis,* some critics have concluded erroneously that behaviorism (the philosophy of behavior analysis) is based on naive conceptual and philosophical assumptions about the behavior of organisms and the conduct of science (e.g., Bethlehem, 1987; Brand, 1989; Koch, 1964; Mahoney, 1989; Robinson, 1994; see also peer commentary on Skinner in Catania & Harnad, 1988), including environmentalism (J. L. Gould, 1982; J. L. Gould & Marler, 1987) and logical positivism (Mackenzie, 1977).

Although the characterizations of contemporary behaviorism cited above are based on profound misconceptions (see Baum, 1994; Blackman, 1991; Chiesa, 1994; Dinsmoor, 1992; Todd & Morris, 1983, 1992, 1993, 1994; Wright, 1987; Zuriff, 1979a), they have become common enough that the actual historical development and current state of behaviorism have become obscured. Behaviorism's founders (e.g., Skinner, 1973, 1974; Watson, 1930) recognized and attempted to correct this problem, as have other scholars and historians who take behaviorism and its development to be subjects worthy of serious consideration (e.g., Boakes, 1984, 1994; Buckley, 1989, 1994; Burnham, 1968, 1994; Chiesa, 1994; Coon, 1994; Harris, 1979; O'Donnell, 1985; Pauly, 1987; Samelson, 1980, 1981, 1994; L. D. Smith, 1986; Todd & Morris, 1994; Zuriff, 1985). During the last ten years especially, the careful and reasoned analyses of scholars within the emerging historicist tradition in psychology have set new standards for discussions of evolution of behaviorism. Superficial scholarship and ad hominem attacks (e.g., Mahoney, 1989) are increasingly seen for what they are (see, e.g., Lattal, 1992), and historians of psychology are demanding greater attention to archivel historical evidence and conceptual rigor (see e.g., Coleman, this volume; Morris et al., this volume). It is within this new tradition that the present volume is set. Its purpose is to commemorate the fiftieth anniversary of the publication of *The Behavior of Organisms* (Skinner, 1938), not with celebratory pieces, but with a modest attempt to expand on the foundation of serious scholarly investigation of classical and contempary behaviorism already under way by historians, behavior analysts, and other scholars (e.g., Bjork, 1993; Boakes, 1984; Buckley, 1989; Catania & Harnad, 1988; Chiesa, 1994; Coleman, 1987; Day, 1980; O'Donnell, 1985; Pauly, 1987; Richelle, 1993; Samelson, 1980, 1981; L. D. Smith, 1986, 1992, 1993; Todd & Morris, 1994; Zuriff, 1985).

This book cannot address all aspects of the conceptual and historical development of radical behaviorism, but it does cover a broad array of substantive issues and important incidents that add depth and detail to its emerging reassessment. It thus includes a mixture of personal views, modern historical analyses, conceptual analyses, and other material. This mixture is offered instead of a set of chapters of homogenous length, style, and perspective because we believe that behaviorism cannot and should not be understood from any single perspective or through one type of analysis. Thus, personal perspectives such as Keller's opening lecture to his introductory learning theory class at Columbia University and Dinsmoor's description of his first encounter with behavior analysis in that same Columbia University program illustrate important aspects of behaviorism's evolution that could not be expressed by accounts of scientific advance couched in terms of theory development or paradigm shifts. That is, an analysis that does not consider the manner in which students of a discipline are educated and by whom is likely to be of limited value in understanding science. Keller and Dinsmoor's contributions (Chapters 1 and 3) offer insights and information about how, through its use in Keller's inspiring graduate classes at Columbia University, Skinner's then-obscure *The Behavior of Organisms* (1938) became a classic while other more successful contemporary competitors such as Hull's *Principles of Behavior* (1943) have largely dropped out of sight. Knapp's descriptive account of the publication history of *The Behavior of Organisms* reinforces the accounts of Keller and Dinsmoor and shows, moreover, how commercial considerations, along with theoretical concerns, can determine what ideas are disseminated. Had Appleton-Century not been willing to risk publishing a book with little or no potential for profit (and reprint it later at the instigation of Edwin Boring and Fred Keller, among others), radical behaviorism might possibly have become an interesting historical sidelight rather than an important philosophy of science.

Because personal and descriptive accounts sometimes do not illustrate important aspects of the theoretical and philosophical development of a scientific discipline, this volume includes several chapters of conceptual and philosophical analyses such as Smith's detailed exploration of the Baconian and Machian roots of Skinner's thinking (Chapter 4), Marr's discussion of parallels between concepts in quantum physics and radical behaviorism (Chapter 8), and Moore's analysis of the role of logical positivism in shaping methodological behaviorism and modern cognitive psychology—but *not* radical behaviorism (Chapter 5). Smith and Moore also show that Skinner's views were not without important intellectual antecedents, as is sometimes alleged (see Knapp, this volume), and that Skinner managed to avoid the philosophical trap of logical positivism which encourages cognitive psychologists to attend primarily to their theories rather than to what their theories are about (see, e.g., Skinner, 1974, 1977b; Watkins, 1990). Indeed, Smith and Moore, reinforced by Marr, show that radical behaviorism's roots are deeply and firmly planted in history of science.

The body of this book consists of two parts: main chapters on Skinner and his work and integrative commentary on those chapters. Within Part I, we have placed the descriptive chapters (e.g., Knapp) ahead of the more analytical contributions (e.g., Marr), and chapters containing background information (e.g., Keller) ahead of chapters that may be better appreciated with additional preparation (e.g., Dinsmoor). Thus, the reader will find that the contributions of Keller, Dinsmoor, and Knapp precede Day and Moore's consideration of the often difficult relationship between radical behaviorism and modern philosophy, as well as Hineline's attribution theory–based account of the language of behavior analysis. Day and Moore point out how behaviorists' and philosophers' different uses of the term behaviorism virtually guarantee that misunderstandings will occur. Similarly, Hineline's contribution demonstrates why listeners to behavior-analytic discourse, with its seemingly odd locutions, often find such discourse difficult to understand. Coleman (Chapter 9) takes this analytic focus further by describing the empirical, conceptual, philosophical, and social functions served by study of the history of behavior analysis. Skinner's contribution, the last in Part I, describes the circumstances of the birth of the experimental analysis of behavior and what happened to selected aspects of it after five decades. The purpose of this organization is to give the book a conceptual flow—from data to theory—when read as a whole. We did not attempt to organize the chapters by topic or to emphasize by formalistic means any one aspect of behaviorism's development over another. Rather, because the development of behaviorism was brought about by the interaction of numerous factors, the book takes an inductive approach and allows the reader to discover general themes and important details of the development of behaviorism as they appear and recur with variations in different chapters.

Because behaviorism should not be understood from one single perspective, or even the ten offered in Part I, we have included commentaries by respected scholars on the relevance of the material in the first ten chapters to the understanding of the development and current historical status of contemporary behaviorism. These commentaries should not be viewed as critiques, however. Rather, their purpose is to illuminate common themes among the chapters and discuss specific issues not directly addressed by their authors. Thus, Lee (Chapter 11) expands on terminological issues implicit in the contributions of Day, Moore, and Hineline. Even the word "behavior," she argues, obscures the real subject matter of behavior analysis—"causal relations between a change at an operandum and a change mediated by an operandum." Zuriff leads the reader somewhat away from the descriptive and conceptual focus of Part I to discuss the influence of methodological developments on conceptual advancement in basic research and clinical application. For instance, the use of the lever press as a functional representative of responding helped behavior analysts resolve the problematic issue of defining behavior on formal grounds—the lever had defined behavior for them. Rachlin (Chapter 13), concerned about the difficulties inherent in Skinner's private event concept as discussed by Day and Moore, offers "teleological behaviorism" as an alternative to "Skinnerian behaviorism." Skinnerian behaviorism, Rachlin claims, has erred by rejecting mental terms. Teleological behaviorism, in contrast, is conceptually superior because it accepts mental terms not as internal mediators but as references to the overt behavior of organisms. Last, Catania's analysis of historical parallels between Darwin's and Skinner's selectionist perspectives (Chapter 14) reveals some fundamental reasons behind the resistance to behavior analysis among psychologists and the public. As a causal mode, selection continues to be misunderstood (Catania, 1987; Skinner, 1981b). Its application to behavior in the form of operant conditioning has been difficult for some traditional psychologists to accept—seemingly because selection as a causal mode is incompatible with the view of the person as an automomous intiating agent (Skinner, 1981b). Skinner (1990) himself described how many psychologists' arguments against behavior analysis mirror arguments against Darwin's views.

In order to facilitate further investigation of Skinner and radical behaviorism, the book concludes with a detailed account of the state of the art in the historiography of behaviorism and includes an appendix consisting of a comprehensive bibliography of Skinner's published works. Chapter 15 amplifies and extends some of the themes raised in Coleman's contribution and suggests numerous directions for further investigation based on the contents of Chapters 1 to 10 and commentaries on those chapters. The bibliography, created by means of an exhaustive search of journals, books, magazines, data bases, archives, and other sources, is the most complete and authoritative available. Its contents reinforce the contributors' view of contemporary behaviorism as an important philosophy of science which attempts to encompass the full range of human and nonhuman behavior. The bibliography also demonstrates how, over a span of six decades, Skinner worked tirelessly and sometimes almost single-handedly to promote the experimental analysis of behavior and the philosophy of radical behaviorism. Skinner wrote on seemingly every aspect of the behavior of organisms and about the implications of a complete understanding of behavior for the continued evolution and improvement of human culture. Moreover, as an examination of the bibliography will show, Skinner may have borrowed a tactic from Watson and did not confine his output to scientific and academic forums (see Burnham, 1994). Rather, by writing for an educated popular audience, Skinner introduced his views to a much broader academic audience than he could have if he had confined his output to psychology journals.

We should note that this volume was not intended to be a forum for sweeping "reappraisals" of behaviorism or a platform for its critics. Even so, the generally positive tone of the chapters does not arise from a universal acceptance of behaviorism by their authors but from a respect for behaviorism as a subject of serious scholarly investigation. Radical behaviorism has certainly not always produced perfect science. But the purpose of this book is not so much to evaluate behaviorism as to help clarify Skinner's behaviorism so that future critical analyses and reappraisals might be based on a deeper and broader understanding than is now often the case. Our intended audience includes, therefore, students, historians, researchers, and, especially, critics of behaviorism. We suggest then that this book may serve as a textbook, professional reference, and a guide to further study. We do not intend that the audience be limited only to those who work at the intersection of the fields just described. It may be read by any person with an interest in behaviorism, the history of psychology, or history in general. We will add again, however, that this book is not a comprehensive account of the development and implications of behaviorism. And despite the wide variety of viewpoints and topics covered, many questions will remain unanswered. Our goal was not to provide any final judgment about behaviorism but to stimulate interest. Sincere critics of behaviorism will welcome the opportunity to gain further insights.

Part I

Perspectives on B. F. Skinner and Contemporary Behaviorism

Chapter 1 _____

Psychology 161

Fred S. Keller

Good Morning! This is Psychology 161, listed in the catalog as *Basic Concepts in Modern Psychology*. Actually, the course is an introduction to *reinforcement theory*.

1. It should not be attended by persons who have passed through their undergraduate training at Columbia University or who have had a comparable course elsewhere.

2. It is to be pitched at a level which your instructor thinks suitable for M.A. candidates, and your instructor is fully aware of the difficulties involved in meeting such a requirement. He means that he will ask you to do reading that he could probably not get an undergraduate to do; to listen to talk that sometimes requires a captive audience; to answer questions on examinations that demand a more analytical attack than can be asked of most undergraduates.

3. The brand of reinforcement theory dealt with here will be of the sort initiated in 1938 and earlier by B. F. Skinner and which is now taught at various universities in this country and abroad. The other, and not unrelated, brand is that associated with the name of Clark L. Hull and his pupils at Yale University. Our emphasis will be "Skinnerian."

4. The *theory* involved, as you may or may not know, refers to the systematic organization of experimental fact that was first suggested by Skinner in *The Behavior of Organisms* (1938), and which has now been extended in many directions and with some modification. It will *not* deal to any marked degree with the "testing" or "proving" of statements, experimentally grounded or otherwise. Nor will it be concerned with "explanations" of behavior in terms of either physiological or psychic events. Stress will be on the *organization* of laboratory findings, in the interests of *clarity, economy,* and *usefulness*—but I'd have a hard time in trying to define the last three terms.

5. *Basic concepts* refers to the basic concepts of reinforcement theory, suggested by such terms as *conditioning, extinction, discrimination,* and, especially, *reinforcement.* Although the course title says "basic concepts in modern psychology," the narrowness here may not be so great as you now feel.

Reinforcement theory is sometimes called "behavior theory," "learning theory," and "operational behaviorism," among other things. It has come to deal with a great deal more than a few experiments on dogs in a frame or rats in a box. The concepts with which we shall deal will be basic to *all psychology*—at least in our opinion.

This introduction to reinforcement theory will be approached quite conventionally through *readings* in selected sources (books and papers), *lectures* by your instructor on key experiments and issues in the development of this system, and *discussion* whenever it is generated.

Readings: The principal book that we shall deal with in this course is *The Behavior of Organisms* by Professor Skinner, published in 1938 by the Appleton-Century Company. There are other, related books, however, that deserve mention here.

Principles of Psychology, by Keller and Schoenfeld (1950), is an elementary text based primarily on *The Behavior of Organisms*. It is a sort of "Skinner for the Beginner," not a primary source.

Science and Human Behavior, by Skinner (1953)—presumably an introductory text, with much extrapolation of laboratory science, full of interesting and provocative ideas, and better appreciated *after* this course.

Principles of Behavior, by Clark L. Hull (1943), also a book on reinforcement theory but with a different orientation, a different experimental model, and a different conception of *theory*. The two positions are different but have quite a bit in common. I'm not interested in furthering a war between Hull and Skinner. I'll do well to give you a positive account of *one* position; let someone else give you the other view.

Theories of Learning, by Ernest R. Hilgard (1948). Hilgard tries to cover nine or ten "learning theories," an impossible task, with an outcome that satisfies the members of no single camp. Some catch phrases, some abbreviated experimental reports, some forced comparisons—these are almost certainly the outcome of such attempts. Since most of the views are practically defunct, the net gain can't be very great.

Modern Learning Theory, by Estes, Koch, MacCorquodale, Meehl, Mueller, Shoenfeld, and Verplanck (1954). This book is a heroic summertime assault at Dartmouth University upon the Hilgard territory. Different viewpoints were assigned to different men for examination in accord with an agreed-upon manner of attack. The dead systems become deader, if possible, but with impressive funerals; and the breath of life, where it still existed, was not captured by these sturdy reviewers. An interesting historical document.

Verbal Behavior, also by Skinner (1957). An interpretation of what most people would call *language*, which cannot be fully understood without a prior understanding of *The Behaviors of Organisms*.

Schedules of Reinforcement, by C. B. Ferster and Skinner (1957), also published last year. An impressive advance within a new sphere of psychology—*behavior maintenance*. We may sample this book later on.

Something about *The Behavior of Organisms,* the *B of O* (By F. S. K., with whom you may not agree when you read it).

1. It is a *must* for anyone who would understand reinforcement theory today, and it is still a source of ideas for the would-be researcher.

2. It is one of the two important books for psychologists in our times. The other is Pavlov's *Conditioned Reflexes* (1927). It is also an *individual* achievement of the highest magnitude; Pavlov was aided by his pupils.

3. Published in 1938, in the Century Psychology Series, it was a feather in the cap of R. M. Elliott, the editor of the series. Elliott was then Chairman at Minnesota, where Skinner got his first teaching job.

4. It embodies researches, almost all of them Skinner's, from 1930 on at Harvard and at Minnesota. Of the eighty-three references noted, twenty-three are to Skinner's own studies—as a graduate student, as a member of the Society of Fellows at Harvard, and as a staff member at Minnesota.

5. In the index are seventy-one names. About half of them are psychologists, an unusually small percentage in a book that presumably deals with psychological theory. The four most-referred-to names are Pavlov (44 references), Sherrington (14), Hull (9), and Magnus (8). Skinner clearly owes most to the physiologists Pavlov and Sherrington. But there are others, perhaps unmentioned but important: Ernst Mach, Percy Bridgman, Francis Bacon, Henri Poincaré, John B. Watson, and Walter S. Hunter. Others seem to have been indirectly important: Auguste Comte, John Dewey, Edwin G. Boring, Wolfgang Köhler, and E. C. Tolman—perhaps some others.

When the *B of O* arrived in 1938, it was *not* selected by the Book-of-the-Month Club. Many found it difficult to read and gave up before finishing the first chapter. Some of you may have this experience. A hard-to-read writer becomes aversive—we avoid him or we damn him; we give up trying to understand him.

Others found the book a kind of sport or freak—a mutation in psychology, without obvious antecedents, possessing no continuity with the psychological past. Others saw only Sherrington's differences between reflex arc and nerve–trunk conduction, Pavlov's conditioning and extinction, and Thorndike's puzzle box, all mixed up with "a lot of high-sounding jargon."

Some saw no reference whatever to their own "highly relevant" research or theoretical publications; the man was obviously not "up with the literature." Some bogged down when they found the *reflex* treated as a *correlation*; others groaned about the acceptance of *volition* and *spontaneity* under the "thinly disguised rubric of 'operant' behavior."

A few people found the book worth reading. One of these was E. C. Tolman, who said that Skinner's place in history was assured with the publication of the book.

Your instructor was polled in 1948 with respect to the wisdom of reprinting the book. Everything was against it except the fact that as many copies were sold in 1948 as in the nine preceding years. I was polled because most of the sales were at Columbia.

On Monday we shall examine the book's first chapter—the most frightening one—in some detail.

That's all for today. The suggested reading is on the blackboard. Are there any questions?

AUTHOR'S NOTE

This chapter is a transcript of my lecture notes for the first class meeting of Psychology 161 at Columbia University in the fall of 1958. These notes were read at the symposium on *The Behavior of Organisms at Fifty* on Monday, May 30, at the 14th Annual Convention of the Association for Behavior Analysis at the Wyndham Franklin Plaza in Philadelphia, PA.

Chapter 2

A Natural History of *The Behavior of Organisms*

Terry J. Knapp

"As time goes on I may be glad I wrote it."

—B. F. Skinner

In May of 1938, an advertisement for two books offered by the Appleton-Century Company of New York appeared in *Psychological Abstracts*. One of the advertisements read: "This book presents a formulatio or system of behavior. By drawing generously upon the author's own experiments, it shows that when behavior is approached experimentally in ways suggested by the system, lawful and reproducable processes emerge which may be described quantitatively." The advertisement suggested that "an important new method of determining changes in the strength of behavior" had been found. "This is a significant work," it reported, "probably the most extensive contribution yet made to the problem of describing the behavior of individual organisms. Although it makes no application to human behavior, many implications suggest themselves."

More than fifty years have now passed, and it is true: Many implications have suggested themselves. *The Behavior of Organisms: An Experimental Analysis* by B. F. Skinner has become a significant volume in the history of twentieth-century psychology and, by the reckoning of some persons, the most significant work to emerge when pre– and post–World War II psychologies are compared. The existence of related works, journals, a division of the APA, other organizations, and university- based training programs is one kind of supporting evidence for such a claim. That historians of psychology have ranked "Skinner's contributions" as the second-most-influential development in the field since World War II (the "general growth of the field" was ranked first, and the "growth of cognitive theory" was tied with "Skinner's contributions") is another kind of evidence (Gilgen, 1982). Introductory psychology textbooks form a third category of evidence. When they are examined, Skinner is the second-most-cited authority, and *The Behavior of Organisms* is his second-most-often-cited work (Knapp, 1985). *Beyond Freedom and Dignity* (Skinner, 1971) is his first. Few participants in the experimental and applied analysis of behavior require evidence of these kinds, for *The Behavior of Organisms*—and the works by Skinner that followed—have been significant influences in the personal and professional lives of many of them.

The purpose of this chapter is not to provide a retrospective review of *The Behavior of Organisms,* or even a contemporary appreciation, but rather to describe its publishing history, the various printings it has undergone, the sales record for a portion of its life, and something of what has been said about it over the years since 1938. I refer to this chapter as a "natural history" because the emphasis is on the various morphological forms the book has taken. In other circles, my purpose might be termed a *descriptive bibliography.*

THE CENTURY PSYCHOLOGY SERIES

The Behavior of Organisms was a volume in the Century Psychology Series (possibly the twentieth), a series begun by the Century Company in 1924, continued in 1933 when Century was acquired by D. Appleton, and enlarged when Crofts was added to Appleton-Century in 1948 to form the familiar Appleton-Century-Crofts (1950).

Richard Elliott, the first editor of the series, has described its beginning in an unpublished manuscript. He wrote, "In the Spring of 1924 Dana H. Ferrin, then head of the College Department of the Century Company . . . went to E. G. Boring to seek his aid in finding an editor for a projected new series of textbooks in the combined fields of psychology and philosophy. Boring thought the time for such a combined venture had passed, but told Ferrin if he persisted in this plan he might try his chances of interesting me in the project." After six months of discussion, during which Elliott persuaded Ferrin to drop the idea of a combined series, (later there was a separated series in philosophy and another in the social sciences), the plans were laid for the Century Series in Psychology, with Elliott to serve as editor and with the understanding that the series was to include "some books which by themselves would not & should not be expected to pay their way" (Elliott, undated).[1] This proviso was to prove an important one for *The Behavior of Organisms* and other memorable books in the series.

A volume on learning by Karl Lashley was planned as the first issue. It was scheduled to be completed by New Year's Day 1926 but was never written. Another three years would pass before the first of the Century Psychology Series arrived in stores. Skinner had witnessed E. G. Boring building a shipping box for the manuscript of this initial volume in the shop of the Harvard

Psychology Department in the spring of 1929 (Skinner, 1979, p. 7). *A History of Experimental Psychology* (Boring 1929, 1950b) proved to be one of the most successful books in the Century Psychology Series. By the time the second edition appeared in 1950, it had sold more than ten thousand copies and is today one of the few early volumes in the series that remains in print.

Other significant volumes followed: Tolman's *Purposive Behavior in Animals and Men* in 1932, Hull's *Suggestion and Hypnosis* in 1933, Edna Heidbreder's *Seven Psychologies* (originally to be titled *Systems in Psychology*) in 1933, Fred S. Keller's *The Definition of Psychology* in 1937, and lesser-known but equally skillful works such as Henry E. Garrett's *Great Experiments in Psychology* in 1930, and Albert R. Chandler's *Beauty and Human Nature* in 1934. Other important works were to come in the 1950s and 1960s. The rise of contemporary cognitive psychology (Knapp, 1986b) is often traced to the volume in the Century Series, *Cognitive Psychology*, authored by Ulric Neisser (1967). Skinner, himself, has had seven books in the series in addition to *The Behavior of Organisms*.[2]

When Appleton-Century-Crofts was acquired by Prentice-Hall, the series was continued, although some volumes were allowed to go out of print, others were reprinted, and in the case of a few works (such as *Schedules of Reinforcement*, [Ferster & Skinner, 1957]), rights were transferred to other reprinting firms. The series continues today, and Skinner's last contribution to it was *Upon Further Reflection* (1987b).

THE FIRST PRINTING OF *THE BEHAVIOR OF ORGANISMS*

Professor Skinner has told his own story of *The Behavior of Organisms* in the second volume of his autobiography (1979). The title was descriptive of the subject matter ("the behavior of organisms") and of the method to be employed in studying it ("an experimental analysis").

Skinner began planning *The Behavior of Organisms* near the end of 1934, describing it in a letter to Fred Keller as simply the "experimental book" (Skinner, 1979, p. 177). He had drawn up a list of "resolutions" to follow in its composition (see Skinner, 1979, pp. 361–362), and had written the book over a number of years (Skinner, 1979, pp. 201–207), incorporating most of the experimental studies he had conducted while a member of the Harvard Society of Fellows (Coleman, 1984).

Skinner arrived at the University of Minnesota in Minneapolis during the fall term of 1936 after being recruited by Richard M. Elliott, the Chair of the Department and editor of the Century Series in Psychology.

Elliott played a significant role in obtaining Skinner's manuscript for the series and in seeking a subsidy to assist with its publication from the Harvard Society of Fellows. On December 11, 1937, Elliott wrote to L. J. Henderson, Head of the Harvard Society of Fellows. The letter was extremely supportive and, in one respect, prophetic:

Skinner is writing you a letter of appeal which is self-explanatory. He has showed it to me and I feel that it lacks, quite naturally, the most important point of all, namely, reference to the extreme value of his book. What he has worked out, and supported with extremely ingenious experimentation, is to my mind the most sustained analysis of an organism's behavior which has ever appeared. Believing this, in my capacity as editor of the Appleton-Century, I have persuaded them to take over its publication, unquestionably at a very sizable loss. . . . I am familiar with the views of Hull, Tolman, Thorndike and other psychologists, all of whom share my hope that a way can be found to bring out this brilliant study without mutilation. If you can help Skinner now, as you have in the past, it will be a boost for the career of a young man whose contribution to psychology promises to be unsurpassed by any of his generation.

Skinner had agreed to forgo the royalties on the first 1,000 copies (Skinner, 1979, p. 214), as had other Century Series authors, and the Society of Fellows provided a subsidy of $500, most of which apparently went toward the cost of figures.

By late July 1938, "Skinner's book [was] getting into shape as far as its manufacture is concerned" (Ferrin to Elliott, July 22, 1938). The book had been announced for publication in June 1938 (see Figure 2.1), and finally appeared in the Century Psychology Series on September 2, 1938, in time for the fall term at most universities. The book was dedicated to Skinner's wife, Yvonne Blue. Skinner sent inscribed copies to his mother and father, Bugsy Morrill,

Figure 2.1
Original and Revised Advertisements for Skinner's *The Behavior of Organisms* (1938) that Appeared in *Psychological Abstracts* (May and October 1938, Respectively)

THE BEHAVIOR OF ORGANISMS
AN EXPERIMENTAL ANALYSIS

BY B. F. SKINNER, Ph.D., Assistant Professor of Psychology, University of Minnesota. This book presents a formulation or system of behavior. By drawing generously upon the author's own experiments, it shows that when behavior is approached experimentally in ways suggested by the system, lawful and reproducible processes emerge which may be described quantitatively. An important new method of determining changes in the strength of behavior is described. This is a significant work, probably the most extensive contribution yet made to the problem of describing the behavior of individual organisms. Although it makes no application to human behavior, many implications suggest themselves. *To be published in June.*

THE BEHAVIOR OF ORGANISMS;
AN EXPERIMENTAL ANALYSIS

BY B. F. SKINNER, Ph.D., Assistant Professor of Psychology, University of Minnesota. This book presents the most successful quantitative description of the behavior of the individual organism so far achieved, not excepting the work of Pavlov. In it a new and highly productive method of investigating behavior is developed, which makes possible the identification and treatment, experimentally, of a considerable number of fundamental behavior variables. A long series of original experiments is reported, with the aid of 148 figures. No application to human behavior is attempted in the book, but the far-reaching implications of the analysis are obvious throughout the work. $5.00

who had been his biology professor at Hamiliton College, L. J. Henderson of the Harvard Society of Fellows, and John Tate, the Dean at the University of Minnesota. (Some of the inscriptions may be found in Skinner, 1979, pp. 219-220.) The Tate presentation copy, and perhaps others, has survived. The volume was recently sold through a dealer for $600.

The advertisement for *The Behavior of Organisms* that had appeared during the late spring prior to its publication was not to the satisfaction of Skinner or Elliott. Elliott wrote to Ferrin that both he and Skinner "were not very much impressed with the ad." It had failed to "concentrate enough on the really unique character" of the book; it was a "general smear of praise" (Elliott to Ferrin, May 27, 1938). Elliott enclosed a revised copy and indicated he was largely responsible for its content. Both the original advertisement, which had appeared in the May 1938 issue of *Psychological Abstracts*, and the revision, which was in the October issue, are reproduced in Figure 2.1.

The revised copy emphasized that the method employed was a new one, that it had already proved successful in yielding a "quantitative description of the behavior of the individual organism" (bettering Pavlov in this regard) and that it was supported by more than one hundred figures.

The first edition of *The Behavior of Organisms* was bound in black cloth. The spine bore in gilded print the complete title in uppercase; the author's last name; the logo; "The Century Psychology Series"; and the name of the publisher, Appleton-Century. The front cover bore in the upper one-third in relief and in uppercase "THE CENTURY PSYCHOLOGY SERIES," followed by the complete title of the book and name of its author. Appleton-Century employed a variety of means to identify the printings and editions of their works (Zempel & Verkler, 1984). A first edition, first printing of *The Behavior of Organisms* is distinguished by its black cloth cover, a number on the back of the face page, "378," indicating that the book was processed in July 1938; and, it is generally believed, the Roman numeral "I" inside parentheses on the final page of the index below and to the right of the last entry. Skinner has indicated that "eight hundred copies were printed, but not all of them were bound" in 1938 (Skinner, 1979, p. 219).

The signature page identified the author as "Assistant Professor of Psychology" at the University of Minnesota. This page is reproduced in Figure 2.2, and is unique to the black cloth first edition.

The Behavior of Organisms was abstracted in the *Psychological Abstracts* in late 1938 and in the *Biological Abstracts* in January 1939. The original abstracts are reproduced in Figures 2.3 and 2.4.

THE SALES RECORD

Figure 2.5 displays the number of copies of *The Behavior of Organisms* sold from September 1938 until December 1962. For comparative purposes a plot of the sales record of Clark Hull's *Principles of Behavior: An Introduction*

Figure 2.2
Signature Page of the First Edition of *The Behavior of Organisms* **(1938)**

The Century Psychology Series
RICHARD M. ELLIOTT, *Editor*

THE BEHAVIOR OF
ORGANISMS

An Experimental Analysis

BY

B. F. SKINNER

ASSISTANT PROFESSOR OF PSYCHOLOGY
UNIVERSITY OF MINNESOTA

D. APPLETON-CENTURY COMPANY
INCORPORATED

NEW YORK   LONDON

Figure 2.3
Abstract of *The Behavior of Organisms* **(1938) that Appeared in** *Psyshological Abstracts* **(1938)**

56. **Skinner, B. F. The behavior of organisms: an experimental analysis.** New York: Appleton-Century, 1938. Pp. 457. $5.00.—Skinner outlines a science of behavior which generates its own laws through an analysis of its own data rather than securing them by reference to a conceptual neural process. "It is toward the reduction of seemingly diverse processes to simple laws that a science of behavior naturally directs itself. At the present time I know of no simplification of behavior that can be claimed for a neurological fact. Increasingly greater simplicity is being achieved, but through a systematic treatment of behavior at its own level." The results of behavior studies set problems for neurology, and in some cases constitute the sole factual basis for neurological constructs. The system developed in the present book is objective and descriptive. Behavior is regarded as either respondent or operant. Respondent behavior is elicited by observable stimuli, and classical conditioning has utilized this type of response. In the case of operant behavior no correlated stimulus can be detected when the behavior occurs. The factual part of the book deals largely with this behavior as studied by the author in extensive researches on the feeding responses of rats. The conditioning of such responses is compared with the stimulus conditioning of Pavlov. Particular emphasis is placed on the concept of "reflex reserve," a process which is built up during conditioning and exhausted during extinction, and on the concept of reflex strength. The chapter headings are as follows: a system of behavior; scope and method; conditioning and extinction; discrimination of a stimulus; some functions of stimuli; temporal discrimination of the stimulus; the differentiation of a response; drive; drive and conditioning; other variables affecting reflex strength; behavior and the nervous system; and conclusion.— *W. S. Hunter* (Brown).

to Behavior Theory has been included. Hull's *Principles* appeared in the Century Psychology Series in the spring of 1943. Both plots are based upon the semiannual royalty records retained in the Richard M. Elliott Archives at the Walter Library of the University of Minnesota.

Several conclusions seem safe based upon an inspection of the sales records. *Principles of Behavior* outsold *The Behavior of Organisms* in each year in which comparison is possible (i.e., from 1943). The general patterning of sales, however, is remarkably related. Both works showed a substantial increase in sales following World War II, though *The Behavior of Organisms* had a larger percentage of increase. No copies of *The Behavior of Organisms* were sold during the latter half of 1946, while 208 copies were

Figure 2.4

Abstract of *The Behavior of Organisms* **(1938) that Appeared in** *Biological Abstracts* **(January 1939)**

16112. **SKINNER, B. F. The behavior of organisms. An experimental analysis.** ix + 457p. D. Appleton-Century Co.; New York, 1938. Pr. $5.—The author sets out to build a systematic description of behavior in the individual organism, based upon an integrated report of his conditioning experiments with the rat as subject. The system is outlined in an introductory chapter, and is developed in further chapters. Throughout, conditioning of type S (Pavlovian conditioning) is compared analytically with the type R conditioning (the "operant" type) in which the environment-altering character of the response is emphasized. The act of pressing a lever, controlling delivery of a food-pellet, was the operant studied analytically in terms of its dynamic properties. The rate of this response was its critical measure. Drive and conditioning are the 2 chief factors affecting "reflex strength," and thus indirectly affecting "reflex reserve." The body of the book includes chapters upon "Conditioning and Extinction;" "Periodic Reconditioning;" "The Discrimination of a Stimulus;" "Some Functions of Stimuli;" "Temporal Discrimination of the Stimulus;" "The Differentiation of a Response;" "Drive;" "Drive "Other Variables (e.g., emotion, drugs) Affecting Reflex Strength." Since the author regards an item of behavioral evidence as "a scientific datum in its own right," the report of evidence is essentially qualitative, and a chapter upon "Behavior and the Nervous System" is placed near the end of the book. In a final chapter the system is compared with certain other contemporary systems; is found very preferable to Hull's system, and most like Tolman's system. (Bibliography of 83 titles.)—*T. C. Schneirla.*

sold in the spring of 1947, and 359 for the entire year. The sudden increase is probably explained by the program in the experimental analysis of behavior developed at Columbia University by Fred S. Keller and William N. Schoenfeld. The program was committed to reinforcement theory, and the founders explained, "We think that reinforcement theory has been given its most useful and comprehensive exposition by B. F. Skinner in his major work, *The Behavior of Organisms*" (Keller & Schoenfeld, 1949, p. 166).

The peak of sales occurred in 1947 for *The Behavior of Organisms* and two years later for *Principles of Behavior.* Both volumes underwent substantial declines in sales during the early 1950s. By then, Skinner had abandoned some concepts contained in *The Behavior of Organisms*, namely, the reflex reserve. Moreover, a fresh secondary account had become available in the form of Keller and Schoenfeld's *Principles of Psychology: A Systematic Text in the Science of Psychology* which had appeared in the Century Series in 1950. *The Behavior of Organisms* underwent a resurgence of sales from 1960

Figure 2.5
Comparative Sales of Skinner's *The Behavior of Organisms* (1938) and Hull's *Principles of Behavior* (1943)

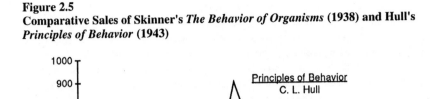

to 1962. The increase may be related to the program in operant psychology which was at that time in the process of development at Arizona State University. *Principles of Behavior* was soon overshadowed by Hull's other books, though it underwent a slight revival in the mid- to late 1950s.

THE REPRINTINGS

The issue of reprinting *The Behavior of Organisms* arose in October 1947 when Dana Ferrin wrote to inform Skinner that the stock was nearly depleted. By Boring's account, Skinner solicited his aid in getting the book reprinted. Boring initiated a series of exchanges with Ferrin beginning on April 1, 1948. He indicated that Skinner was "very much exercised about the exhaustion" of the book and had sought Boring's influence in obtaining a reprinting. Boring noted that "all I can do is tell you how locally useful it would be and that Fred is getting an increasing following and that his appointment at Harvard [Skinner had accepted a Professorship there in 1948] will increase it still further." Ferrin replied that "the book manufacturing situation is most difficult . . .Printing and binding costs have more than doubled in the past four or five years, making it impossible for us to run reprints of five hundred or a thousand copies without substantial financial loss." However, he admitted that 300 copies of *The Behavior of Organisms* had been sold in the last year alone, and that "it is conceivable, if not probable, that we will run another printing, making plates by photographic process" (Ferrin to Boring, April 5, 1948). A few days later Boring was writing to Ferrin again, after conferring with Skinner. He quoted extensively from a letter Skinner had written him, outlining the case for reprinting 1,000 copies. Boring added, "He [Skinner] has got disciples at Columbia and at Indiana. As the Skinner-box people increase in number, the use for *The B of O* ought to increase" (Boring to Ferrin, April 12, 1948).

The outcome of these exchanges is reported by Skinner in the second volume of his autobiography. "In their revolutionary changes at Columbia, Fred Keller and Nat Schoenfeld began to use *The Behavior of Organisms*, and the resulting sales came just in time. . . . The 'adoption' at Columbia saved the day. Another modest batch of copies was printed" (Skinner, 1979, p. 315–319).

The reprinting occurred in 1948, after Appleton-Century had acquired Crofts. *The Behavior of Organisms* was issued in a light-green cloth volume, a color E. G. Boring had described as "vomit green" (Boring to Ferrin, April 1, 1948) when it was employed during war years for his *A History of Experimental Psychology*. These volumes resembled the black first printing in most respects, except for color of cloth, the addition of "Crofts" to the spine, and a signature page that was now inscribed with both the Appleton-Century-Crofts new logo, in place of the former Appleton-Century logo, and the name "Appleton-Century-Crofts, Inc.," which only listed New York as the address of the publisher. Skinner is still identified as an Assistant Professor at Minnesota. This is the signature page that appeared in all subsequent printings until the paperback edition of 1966. The copyright page bore the name of the original publisher (D. Appleton-Century Company, Inc.), but in the copies I have seen there is no Roman numeral "I" on the last page of the index. Also, the paper is of inferior quality to the first printing. These green bindings may have been issued for only a brief time in the late 1940s or perhaps until the early 1950s.

Sales records indicate that the original 800 copies printed in 1938 would have expired sometime during 1947 and that the number of green bound volumes issued may have been very few, making it possibly as scarce as the original black first printing. Dana Ferrin explained to E. G. Boring in the spring of 1948 that "for the past three or four years it has been pretty much a case of catch as catch can. In other words," he said, "publishers have had little choice and have been obliged to use whatever cloth they can get hold of. As a result, it has been impossible for us to maintain any series of color scheme, and some of the books we have bound in this period have frankly been hideous in appearance" (Ferrin to Boring, April 5, 1948). Ferrin went on to explain that Appleton-Century-Crofts was now issuing the new volumes in the series (*Theories of Learning* by Ernest Hilgard [1948], had just appeared) in a "light tan with fairly dark panels on the backbone."

Sometime in the late 1940s or early 1950s, *The Behavior of Organisms* was issued in the new tan and burgundy color scheme. With this issue, the subtitle, "An Experimental Analysis," was deleted from the spine and front cover. The signature page remained unchanged. The printings of *The Behavior of Organisms* remained in this form (the fifth printing appeared in December 1963), with slight variations in color shading until 1966 when a paperback edition was issued.

The Paperback Printing

The paperback printing was the seventh for *The Behavior of Organisms*; with it, the copyright was renewed and a six-page preface added. There were other changes as well. The cover became a reddish brown with a black spine that spilled over one-fifth of the cover. The main title was printed vertically in white on the spine, with "Skinner," printed at the very top and "Appleton-Century-Crofts" at the bottom in the same color as the cover. The cover featured the main title at the lower right side in white, and "B. F. Skinner" under it in black. The words "Century Psychology Series" appeared across the middle of the cover on the reddish brown background, and a part of the Appleton-Century-Crofts logo appeared opposite it in the black trim portion of the cover.

Inside there were more changes. On the title page, Skinner's affiliation was changed to Harvard University, as it had been since the late 1940s, and his former title at the University of Minnesota, "Assistant Professor," was dropped and no rank indicated. This is the only printing of *The Behavior of Organisms* to indicate that Skinner was affiliated with Harvard University. A new Appleton-Century-Crofts logo replaced the old one, and the firm was identified as a division of the Meredith Publishing Company.

The Preface (Skinner, 1966b) was inserted following the original acknowledgment page and numbered in Roman numerals beginning with ix and titled simply, "Preface to the seventh printing." The Table of Contents page followed the Preface, and a new page was inserted after the Table of Contents, which bore the main title centered and in capital letters. This had appeared as the first page in all previous printings. In the earlier printings, the page following the Table of Contents bore the full title in uppercase on one line and the subtitle below it, both between heavy black rules on the upper one-third of the page. In the paperback printing, this page was moved to the first-page location.

The Preface is dated June 1966, and the Appleton-Century-Crofts date on the copyright page indicated May 1966, that is the number 656, which is followed by a dash and another 6. This would normally indicate that the book is receiving its sixth printing. With the fifth printing having appeared in December 1963, it does not seem likely that two additional printings would have been required by 1966. Thus, there is some uncertainty about the accuracy of the paperback printing as the seventh.

Hull's *Principles of Behavior* was also issued in paperback at the same time. It also was identified as the seventh printing. Hull had died in 1952, and it was left to Kenneth Spence (1966) to write the foreword to *Principles*. Though writing independently, both Skinner and Spence began their introductions with a comparative analysis of *The Behavior of Organisms*, the *Principles of Behavior*, and a third classic in the Century Series, Edward C. Tolman's *Purposive Behavior in Animals and Men.*

The Last A-C-C Printing

The final A-C-C (Appleton-Century-Crofts) printing of *The Behavior of Organisms* was issued in 1981, when Prentice-Hall acquired Appleton-Century-Crofts and reissued some of the works in the Century Psychology Series. This volume bore a black cover. A bright burgundy was used on the spine, against which was printed in gold the title, author's last name, "Century Psychology Series," and the new publisher's name. The signature page is a reprint of the one employed since the late 1940s (Skinner is once again identified as an Assistant Professor), with the exceptions of the deletion of "Richard M. Elliott, Editor" under "The Century Psychology Series," and the replacement of Appleton-Century-Crofts with Prentice-Hall, Inc. The A-C-C logo was retained, however. The Preface written by Skinner for the paperback edition was included. (In some number of copies, mine among them, an apparent binding error allowed only the first page of the Preface to be included. Moreover, in other copies the Preface was deleted altogether. I have not been able to discover how these errors came about nor how many copies contain them.) In 1991, the B. F. Skinner Foundation began issuing copies of those works by Skinner that had gone out of print, with *The Behavior of Organisms* as the first volume to appear.

EARLY REACTION TO *THE BEHAVIOR OF ORGANISMS*

The numerous published works by B. F. Skinner have yielded well over 1,000 published responses of one sort or another (Knapp, in press), and it may be said the *The Behavior of Organisms* in large measure led to the nearly fifty volumes that constitute the *Journal of the Experimental Analysis of Behavior* and to the more than 8,000 references in the *Psychological Abstracts* indexed since 1940 under the term "operant conditioning."[3]

There is, however, only a small body of critical and historical literature which directly takes *The Behavior of Organisms* as its object. I have in mind here the original reviews that appeared shortly after its publication and the later occasional pieces which, for the most part, have limited their focus to

Skinner's views as presented in *The Behavior of Organisms*. Though circumscribed in number and limited in length, it is possible only to survey this literature here. The number of such pieces will undoubtedly increase in the future, as the symposium at the Association for Behavior Analysis in 1988 (Todd & Morris, 1988), the collection of commentaries published (Catania, 1988b) in the *Journal of the Experimental Analysis of Behavior*, and the recent retrospective review of *The Behavior of Organisms* by Thompson (1988) attest.

Ernest Hilgard wrote a review for the *Psychological Bulletin* (Hilgard, 1939). He thought *The Behavior of Organisms* was within the current trends by eschewing neuroanatomy but outside them in its inductive rather than deductive approach and in its "laws" which might by better termed "collections of variables" (p. 122). Hilgard felt that the real laws are not those summarized verbally in connection with the data in the book but the curves that fit the data. He found that the distinction between operant and respondent conditioning, though implicit in Edward Thorndike's discussion of associative shift versus trial-and-error learning, is "perhaps Skinner's most significant conceptual contribution" (p. 122) and he thought that "the difficulties in making the extensions of the system" (a consequence of Skinner's failure to include relevant experimental studies by other psychologists), "may result in the book's being less useful, and perhaps less influential, than it ought to be" (p. 124). Hilgard would later provide in his *Theories of Learning* (published in 1948), the first systematic secondary account of Skinner's system. When *Theories of Learning* appeared in the fourth edition, *The Behavior of Organisms* was described as a "historically significant book" (Hilgard & Bower, 1975, p. 207).

David Krech, a student of Tolman's (writing as I. Krechevsky), agreed with Hilgard that "it is to be profoundly regretted that Skinner did not attempt to tie up his work and his thinking with the rest of psychology's experimental data and concepts" (Krechevsky, 1939, p. 407). Krech, in a review written for the *Journal of Abnormal and Social Psychology* and characterized by Skinner as "scurrilous" (Skinner, 1979, p. 227), desired "a more 'social' and a more generalized product"; but he applauded *The Behavior of Organisms* for its "lawfulness, regularity, and new 'high' in experimental achievement" (p. 404). The greater part of Krech's review is devoted, however, to arguing that Skinner's system is not incompatible with the views of the gestalt psychologists and that their criticism of 'molecular' systems does not—despite what Krech regards as Skinner's attempts to respond to the Gestalt position—in fact, apply to Skinner's analysis. Krech wished "to emphasize the point that Skinner's reflex is *not* a "molecular" unit, as understood and criticized by the Gestalt's psychologists" (p. 406).

A brief and descriptive review was offered by F. Nowell Jones (1939) in the *American Journal of Psychology*. He concluded that whatever modification future experiments might bring, "The basic position should always deserve respectful consideration" (p. 660). He noted, "The emphasis upon operant rather than respondent behavior should be hailed by all who object to the forcing of behavior into falsely simplified explanatory system" (p. 660). He is referring, of course, to the simple system of stimulus–response.

Ernest Wolf (1939), a physiologist with the Biological Laboratories of Harvard University and a student of W. J. Cozier, reviewed *The Behavior of Organisms* for the *Journal of Genetic Psychology*. He began by noting that the title of Skinner's work suggested "by its generality something in which every experimental physiologist and biologist should be generally interested" (p. 475), but he concluded that the work would be better titled "properties of certain specific complex reflex mechanisms in the white rat" (p. 479). Wolf asserted that "experiments with the albino rat are certainly not enough to establish a system of behavior . . . only one strain of rats has been used [and] it . . . seems doubtful whether a system of behavior can be of any value as long as its applicability has not stood the test of numerous other animals . . . Skinner really ought to furnish proof" (p. 478).

A final review appeared in the *Journal of General Psychology*, the outlet for most of Skinner's early papers that had preceded *The Behavior of Organisms*. John L. Finan, a former student of Hull's and a professor at the University of Illinois, recognized that several readings of the book were possible. He described *The Behavior of Organisms* as either "a detailed monograph on conditioning studies with albino rats, or . . . a theory of scientific methodology" (Finan, 1939, p. 441). The book avoids the difficulties of a "strict S-R formula" (p.441), lacks the "fortification of statistical convention" (p. 444), and makes "no serious attempt [to] relate the results to the accumulated literature on learning and conditioning" (p. 445). In the end, though, the reviewer concluded that the book would take its place with those of Tolman, Hull, and Guthrie, that is, as a foundational work in the *psychology of learning* (which in the 1930s and 1940s was psychology).

The early reviewers shared the opinion that *The Behavior of Organisms* failed to make contact with relevant contemporary literature, and to utilize the then-emerging techniques of statistical analysis. Finan, for example, intimated that the experimental results of *The Behavior of Organisms* might require the treatment accorded Pavlov, wherein "the ruthlessly accurate demands of the laboratory, [made] it necessary to re-examine experimentally almost in their entirety the non-statistical data of the Pavlovian system" (Finan, 1939, p. 444). Moreover, he suggested, Skinner's work lacked the widely accepted practice of hypothesis testing. In short, as one reviewer said, the book is "undoubtedly too exclusively personal" (Wolf, 1939, p. 478)—too outside the philosophical and methodological mainstream of American psychology.

Skinner's reaction to these reviews may be found in his autobiography (1979, p. 231–233), along with the opinions of friends and colleagues who wrote to him following the publication of the book (1979, pp. 219–222).

ANCILLARY AND LATER REVIEWS

Douglas Ellson, a student of Hull's, published a study based upon his dissertation, in which the system presented in *The Behavior of Organisms* was reduced to five principles, the most critical of which, by Ellson's account, was the "reflex reserve" concept. Based upon his own data and an analysis of the data contained in *The Behavior of Organisms*, Ellson concluded, "The size of the reflex reserve was found to be unmeasurable and statements expressing a relationship between the size of the reserve and other variables are unverifiable" (Ellson, 1939, p. 575). Skinner later abandoned the reflex reserve, the history of which deserves a paper itself. Ellson's dissertation, and earlier empirical papers, some of which appeared concurrently with the publication of *The Behavior of Organisms*, constitutes the first systematic and direct response to the book. It is difficult, though, to discern what later experimental work was directly prompted by the book's appearance, since Skinner had regularly published studies in the 1930s, the results of which were incorporated into *The Behavior of Organisms*.

Roger Brown Loucks in 1941 responded to arguments against physiological explanations of behavior contained in *The Behavior of Organisms* (Loucks, 1941). Loucks took Skinner's position as one of the most consistently argued but also as a position which was representative of most psychological theories of the time, theories that sought explanations of behavior independently of physiology (or neurology) and that, in Loucks's view, relied upon an artificial distinction between "overt response and the internal activity of the organism" (p. 105). Loucks's paper was originally prepared for the celebration of a new life science building at UCLA, and Skinner had corresponded with Loucks on an earlier draft (Skinner, 1979, p. 255).

The most extensive, analytic review of *The Behavior of Organisms* appeared many years after its publication in *Modern Learning Theories* (Verplanck, 1954). Willard Day described this analysis as "the finest critical assessment of *The Behavior of Organisms* to date" (Day, 1980, p. 242). The Verplanck chapter is an exceedingly important secondary work, and it has deservedly received a recent retrospective analysis by Schneider and Morris (1988). Verplanck importantly recognized that Skinner's system bore "no more than terminological resemblance to Hull's or to Pavlov's" but that it was "at least first cousin to Kantor's system" and that it had "affinities to Tolman's." Most importantly, Verplanck understood that "Skinner attempts a clean break with much of traditional psychology" and that this "fact [had] escaped many psychologists" (Verplanck, 1954, p. 308).

Verplanck grasped nicely the fundamental nature of Skinner's split with the rest of psychology despite the terminological overlap. A good part of what had served as the basis of criticism for the earlier reviewers was, in fact, what made the subsequent success of the experimental analysis of behavior possible. *The Behavior of Organisms* was not really "one more psychology of learning" among others; it was a fundamentally different approach and a fundamentally different subject matter—an experimental analysis that led to a "quantitative description of the behavior of the individual organism," as the revised advertisement put it.

When Kenneth Spence (1966) wrote the Foreword to the paperback edition of Hull's *Principles of Behavior*, he made extensive comments about *The Behavior of Organisms*. He gave Skinner credit for being the "first to describe the role of intervening variables in psychological theorizing" (p. x) and for providing in *The Behavior of Organisms* "the most lucid and intelligible" account for "hypothetical middle terms" that he had ever seen. He later wondered if the fact that "Skinner's book did not receive the attention it deserved" might explain Skinner's abandonment of "the abstract kinds of laws that all sciences have traditionally sought" (p. xi). He expressed regret over the current direction of Skinner's work, moving as it was toward education, teaching, and technology. Spence felt that "*The Behavior of Organisms* showed [Skinner] to be brilliantly qualified" (p. xi) for the more abstract theoretical work of true science. Undoubtedly, Spence regarded Hull as the prototype in such matters.

CONCLUSION

Most psychologists came to behavior analysis having never met B. F. Skinner or any of his few students. Some, to be sure, were influenced by others who had taken up the cause of behavior analysis. But many more had, in isolation, read a book by Skinner and were changed as consequence. Commitments and plans were made. The book read may not have been *The Behavior of Organisms*, but this was Skinner's first professional book, and without it the others probably would not have followed. Of course, the determination of individual lives is more complex than the act of reading a single book. Otherwise, books *might be* the kind of threat that those who seek to ban them make them out to be. Yet, more than other American psychologists, Skinner's views have gained followers because of what he wrote (Krantz, 1972) and what readers found they could do after reading his works.

In the years ahead, *The Behavior of Organisms* will become the object of extensive analysis by biographers, historians, philosophers of science, and others; it is the foundational book in the emergence of a unique phenomenon in the latter half of twentieth-century American psychology. Whatever a person's judgment of the merit and worth of the experimental analysis of behavior, agreement can usually be reached on its significance as a distinctive and influential movement in recent American behavioral science—one without any clear parallel.

In April 1938, the author of *The Behavior of Organisms* offered his own appraisal of the work that began it all in a letter to his friend Fred Keller. It seems that the book was being set in type; and while he had not given much thought to it in some months, he was "beginning to think it may be a good book after all" and was coming to believe that "as time goes on I may be glad I wrote it" (Skinner, 1979, p. 216).

AUTHOR'S NOTE

My appreciation to Colleen Leavens-Knapp, John Gach, and the editors of this volume for assistance in the preparation of this chapter, and to the University of Nevada, Las Vegas, Research Council for a grant to facilitate its completion.

Chapter 3

In the Beginning . . .

James A. Dinsmoor

I stumbled across systematic psychology almost by accident. I had entered the graduate program at Columbia, intending to specialize in social and clinical psychology. But to make ends meet (and to master some of the fundamentals more securely while doing so), I had accepted a stipend of $37.50 per month to serve as the "reader" in the introductory course for male undergraduates (Columbia College). The first two semesters were fairly uneventful intellectually; but in the spring of 1945, Fred S. Keller returned from his Morse Code research with the U.S. Army Signal Corps and resumed his teaching duties, which included that course. When he handed out a mimeographed outline that proposed a "consideration [of] principles derived from the analysis of human and animal behavior by the experimental method," I realized that something was up. Soon he was into such esoteric matters as the static laws of the reflex, Type S and Type R conditioning, extinction, generalization, stimulus discrimination, response differentiation, chaining, and their application to verbal behavior and thinking.

By then I was beginning my fourth semester (plus two summers) of graduate study. That was just enough training for me to have made two disturbing observations: First, in R. S. Woodworth's laboratory course I had discovered that even in "experimental psychology" many of the best-known theories yielded no predictions sufficiently specific to be subjected to empirical test. If they made no predictions, they could not be very useful. Second, the different areas within psychology seemed to be completely compartmentalized, with no broader principles crossing their boundaries to link them together. By contrast, the processes Keller was talking about were objective descriptions of what happened in the laboratory and could readily be replicated. When he further suggested that "the modern psychologist . . . seeks to achieve a systematic interconnection of the basic facts of human and animal behavior,"

I was intrigued. When he proceeded to do so, I was hooked. "Response" as an abstract category seemed to me to be a promising stand-in for whatever specific activity might be of interest in a given situation and laws of "response strength" a promising system for psychology as a whole.

As many readers will recognize, Keller's section on verbal behavior came from a manuscript version of the book that did not appear in print until twelve years later (Skinner, 1957). Almost without exception, the fundamental concepts throughout the rest of the outline could be found in *The Behavior of Organisms: An Experimental Analysis* (1938). Aside from a series of articles that were rarely consulted because the important material was duplicated in the book, that was all there was. In its black cover, the *B of O*, as everyone called it, served in the early days as the bible of our movement.

In the years that followed, a large number of writers have commented on Skinner's work, and they have credited him with many and varied contributions—methodological, empirical, and philosophical. The purpose of the present chapter, however, is to single out the one or two contributions that in my opinion have been most critical to his impact, not only on my own thinking but on the field of psychology as a whole.

A RESEARCH TECHNOLOGY

One factor that could readily be overlooked today is Skinner's contribution to experimental technology. When an innovation is widely adopted, it becomes commonplace, and no one any longer gives it much thought. This is what has happened to the arrangement that serves as the discriminative stimulus for the ubiquitous tact, "Skinner box"—the provision of a switch that springs back into place after it is operated by the subject. As control of the experimental routine by an electronic system requires some sort of switching device as an input, it seems likely that when computers finally entered the behavioral laboratory, psychologists would inevitably have discovered lever pressing, disk pecking, or some similar device. But Skinner adopted the lever back in 1931, and it was the switch that led to the complex networks of electromechanical programming modules—crude equivalents to today's computers—rather than the other way around. In the decades immediately following the publication of the book, there were many investigators who carefully dissociated themselves from the rest of Skinner's thinking but who made use of his lever or his key in their experimental work. Today, a very large part of the research on learning and cognition conducted with nonhuman subjects depends on these devices, including, for example, the use of conditioned suppression and autoshaping to study Pavlovian processes and the use of the matching-to-sample technique to study memorial processes and attention. Research technology with human subjects has also caught up, but in most cases this owes more to the advent of the computer than to the historical influence of Skinner.

Recording the opening or closing of a switch as the subject's response has a number of advantages. Prosaic but important is the fact that it permits automation of the experimental procedure, with its attendant promises of greater precision, more complex contingencies, and much more data for the same investment in human time. Because manipulation of a switch does not ordinarily depend on locomotion, this technology permits greater freedom in programming relationships among events. In the runway or the maze, where the recorded behavior is a change in the subject's location, the ratio of individual steps to reinforcer deliveries, time to reinforcer, effort expended, and change in external stimulation all are likely to be confounded. They are difficult or impossible to disentangle as parameters of the subject's behavior. Furthermore, changing one of these parameters may require time out for the use of a hammer and saw, disrupting the continuity of experimental events. When antecedent stimuli, responses, and consequences are linked by electric circuits, all relationships known to nature or that can be concocted by human imagination should be reproducible and their effects capable of being examined within the laboratory setting. Furthermore, in a manner reminiscent of Watson's remarks about the conditioned response as the unit of "habit" (1924a, pp. 207-208), larger patterns of behavior—such as ratios, chains, simulations of foraging and observing, and those produced by a variety of complex schedules—can be constructed by linking individual stimuli and responses together in complex contingency networks. A great variety of such patterns have been arranged in which single presses or single pecks are still recorded as elementary constituents. The abstract category "response" serves an integrative function at the theoretical level, and in a somewhat different fashion the concrete instance of a switch closure serves to integrate the data at an empirical level.

EXTENDING THE SYSTEM

If the closure of a switch provided a lingua franca at the level of instrumentation and the number of closures per unit of time (rate of responding) provided a lingua franca at the level of measurement, these matters were of concern primarily to experimenters using rats, pigeons, and monkeys to study behavioral processes at the most abstract level. As Skinner noted in the second volume of his autobiography (Skinner, 1979, p. 318), until Fred Keller and Nat Schoenfeld began teaching laboratory courses based on *The Behavior of Organisms*, only 550 copies had been sold (see Knapp, this volume).

The technology did make it relatively easy, once the necessary equipment was obtained, to conduct research on basic behavioral processes, and during the period when grant money was in reasonable supply, the equipment could indeed be obtained. Soon there developed a community of "operant conditioners" who knew each other both professionally and personally, who spoke a common language, and who felt common loyalties. This was the original foundation of the movement that eventually established two of psychology's most frequently cited journals, Division 25 of the American Psychological Association, and later, an independent organization known as the Association for Behavior Analysis (see Laties, 1987; Peterson, 1978). Many of the pioneers in behavior modification were trained initially in the conditioning laboratory.

A technology for studying the behavioral processes of rats or pigeons, however, could never have generated by itself a system that would extend beyond the laboratory to the world of practical affairs. Although the language of *The Behavior of Organisms* may sound archaic to contemporary ears, the seeds were there. To put it in a way that will be accessible to a broad spectrum of readers, Skinner had begun the task of constructing a set of concepts capable of dealing in a scientific fashion with the heartland of psychology. His vocabulary was quite forbidding to those encountering it for the first time. It required an effort to master. On the one hand, it was more tightly tethered to concrete observations than the language of any other systematic treatment. On the other, it was capable of transcending the boundaries between the conventional physical categories used in everyday discourse (for a panorama of application, see Lundin, 1974; Martin & Pear, 1992; Miller, 1975).

CONSTRUCTING A THEORY

Because the presidential address he delivered to the Midwestern Psychological Association in May 1949 was entitled "Are Theories of Learning Necessary?" Skinner (1950), has almost invariably been described in subsequent commentaries as "atheoretical" or even "antitheoretical." But I believe this to be a profound misconception. Finding appropriate terms for the description of behavior is in itself a theoretical enterprise. A revealing glimpse into Skinner's views on theories and how they should be constructed is provided by the remarks he had delivered just two years earlier at a symposium conducted on March fourth and fifth, 1947, at the University of Pittsburgh (Skinner, 1947). There he declared quite explicitly and unabashedly that "a theory is essential to the scientific understanding of behavior as a subject matter" (1947, p. 29). In the preceding paragraph, he had specified what he considered a theory to be: "Theories . . . are statements about organizations of facts. . . . But they have a generality which transcends particular facts and gives them a wider usefulness" (1947, p. 28; see also Skinner, 1961b, p. 230).

After presenting his usual objections to such explanatory fictions as a controlling mind or a hypothetical neural structure, he went on to suggest that "the first step in building a theory is to identify the basic data" (1947, p. 34; 1961b, p. 233). To illustrate this stage of theory construction, he cited the work of Galileo, who chose "to deal with the positions of bodies at given times, rather than with their hardness or size. This decision . . . was not so easy as it seems to us today" (1947, p. 38; 1961b, p. 235). As the psychological counterpart, he pointed to the problem of delineating "the parts of behavior and environment between which orderly relations may be demonstrated" (1947, p. 34; 1961b, p. 233). In its second stage, he suggested, theory should "express relations among data" (1947, p. 37; 1961b, p. 235), preferably in terms as general as possible. Then, in the third stage, new concepts might emerge as the concepts of acceleration had emerged from the second-stage relation between position and time.

Although he never made it to the third stage, I believe this account of the first two stages to be a reasonably accurate description of what Skinner considered his own activities to have been when he was writing *The Behavior of Organisms* some ten years earlier. After choosing "stimulus" and "response" to represent relevant facets of the environment and the behavior, respectively, he began to examine some of the kinds of relations that were possible between these categories of events.

To those who have not read Skinner, the terms *stimulus* and *response* have an unfortunate connotation. They were borrowed, via Pavlov, from the science of physiology, and to the casual observer, the physiology of the reflex appears extremely atomistic. Although stimulus and response may confer an aura of material respectability upon a seemingly more ephemeral subject matter, they also conjure up visions of much too simply determined relations between physical energies impinging on the sensory receptors on the one hand and muscular contractions and glandular secretions on the other (e.g., Breger & McGaugh, 1965). This stereotyped picture of Skinner's views may be responsible for the demand that he and other behaviorists take up the burden of accounting for complex patterns of activity in physiological terms—a task that is actually quite distinct from that of the experimental analysis of behavior—and for some of the charges frequently leveled by critics who do not seem to be familiar with what has actually been said. If the terms stimulus and response were not available, however, others would have to be invented in their stead. As Skinner has pointed out (e.g., 1938, p. 9), there is no way to study changes in the totality of behavior as a function of changes in the totality of the environment. In order to measure, or even to record, it is necessary to select some part of that behavior. When it is shown that a given part of the subject's behavior can be changed by changing some part of the environment, that part is known as a stimulus.

There are other concepts of systematic importance to be found in *The Behavior of Organisms*. Somewhat to my surprise, when I returned to the book after a number of years, I found that these concepts were not represented by formal definitions. Most of the content is devoted to empirical determinations of the behavioral processes governing the rate of lever pressing by the albino rat. This is the second stage of theory construction, as outlined by Skinner. Each of the "dynamic laws of the reflex" has embedded within it a classificatory scheme. One may look in vain, for example, for a direct and explicit definition of what is meant by a "discriminative stimulus." But what might be termed a low-profile and incomplete definition can be found on p. 178: "Only in the presence of S^D is R^O followed by S^{1}" (Skinner, 1938); and a more complete definition is implied in "THE LAW OF THE DISCRIMINATION OF THE STIMULUS IN TYPE R. *The strength acquired by an operant through reinforcement is not independent of the stimuli affecting the organism at the moment, and two operants having the same form of response may be given widely different strengths through differential reinforcement with respect to such stimuli"* (1938, p. 228, italics in original). From *The Behavior of Organisms* it is possible to extract such broad concepts as positive reinforcement, negative reinforcement (meaning punishment in those days), extinction, stimulus generalization (induction) and discrimination, response induction and differentiation, successive approximation (shaping), chaining, and conditioned reinforcement. In later years, as the system has expanded, other concepts have been added.

CONCEPTS AND DEFINITIONS

The full meaning of the word *concept* is difficult to grasp unless one is familiar with at least one illustrative study of the concrete behavioral relationships to which the term is applied. In laboratory studies, the experimental subject is often human, and some new and undefined word has typically been used as the response (e.g., Hanfmann & Kasanin, 1937; Hull, 1920; Kuo, 1923); but the subject may also be nonhuman, in which case the closure of a certain switch will do just as well (e.g., Kelleher, 1958). What is recorded in either case is the subject's response to each member of a population of stimuli that differ in a number of respects. In essence, to have a concept is to react in the same way to a certain group of stimuli that presumably have something in common but not to react in that way to other stimuli that do not share the common characteristic. A variety of different groupings may be possible but only one is currently acceptable to the experimenter.

Outside the laboratory, too, nature may be sliced in a variety of ways. To take a literal example, picture two butchers slicing up a leg of beef, one in Bloomington, Indiana, and the other in Laconia, New Hampshire. They will cut the beef in different places and divide it into different parts. If you ask for "round steak" in Bloomington, you will get a certain cut with certain properties, to be prepared in certain ways; but if you ask for the same cut in Laconia you will get a puzzled look. It is not merely a matter of the name by which they identify it: The butcher in Laconia will have nothing with quite the same properties. The concept does not exist.

Similarly, any population of instances can be divided in a number of ways—for example, according to number, according to shape, according to size, according to color, according to much subtler properties (e.g., Gardner & Gardner, 1984; Herrnstein & Loveland, 1964; Smoke, 1932). Some of these distinctions may be useful for a given purpose, others may not. Technically speaking, what we are dealing with here is the set of discriminative stimuli controlling a given response. In verbal behavior, this relation between stimuli and a response is what Skinner (1957) called a *tact*. Usually, selective reinforcement determines the boundaries. When the rules as to what is included and what is excluded can themselves be verbalized (which is not always the case) we have a definition. Definitions are rules governing the application of the words they define.

A science is no better than its definitions. Rules for the application of words to events are critical steps both in testing a theory and in applying it. In some sense (this is not the place to spell out the details) all scientific theory must ultimately be reducible to a set of propositions of the form that circumstances A (for antecedent) lead to outcome C (for consequent). These are descriptive statements that at their most basic level merely summarize sequences of events. When testing or applying such statements, we make the added assumption that A–C relationships observed in the past will continue to hold for the future.

The statements relating verbal antecedent (VA) and verbal consequent (VC) are isomorphic with the relations between observed antecedent (OA) and observed consequent (OC); and the role of definition is to translate words into observations and observations into words, moving from one level to the other and back again, just as we might translate back and forth between two languages. When testing a theory, we begin with the verbal specification of antecedent circumstances (VA), use a definition to select an experimental procedure (OA), carry out that procedure, observe the outcome (OC), and translate the data by way of definition back into the terms of the theory (VC). If the outcome of the experiment is consistent with the outcome specified by the theory (OC = VC), we keep that theory; if not, we modify what we have said.

In a very broad and abstract sense, the uses we make of theories come under the headings of prediction and control. To make a prediction, we observe the current circumstances (OA), find a theory that applies to those circumstances—that is, has a corresponding antecedent (VA)—take the outcome specified by that theory (VC), and translate that back into an observable outcome (OC), which constitutes the prediction. When we use a theory to control events, we begin with the desired result (OC), find a theory with a corresponding outcome (VC), and translate those conditions back to the necessary practical operations (OA).

Although definitions were not at all conspicuous in *The Behavior of Organisms*, Skinner's behavior at the first Conference on the Experimental Analysis of Behavior less than a decade later confirmed my budding suspicion that they are extremely important. Quite a bit of his time was allocated to tentative specifications for a variety of basic terms to be used in the science of behavior (see also Figure 2 in Dinsmoor, 1987). In the early days of the *Journal of the Experimental Analysis of Behavior*, a number of readers complained about technical vocabulary that made material in the new journal difficult to follow. But without that vocabulary, our authors could not make sensible statements about their procedures, let alone their conclusions. I have discovered that undergraduate students and cognitive psychologists also experience difficulty with behavioral language and often feel that it is merely a pedantic version of ordinary English, capable or almost capable of a literal, one-to-one translation into their mother tongue.

INADEQUACY OF POPULAR VOCABULARY

This is not the case. The linguistic categories that develop and are passed along from generation to generation within a given culture are presumably of some effectiveness in dealing with the exigencies of daily life, but they are not the same as those needed for valid and general scientific statements. Consequently, the words that are reinforced and the circumstances under which they are reinforced in everyday conversation are not the same as those in various scientific communities. To put it succinctly, different concepts are needed.

That Skinner recognized the inadequacies of the boundaries established by popular usage is evident from the following passage:

[The] science of behavior . . . must not take over without careful consideration the schemes which underlie popular speech. The vernacular is clumsy and obese; its terms overlap each other, draw unnecessary or unreal distinctions, and are far from being the most convenient in dealing with data. They have the disadvantage of being historical products, introduced because of everyday convenience rather than that special kind of convenience characteristic of a simple scientific system. It would be a miracle if such a set of terms were available for a science of behavior, and no miracle has in this case taken place. (1938, p. 7)

It is difficult to conceive of a way in which any of the physical or biological sciences could have achieved even a semblance of their current effectiveness without the construction of technical vocabularies. The observations must be classified in appropriate ways to make possible the generation of valid descriptive statements of any substantial degree of generality. If the whale were to be classified as a fish, for example, or the tomato as a vegetable, otherwise correct statements about fish or vegetables would for these cases be rendered incorrect. However, when whales are classified as mammals and tomatoes as fruit, all is well. Consistency is preserved.

A SCIENCE OF BEHAVIOR

Because they do not use a mentalistic vocabulary, Skinner and other behaviorists frequently have been accused by cognitive psychologists of ignoring or denying all that is most interesting and most central to psychology. But what Skinner was avoiding was not the processes themselves, as should be obvious from his later writings, but only words that were inadequately related to their controlling stimuli:

The traditional description and organization of behavior represented by the concepts of "will," "cognition," "intellect," and so on, cannot be accepted so long as it pretends to be dealing with a mental world, but the behavior to which these terms apply is naturally part of the subject matter of a science of behavior. What is wanted in such a science is an alternative set of terms derived from an analysis of behavior and capable of doing the same work. . . . Traditional concepts are based upon data at another level of analysis and cannot be expected to prove useful. They have no place in a system derived step by step from the behavior itself. (1938, p. 441)

In common with those used by other learning theorists, Skinner's concepts occupy a position that is central to psychology as a whole. It was no accident that the first attempts to communicate his views to a broader audience (Keller & Schoenfeld, 1950; Skinner, 1953) took the form of textbooks to be used for introductory courses rather than for some specialty area within the discipline. Almost all behavior of interest to psychologists in such areas as personality and social, clinical, industrial, educational, and developmental psychology is behavior that is greatly influenced if not wholly shaped by a process of learning. Although some interventions by applied psychologists take the form of changes in the situation, more often they take the form of changing the individual's reaction to that situation, a process that in most cases can be classified as learning.

Although they differ greatly in the data bases they employ and in their scientific rigor, there is a curious similarity between behavior analysis and psychoanalysis. Perhaps it is more than a coincidence that they both apply the word *analysis* quite broadly—one to behavior and the other to the psyche. Both have rejected the conscious mind of common-sense psychology as the arbiter of behavior and have presented themselves as alternative systems capable of integrating a large part of their subject matter. The frequent use of the word *dynamic* in *The Behavior of Organisms* is reminiscent of the use of the word *psychodynamic* in clinical writings. Perhaps some reference was intended to the underlying emotions or motivations—whatever these words may mean—that affect the behavior in a way that is orthogonal to its immediate context (see Skinner, 1938, pp. 21–26). But a more rigorous and more inclusive characterization is that both systems attempt to describe the laws of motion governing the characteristic reactions of the individual to certain situations that recur from time to time; that is, there is reference to the prior history of the organism. Writers like Dollard and Miller (1950) and Mowrer (1950), closely associated with Hull, devoted considerable attention to the behavioral interpretation of psychoanalytic mechanisms, and so, in later writings, did Skinner (e.g., 1953, 1972a).

INTERVENING VARIABLES

Some of the terminology used in *The Behavior of Organisms* has virtually disappeared from current usage (e.g., Type S and Type R conditioning, now called by other names, or the reflex reserve, a construct that has since been discarded); but the fruitfulness of other concepts is indicated not only by their continued use in research on conditioning but frequently by their extension to applied settings (see e.g., Bijou & Baer, 1961, 1965; Lundin, 1974; Martin & Pear, 1992; Miller, 1975). The same cannot be said for most of the terms suggested by rival theorists from the same period (e.g., Guthrie, 1935; Hull, 1943; Tolman, 1932), although they, too, were attempting to deal with the central problems of psychology at the most general level.

One of the reasons for the popularity of Skinner's concepts among those interested in the application of psychology may lie in his sparing use of mediating constructs. True, his attitude toward such constructs has never been quite as proscriptive as that ascribed to him by many current writers, both critical and friendly. So far as I can determine, he has never denied their scientific legitimacy; he has only questioned their strategic value for the conduct of research in the science of behavior. In fact, in *The Behavior of Organisms*, he himself made use of such "hypothetical middle term[s]" as reflex strength, the reflex reserve, and particularly the "intermediate state[s]" of emotion and drive concepts that he explicitly identified as corresponding in their status within the system to the mediating constructs that had recently been proposed by Tolman: "What has here been treated as a 'state,' as distinguished from the operation responsible for the state, is called by Tolman an 'intervening variable'" (Skinner, 1938, p. 437; note also on p. 25 his recognition of the distinction between learning and performance). What is more, in a footnote he established his precedence by citing an earlier publication (i.e., Skinner, 1931).

Intervening variables (by which I mean to include hypothetical constructs, which are sometimes considered a separate category) play a central and critical role in such matured sciences as physics, chemistry, and genetics. Examination of the difficulties encountered by Tolman and by Hull with their respective systems suggests that Skinner took the wiser course in staying as close as possible to his data, holding such constructions to a minimum. The problems with Tolman's and Hull's systems were opposite in nature, and the failures at both extremes suggest that such a fate may have been inevitable at any point along the continuum.

In Tolman's case, the proposed variables were borrowed from traditional common-sense psychology and hence were intuitively appealing, but they were largely programmatic. He offered only a tentative list of what the appropriate theoretical terms might be, and he was understandably reluctant to labor over the details of their definition. That could come later. Tolman's strategy allowed considerable flexibility and made it easy for him to "explain" results that posed difficulties for Hull and perhaps even for Skinner. As a consequence of that strategy, Tolman's system never achieved the specificity of prediction needed to compete as a viable alternative to those offered by Skinner and Hull.

Hull went to the opposite extreme. He constructed a highly formalized network of intervening variables in which most of the relationships, including those with observable events, were specified with a degree of rigor that was, within psychology, quite rare. Looking back, the image that often occurs to me is that of Icarus, who strapped on wings of feathers and wax to escape from an island prison. He flew too high, the sun melted his wax, and he fell into the sea. Hull's ambition was too lofty, and his goals could not be achieved. Perhaps he was naive to think that such an enterprise could succeed, but one can still admire his daring and the height to which he flew.

Attempts were made by others to extend Hull's system to the realm of practical affairs. Dollard and Miller (1950) constructed a greatly simplified version of Hull's system—in itself a significant move—and used it to "explain" a variety of psychodynamic processes noted in the clinic. (Unfortunately, these processes were themselves open to question on empirical grounds.) Although in the United States the first behavior modifiers were inspired by Skinner (see Ullmann & Krasner, 1965; Ulrich, Stachnik & Mabry, 1966), in Britain they usually cited Hull (e.g., Eysenck, 1960). However, Skinner's system is still with us, whereas the Hullian contribution seems to have petered out. The essential difficulty, in my view, was that Hull's structure was too complex to be practical in application. It was difficult and time consuming to learn and cumbersome to use. And, errors aside, the benefits simply were not of sufficient magnitude to compensate for the costs.

By avoiding such lengthy verbal linkages between theory and data, Skinner was able to keep his concepts precise, simple, and relatively few in number. They map fairly directly onto the observations themselves, in a manner that Skinner suggested was "purely descriptive" (1938, p. 426). Skinner's descriptions were certainly couched in terms different from those used by the layperson, based on different criteria.

FUNCTIONAL DEFINITIONS

As stated earlier, the stimuli impinging upon an organism can be categorized in a variety of ways. The classificatory scheme used in *The Behavior of Organisms* is especially effective for a systematic science of behavior because it cuts across a number of important boundaries. What Skinner's definitions ignore is almost as important as the criteria to which they attend. They ignore, for example, the species of the subject, the distinction between the laboratory and the natural world, different settings within the natural world, and different topographies of behavior in each of those settings. From a conceptual point of view, at least, there are no barriers to extrapolation across the face of psychology.

Compare the concepts in Skinner's system with the categories normally used by the nonpsychologist. When asked to describe a scene, the average person might simply list the objects that are present, giving each the name supplied by the national language and perhaps its spatial relation to other objects: "two chairs and a table, a window through which one can see some trees outside, . . . " and so on. (Significantly enough, when asked to describe someone's *actions*, the same person might give a highly inferential account, couched in terms belonging to what might best be described as a contemporary folk psychology. One of the things that may be learned from laboratory work with rats and pigeons is to use physical rather than inferential categories in describing behavior.) For inanimate objects, the conventional categories maintained by our culture draw sharp distinctions in terms of immediate physical characteristics, such as shape, size, and color, because these attributes are quickly and reliably discriminated and because the distinctions among different objects are important for everyday uses, such as deciding where to sit, what to eat, when to flee, and so on. If used for psychological systems, this kind of physical specification would impose restrictions that would prevent us from transferring the concept from one experiment to another, let alone to the settings for such target behaviors as studying, personal grooming, inviting on a date, attaching seat belts, or sequences of verbal behavior.

In terms of progress toward a general theory, the situation is not much more encouraging when we turn to the sensory psychologist. There the dimensions used to describe the stimulus are less immediate and, therefore, less convenient for everyday purposes—they require instrumentation—but serve more accurately to interrelate physiology and function within the sensory field. Although dimensions like wavelength, visual angle occluded, luminous flux, angular velocity, auditory frequency, or sound pressure level may be appropriate for the reporting of experiments in vision or audition, in research on conditioning, they occupy center stage only in the methods section; in theoretical discussions, they are relegated to the wings. For the most part, we are not much interested in this type of specification, despite its technical sophistication, but in whether stimuli are discriminative, reinforcing, eliciting, inhibitory, aversive, and so on. These classifications require functional definitions.

The type of definition required for a general science of behavior sounds extremely labored to the untrained ear, and the need for this type of definition is by no means apparent to casual observation. Those who teach this form of analysis encounter substantial resistance from many of their students. The failure to appreciate the inadequacy of the traditional vocabulary and the gains to be achieved through a functional classification may constitute the single most important barrier to more widespread acceptance of a truly scientific perspective among professional psychologists, let alone the lay public. Functional definitions are based not on immediate sense impressions but on the location of the stimulus or the response in question within a network of events stretching across some period of time. To put it another way, a history is required. Such definitions are not the most convenient, to be sure, but they are necessary if we are to break away from the popular mythology of our culture and establish a scientific treatment of our subject matter.

In Skinner's system, stimuli are classified in terms of the operations into which they enter and the effects of those operations on the subject's behavior. As originally described, at least, a (positive) discriminative stimulus is present when the specified is present when the specified response is eligible for reinforcement. The response occurs sooner or at a higher rate in the presence of that stimulus than in its absence. In another example, the stimulus may be delivered a number of times following instances of the designated response; if the response occurs at a higher rate under that circumstance, then the stimulus is classified as reinforcing.

In spite of the fact that these functional definitions transcend the limitations of description in terms of *immediately detectable* physical attributes, as indicated earlier, ultimately they do refer back to concrete physical description, and in a fairly unambiguous manner. Whether a stimulus is present or absent when a reinforcing event arrives is a matter that in most cases can easily, reliably, and objectively be determined by direct observation or by suitable recording apparatus. It can also be verified by an independent observer, and agreement among observers should be nearly perfect. Whether the event that takes place in the presence of the stimulus can be classified as reinforcing is determined by measuring some physically specifiable item of behavior (originally, counting the closures of a switch) across different periods of time.

Although these are not the same observations used by the layperson or the sensory psychologist, they are equally physical in their status; and it is the return to concrete physical specification that provides the objectivity so necessary to scientific discourse. Skinner himself has suggested that effectiveness in controlling behavior is a better criterion for the selection of a scientific vocabulary than is agreement among observers. Perhaps the control must come first, to make the production of a new term reinforcing to its author. To establish the collective body of knowledge known as a science, we need the ability to communicate with other scientists. Eventually, we must transmit our findings to our students and to the general public, who we hope will make use of our verbal behavior and will provide economic support for our efforts. The transmission of scientific information depends upon agreement between the speaker or writer and the listener or reader in the way in which words are used.

In this review, I have argued that even though Skinner largely avoided the use of intervening variables in his work, he nonetheless constructed a theoretical system; and I have argued that the most important source of his influence on the behavior of other psychologists is to be found in the nature of the concepts he proposed for classifying behavioral events. These concepts are the content of the system. Direct testimony concerning the importance of Skinner's definitional structure has been provided by Arnold Buss, who took a course with him in the 1940s. Preparing a reminiscence for the centennial of Indiana University's psychological laboratories, Buss recorded the following observation: "I took a seminar with him, and he asked the class not to necessarily agree with his position but to use his language so that we could understand one another without confusion. By the end of the semester, I discovered his language equaled his position, and once you became accustomed to talking his way, you were a Skinnerian."

Chapter 4

Inquiry Nearer the Source: Bacon, Mach, and *The Behavior of Organisms*

Laurence D. Smith

The Behavior of Organisms is a strikingly positivistic work. Indeed, to read the book is to be reminded of Herbert Feigl's (1981) designation of B. F. Skinner as "America's most brilliantly and consistently positivistic psychologist" (p. 41). *The Behavior of Organisms* was seen as representing a highly descriptive and positivistic approach when it appeared fifty years ago, and it can only be judged more so by today's standards. In the last half century, much of American psychology has moved away from positivistic formulations toward greater tolerance of hypothetical constructs and inferred entities and processes. It is no secret that the dominant philosophy of science in the 1930s—a version of positivism known as "logical positivism"—has fallen from favor in philosophical circles. Yet *The Behavior of Organisms* stands today as the founding monograph of a scientific tradition of research and practice that continues to flourish. This situation poses an interesting historical problem; namely, how has the scheme for psychological science laid out more than fifty years ago in *The Behavior of Organisms* maintained its viability—indeed, vitality—in the face of the general decline of positivism in the intervening years?

One key to tackling this question lies in situating *The Behavior of Organisms* in the tradition of positivist thought to which it properly belongs. Although the works of B. F. Skinner have sometimes been identified with logical positivism (e.g., Suppe, 1984; Wolman, 1968), there is ample evidence in his writings (*The Behavior of Organisms* included) that Skinner all along subscribed to a different strain of positivism—one that antedates logical positivism and, in some respects, stands in opposition to it. The aim of this chapter is to place *The Behavior of Organisms* in the tradition of the descriptive, inductive, *non*logical positivism begun by Francis Bacon in the seventeenth century and championed by Ernst Mach in the nineteenth.[1] This will be done by three means: first, by clarifying what is distinctive about the Baconian–Machian brand of positivism; second, by indicating why *The Behavior of Organisms* is properly viewed as standing in the tradition of Bacon and Mach; and, third, by laying out the crucial differences between this tradition and the failed tradition of logical positivism. It is hoped that connecting *The Behavior of Organisms* with its rightful historical and philosophical precursors will encourage a more perceptive assessment of the place of the book—and the operant behaviorism it spawned—in twentieth-century thought.

THE POSITIVISM OF BACON AND MACH

The general outlines of Bacon's philosophy are well known. Writing in the early part of the Scientific Revolution, Bacon cast himself as the voice of a new empiricism (see Whitney, 1986). He enjoined the scientists of his day to reject the authority of the past and turn to the study of nature rather than books. The new method of science would be induction, in which knowledge arises, as Bacon (1620/1960) put it, "by gradual and unbroken ascent" from particular observations to cautiously tested generalizations (p. 43). No other approach to procuring knowledge would suffice, for "the intellect is not qualified to judge except by means of induction" (p. 23). But before induction could begin, according to Bacon, the mind must be "purged and swept" (p. 105) to remove preconceptions derived from everyday life that obstruct the understanding and lead investigators into "empty controversies and idle fancies" (p. 49). These common preconceptions—referred to by Bacon as the "Idols of the Marketplace"—arise from the "ill and unfit choice of words" found in the vernacular (p. 49). The problem with the vernacular, Bacon stated, is that it follows "those lines of division which are most obvious to the vulgar understanding" rather than those lines which "suit the true divisions of nature" (p. 56). Only the careful use of the inductive method would reveal the true lines of nature to which scientists would otherwise be blinded by the verbal habits of daily affairs.

Bacon (1620/1960) also described a second class of "idols" that must be swept from the mind before proceeding with inductive science, these being the "Idols of Systems" (or the "Idols of the Theater"). The systems to be eschewed include those that are boldly constructed by philosophers from "too narrow a foundation of experiment and natural history" and based on "the authority of too few cases" (p. 59). Abstract systems of this sort are easily multiplied, according to Bacon, but they have no bearing on the "fortunes of men" and can thus be rejected as "speculative and withal unprofitable" (p. 106).

Once the "arbitrary abstractions" of common parlance and of philosophical systems have been rejected, the process of Baconian induction could commence. This method, in Bacon's (1620/1960) words, "depends on keeping the eye steadily fixed upon the facts of nature and so receiving their images simply as they are" (p. 29). The simple facts are to be arrayed in tables according to the presence, absence, and varying degrees of simple natural properties. After the facts have been "duly ordered and digested" (p. 80) in this fashion, the scientist may rise by gradual steps to the establishment of descriptive laws, or what Bacon called "middle axioms." The extension of laws to novel cases must always be checked by experience, and "the understanding must not . . . be allowed to jump and fly from particulars to axioms remote" (p. 98). Indeed, science can progress without ever ascertaining the abstract "remote axioms" or "first principles" because the middle axioms are "the true and solid and living axioms, on which depend the affairs and fortunes of men" (p. 98).

For Bacon, the fortunes of humankind would depend on descriptive laws derived from induction, and they would do so in two ways. First, the results of induction would give rise to new experiments and thus to new discoveries. By providing a method of discovery, the generation of experimental results from prior results would ensure for science the kind of steady progress enjoyed by the "mechanical arts" (i.e., skilled craft, artisanship, technological pursuits). Second, the descriptive laws arrived at through induction would benefit humanity by virtue of their being equivalent to rules of operation for mastering nature. "Nature to be commanded must be obeyed," wrote Bacon (1620/1960), and "that which in contemplation is as the cause is in operation as the rule" (p. 39). To know a cause is to have the ability to produce an effect, an insight conveyed in Bacon's well-known dictum that "human knowledge and human power meet in one" (p. 39). Thus, the two great sides of natural science—what Bacon (1623/1937) called the "Inquisition of Causes" and the "Production of Effects"—are merged. The "Inquisition of Causes" would involve "searching into the bowels of nature," while the "Production of Effects" (also referred to as "the Operative" part of science) would involve "shaping nature as on an anvil" (p. 413).

Bacon made clear that the "power of operation" found in inductive laws— and hence the success of the whole Baconian enterprise—depends from the outset on close contact with nature. A true understanding of nature cannot be achieved, wrote Bacon (1620/1960), "without a very diligent dissection and anatomy of the world" (p. 113). A dissection of the world must, in turn, be done in accordance with the "true and exquisite lines" by which underlying order is expressed in nature (p. 114). The discernment of these "exquisite lines" of order, though aided by naturalistic observation, is best pursued through experiment. If humans are to learn efficiently from nature, says Bacon, it will be from nature "forced out of her natural state, and squeezed and moulded" because "the nature of things betrays itself more readily under the vexations of art [i.e., experiments] than in its natural freedom" (p. 25). In Bacon's philosophy, therefore, the human capacity to manipulate nature is the beginning and end of science: the beginning when nature is "squeezed and moulded" by experiments to reveal its order, and the end when its laws permit the "shaping [of nature] as on an anvil" for the betterment of the human condition.

The strict empiricism of the Baconian tradition found one of its greatest nineteenth-century advocates in the Austrian physicist-philosopher Ernst Mach. Again, the general outlines of the Machian view of science are well known. Like Bacon, Mach emphasized the gradual inductive establishment of laws through careful observation and experimentation, and he stressed the need to avoid hasty overgeneralization and metaphysical speculation. Also like Bacon, Mach spoke of the need to purify concepts of their prescientific meanings—whether derived from everyday speech or from philosophical discourse—and to ground all concepts in observation. The reason for purifying concepts in this way, Mach wrote in *The Science of Mechanics* (1883/1942), is to "clear up ideas, expose the real significance of the matter, and get rid of metaphysical obscurities" (p. xiii). Mach's positivistic treatment of the concept of "cause" stands as a case in point. Most thinkers, Mach states, conceive of a cause as pushing or pulling to produce its effects; but such a notion of cause is metaphorical, superfluous, and to be rejected in scientific formulations. Instead, Mach advocated a purely descriptive notion of cause and effect as correlated changes in two classes of phenomena, a correlation that could be represented concisely as the functional relation between two variables in a mathematical equation (e.g., Mach, 1883/1942, p. 325; see Abbagnano, 1967, p. 418).

As the example of causality suggests, the Machian approach to science is purely descriptive. For Mach, science is simply the economical description of facts; the aim of science, as stated in *The Science of Mechanics*, is to provide "the concisest and simplest possible knowledge of a given province of natural phenomena" (Mach, 1883/1942, p. 7). Once direct contact is made with a domain of phenomena through unprejudiced observation, the phenomena are always seen to occur in varying relationships of interdependence and are thus naturally described in terms of such dependencies. According to Mach, though, these descriptions of dependencies are nothing other than the laws of science, inductively derived and expressed as functional relations between classes of events.

As Bacon had done, Mach emphasized that the chief value of scientific laws lies in their utilitarian capacity to benefit people in their interaction with the world. The "task of science," wrote Mach (1886/1959), "is to provide the fully developed human individual with as perfect a means of orienting himself as possible. No other scientific ideal can be realized, and any other must be meaningless" (p. 37). The role of scientific laws in promoting adjustment to the environment is starkly revealed in Mach's assertion that "the ways even of science still lead to the mouth" (p. 23). Mach attributed the esteem in which the laws of science are held to their "high practical value" (1894/1943, p. 222) and held that the worth of scientific enquiry can be judged by the extent to which the investigator's "behaviour really leads to practical and intellectual advantages" (1905/1976, p. 11).

In his writings, Mach (1894/1943) once posed the question, "Does description accomplish all that the enquirer can ask?" His unhesitating reply was, "In my opinion, it does" (pp. 252–253). To go beyond description by seeking explanations of regularities in terms of hidden forces or hypothetical entities, that is, to supplement laws with theories, was to violate the demands of simplicity and economy in science. As Bacon warned against "flying to remote axioms," so Mach rejected any role for theories and hypotheses in science, except perhaps as "provisional helps" that would be abandoned once the aim of complete description was fulfilled (1883/1942, p. 590). Echoing Bacon's denunciation of the method of hypothesis (or of what he called "Anticipations of Nature"), Mach wrote in *The Science of Mechanics* that "we err when we expect more enlightenment from an hypothesis than from the facts themselves" (p. 600).

As a devout Darwinian, Mach viewed the demand for intellectual economy in science as a natural outgrowth of the demands of biological economy in nature. "Economy of communication and apprehension is of the very essence of science," he wrote (1883/1942, p. 7). At root, then, the problem with theories and hypotheses in Mach's view is that they are uneconomical in the sense of diverting attention away from the facts and impeding direct and efficient contact between an investigator and a domain of phenomena. The tradition of inductive positivism begun by Bacon was thus given a Darwinian twist by Mach, and the descriptive positivists' insistence on direct observation and simplicity of expression could now be justified on grounds of intellectual parsimony and efficiency of investigation as they are related ultimately to biological economy.

BACON, MACH, AND *THE BEHAVIOR OF ORGANISMS*

We are now in a position to point out the respects in which *The Behavior of Organisms* can properly be said to belong to the tradition of Bacon and Mach. That *The Behavior of Organisms* stands squarely within this tradition and represents an extension of descriptive positivism to the study of behavior may already be apparent from the foregoing account of that tradition. Indeed, the preceding characterization of the views of Bacon and Mach was drawn almost entirely from those of their works that B. F. Skinner read as a young man and subsequently acknowledged as having influenced his work. In his autobiography, we are told that the young Skinner became acquainted with the works of Francis Bacon while in the eighth grade, reading not only Bacon's *Essays*, *New Organon*, and *Advancement of Learning*, but also biographies of Bacon and books on his philosophy, and becoming an "ardent Baconian" in the process (Skinner, 1976b, p. 129; 1983, p. 406). Not coincidentally, Skinner returned to explicitly Baconian themes in the Epilogue of his final autobiographical volume, *A Matter of Consequences* (1983, pp. 406–407, 412; see also Kaufman, 1968). As for Mach, Skinner read *The Science of Mechanics* while in graduate school and adopted its historiocritical approach in his own dissertation of 1930 (Skinner, 1931). He later delved into Mach's *The Analysis of Sensations* (1886/1959) and *Knowledge and Error* (1905/1976), and continued to embrace a distinctly Machian outlook on science (see Day, 1980, p. 227; Marr, 1985; L. D. Smith, 1986, pp. 257–297).

In what ways, then, does *The Behavior of Organisms* embody the positivist heritage of Bacon and Mach? At the most general and obvious level, it is an avowedly *positivistic* work. Summarizing the approach laid out in the opening chapter, Skinner (1938) writes:

So far as scientific method is concerned, the system set up in the preceding chapter may be characterized as follows. It is positivistic. It confines itself to description rather than explanation. Its concepts are defined in terms of immediate observations. . . . Terms of this sort are used merely to bring together groups of observations, to state uniformities, and to express properties of behavior which transcend single instances. They are not hypotheses, in the sense of things to be proved or disproved, but convenient representations of things already known. (p. 44)

The emphasis on *descriptive* positivism is conspicuous throughout the book. Skinner argues that what is needed is a "directly descriptive science of behavior" (p. 5); he speaks of his concepts as having "sharp reference to behavior," the chief advantage of which is said to be that "the descriptive value of the term is kept at a maximum" (p. 440). Less descriptive approaches to behavioral science are criticized on these grounds, as when Skinner complains that mentalistic terms are lacking in "the immediacy of their reference to actual observations" (p. 441), or that Tolman's "behavior ratio" is a poor substitute for "measuring behavior directly" (p. 437), or that the methods of inferential statistics are guilty of "a general neglect of the problem of direct description" (p. 443). By way of contrast, the extensive use of cumulative records in *The Behavior of Organisms* is justified by the author in terms of their remaining "as close to the experimental data as possible" and by noting that they are "made directly by the rats themselves" without human intervention (p. 60).

The scheme laid out in *The Behavior of Organisms* is also avowedly *inductivist*. The system developed there is said to be "derived step by step from behavior itself" (p. 441) and is described as proceeding "through *induction* to the establishment of laws" (p. 437). In addition, the laws arrived at by induction are construed, in solid Machian fashion, as correlations between classes of observable events—stimuli and responses in the case of the static laws of the reflex—or as functional relationships between third variables and response rates in the case of the dynamic laws of the operant. Equally Machian is the treatment of causality given in the book, as when Skinner endorses "the substitution of correlation for cause" (p. 443). In its application to the reflex, this conception entails that the terms *stimulus* and *response* refer "to correlated entities, and to nothing more," that "the notion of a reflex is to be emptied of any connotation of the active 'push' of the stimulus," and that "all metaphorical and figurative definitions should be avoided as far as possible" (p. 21).

Echoing the Baconian–Machian aversion to hypotheses and theories in science, Skinner states outright that the system presented in *The Behavior of Organisms* "does not require them" (p. 44); hypotheses are needed neither as incentives to experimentation nor as means of organizing facts (pp. 44–45). He chastises those scientists "whose curiosity about nature is less than their curiosity about the accuracy of their guesses" (p. 44) and decries the "misdirected experimentation and bootless theorizing" about behavior that have arisen from gratuitous neurological hypotheses (p. 426). When hypothetical concepts *are* introduced in *The Behavior of Organisms*—as in the case of drives and emotional states—they are clearly indentified in terms of operations and their dispensability in favor of operations is carefully noted. Even the reflex reserve, the closest thing to a truly theoretical construct to be found in the book, is closely tied to direct graphical representations of data and is said to be measurable in terms of the process of extinction that exhausts it (p. 26).[2]

All of these points of congruence between *The Behavior of Organisms* and the Baconian–Machian tradition of positivism will likely be apparent enough to anyone who has read the book with care. There are other more specific ways in which the book reflects its heritage that are perhaps less evident. Consider the distinctive Machian theme of economy that runs through *The Behavior of Organisms* as a largely unstated but often-invoked premise. The criteria according to which a scientific system may be judged, says Skinner, are "the usefulness and economy of the system with respect to the data at hand" (p. 438). The Pavlovian interpretation of extinction as due to an active inhibitory force is rejected on the grounds that "the number of terms needed in the system is unnecessarily increased" (p. 97; see Donahoe & Palmer, 1988). Similarly, the Hullian system is attacked for its unguarded proliferation of unnecessary terms—its "supernumeraries," as Skinner calls them— and for its failure to strive for "that ultimate simplicity of formulation that it is reasonable to demand of a scientific system" (Skinner, 1938, p. 436). As in Mach's writings, the theme of economy in science in *The Behavior of Organisms* goes beyond that of conceptual parsimony to encompass the economy of scientific investigation. The descriptive approach to science is defended by Skinner as possessing "greater efficiency" than the hypothetico-deductive approach (p. 44). The singling out of variables for study is said to be done "for the sake of convenient investigation and description" (p. 434), and the order in which they are studied may be dictated by considerations of "experimental convenience" (p. 46). The choice of the white rat as a subject is also defended in terms of its experimental convenience (pp. 47–48), and "limitations of time and energy" are cited as part of the justification for the use of small numbers of subjects (p. 442). The language of economy, expedience, convenience, and simplicity is found throughout *The Behavior of Organisms*; and the language of truth, hypothesis, deduction, and theory testing is everywhere notably absent.

Another way in which *The Behavior of Organisms* can be seen to reflect its heritage in the Bacon–Mach tradition lies in its treatment of terms drawn from the vernacular. Just as Bacon complained that popular language is afflicted with the "ill and unfit choice of words," Skinner (1938) states that the vernacular is "clumsy and obese" (p. 7). Bacon's statement that ordinary language follows "lines of division" based on "the vulgar understanding" rather than on the "true divisions of nature" is paralleled by Skinner's claim that the terms of the vernacular "draw unnecessary or unreal distinctions" (p. 7). For Skinner, vernacular terms will be admissible only if their "experimental reality" can be demonstrated (pp. 41–42), and the "points of contact between a popular and a scientific system will presumably not be many" (p. 8). Moreover, Skinner eschews the practice, not uncommon among other behaviorists of the time, of attempting to translate the mentalistic terms of everyday discourse into the terms of his scientific system. Indeed, just as Bacon (1620/1960) noted that words describing actions (as opposed to objects) are especially prone to distortion and error (p. 58), Skinner (1938) shows a special concern with the problematic nature of vernacular verbs that purport to name meaningful units of action. In Skinner's extended analysis (pp. 6–8, 41–43), even a verb such as "to hide," which would seem to have relatively clear-cut reference to behavior, must be rejected from scientific discourse on the grounds that it cannot adequately meet the test of experimental reality.

The heavy reliance in *The Behavior of Organisms* on visual displays of data represents yet another indication of its author's affinity with the descriptive positivism of Bacon. Bacon's telling statement that "all depends on keeping the eye steadily fixed upon the facts of nature and so receiving their images simply as they are" is but one of many expressions in his writings of his overriding faith in visual evidence and its organization into visible patterns. The tables of induction for which Bacon is renowned were developed by him with the explicit aim of promoting the easy discernment of patterns in the data and as a visual aid to remembering and using the findings. "Natural and experimental history is so various and diffuse that it confounds and distracts the understanding, unless it be ranged and presented to view in a suitable order" (Bacon, 1620/1960, p. 130). In similar fashion, the 148 figures contained in *The Behavior of Organisms* comprise simple images of natural facts, ordered in such a way as to facilitate comprehension, induce relevant comparisons, and suggest inductive generalizations. Bacon also advocated the use of his tables as a means of promoting the discovery of new facts and the design of new experiments. We know from Skinner's (1956) account of the research that went into *The Behavior of Organisms* that the cumulative records served just such a function for him.

Last, the tradition of descriptive positivism is naturally committed to the assumption that there is order in nature to be discerned by the attentive investigator. In science, Bacon (1620/1960) states, "Order must be our pattern," (p. 114) and that order is found in nature in the form of those "true and exquisite lines" (p. 114) of division that mark the natural world. For purposes of dissecting and analyzing this order, the experimental method is especially well suited. So it is with the approach presented in *The Behavior of Organisms*. When it comes to defining natural units of behavior, Skinner adopts Baconian language in introducing what is arguably the central idea of the book:

The analysis of behavior is not an act of arbitrary subdividing. We cannot define the concepts of stimulus and response quite as simply as "parts of behavior and environment" without taking account of the natural lines of fracture along which behavior and environment actually break. (p. 33)

In discussing the generic nature of the stimulus and response, an insight fundamental to the discovery of the operant, Skinner appeals to the orderliness of experimentally induced dynamic changes to mark the level of restriction at which a genuine unit of behavior emerges. As with Bacon, the order of nature—its lines of fracture—has betrayed itself, and it has done so not in its natural freedom but only when forced out of its natural state by the hand of the experimenter. The resulting natural unit of behavior, as Skinner notes, considerably broadens the field of operation for a science of behavior by virtue of the identification of those parts of behavior and environment that have "experimental reality" (p. 41). The concept of "experimental reality"—in some respects, a bold notion for a positivist—neatly captures the deep relation seen by descriptive positivists, from Bacon to the present, between the order of nature and the human capacity to manipulate the world.

The ways in which *The Behavior of Organisms* embodies the positivism of Bacon and Mach, however striking, represent only a limited subset of the ways in which Skinner's work as a whole evinces the influence of these two thinkers. The foregoing review of Skinner's philosophical roots was limited to those aspects of descriptive positivism that find expression in *The Behavior of Organisms*, but there are further themes in the Skinnerian corpus that derive from the Bacon–Mach heritage. Prominent among these are Skinner's notion of the egoless individual (1957, p. 313; 1947/1961b, p. 236; 1983, pp. 410–413), which has its counterpart in Mach (Blackmore, 1972, p. 37) and even Bacon (Whitney, 1986, pp. 198–199); Skinner's use of the history of science to criticize opposing views of science and to justify his own (compare Skinner, 1931, with Bacon, 1620/1960, pp. 59–62, 69–75, and Mach, 1883/1942); his tracing the roots of science to skilled artisanship (Skinner, 1953, p. 14; 1974, p. ix; Bacon, 1620/1960, pp. 8, 25, 72; Mach, 1883/1942, pp. 1–6, 613–616; 1905/1976, p. 55); his belief in a crucial role for serendipity in scientific discovery (Skinner, 1956; Bacon, 1620/1960, p. 100; Mach, 1894/1943, p. 265); his antipathy to overreliance on logic in science (Skinner, 1945,

1956; Bacon, 1620/1960, pp. 66–67, 79; Mach, 1905/1976, p. xxxi); his psychologistic epistemology (Skinner, 1957, chap. 18; Mach, 1905/1976; on Bacon's psychologism, see Jardine, 1974, chap. 4); his belief that the methods of science are not foreordained but rather evolve as science evolves (Skinner, 1945, p. 277; 1957, p. 430; Bacon, 1620/1960, p. 120; Mach, 1905/1976, p. xxxiii); his assumption of a close connection between science and technology (Skinner, 1969, pp. 95–98; Bacon, 1620/1960, p. 39); and his social meliorism and utopianism (Skinner, 1948; Bacon, 1624/1942). In sum, although *The Behavior of Organisms* stands as an important and seminal work, both in Skinner's career and for the operant tradition at large, it by no means exhausts the ways in which Skinner assimilated the Baconian and Machian legacy and adapted it to the context of twentieth-century psychology.

DESCRIPTIVE POSITIVISM AND LOGICAL POSITIVISM

Having indicated why *The Behavior of Organisms* is properly viewed as representing the branch of positivism that can be traced to Bacon and Mach, the remaining aim of this chapter is to sketch the crucial differences between this brand of *descriptive* positivism and the *logical* positivism that is widely regarded as having been discredited since its heyday in the 1930s. To do so will help us understand why the positivistic scheme laid out in *The Behavior of Organisms* fifty years ago has continued to flourish despite the much-publicized decline of positivistic thought during those five decades.

Because the differences between Skinnerian positivism and logical positivism have been discussed in depth by others (e.g., Day, 1969a; Moore, 1985; L. D. Smith, 1986; Zuriff, 1980, 1985), it will suffice here to summarize the chief distinctions that bear most directly on Skinner's Baconian–Machian heritage. First, as a form of so-called "linguistic philosophy," logical positivism focuses on the analysis of language rather than on the analysis of the world as it exists outside of language. This focus, in itself, constitutes a violation of Bacon's dictum that scientists should study nature, not words. Descriptive positivism, by way of contrast, focuses on the natural world—including the enquirers who operate in it—and studies words with an eye to determining their actual effects, beneficial or otherwise, on the conduct of investigation. In a related vein, logical positivism stresses the formal analysis or "rational reconstruction" of the *end products* of science (i.e., its finished theories). The positivism of Bacon, Mach, and Skinner concerns itself with the *process* of science as it is carried out and used in the world. It is utilitarian rather than formalist; it speaks the language of economy, contingency, and control over nature rather than the language of logic, necessity, and truth by correspondence. In logical positivism, the data of observation are to be organized by the formal means of mathematics and logic; in descriptive positivism, as we have seen, data are more likely to be organized in the directly useful form of visual patterns and displays.

Logical positivism allows a role for theories, hypotheses, and hypothetical constructs that go beyond the observable; descriptive positivism, of course, strives to avoid such devices, preferring to remain at the level of laws, which are conceived as functional relations among classes of observable events. Logical positivism endorses the hypothetico-deductive method and gives it a logical formulation; descriptive positivism shuns the method of hypothesis as wasteful guesswork and a harmful diversion from the task of providing complete descriptions. Similarly, logical positivism encourages explanation and formalizes it in the deductive–nomological model; descriptive positivism holds that explanation amounts to nothing more than complete description.

As a final point, logical positivism gladly accepts vernacular terms, including those of common-sense mentalistic psychology, as legitimate scientific discourse as long as they are defined in an intersubjectively verifiable way (cf. Carnap's classic 1935 treatment of "anger"). Descriptive positivists hold that vernacular terms should be subjected to the test of "experimental reality." Logical positivists, in fact, cannot even speak meaningfully of "reality," whereas the descriptive positivist can speak of real and unreal divisions of reality when there are good inductive grounds for doing so.

CONCLUSION

When *The Behavior of Organisms* was published more than fifty years ago, its appearance coincided with both the ascendancy of logical positivism in philosophy and the beginnings of its rise to popularity and influence among psychologists. In the 1930s and early 1940s, much of American psychology was turning to logical positivism, with its stress on rigorous formal methods, as a scientific philosophy that would give psychology the grounding it required to become a legitimate science (see Bergmann & Spence, 1941; Kattsoff, 1939; Koch, 1941; Stevens, 1939; and discussion in L. D. Smith, 1986).[3] This temporal coincidence helps account for why the tradition of operant behaviorism established by *The Behavior of Organisms* has sometimes been associated with logical positivism. By now, however, it should be clear that the positivism embodied in the book—the positivism of Bacon, Mach, and Skinner—is of a very different order. Intellectual frameworks, like the human activity that gives rise to them, have their natural lines of fracture; and to fail to see those natural divisions for what they are is to misunderstand the philosophical allegiances that are manifested in scientific works.

Given that logical positivism was the reigning philosophical outlook at the time *The Behavior of Organisms* was being written, Skinner's independence of it testifies to his Baconian skepticism toward authority. In this degree at least, Skinner's iconoclasm served him well. If Feigl is right that Skinner was both brilliant and consistent in his positivism, it is because he sufficiently withstood the philosophical currents of his time to embrace an older version of positivism that was free of some of the obvious defects of the twentieth-century version and because he embraced it with the consistency and determination that was required to translate it into a viable tradition of behavioral science.

The recognition that Skinner's work is not to be identified with the failed tradition of logical positivism leaves unanswered the question of exactly what strengths and liabilities his work may have derived from its very real historical and conceptual associations with Baconian–Machian positivism. Attempts to answer this question, however, will not meet with easy success. To see that the assessment of Bacon and Mach is germane to the assessment of Skinner is by no means to be in possession of a verdict about their shared brand of positivism, if only because history has not yielded any clearer a consensus about Bacon or Mach than it has about Skinner.[4] Still, the benefits of accurately identifying the philosophical allegiances of any scientific tradition should not be underestimated. For example, those critics of Skinnerian psychology who are puzzled by its strident antiformalism in matters of methodology, or by its seemingly anachronistic conflation of science and technology, or by its incongruous incorporation of utopianism will do well to understand that its philosophical roots lie more in the positivism of centuries past than in the positivism of the twentieth century. Only then will the operant tradition that stems from *The Behavior of Organisms* be understood correctly as part of a wider legacy and the implications of its genuine philosophical affiliations begin to be unraveled.

AUTHOR'S NOTE

An earlier version of this chapter was presented as "*The Behavior of Organisms* in Historical Perspective: Bacon, Mach, and Skinner" in the symposium "*The Behavior of Organisms* at Fifty" at the meeting of the Association for Behavior Analysis, Philadelphia, May 27, 1988. The present title—chosen for its applicability to historical, no less than scientific, inquiry—derives from Bacon's (1620/1960) injunction to "begin the inquiry nearer the source than men have done heretofore" (p. 21). I wish to thank Terry Knapp for bibliographical assistance with this chapter and Tony Nevin for imparting his insights about the conceptual underpinnings of behavior analysis.

Chapter 5 _____

Some Historical and Conceptual Relations among Logical Positivism, Behaviorism, and Cognitive Psychology

Jay Moore

Logical positivism, behaviorism, and cognitive psychology are three of the most influential intellectual positions of the twentieth century. Logical positivism is an approach to philosophy, whereas behaviorism and cognitive psychology are generally regarded as competing orientations in contemporary psychology. The purpose of this chapter is to examine the historical and conceptual relations.

We will begin by briefly reviewing the history and principal features of the three positions. We will then consider three specific conceptual issues germane to the relation among the three positions: (1) the interpretation of theoretical terms, (2) type–identity physicalism, and (3) epistemological dualism. After examining these three conceptual issues, we will turn to Skinner's radical behaviorism to examine how it differs from the positions reviewed to that point.

This chapter is not concerned so much with examining the technical features of the positions, as would a philosopher of science. Rather, it will examine the positions from the point of view of an informed reader of the psychological literature. Let us begin, then, by briefly examining the history and principal features of the three points of view.

HISTORY AND PRINCIPAL FEATURES OF LOGICAL POSITIVISM, BEHAVIORISM, AND COGNITIVE PSYCHOLOGY

Logical Positivism

Logical positivism is an orientation to philosophy which holds that all meaningful statements must either be verifiable in terms of directly observable phenomena or reducible by logical operations to such phenomena. Logical positivism originated during the 1920s, when a distinguished group of scholars, known as the Vienna Circle, began to meet and discuss the changing nature of scientific knowledge (see also L. D. Smith, 1986; Suppe, 1977). Although the leader of the Circle was the philosopher Moritz Schlick, many of its members were not philosophers but, rather, were mathematicians, physicists, and logicians (Rudolf Carnap, Herbert Feigl, Philipp Frank, Friedreich Waismann). One was even a social economist (Otto Neurath).

A particularly strong impetus for the Circle's discussions were the stunning conceptual advances of the "new physics." Until perhaps the first quarter of the twentieth century, science was presumed to progress via the ever more careful observation of nature's mechanisms at work. However, the success of the "new physics" was specifically attributable to its proposals of a host of unobserved entities at the "atomic" level. Clearly, the "new physics" implied that science was more than simply a matter of carefully charting nature's observable mechanisms. Given these developments, was an alternative approach to scientific knowledge required, such as a return to idealism?

The logical positivists strongly felt that it was not. More specifically, they sought to guarantee the meaningfulness of scientific statements and, indeed, statements in general by linking Mach's empiricist thesis—that science was fundamentally the description of the scientist's experience—with formal logic. That is, appeals to unobservables were perfectly reasonable, so long as the entities were derived according to the approved techniques of formal logic. In particular, Wittgenstein's (1922) *Tractatus Logico-Philosophicus* was regarded as setting the standard for securing the requisite meaningfulness of statements via a logical analysis.

An important milestone in the historical development of the new position was the publication of Carnap's (1928) monumental *Der Logische Aufbau der Welt*, which knit the various epistemological threads into comprehensive fabric. The 1930s evidenced further concern with establishing the meaningfulness of statements in general and of scientific statements in particular. An overarching concern during the 1930s was the "unity of science," a heroic attempt to reduce all scientifically meaningful statements of whatever discipline to the physicalist observation language. The 1930s also witnessed a slow series of modifications that would result in logical positivism's becoming known as "logical empiricism." More will be said later about certain of these modifications. At this point, suffice it to say that under political pressure from Nazism during the 1930s, the Circle was forced to disperse. The members ended up primarily in England and the United States, where concerns with pragmatism and operationism had produced a particularly sympathetic intellectual environment.

Through the 1940s and into the 1950s, the logical empiricists grappled with distinctions between observational and theoretical terms and between factual (synthetic) and logical (analytic) truths. Perhaps the major concern among logical empiricists, as reflected in the contents of the Minnesota Studies during the later 1950s and into the 1960s, was the clarification of physicalism and the physicalistic treatment of mental terms and the mind–body problem. The influence of logical empiricism diminished in subsequent decades, although it remains a major force in "philosophy of science" among natural and social science departments in universities, if not among philosophy departments.

In brief, the logical positivists set out to provide a "rational reconstruction" of scientific epistemology that "did justice" to the theoretical accomplishments of modern physics, through the blend of empiricist principles and formal logic. From their beginning concern with scientific statements, the logical positivists extended their principles to all forms of discourse, in an effort to bring some sort of order to the human intellectual endeavor. They felt that only cognitively significant statements were meaningful, and those statements were either (1) verifiable in terms of public observations or (2) reducible by logical operations to public observations. Statements of emotional significance only, as judged by an inability to be verified against a formal analysis involving the facts of experience, were to be rejected.

Overall, logical positivism evinced an antimetaphysical disdain for pseudoproblems that could not be reduced to a matter of the description of experience. Questions of "why" were to be engaged as questions of "how." Statements involving untestable a prioris, which could not be checked against the facts of experience, were not allowed. Verifiability in terms of publicly observable phenomena or logical constructions from publicly observable phenomena was the touchstone for determining meaningful statements. To the extent there could be a "philosophy," that philosophy was not about the world itself. That enterprise would almost surely end up in a morass of pointless metaphysical speculation. Rather, philosophy was about the formal, symbolic properties of the language used to speak of the world.

Behaviorism

Behaviorism is generally regarded as an orientation to psychology that advocates studying observable behavior according to the methods of natural science rather than making inferences about mental life from introspective verbal reports. Behaviorism is largely an American orientation to psychology, springing from background interests in animal psychology, the school of functionalism, and a pragmatic philosophical orientation (see Boakes, 1984; Day, 1980; L. D. Smith, 1986; Zuriff, 1985).

Distinctions are commonly made among several varieties of behaviorism. Classical behaviorism applies to the positions of such figures as Pavlov, Watson, and Guthrie from the early 1900s until the 1930s. Of importance in this variety is the concept of the conditioned reflex, with an immediately antecedent stimulus, S, and the ensuing response, R. The concepts were molecular; and many, such as excitation and inhibition, were taken from physiology (e.g., Watson, 1913, 1919).

Neobehaviorism is, in general, the chronological successor to classical behaviorism. It employed larger-scale ("molar") concepts of stimulus and response rather than the molecular concepts of classical behaviorism. In addition, neobehaviorism incorporated mediating organismic variables which were not directly observable but which were thought to be necessary to secure an adequate explanation of behavior. Tolman (1932) was particularly energetic in introducing theoretical terms, but his application was soon matched by other neobehaviorists, such as Hull (1943) and Spence (1948). Thus, neobehaviorism may also be referred to as mediational S-O-R (stimulus-organism-response) neobehaviorism, to indicate the confluence of these several traditions (see also Leahey, 1987a; Moore, 1987).

Among the principal features of mediational neobehaviorism are (1) the insistence on intersubjective techniques for securing and expressing empirical data; (2) the advocacy of stimulus-and-response variables as the only legitimate independent and dependent variables, with conventional operational definitions of hypothetical, mediating variables; (3) the accommodation of causal processes in terms of the model of antecedent causation, where causal efficacy is vested in a chain beginning with the independent variable, continuing with the mediational, intervening variable, and terminating with the dependent variable; and (4) the position that psychological knowledge is to be regarded as a theoretical inference about the mediating processes or events going on somewhere else, at some other level of observation, described in different terms, and using behavior as evidence to support the inferences.

Radical behaviorism, or behavior analysis, is the particular position associated with B. F. Skinner (for discussion of historical context of the phrase radical behaviorism, see Schneider & Morris, 1987; see also Day, 1980). It differs appreciably from mediational neobehaviorism (Moore, 1987). Among its principal features are (1) an embrace of monism and determinism; (2) an emphasis on functional explanatory concepts; (3) an embrace of the metatheoretical perspective of Darwinian theory; (4) an inclusion of psychology among the biological life sciences, with methods and concepts appropriate to those disciplines; (5) a vigorously antimentalistic posture that rejects any theoretically critical distinction between subjective and objective (or any comparable dichotomy) as it pertains to mediating processes from non-behavioral dimensions, but which nevertheless accommodates the contributions of private phenomena at a behavioral level; (6) a rejection of verbal behavior as essentially a referential activity, which leads further to the rejection of most forms of explanation tacitly employed by mediational neobehaviorism, and the accompanying appeal to mediating theoretical terms (intervening variables, hypothetical constructs); and (7) an insistence that behavior be studied at its own level and not studied to provide the basis for inferences about mediating causal variables in a neural, psychic, or conceptual dimension.

Cognitive Psychology

Cognitive psychology is generally regarded as an orientation to psychology in which consideration of various internal phenomena (acts, states, mechanism, processes, presumed to be operating in a "mental" dimension) is taken as a unique, necessary, and the primary contribution to a causal explanation of behavior. Cognitive psychology is a relatively recent development, and much of its historical background concerns events since World War II (see Baars, 1986; Flanagan, 1984; Gardner, 1987; Knapp & Robertson, 1986). Among the precursors of cognitive psychology are developments in (1) information and communication theory, (2) cybernetics and engineering technology, and (3) mathematics and computer technology. Of course, cognitive psychology grew from a base in the discipline of psychology. Consequently, two other, explicitly psychological themes may be acknowledged as precursors: (4) the verbal learning and memory tradition, and (5) mediational neobehaviorism itself.

Historical highlights in the development of cognitive psychology include September 11, 1956, the date of the Symposium on Information Theory at MIT, which Gardner (1987, p. 28) marks as the birthdate of cognitive psychology (although Knapp, 1986b, pp. 16–17, reports that the first book in the English language explicitly titled *Cognitive Psychology* was actually written by T. V. Moore and published in 1939). The Harvard Center for Cognitive Studies opened in 1960, a year which also marked the publication of Miller, Galanter, and Pribram's (1960) influential book, *Plans and the Structure of Behavior*. Neisser's seminal text, formally titled *Cognitive Psychology,* was published in 1967. During the 1970s, the number of textbooks and journals in the area rapidly increased, and cognitive psychology began to receive strong support from the Sloan Foundation. At present, cognitive psychology is flourishing in universities and research centers across the country (Gardner, 1987).

In general, cognitive psychology adheres to an "informational" description of psychological events. Input is converted to a representation, an operation is then performed on the representation, and an output is produced from the new representation. It follows a principle of "recursive decomposition," where the input is decomposed into a number of components, followed by a specified ordering of how the representation flows through the system of components in time. The process can be described in terms of flowcharts. The emphasis is on the abstract, conceptual description of functional properties of a system. The enterprise follows a top-down, design stance. There is further a heavy use of the computer metaphor, where the aim is to infer an operating system or a program. This objective is neutral with respect to hardware (see Palmer & Kimchi, 1986).

Cognitive psychology emphasizes the universal principles that describe abstractly the biological properties that enable organisms to behave as they do in a context. It does not heavily emphasize affect, context, culture, or history as variables that need to be incorporated into the causal explanation of behavior. The enterprise bears the imprint of Kantian rationalism and the concern with how form and structure are supplied to experience by way of a rich system of a priori mental structures (Wessells, 1981, 1982).

Functionalism is generally regarded as the philosophy of mind that supplies the philosophical underpinnings of cognitive psychology. According to functionalism, mental states are functional states that can be realized in multiple ways; their actual physical embodiment is an incidental consideration. The position is at once intentional, agent oriented, and intentional.

Last, a central claim in cognitive psychology is that any form of behaviorism, including Skinner's radical behaviorism, either ignores phenomena that are necessary for the proper understanding of behavior or tries to deal with mental phenomena inappropriately, as a consequence of its heritage from logical positivism. In connection with this claim, cognitive psychology argues that behaviorism needs to be theoretically liberated to talk of underlying processes and mechanisms and not just the relation between environment and observable behavior because a genuine understanding cannot be achieved by restricting the analysis to the level of observable behavior. A causal explanation of behavior is incomplete unless it specifies the underlying mental phenomena. The mental phenomena are therefore not identical with behavior, and they should not be defined in terms of behavior, as they say behaviorism attempts to define them because of the influence of logical positivism.

COMPARISON AND CONTRAST AMONG LOGICAL POSITIVISM, BEHAVIORISM, AND COGNITIVE PSYCHOLOGY

As noted above, logical positivism is an approach to philosophy. In contrast, behaviorism and cognitive psychology are instances of concrete laboratory science. At a broad level, certain general points of similarity do exist among the three. All claim to be materialist and antimetaphysical. All emphasize empirical and objective methodologies rather than introspection. All advocate formulating general laws and theories, in which formal, quantitative treatments of the data play a major role. Last, all view themselves as turning points in the histories of their disciplines, offering fresh starts and a new basis for progress.

Nevertheless, despite the foregoing similarities, most treatments suggest that a greater continuity exits between logical positivism and behaviorism than between logical positivism and cognitive psychology, as indicated by behaviorism's heavy emphasis on observable behavior and objectivity in attempting to secure an understanding of behavior (see L. D. Smith, 1986, and Toulmin & Leary, 1985, for further discussion of the relation between behaviorism and logical positivism). Indeed, such sources as Baars (1986), Flanagan (1984), Fodor (1968), Gardner (1987), and Sober (1983), among others, have contributed to a sort of "received view" regarding the relations among logical positivism, behaviorism, and cognitive psychology (although admittedly no single source may embody all aspects of the view).

Figure 5.1 attempts to present the received view graphically. As suggested in Figure 5.1, classical S-R behaviorism in the Watsonian tradition, mediational S-O-R neobehaviorism in the Hull–Spence tradition, and modern radical behaviorism and behavior analysis are viewed as nothing more than instances of the same moribund viewpoint. Their adherence to empiricistic, logical positivist–inspired principles has prevented them from dealing effectively with certain underlying phenomena that must be dealt with to secure the proper understanding of behavior. As a result, they are forever bound to crawl along at their own slow pace (see L. D. Smith, 1986, for development of this point).

In contrast, the received view assumes the greatest increase in the scientific understanding of behavior has occurred because of the rejection of logical positivist–inspired behaviorist principles and the introduction of cognitive concepts, beginning in the mid-1950s. These concepts are not defined in terms of observable behavior. Rather, they are concerned with the mental states and processes that underlie behavior, knowledge of which is regarded as essential for the proper understanding of behavior.

An alternative to the received view is presented in Figure 5.2. According to this view, behavior analysis constitutes the fresh approach. Cognitive psychology is actually the intellectual position that continues in the tradition of

Figure 5.1
The "Received View"

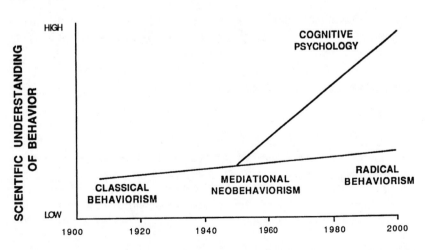

Figure 5.2
An "Alternative View"

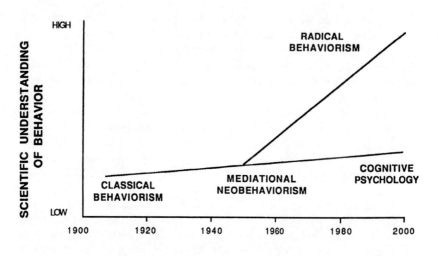

logical positivist–inspired mediational neobehaviorism rather than behavior analysis. Some of the criticisms that cognitive psychologists direct at mediational neobehaviorism simply do not apply. Ironically, others apply equally, in principle, to cognitive psychology. Any claims that scientific understanding has increased as a consequence of the so-called cognitive revolution are regarded as simply mischievous.

To be sure, the interpretation presented in Figure 5.2 is decidedly unconventional. What evidence would support it? From the perspective of this chapter, consideration of at least the following three points will do so: (1) the interpretation of theoretical terms, (2) type–identity physicalism, and (3) epistemological dualism. Let us begin, then, by considering the interpretation of theoretical terms.

THE INTERPRETATION OF THEORETICAL TERMS

Historical Background

According to standard accounts, the "behavioral revolution" took place in the first quarter of the century when Watson's (1913, 1919) classical S-R behaviorism overthrew the prevailing concern with the contents of consciousness as revealed through introspection. As noted earlier, classical behaviorism advocated instead a concern with observable behavior in terms of the S-R elicitation model. Although the resulting emphasis on observable behavior was valuable, psychology did end up ignoring many factors relevant to the understanding of human behavior. During the 1930s, psychologists came to question the wisdom of restricting their concerns to observable behavior. As a consequence, the pendulum then swung the other way. Mediational S-O-R neobehaviorism was born as psychologists reintroduced mental phenomena into explanations as mediating "organismic" variables. The problem was how to remain scientifically respectable in the process.

Logical positivism and the allied doctrine of operationism offered some support. Neither logical positivism nor operationism ever advocated that science consider only observable phenomena (Boring, 1950b, pp. 653–659; Moore, 1985; Suppe, 1977, pp. 13–15). However, the appeals to unobservable phenomena had to be handled correctly, that is, as statements involving "theoretical" terms. More now needs to be said regarding the historical context of these events, both within logical positivist philosophy and behavioral psychology.

During the late 1920s and early 1930s, a philosophical position developed under the auspices of logical positivism that was called "logical behaviorism" (see Hempel, 1935/1949). According to this position, "mental" concepts in psychological explanations were to be treated as "dispositions." Dispositions were then to be treated as instances of theoretical concepts and defined explicitly and exhaustively in terms of behavior; that is, all mental or dispositional terms were to be reducible without remainder to observable behavior. An emphasis on observable behavior seemed entirely consistent with the classical behaviorism of the time, and thus behaviorism and logical positivism seemed to be progressing in parallel.

From Logical Positivism to Logical Empiricism

Unfortunately, there were technical problems brought about by the logical structure of explanations that appeal to intervening variables and dispositions. For example, intervening variables are logically superfluous. If they are entirely reducible to public observations, then they do not contribute anything more than the public observations from which they are derived. In effect, they are redundant and unnecessary (see Hempel, 1958, for technical discussion of this problem, also known as the "theoretician's dilemma").

In addition, there is the problem of the "counterfactual conditional." Suppose a substance dissolves in water, and the explanation of its dissolving appeals to the dispositional property of "solubility." The dispositional property of solubility is then defined in terms of a conditional statement: "If a substance is placed in water, then it will dissolve." However, by truth functional logic, a conditional statement is true even if the antecedent is false. Hence, in the absence of the test condition (i.e., being placed in water), solubility could be attributed to a rock just as well as to salt (for further discussion of this matter, see Zuriff, 1985, p. 59ff.; Suppe, 1977, pp. 36–45).

In the mid-1930s, Rudolf Carnap, a leader of the logical positivist movement, introduced partial definitions, reductive chains, and bilateral reduction sentences to correct these problems (e.g., Carnap, 1936, 1937). The upshot was that logical positivism dropped the requirement that theoretical terms, such as mental concepts, be exhaustively defined with reference to observable events and required only that they be linked via logic to observable events. As alluded to earlier in this chapter, the changes were of sufficient magnitude to warrant a new name for the movement—logical empiricism rather than logical positivism (L. D. Smith, 1986, p. 28). In any event, by the 1960s, Feigl (1963), an eminent logical positivist and logical empiricist, was able to write:

> Given this general outlook it becomes obvious that the naive peripheralistic forms of behaviorism must be repudiated and their shortcomings remedied by the admission of central states and processes as the genuine referents of psychological terms. Although at the current state of neuropsychological research specific identifications of these states and processes are mostly quite problematic, this does not make the idea in principle objectionable. . . . Concepts such as memory trace . . . may plausibly be taken to refer to (as yet very incompletely specified) central conditions. (p. 252)

This statement indicates the remarkable liberalization of logical positivist theoretical outlook that occurred during the 1940s and 1950s.

Behaviorism and Its Theoretical Terms

After behaviorism began to embrace mediating organismic variables, it similarly had to deal with the question of whether those variables were to be defined exhaustively in terms of publicly observable behavior. Behaviorism made contact with the issues faced by logical positivist philosophy in connection with theoretical terms via its commitment to operationism. The original interpretation of operationism was that the mediating theoretical terms, in fact, did need to be explicitly and exhaustively defined with reference to observables.

However, as had logical positivism, behaviorism soon began to question whether its theoretical terms referred to only publicly observable behavior, or whether they had "surplus meaning" beyond phenomena that were publicly observable (although see Toulmin & Leary, 1985, p. 605). Recognizing that psychologists used more and more "theoretical" terms that were not exhaustively defined and that psychologists often used those terms that did and those terms that did not require exhaustive definition interchangeably, MacCorquodale and Meehl (1948) eventually suggested a linguistic convention to calm the epistemologically troubled waters. They suggested that theoretical terms that were exhaustively reducible to a set of publicly observable operations, without surplus meaning, be designated "intervening variables." This interpretation was the original interpretation and was the interpretation involved in the original sense of operationism. They further suggested that theoretical terms with meaning beyond the set of publicly observable operations to which they were related be designated "hypothetical constructs." Both kinds of theoretical terms were permissible, so long as the usage was consistent. This second interpretation was akin to that proposed by Carnap some years earlier. In addition, it was probably more in keeping with how scientists were actually going about their business.

The upshot was that the distinction liberalized the principle of operationism substantially; behavioral theorists once again felt reassured their verbal–theoretical practices were congruent with their experimental practices. Thus, Tolman (1949), who introduced theoretical terms to psychology, eventually abandoned his original intervening variable interpretation of theoretical terms, coming to favor the hypothetical construct interpretation:

I am now convinced that "intervening variables" to which we attempt to give merely operational meaning by tying them through empirically grounded functions either to the stimulus variables, on the one hand, or to response variables, on the other, really can give us no help unless we can also imbed them in a model from whose attributed properties we can deduce new relationships to be looked for. That is, to use Meehl and MacCorquodale's distinction, I would abandon what they call pure "intervening variables" for what they call "hypothetical constructs," and insist that hypothetical constructs be parts of a more general hypothesized model or substrate. (p. 49)

This issue is important because a major premise of the received view is that both logical positivism and behaviorism define theoretical concepts exhaustively in terms of intersubjectively verifiable behavior. For example, Fodor (1968), a cognitive psychologist and one of the most vocal critics of behaviorism, formally distinguishes between behaviorism and the mentalism of cognitive psychology on the basis of whether theoretical and mental concepts are defined in terms of observable behavior:

To qualify as a behaviorist in the broad sense of that term that I shall employ, one need only believe that the following proposition expresses a necessary truth: For each mental predicate that can be employed in a psychological explanation, there must be at least one description of behavior to which it bears a logical connection. (p. 51)

A mentalist is, then, simply someone who denies "necessarily P." . . . The distinction between mentalism and behaviorism is both exclusive and exhaustive. (p. 55)

The implication of the received view is that cognitive psychology is different from, and superior to, mediational neobehaviorism precisely because cognitive psychology is not constrained to conceive of unobservables in terms of physicalistically defined, intersubjectively verifiable measures.

However, this picture may not be as clear cut as one might expect from reading Fodor (1968). As the passage from Tolman (1949) indicates, mediational neobehaviorists came to abandon the exhaustive operational definition and intervening variable interpretation of theoretical terms in favor of the more liberalized hypothetical construct interpretation. For example, Hull's "oscillation factor" (1943, p. 304ff.) and "afferent neural interaction" (1943, p. 349ff.) do not refer to publicly observable behavior. Similarly, although Hull–Spence r_g-s_g mechanisms were originally intended to refer to material and peripheral phenomena, those mechanisms grew to be highly chimerical as they were called on to explain more and more research findings. Thus, Fodor may be characterizing a behaviorism to which no one actually adheres, or at least has not adhered for well over thirty years.

Theoretical Terms in Mediational Neobehaviorism and Cognitive Psychology

Recent treatments of the history of behaviorism and cognitive psychology point out that many cognitive psychologists actually began their scientific careers as Hull–Spence theorists in the tradition of mediational S-O-R neobehaviorism (Baars, 1986; Leahey, 1987b). These Hull–Spence theorists quite naturally carried forth certain of their theoretical practices. To the extent they did, their application of theoretical terms as hypothetical constructs was the same.

Leahey (1987b) explicitly points out the strong relation between the practices of mediational neobehaviorism and cognitive psychology in the following three passages:

The mediationalists' commitment to internalizing S-R language resulted primarily from their desire to preserve rigor and avoid the apparent unscientific character of "junkshop psychology." . . . However, when a new language of power, rigor, and precision came along—the language of computer programming—it proved easy for mediational psychologists to abandon their r-s life raft for the ocean liner of information processing. (p. 393)

Herbert Simon, one of the founders of modern information processing psychology, betrays the continuity of information processing with behavioralism, and even its affinity with behaviorism, very well. (p. 437)

Lachman, Lachman, and Butterfield's explication of the information processing "paradigm" makes it clear that information processing psychology is a form of behavioralism with strong affinity to all but radical behaviorism. . . . In short, though Lachman, Lachman, and Butterfield specifically deny it, information processing adopted a modified logical positivism from neobehaviorism. (pp. 445–446)

Note that "behavioralism" is a neologism coined by Leahey to designate the attempt to predict, control, explain, or model behavior through reference to unobserved mental processes. The concern is fundamentally with achieving an understanding of behavior in terms of the purported internal processes that are responsible for it. The explanation of behavior is secured in terms of these processes.

The received view suggests that cognitive psychology was a revolutionary development, but closer inspection of the historical record indicates the development was more evolutionary than revolutionary. Notwithstanding the "received view" in Figure 5.1, closer analysis of the historical record suggests a certain continuity has always existed among logical positivism, mediational neobehaviorism, and cognitive psychology and that this continuity is evidenced in an analysis of the way theoretical terms are deployed in explanations. More specifically, we can see that once exhaustive definitions of theoretical concepts in terms of observable behavior are not required, the mediational phenomena of the neobehaviorist may be understood as essentially similar to the "mental states" of the cognitive psychologist, who might use reaction time as evidence to support a theory about the role of those mental states in information processing. The continuity in theoretical terms was provided by the theorists themselves as they transported general concepts from one view to the next. Perhaps cognitive psychologists use more hypothetical constructs than intervening variables, whereas mediational neobehaviorists use more intervening variables than hypothetical constructs. Nevertheless, both mediational neobehaviorists and cognitive psychologists employ mediating phenomena that are quite consistent with each other, as well as with logical empiricist philosophy, notwithstanding the received view of Figure 5.1.

TYPE-IDENTITY PHYSICALISM

How Are the Mediators to Be Defined?

A second critical point germane to the relation among logical positivism, behaviorism, and cognitive psychology concerns the thesis of "type–identity physicalism." In brief, type–identity physicalism is the thesis that instances of a given class of mediating phenomenon are to be identified by some common physical (i.e., behavioral or physiological), intersubjectively verifiable property across the several occasions where they might be observed (Flanagan, 1984; Schnaitter, 1984). How is this thesis relevant?

As noted above, a conspicuous feature of cognitive psychologists is the use of mediating phenomena (i.e., mental states) in psychological explanations. For example, Sober (1983) states quite explicitly that "mental states are inner. They are the causes of behavior and therefore are not identical with behavior. . . . Besides claiming that mental states cause behavior, mentalism goes on to say how these inner states manage to do so" (p. 113). Cognitive psychologists point out that behaviorists typically draw on logical positivist doctrine and operationally define their theoretical concepts in terms of physical, publicly observable phenomena, such as behavior or physiological pointer readings. Cognitive psychologists claim that when behaviorists do so, behaviorists are committing themselves to type–identity physicalism because operationally defining theoretical concepts necessarily involves postulating that some physical property links the several instances where the concepts are employed. Thus, cognitive psychologists criticize behaviorism for its supposed adherence to type–identity physicalism.

Functionalism

The brief description of cognitive psychology earlier in the chapter mentioned the importance of the philosophical position known as "functionalism." Cognitive psychologists do feel that the inner, "mental" phenomena used in their explanations are physical and material. However, cognitive psychologists contend that instances of mediating phenomena are not members of a given type because they share some physiological or behavioral property. For example, some mediating phenomena may be grouped as relating to pain, others may be grouped as related to pleasure, and still others to other ascriptions. However, cognitive psychologists argue that there does not need to be anything physiological or behavioral in common among occasions where pain is ascribed or among occasions where pleasure is ascribed. Cognitive psychologists argue that a given psychological function can be accomplished by a variety of physiological structures; and, conversely, two physiological structures whose outward appearances are identical should not be assured of performing identical psychological functions. An organism might well be in pain but show some Spartan-like tendency not to pain-behave. Therefore, cognitive psychologists argue that type–identity physicalism is overwhelmingly likely to be false; and any position committed to type–identity physicalism, as they argue behaviorism is, must necessarily be inadequate (Block, 1980).

Cognitivists contend that what makes instances of a type identical for purposes of psychological explanation is their function rather than a common behavioral or physiological property. Cognitivists contend further that to define a mental state in terms of behavior or physiology, instead of in terms of its function, is to fall victim to the constraints of a logical positivist–inspired behaviorism as they have been imposed on psychology.

Cognitive Psychology and Mediational Neobehaviorism

Despite the attractiveness of the functionalist argument, cognitive psychologists may not have correctly characterized the issues involved. For example, the material cited in the section about theoretical terms shows that neither the logical positivists nor the mediational neobehaviorists conceived of their mediational concepts exclusively in terms of observable behavior. Thus, cognitive psychologists may be tarring their purported opposition with too broad a brush.

Consider also the following argument taken from Hocutt (1985). Suppose two persons engage in the same behavior. In addition, suppose that an explanation of the behavior of one of the persons appeals to an underlying mental state. The argument advanced by cognitive psychologists is that insofar as behaviorists appeal to mental states, behaviorists are obliged also to argue that some intersubjectively verifiable measure must reveal the brain of the second person to be in the same neurophysiological state as the brain of the first person. Cognitive psychologists point out that because there is general agreement that this state of affairs does not obtain, behaviorism is false, and argue that psychological explanations should make use of mental states that do not reduce to publicly observable measures.

Hocutt (1985) rebuts this argument by suggesting it is sufficient to say that when individuals are engaged in a given form of behavior, their brains are in a different state than when they are engaged in a different form of behavior. There does not need to be a commitment to anything about the neurophysiological state of anyone else's brain, and how the brain states compare, when that other person is engaged in either form of behavior. To be certain, the principle identified as type–identity physicalism may be criticized on valid grounds. However, as Hocutt's (1985) argument shows, the relation between internal phenomena and behavior may be dealt with in the dimension of physics and biology. The claim by cognitive psychologists that such efforts are flawed in principle simply does not hold up.

EPISTEMOLOGICAL DUALISM

A third critical point germane to the relation among logical positivism, behaviorism, and cognitive psychology concerns "epistemological dualism." In brief, epistemological dualism is a stance that concedes the existence of not only an objective world of material objects but also a pre-analytical complex of subjective immediate experience (see also Boring, 1950b, p. 667; L. D. Smith, 1986, p. 96ff.). Traditional metaphysical dualists assume two dimensions for both the object that is known and the person who does the knowing. In contrast, epistemological dualists argue they are different: They assume only one dimension in the known, although they do assume two dimensions in the knower. The thesis of this section is that logical positivism, mediational neobehaviorism, and cognitive psychology all embrace epistemological dualism.

The evidence may be seen in the writings of the theorists themselves. For example, consider the following quotes. According to Reichenbach (1938),

We do not see things . . . as they objectively are but in a distorted form; we see a substitute world—not the world as it is, objectively speaking. . . . Our immediate world is, strictly speaking, subjective throughout; it is a substitute world in which we live. (p. 220)

According to Spence (1948),

The data of all sciences have the same origin—namely, the immediate experience of an observing person, the scientist himself. [The scientist] simply takes it for granted and then proceeds to his task of describing the events occurring in it and discovering and formulating the nature of the relationships holding among them. (p. 68)

According to Attneave (1974),

The statement that the world as we know it is a representation is, I think, a truism—
there is really no way in which it can be wrong. . . . We can say in the first place, then,
that knowing necessarily involves representation. (p. 493)

All three passages make essentially the same point about the significance of
the mental processes supposed to underlie behavior. Yet the first author is a
logical positivist, the second is a neobehaviorist, and the third is a cognitive
psychologist. Thus, epistemological dualism is prevalent in all three positions.

Three Problems Raised by Epistemological Dualism

From the perspective of the present analysis, epistemological dualism
raises at least the following three problems. First, epistemological dualists
need to account for how psychologically meaningful action follows as a consequence of the "underlying" mental processes. All too often, the mental processes end up being endowed with just the right powers and forces necessary
to account for the behavior in question (Skinner, 1974, 1989a). The concern
with the causal role of these supposedly underlying processes then becomes
central for a science of behavior as it has for mediational neobehaviorism and
contemporary cognitive psychology.

Second, epistemological dualism leads directly to solipsism. Solipsism is
the position that all one knows is one's subjective experiences. Recall that the
fundamental premise of logical positivism, neobehaviorism, and cognitive
psychology, manifest in the three passages above, is that all one sees is one's
own constructed copy of public phenomena. Indeed, Fodor (1980) used
Carnap's phrase "methodological solipsism" in the title of a recent publication. As Gardner (1985, p. 84) indicates, Fodor's use concedes that this issue
constitutes a significant concern of both cognitive psychology and logical
positivism. The question is: How does an appeal to verifiability in terms of
public phenomena resolve the problem when public phenomena are not seen
anyway? To accept public verification as a solution to one's epistemological
problems is to tacitly surrender to the very kind of problem one is trying to
resolve.

Third, epistemological dualists need to better defend their position against
the liabilities of traditional metaphysical dualism. The logical positivist,
mediational nebehaviorist, and cognitive psychologist argue against traditional, metaphysical dualism, saying that explanations should entail only
material phenomena. However, they fail to consider the following important
implication of their own position.

The dimension of immediate experience, which is central to epistemological dualism, is supposedly ineffable. Its features cannot be communicated
from one sentient being to another. If such is the case, how does language

descriptive of one's personal experience develop, which it obviously does? How does language descriptive of the pain of a toothache develop? Indeed, how do scientists operate on the contents of their immediate experience when they do science and follow the appropriate logical rules that enable them to predict and control events?

Epistemological dualists have difficulty providing an answer that is internally consistent with a materialist position. In many cases, they end up assuming that humans must somehow possess the capacity for a "private language" that enables them to talk about their immediate experience. This conception of a private language with a set of private logical rules, private operations, and private categories of meaning seems integral to the general orientation to epistemological issues associated with logical positivism, mediational neobehaviorism, and cognitive psychology. Yet it is hard to imagine anything more nonmaterialistic than an appeal to a "private language." Indeed, Wittgenstein, among others, has found this appeal untenable and a prime indicator of dualism (see Day, 1969a, pp. 495–496, for further development of this point).

In any event, an assumption of epistemological dualism is the foundation of psychological theories of knowledge that appeal to representational or mediational processes. Skinner (1969, 1974) has repeatedly criticized this position in the context of the "copy theory." Logical positivism, mediational neobehaviorism, and cognitive psychology all embrace mediational processes and the copy theory. Thus, all three positions share this significant metatheoretical assumption, despite their arguments to the contrary, showing their common orientation to the problem of knowledge and explanation.

SKINNER'S RADICAL BEHAVIORISM

Explanations

As noted earlier in this chapter, Skinner's radical behaviorism differs markedly from logical positivism, mediational neobehaviorism, and, of course, cognitive psychology. The issues addressed thus far in the chapter have concerned the topic of explanations in psychology. How then does Skinner's radical behaviorism approach these issues, particularly with regard to the role of internal, unobservable phenomena in causal explanations?

For radical behaviorism, explanations are primarily instances of verbal behavior that serve as guides for future action (see Moore, 1987). As instances of verbal behavior, explanations may therefore be analyzed in terms of the conditions that occasion them.

In a science of behavior, the most effective explanations are presumably occasioned by (1) contingencies—either contingencies of survival or contingencies of reinforcement—and the elements that constitute them, and (2) the physiological factors that make up the organism itself. Let us now speak to these factors, beginning with contingencies.

Contingencies

Contingencies of survival operate during the lifetime of the species. They are responsible for a wide range of behavior, ranging from simple cases (such as reflexes and tropisms) to complex cases (such as fixed action patterns). The stimuli in these contingencies generate behavior that has survival value. The behavior has been selected by the environment as the species has existed in its particular ecological niche over the course of evolution.

A contingency of reinforcement is concerned with the effects of the environment on the organism during its lifetime. A contingency is the interrelation among (1) the prevailing (antecedent) circumstances at the time a response is made, (2) the response itself, and (3) the consequences of a response in those prior circumstances. Behavior generated by contingencies of reinforcement is selected by the environment as the organism lives its life in a particular set of circumstances.

The relative emphasis given to contingencies of survival and contingencies of reinforcement in interpreting behavior is an empirical matter. For some organisms, a relatively large proportion of their behavioral repertoire is a function of contingencies of survival, and a relatively small proportion a function of contingencies of reinforcement. For other organisms, a relatively small proportion is a function of contingencies of survival and a relatively large proportion of contingencies of reinforcement. Humans presumably fall in the second category. In any case, as Skinner (1969, p. 199) has stated, the basic issue is not whether a given instance behavior is instinctive or learned, as if the use of such terms attributes some essence to the behavior in question. Rather, the issue is whether the variables responsible for the provenance of the behavior, as well as those currently in control, have been correctly identified.

Private Events

Ordinarily, elements in contingencies—and the emphasis here is on contingencies of reinforcement—are intersubjectively verifiable. However, in some cases, explanations may be partially occasioned by factors that are private. We now come to the radical behaviorist conception of private events (Skinner, 1953, Chap. 17; see also Moore, 1980, 1987). Incorporating private events into a naturalistic science of behavior is one of the principal concerns of radical behaviorism. Its conception of private events cuts across traditional distinctions between objective and subjective, public and private, mental and physical, external and internal (Skinner, 1945).

In brief, some private events are internal behavioral processes that serve as sources of stimulation for subsequent behavior, in the sense of being links in a chain of events. Others are private sources of interoceptive stimulation, not related to ongoing behavior (Moore, 1980, 1984b, 1987; Skinner, 1953). In any case, private events are distinguished by their accessibility, not by their structure: Private events are accessible only to one person rather than to other members of the verbal community.

When advocates of the received view are concerned with theoretical terms (i.e., intervening variables, hypothetical constructs) or with mental terms (i.e., mental states), the radical behaviorist asks about the dimensions of phenomena cited in their explanations and the causal role of those phenomena. Are the phenomena from the same dimension as behavior, or do they need to be accommodated at some superordinate level? Are they assigned some mysterious powers or forces that cause the behavior in question?

For Skinner's radical behaviorism, private events are physical, material events, just as are public events. As a consequence of certain prior, public events, private events may come to serve a discriminative, controlling function or an eliciting function (Moore, 1980, 1984b; Skinner, 1953). They do not serve an initiating, originating function. Unfortunately, Skinner's conception of the behavioral dimensions of private phenomena is controversial because many (e.g., cognitive psychologists) reject in principle the possibility that private events included in psychological explanations can be behavioral. The problem for a naturalistic science of behavior is that if the discriminative influence of private events is not dealt with in the same dimension as other behavioral phenomena, then dualistic interpretations of the causes of behavior come to predominate. As a consequence, the environmental conditions of which behavior is a function remain unanalyzed, the contribution of private stimuli and responses goes unrecognized, and the explanatory integrity of a naturalistic science of behavior is compromised.

The Contribution of Physiology

As noted above, radical behaviorism also contends physiological factors making up the organism are relevant to a science of behavior. From a physiological perspective, a purely behavioral analysis has two temporal gaps. One is the gap within the behavioral event itself, between stimulus and response. The other is the gap between today's events and their effects tomorrow (Skinner, 1974).

Skinner has written extensively on how physiological information relevant to either of these two gaps will contribute to a science of behavior. In some cases, information about physiological factors may be regarded as supplemental stimuli that provide additional discriminative control over predictions of behavior. For example, if an organism's physiology reveals independent evidence of how it stands at the moment in question, such as how it has already been affected by the environment, then the prediction of how the organism will behave when it does confront a given kind of stimulation becomes easier. Thus, although there can be psychology without physiology, physiological information can play a meaningful role in the absence of relevant information about the behavioral history of the organism. In other cases, knowledge of the physiology may actually lead to intervention. Pharmacology, surgery, or other interventions may change the organism that exists in a particular environment so that the features of that environment produce different effects than otherwise. Interventions at the level of physiology supplement those at the level of contingencies and expand the possibilities for control of behavior (e.g., Skinner, 1969, p. 283).

This position is not necessarily equivalent to the type—identity physicalism discussed above. There is no commitment to an operational definition of a theoretical concept in terms of physiology. The concern is with the actual physiology of an individual organism. How closely the physiological structure of one person will prove to resemble that of another is an empirical matter. Certainly there is no commitment to the status of a neuron at a given set of stereotaxic coordinates or to the unvarying effect of an intervention at a given anatomical site.

In any case, although Skinner does not conceive of the organism as actually empty, he does feel it would be a remarkable coincidence if what is currently being used to refer inferentially to inner events will find a place in future explanations (Skinner, 1945; 1972b). Indeed, in a more advanced account of the behaving organism, information about its momentary physiological state might even be preferred to a possibly inadequate specification of contingencies when it comes to prediction (Skinner, 1953, p. 34; 1969, p. 283). A representative quote is as follows (Skinner, 1974):

The physiologist of the future will tell us all that can be known about what is happening inside the behaving organism. His account will be an important advance over a behavioral analysis, because the latter is necessarily "historical"—that is to say, confined to functional relations showing temporal gaps. . . . No matter how clearly that fact can be established, a step is missing, and we must wait for the physiologist to supply it. He will be able to show how an organism is changed when exposed to contingencies of reinforcement and why the changed organism then behaves in a different way, possibly at a much later date. What he discovers cannot invalidate the laws of a science of behavior, but it will make the picture of human action more nearly complete. (p. 215)

COMPARISON OF RADICAL BEHAVIORISM WITH LOGICAL POSITIVISM AND MEDIATIONAL NEOBEHAVIORISM

Skinner's entire outlook is very different from that of logical positivism and mediational neobehaviorism. As L. D. Smith (1986, pp. 278–287) notes, although Skinner was not a mediational neobehaviorist, his early work took place during the 1930s, when all psychologists (especially neobehaviorists) were discussing how to establish a more scientific foundation for psychology. What was needed was a fresh set of concepts derived from the analysis of newly emphasized data. Logical positivism, which was more often talked about than understood at the time, seemed to offer some promise. Skinner's book, *The Behavior of Organisms* (1938), explicitly acknowledged its underpinnings:

> The system set up in the preceding chapter may be characterized as follows. It is positivistic. It confines itself to description rather than explanation. Its concepts are defined in terms of immediate observations. (p. 44)

However, Skinner viewed his radical behaviorism from its inception as a comprehensive approach to the analysis of all human endeavors, including philosophy and especially epistemology. Even though he was generally aware of logical positivism, Skinner never embraced its formalism, and was actually antiformalist in many important respects (L. D. Smith, 1986, p. 280). Similarly, even though Skinner was concerned with operationism, and even though operationism became synonymous with the physicalistic foundations of logical positivism, Skinner's unique interpretation of operationism has always kept him apart from the mainstream of experimental psychology (Moore, 1975, 1984b, 1985; Skinner, 1945).

For their part, the logical positivists viewed behaviorism as but a "gentleman's agreement" regarding the application of the underlying philosophical doctrine of physicalism within the broader context of the importance of formal logic and the unity of science movement (e.g., L. D. Smith, 1986, p. 279). The logical positivists were interested in bringing a new standard of rigor to all aspects of science. They were sympathetic to behaviorism primarily because they felt they had less work to do with behaviorism than with any other version of psychology (e.g., L. D. Smith, 1986, pp. 60–64, 318). By 1945, Skinner had become fully aware of where logical positivist–inspired mediational neobehaviorism was headed (see Day, 1969a; Moore, 1985), and his own position has been evolving in a different direction ever since.

Exegesis

When Skinner argues for behavioral interpretations of "mental" terms, he is not arguing that the way to make mental terms meaningful is by referring to observable behavior. Such a position entails a commitment to the "operationism of Boring and Stevens" (Skinner, 1945, p. 292). Rather, Skinner is arguing that ontologically, any facts to which "mental" terms are thought to refer have never been anything more than facts from a behavioral dimension. Some mental terms are occasioned by private phenomena, some are occasioned by public phenomena, and some by both. Some mental terms are occasioned by stimuli, some by responses, and some are occasioned by behavioral relations, either public or private. Some are presumably occasioned by physiological phenomena. None are occasioned by phenomena from a mental, cognitive, or subjective dimension, which then need to be defined in terms of observable behavior so that two people can agree on them (Skinner, 1945, 1989a).

Inner states may well be involved in explanations but generally as aspects of an organism's physiology. If the term *disposition* happens to be used, in some cases the usage might indicate that stimulus control exists. In other cases, the usage might indicate motivationally relevant operations have been carried out that alter the effect of environmental stimuli. At some point, however, there will be an interest in control. At that point, the Skinnerian radical behaviorist becomes primarily interested in the relation between the events that have established the inner state in question and the ensuing responses. As Skinner (1953) states in a well-known passage objecting to the "theoretician's dilemma" of conceiving of inner states as intervening variables:

The objection to inner states is not that they do not exist, but that they are not relevant in a functional analysis. We cannot account for the behavior of any system while staying wholly inside it; eventually we must turn to forces operating upon the organism from without. Unless there is a weak spot in our causal chain so that the second link is not lawfully determined by the first, or the third by the second, then the first and third links must be lawfully related. If we must always go back beyond the second link for prediction and control, we may avoid many tiresome and exhausting digressions by examining the third link as a function of the first. Valid information about the second link may throw light upon this relationship but can in no way alter it. (p. 35)

Of course, we should not suppose that Skinner's emphases on description and observable processes constitute a naive commitment to a post hoc psychology, using only observed events. Consider the following passage from Skinner (1961a):

A science must achieve more than a description of behavior as an accomplished fact. It must predict future courses of action; it must be able to say that an organism will engage in behavior of a given sort at a given time. But this raises a special problem. We want to believe that a prediction is in some sense a description of a condition at the moment before the predicted event has taken place. Thus, we speak of tendencies or readinesses to behave as if they corresponded to something in the organism at the moment. . . . We look for neurological or psychic states or events with which habits, wishes, attitudes, and so on may be identified. In so doing we force extraneous properties on behavior which are not supported by the data and which may be quite misleading. (pp. 70–71)

This passage is significant because it indicates Skinner's commitment to the practical concerns of doing science. It also indicates his rejection of the distinctively unpragmatic and unparsimonious flavor of mediational neobehaviorism, which seeks to validate the appeal to phenomena from other dimensions, such as psychic events, habits, wishes, attitudes, and so on, in terms of intersubjectively verifiable phenomena, such as behavior or neurological states. Absent is any concern among mediational neobehaviorists that their appeals to phenomena from other dimensions might possibly interfere with doing science (see discussions in L. D. Smith, 1986, pp. 271–272; Zuriff, 1985, pp. 68–69, 257–261).

In broader perspective, we see that two questions are relevant to a science of behavior. The first is, "What are the various aspects of the world to which an organism's body responds?" This question concerns an analysis of environmental contingencies. The second question is, "How does an organism's body work when it responds to various aspects of the world?" This question concerns the anatomy and physiology of the behaving organism. For logical positivism, mediational neobehaviorism, and cognitive psychology, the second question supersedes the first. In contrast, radical behaviorism keeps the two questions coordinated but distinct. Although answers to both questions may well be relevant to predictions in a science of behavior, information about the fundamental control of behavior is to be found in the answer to the first question.

SUMMARY AND CONCLUSION

In summary, this chapter has examined historical and conceptual relations among logical positivism, mediational neobehaviorism, and cognitive psychology. The results indicate there is great continuity, rather than discontinuity, among them on this matter, as suggested in Figure 5.2.

Skinner's radical behaviorism stands in distinct contrast to logical positivism, mediational neobehaviorism, and cognitive psychology. For radical behaviorism, any concern with the contribution of internal phenomena to explanations is a specific case of the more general concern with the factors that the psychologist should entertain in order to predict, control, or interpret behavior accurately. First, radical behaviorists feel that it is useful for psychologists to be concerned with elements of contingencies. These elements may be public or private, and radical behaviorism's inclusion of private behavioral events is one of its most salient features.

Second, radical behaviorists feel that important factors may be gleaned from the study of the anatomical and physiological features of the organism itself. Information about these factors can contribute to predictions in the absence of information about organism–environment interactions. In addition, manipulations may actually be possible at the level of physiology to control behavior, supplementing manipulations of contingencies.

Thus, a science of behavior does have a place for the study at the abstract level of the functional design of the internal mechanisms that allow organisms to behave in context. The study of such phenomena, a kind of theoretical neurophysiology, is sufficiently different from the study of behavior that it need not conflict with the study of behavior (see Schnaitter, 1984, 1986, 1987).

To repeat, however, the foregoing acknowledgment of the relevance of information about internal phenomena does not imply that that information has any privileged epistemological status. Under logical positivism, mediational neobehaviorism, and cognitive psychology, the information does assume a privileged status. Although physiology will eventually support a behavioral formulation, a behavioral formulation will always be needed for at least two reasons, even when the physiology of the behaving organism is better understood, just as much of chemistry remains useful even though an account of a chemical interaction may be given at the level of molecular or atomic forces (Moore, 1987, p. 468; Skinner, 1978, p. 70). First, knowledge of environmental events is still necessary at some point to ascertain the significance of a given set of physiological variables, as those variables participate in the interaction between the environmental events and subsequent behavior. Second, prediction and control of behavior will nearly always be accomplished through manipulation of standard environmental variables in ways that do not depend upon the knowledge of the physiology involved. Indeed, interactions between organisms ordinarily take place at the level of their behavioral repertoires, not at the level of their physiology.

Does cognitive psychology as it is currently practiced contribute to an understanding of the private events or the physiology relevant to the prediction and control of behavior? Contrary to the received view of Figure 5.1, the conclusion here is that it does not. However, the concern is not so much with its mentalism. Rather, the following conclusion seems more appropriate: Cognitive psychology is concerned more with use of unobservables of metaphorical origin to secure a causal explanation of behavior as an event and less with an abstract functional account of acts, states, mechanisms, and processes purportedly inside the organism (Skinner, 1989a). As noted at the beginning of the chapter, cognitive psychology, therefore, stands as the culmination of methodological and epistemological trends that began in mediational S-O-R neobehaviorism under the auspices of logical positivism and that have misled psychologists for at least fifty years.

A final caution seems appropriate. Logical positivism has influenced a great deal of psychological science, including radical behaviorism. A better identification of the origins of our existing thought, particularly in the literature of the applied and experimental analysis of behavior, might prevent radical behaviorists from doing more of the same just renamed, as cognitive psychologists seem to be doing. Ringen (1976) has captured the spirit of the present argument:

Radical behaviorism appears to be the only serious existing alternative to common sense mentalism, and serious conceptual analysis of its technical terms will contribute to our understanding of what the alternatives are. If current assessments of the revolutionary character of operant behaviorism are correct, such a clarification will be no small task. It will require something of at least the magnitude of Galileo's critical discussion of Aristotelian physics and cosmology. (p. 250)

Just so.

Chapter 6 _____

On Certain Relations between Contemporary Philosophy and Radical Behaviorism

Willard F. Day, Jr., and Jay Moore

Most of this chapter concerns certain relations between contemporary philosophy and radical behaviorism at this particular moment in the history of those two disciplines. The chapter was undertaken in recognition of two exciting developments in the recent literature. First, there is the conspicuous increase in the extent to which people interested in the analysis of behavior are turning to historical analysis in an effort to shed light on professional issues. The recent work of S. R. Coleman (1981, 1984, 1985a, 1985b, 1987) is but one illustration of this trend. L. D. Smith (1986) and Zuriff (1985) are book-length treatments of significant issues in the historical and conceptual analysis of behaviorism. Morris and Larsen's (1986) paper on contextual conditions in the experimental analysis of behavior, Schneider and Morris's (1987) work on the history of the term *radical behaviorism*, and recent attempts to piece together evidences of the control exercised over Skinner's work by the thought of Bertrand Russell (Wood, 1986) are all further examples of the kind of current behavior-analytic scholarship that makes one want to get up in the morning and peck away at the typewriter again.

Second, there is the recent publication of several canonical papers of B. F. Skinner, along with invited commentary and Skinner's responses to that commentary (Catania & Harnad, 1988). There is no question but that this penetrating peer commentary—each among which generates an explicit and considered, if brief, response from Skinner—is destined to constitute a highly stable benchmark in enabling future critical analysis of Skinner's thought to stay reasonably close on target. As in no place else in connection with the intellectual assessment of radical behaviorism, the extensive discussion and commentary on the heart of Skinner's systematic views that are made available in Catania and Harnad (1988) makes it possible for the first time to think in terms of a comprehensive, up-to-date, and technically competent assessment of the heart of Skinner's views at a philosophical level.

Let us move on then. As noted above, this chapter is concerned with certain aspects of the current situation in professional philosophy as they pertain to behaviorism. First, we will consider a general characterization of what philosophers mean these days by the term *behaviorism*. Then we will discuss one of the dominant intellectual stances in contemporary professional philosophy, functionalism, which we think it would be worth the time and trouble for behavior analysts to know something about, as they engage issues relevant to that most noble tradition within professional psychology, behaviorism.

WHAT DO PHILOSOPHERS MEAN BY THE WORD *BEHAVIORISM?*

Interestingly, what philosophers mean by *behaviorism* is likely to have very little to do with what behavior analysts mean by *behaviorism*. Moreover, behavior analysts should be on their guard when listening to what philosophers have to say about behaviorism, since philosophers will often want to give the impression that what is being said really has a great deal to do with what one should think about behavior analysis. And, as a general rule that is likely to be bad.

With regard to behaviorism, philosophers today commonly distinguish between what they call "methodological behaviorism," on the one hand, and "philosophical behaviorism," on the other. A representative passage on this distinction is from a book by Arthur Collins called *The Nature of Mental Things* (1987):

It is customary to distinguish between methodological behaviorism and philosophical . . . behaviorism. Methodological behaviorism takes no stand on inner mental realities. It merely emphasizes the principle that scientific understanding has to rest entirely on appeal to matters that are publicly observable. Thus, mental phenomena which are intuitively thought of as private ought to be excluded from the evidential basis of psychology. [Philosophical behaviorism] rejects inner states and mental processes, not because they are not accessible for public scrutiny, but because there are no such things to be scrutinized. Philosophical behaviorists attempt an analytical reduction of mental concepts to concepts of dispositions, all of the manifestations of which are publicly observable behavior. This radical project has not got many adherents left. (p. 16)

The basic point is that neither of these two varieties of behaviorism as conceptualized by philosophers engage very relevantly or accurately what it is either about Skinner's thought or the practice of behavior analysis that is significantly interesting, or appropriately controversial, as the case may be. Of course, the distinction has been set up by philosophers to serve their own needs, and the distinction obviously functions successfully in some way or other in connection with the scholarly work of that discipline. However, serious questions must be raised whether everybody correctly understands the extent to which Skinner's views have been engaged in such philosophical work. Let us now more specifically consider methodological behaviorism.

METHODOLOGICAL BEHAVIORISM

Methodological behaviorism is generally regarded as a position within professional psychology. According to Churchland (1984), a prominent professional philosopher,

[The central principles of methodological behaviorism] are not difficult to understand. According to behaviorism, the first and most important obligation of the science of psychology is to *explain the behavior* of whatever creatures it addresses, humans included. By "behavior" the behaviorists mean the publicly observable, measurable, recordable activity of the subjects at issue: bodily movements, noises emitted, temperature changes, chemicals released, interactions with the environment, and so forth. . . . In sum, explanations in psychology are to be based entirely on notions that either are outright publicly observable, or are operationally defined in terms of notions that are so observable. (pp. 88–89)

How does this position relate to Skinner's radical behaviorism? The radical behaviorist first asks, "Why the italics?" At some point, we are all interested in the behavior we can observe in others, but Churchland's emphasis of the matter seems to invite some comparison with Skinner and to imply that Skinner's views are among those properly classified as methodological behaviorism. To be sure, Skinner's position has much to say on such matters as public observability, explanation, and operational definitions (Skinner, 1974, pp. 13–18; see also Day, 1969a, 1976, 1980, 1983; Moore, 1975, 1981, 1984a, 1984b, 1985, 1987; L. D. Smith, 1986, pp. 284–287). Nevertheless, the point is that these sources take great pain to *dissociate* radical from methodological behaviorism, precisely along the dimensions of public observability, explanation, and operationism. To mouth platitudes about prediction and control of publicly observable behavior, as do many of Skinner's critics, is simply not to deal with the realities of Skinner's thought at all. At least a tacit scanning of representative radical behaviorist material cited above on explanation and operationism is explicitly required of professional philosophers interested in assessing radical behaviorist or behavior-analytic explanatory accounts. At the very least, a far better word to use in speaking of explanatory accounts given by radical behaviorists or behavior analysts is the term *interpretation*. Skinner often speaks of interpretation in connection with matters of prediction and control (e.g., Skinner, 1974, pp. 209, 228).

Churchland (1984) explicitly brings up Skinner's work toward the end of his discussion of methodological behaviorism. Churchland says that Skinner "has recently urged a version of behaviorism in which the reality of internal phenomena is asserted, as well as our introspective access to them, and in which internal phenomena are assigned a perfectly legitimate role in psychology" (1984, pp. 90–91). No doubt much of what Churchland is saying here is under the control of relevant material on the importance of private events from Skinner (1974), with which Churchland indicates some familiarity. In any case, although Churchland's accounting of Skinner's views on private events is accurate as far as it goes, it fails to engage the wide, wide world opened in Skinner's book, *Verbal Behavior* (1957). Moreover, Churchland has unfortunately presented Skinner's views on private events as relatively "recent" and as having been arrived at as "concessions" to the force of the arguments against behaviorism that he has just recounted. The core of Skinner's views, however, was clearly present in Skinner's landmark paper on operationism (Skinner, 1945) and again in *Science and Human Behavior* (Skinner, 1953) and *Verbal Behavior* (Skinner, 1957)—all of which is appropriately regarded as reasonably early, but fully mature, Skinner. Thus, Churchland seems right on target when he criticizes methodological behaviorism. However, Churchland strays off target when he implies that because Skinner is a behaviorist, he must necessarily be subject to the same criticisms as a methodological behaviorist. Let us now consider philosophical behaviorism.

PHILOSOPHICAL BEHAVIORISM

Philosophers commonly take philosophical behaviorism to be a position within academic philosophy and, unlike methodological behaviorism, something which no longer has much vital relevance to the affairs of professional psychology. For that matter, as Collins (1987) suggests, it is not especially popular among professional philosophers either. Plainly and simply, as a philosophical position, philosophical behaviorism stands for analyzing or reducing mental states into dispositions to behave; that is, philosophical behaviorism attempts to secure a *conceptual* analysis of behavior.

To be sure, radical behaviorism does have some superficial similarities with philosophical behaviorism (see Schnaitter, 1985, for discussion), but we need to address the relations more directly. Specifically, how does radical behaviorism deal with dispositional analyses of "mental" terms? Suffice it to say that for radical behaviorism, any particular *description* of behavior will make use of whatever *descriptive* vocabulary is occasioned by the behavior being described, given the idiosyncrasies of the circumstances under which the description is made. The supposedly "mental" implications of some descriptors do not indicate mental properties of the behaving organism to which the descriptors directly or indirectly refer. Instead, the descriptors are regarded as simply instances of verbal behavior, influenced by the particulars of the verbal environment shaping that person's verbal repertoire. Dispositional terms are, therefore, perfectly reasonable *descriptors* to employ.

The major problem concerns trying to generate a causal explanation, rather than a description. The use of dispositions may lead a wide variety of people—from the lay community and especially philosophers and psychologists, who ought to know better—to think that because psychology can be taken to be the study of behavior, behavior itself can be taken as nothing but "evidence" for a disposition to behave at a particular time in one way rather than another. The dispositions then become inner entities of focal importance in any analysis. As a result, when persons speak of dispositions to behave, the opportunity all too conveniently presents itself for reifying these dispositions to behave back into some special kind of causal inner states. Doing so, of course, turns dispositions into causes that are just as occult as any mental cause, an ironic turn of events for a position trying to circumvent *any* appeal to mental events.

What then do philosophical behaviorists do when asked to give causal explanations of behavior? Either they must remain silent—a curious posture at best for any philosopher (as well as for any psychologist!)—or else they must abandon their program of conceptual analysis and tacitly turn the dispositions into mental causes. Neither of these alternatives seem especially desirable (for further discussion, see Schnaitter, 1985).

Most philosophical behaviorists are aware of these two difficulties and attempt to stay on the safe middle ground. However, when dealing with mental terms as dispositions, most philosophical behaviorists nevertheless rely on publicly observable behavior and appeal to "operational definitions." It is, therefore, all too easy to lapse, however inadvertently, into methodological behaviorism.

No doubt many "mental" terms can be treated in terms of publicly observable behavior (Skinner, 1989a). However, radical behaviorists say not all can be so treated. Some mental terms are occasioned by private events, rather than by publicly observable phenomena. Some are occasioned by behavioral relations. If dispositions happen to be used in the language of behavior analysis, they typically indicate that motivationally relevant operations have been carried out, or that the behaving organism is in contact with antecedent conditions that have gained a particular significance during the lifetime of the organism. Thus, radical behaviorists do differ appreciably from philosophical behaviorists and their conceptual analyses employing dispositions.

PHILOSOPHICAL FUNCTIONALISM

Philosophical functionalism is "probably the most widely held theory of mind among philosophers, cognitive psychologists, and artificial intelligence researchers" (Churchland, 1984, p. 37). It has been defined in the following way:

According to *functionalism*, the essential or defining feature of any type of mental state is the set of causal relations it bears to (1) environmental effects on the body,

(2) other types of mental states, and (3) bodily behavior. Pain, for example, characteristically results from some bodily damage or trauma; it causes distress, annoyance, and practical reasoning aimed at relief; and it causes wincing, blanching, and nursing of the traumatized area. Any state that plays exactly that functional role is a pain, according to functionalism. Similarly other types of mental states (sensations, fears, beliefs, and so on) are also defined by their unique causal roles in a complex economy of internal states mediating sensory inputs and behavioral outputs. (Churchland, 1984, p. 36)

Churchland goes on to indicate that functionalism goes to great lengths to contrast its position with behaviorism, of either the methodological or philosophical variety, when he notes that functionalism may remind the reader of behaviorism; and indeed it is the heir to behaviorism. However, there is one fundamental difference between the two theories. Where the behaviorist hoped to define each type of mental state solely in terms of environmental input and behavioral output, the functionalist denies this is possible. As he sees it, the adequate characterization of almost any mental state involves an ineliminable reference to a variety of other mental states with which it is causally connected, and so a reductive definition solely in terms of publicly observable inputs and outputs is quite impossible (1984, p. 36). Block (1980), another prominent contemporary philosopher, covers similar territory:

First, while behaviorists defined mental states in terms of stimuli and responses, they did not think mental states were themselves causes of the responses and the effects of the stimuli. Behaviorists took mental states to be "pure dispositions." Gilbert Ryle, for example, emphasized that "to possess a dispositional property is not to be in a particular state, or to undergo a particular change" (1949, p. 43). Brittleness, according to Ryle, is not a *cause* of breaking, but merely the fact of breaking so easily. Similarly, to attribute pain to someone is not to attribute a cause or effect of anything, but simply to say what he would do in certain circumstances. Behaviorists are fictionalists about the mental, hence they cannot allow that mental states have causal powers. Functionalists, by contrast, claim it to be an advantage of their account that it "allows experiences to be something real, and so to be the effects of their occasions, and the causes of their manifestations." (pp. 175–176)

In brief, functionalism makes two arguments against the adequacy of behaviorism. Churchland (1984, pp. 23–25) discusses the first, which he called "Argument X." The upshot of Argument X, functionalists contend, is that whenever one tries to place a particular dispositional definition of mental state notions in a specifically imaginable context, one ends up having to bring in new mental-state terms in order to describe the realities of the situation. For example, in a behavioral, operational, and dispositional analysis of the mental state notion of wanting, as in "Anne wants a vacation," Churchland suggests that the number of conditionals necessary for an analysis of wanting is either indefinite or infinite. That is, if we ask Anne if she "wants" a vacation, her answer "yes" is true only if she is not being *secretive* about her real plans, which we can only determine if we know whether she is simply *bored* with talking about her vacation plans, and so on. Thus, functionalists argue why not appeal directly to the underlying mental states, as does functionalism, instead of staying with the incomplete specification of observable behavior, as does behaviorism?

The second objection to the adequacy of behaviorism is provided by the "'perfect actor' family of counterexamples" (Block, 1980, p. 175). For the methodological behaviorist, pain is something that must be operationally defined in terms of publicly observable behavior. For the philosophical behaviorist, pain is a disposition, talk of which is made meaningful on the criterion of publicly observable pain behavior. In arguing against the adequacy of either variety of behaviorism, the philosopher of science Hilary Putnam has proposed the existence of a world populated by Spartans (see Block, 1980, pp. 24–36). These stalwart citizens have pains but neither moan, groan, nor show any other overt signs of distress. In fact, they act perfectly normal. Presumably, the "mental" concept of pain applies to them, despite the absence of publicly observable pain behavior, thereby proving any variety of behaviorism false.

What does radical behaviorism have to say about this state of affairs? First, of course, the talk of the causal efficacy of mental states is pure mentalism. Being opposed to mentalism is at the very heart of what radical behaviorism is all about. This is not to say that radical behaviorists reject the importance of functional considerations. In point of fact, Skinner has long-term squatter's rights when compared with philosophical functionalists, since he has been expounding the functional position at least since *Science and Human Behavior* (Skinner, 1953).

In addition, radical behaviorism does not define all "mental" concepts in terms of behavioral dispositions. In radical behaviorism, mental terms, just as any other terms, are defined by an analysis of the factors governing their emission as an aspect of language in use. The notion that psychological terms are defined through an analysis of the contingencies controlling their functioning in actual verbal behavior, rather than an enumeration of relevant dispositions, is perhaps the centrally most important idea in Skinner's landmark paper on operationism (Skinner, 1945). When talking of inner states, Skinner does not deny that they exist. Rather, he disputes the causal role that functionalism assigns to them (see Skinner, 1953, pp. 34–35). To assign a causal role is to wander into the endless forest of mentalism, from which there is no escape.

Lycan (1984), another contemporary philosopher, also discusses the purported superiority of functionalism over behaviorism. As with Churchland (1984) previously, the implication is that Skinner's radical behaviorism should be considered as among those exemplars of behaviorism that are inadequate. In advocating the functionalist position, Lycan argues that "the positing of underlying mechanisms in the form of mental-functional states affords a deeper explanation of behavior than does the mere subsuming of the behavior under a nakedly empirical S-R generalization" (1984, p. 634). This statement is similar to Lycan's later observation that an inner-state explanation can succeed as an explanation even though its relation to prior environmental causes has not been specified, although "a more complete explanation would go further back along the causal chain" (Lycan, 1984, p. 635). Yet, in his interest in depth and completeness of explanation, Lycan is insisting on a kind of ontological engagement which is orthogonal to the basic aims of radical behaviorist analysis. Nobody disagrees that explanations should be as "deep" or as "complete" as is of interest to anybody. Both sides agree that the ability to predict is important. So? Everybody agrees that prediction is not the only objective in scientific research. So?

Lycan's most significant challenge to Skinner is the claim that only by postulating mental states can we overcome the objections to behaviorism that stem ultimately from the familiar Argument X. Lycan (1984) puts the point this way:

Functional states also seem to be required in light of a powerful objection standardly put to Skinner at least by philosophers and linguists (Chomsky 1959; Dennett [1978]; Fodor 1975): that for the most part, S-R correlations in humans are established or presumable only with the aid of tacit but massive assumptions about the subjects' internal organization (utilities, modes of representation, background beliefs, and the like). (p. 634)

However, it is simply not true that overcoming this objection requires the postulation of causal mental states, as does functionalism. Suppose a behavior analyst is interested in predicting or explaining someone's behavior. Suppose further that it is thought the behavior analyst should or should not in some sense take into account utilities, modes of representation, or background beliefs (or for that matter, assessments of the relevant aspects of the controlling environment, or reference to relevant reinforcement history). To begin with, causal mental states are not involved at all—in anybody's head. What is actually involved are the interpretive behaviors of the behavior analyst. Some of these interpretive behaviors are publicly observable. Others are only privately so. These interpretive behaviors are to be analyzed with reference to the discriminative stimuli, reinforcers, and contingencies that control them. The claim that the mental states of the one being observed are involved is only an assumption, predicated in turn on a long-standing series of preconceived notions about the inherent nature of scientific explanation. We are concerned here with the conceptual equipment employed in the interpretation of behavior, and there is absolutely no reason to take it for granted that the only way to make sense out of making sense is to postulate causal mental states within any human head.

To be sure, issues of ontology are inevitably raised in discussion of the mental. Yet Skinner does not shrink from that discussion. Consider, for instance, the following passage from Day (1969b):

In response to a question raised by Scriven in the Rice symposium concerning how he can justify calling himself a radical behaviorist, Skinner replies that, "I am a radical behaviorist simply in the sense that I find no place in the formulation for anything which is mental." . . . These comments by Skinner are likely to appear somewhat cryptic to someone who has not studied Skinner's published work extensively. It is clear that Skinner is objecting here not to things that are private but to things that are mental. It is true that the distinction between radical and conventional behaviorism hinges in a number of ways on the issue of mentalism. It is also true that one of Skinner's most persistent objections to conventional behaviorism is directed at a fundamental mentalism which he sees as all too thinly disguised. Yet actually, the issues involved in what Skinner means by "mentalism" are quite complex. (pp. 317–318)

[The radical behaviorist's resistance to hidden epistemology] leads at times to an obstinate refusal to think in terms of a particular common-sense theory of what it is to have knowledge about one or another subject matter. This is the notion that whenever we have significant knowledge, this knowledge consists of an at least partial identification of the inherent nature of what it is that is known about. The notion is, in other words, that in knowing about something the expression of our knowledge consists in a comment on the *nature* of the object of knowledge or of a statement of what the object of knowledge *is*. It is as if in verbalizing our knowledge of things we have always to express an identification of one or another aspect of the permanent structure of nature. Yet the radical behaviorist is aware that we may attribute thingness to events largely because we are accustomed to speak of the world about us as composed of objects which are felt to possess an inherent constancy or stability. He is reluctant to take for granted that all useful knowledge must be conceptualized in terms of verbal patterns of thought derived simply from our experience with material objects. Consequently, he is led to a position which is peculiarly anti-ontological. (p. 319)

The radical behaviorist claims that the question of ontology is needlessly raised by the functionalist, whose talk of the mental as being different from the private keeps current the concerns with events in other dimensions, to be talked about in different terms and engaged according to different techniques. Far from resolving questions of ontology, functionalism actually creates and perpetuates them, much to the detriment of scientific and philosophic progress.

SUMMARY AND CONCLUSION

In conclusion, what can we say about the relation between contemporary philosophy and radical behaviorism? Clearly, there is a regrettable lack of communication between the two. At the very least, most philosophers fail to recognize that radical behaviorism is an intellectual position that differs appreciably from both methodological and philosophical behaviorism. Although the term *behaviorism* does have a generic usage that makes it applicable to certain aspects of radical, methodological, and philosophical behaviorism, important differences among the positions nevertheless remain (and one should not make too much of any similarities).

On the other hand, radical behaviorists would do well to recognize that an analysis of Skinner's thought at an essentially *philosophical* level may result in an intrinsically more stable radical behaviorism. For example, the philosophically oriented Princeton psychologists Richard Brinker and Julian Jaynes (1988) commented in Catania and Harnad (1988) on one of Skinner's canonical papers, "The Operational Analysis of Psychological Terms" (1945; 1972c). Basically, Brinker and Jaynes accuse Skinner of an exceedingly unfortunate and professional damaging change in epistemological position from the reasonably early 1945 paper on operationism to the considerably later work in 1969 from which they extract verbal material to support their charge of significant epistemological change. The change concerns a shift from the possibility of understanding any behavior, verbal or otherwise, through an analysis of natural contingencies, to an emphasis (perhaps it is appropriate to say *over*emphasis) on standard techniques of demonstrating experimental control. The upshot is that they accuse Skinner of shying away from any significant empirical concern with certain subject matter, such as human verbal behavior, simply because experimental control is so difficult to demonstrate.

The important thing to glean from Brinker and Jaynes's (1988) commentary is that the charge grew from an essentially philosophical analysis of Skinner's work. Even though the force of Brinker and Jaynes's charge may be softened by Skinner's comment that he has always recognized the need for closer study of controlling variables, the particular issues identified by Brinker and Jaynes need to be really engaged on explicitly *philosophical* grounds. Brinker and Jaynes need to spell out in clear and, if necessary, in technical philosophical detail the nature of their charge of intellectual inconsistency. Radical behaviorists, for their part, need to be able to specify, clarify, and (if necessary) defend the methodological practices that have occasioned Brinker and Jaynes's accusations to begin with. Therein lies, in the most meaningful sense, the basis for productive interplay between contemporary professional philosophy and radical behaviorism.

AUTHORS' NOTE

This chapter was conceived by Professor Willard F. Day, Jr., who delivered parts of it at the symposium on "History, Philosophy, and Behavior Analysis" at the convention of the Association for Behavior Analysis in Philadelphia, May, 1988. As is known to his many students and colleagues, Professor Day died before the chapter was completed. Using the text that Professor Day had completed as a guide, Jay Moore prepared the chapter for this book. The chapter is respectfully dedicated to his memory.

Chapter 7

The Origins of Environment-Based Psychological Theory

Philip N. Hineline

One of the most impressive aspects of B. F. Skinner's *The Behavior of Organisms* (1938), as a fifty-year-old book, is its introducing features of theory that continue to be among the most subtle to be found in psychology. While they seem not to be widely understood among contemporary psychologists, some of these subtleties have been appreciated throughout the years by those working within the tradition that developed from Skinner's work. A fundamental example is seen in Skinner's characterization of the reflex—the presumed simplest of functional units—as a relation between classes of events rather than as bundled connections between individual stimuli and responses. This conception construes the reflex as intrinsically abstract while directly observable; the more usual conceptions of the reflex treat it as a tangible mechanism, although that mechanism is usually inferred rather than observed. In amplifying his conception, Skinner asserts, "In general, the notion of a reflex is to be emptied of any connotation of the active 'push' of the stimulus. The terms refer here to correlated entities, and to nothing more" (Skinner, 1938, p. 21). Thus, in its very beginnings behavior-analytic theory moved beyond the primitive metaphors of billiard-ball causation or of an organism as a purely reactive machine. Similarly, Skinner's version of the reflex is at least as abstract as the mental connections that other psychologies have taken as basic. Even though clearly stated at this beginning, other subtleties have been less appreciated even by Skinnerian theorists. For example, in introducing the operant, Skinner (1938) included a new way of incorporating time into descriptions of psychological process. He provided this matter-of-fact introduction: "One important independent variable is time. In making use of it I am simply recognizing that the observed datum is the appearance of a given identifiable sample of behavior at some more-or-less orderly rate" (p. 20). While

Skinner explicitly identified the use of rate as distinctive of his approach, most of us have only slowly come to understand its implications. Among these:

1. Behavior analysis is essentially the study, definition, and characterization of effective environments as arrayed over time, with *effective* defined by the dynamics of behavior. That is, in behavior-analytic theory the world is characterized through categories of transaction with behavior. Those categories do not consist of punctate, individual events; rather, they are sets of contingent relations or correlations between events or patterns of events over time.

2. Psychological process is construed as behavior–environment interaction. It does not consist of phenomena that underlie that interaction. At the same time, this is not a psychology of empty organisms. As will be described below, Skinner explicitly acknowledges the legitimacy of physiologically-based explanations of behavior, although he requires that physiological interpretive terms be supported by relatively direct experimental observations; a purely metaphorical physiology is not essentially different from a mentalistic metaphor.

3. Rate, while comprised of tangible, observable events, is transparent. You can look right through a rate as it proceeds, even though none of the events that comprise the rate is occurring at a given moment. Thus, rate is an abstraction; and interpreters of human action commonly ignore diffuse but directly observable events and instead appeal to impalpable entities, such as mental or presumed physiological processes, as causing overt behavior. Apparently, the fact of seeming to be localized in time and space (i.e., right now, behind the eyes) makes those presumed events seem to provide for more satisfactory explanation. Thus, Skinner's persistent criticisms of mentalistic explanation have continued to inspire controversy.

INTERPRETIVE DIRECTIONALITY IN PSYCHOLOGICAL THEORIES

Skinner's focus on mentalistic versus antimentalistic explanation as a key issue of contention may have obscured a more fundamental yet more tractable point of disagreement between his and the more conventional viewpoints. The essential differences of interpretation may concern not the status of hypothetical terms for explaining behavior but, rather, a dimension of interpretive prose that, just like rate of occurrence, is right before our eyes yet seldom noticed. The key issue may concern not mentalism but, rather, the directionality of interpretive talk.

Interpretive or explanatory prose seems to be intrinsically bipolar, whether it is cast in terms of cause–effect, of noun–verb, of independent variable–dependent variable, or of agent–action. This bipolarity, then, constrains psychological theory to one of two general types: In one, interpretive statements take the form of organism–behavior locutions; in the other, the form is that of environment–behavior locutions. Heated disagreement or misunderstanding occurs when proponents of one theoretical type address interpretive contributions of the other type, as illustrated by the familiar and venerable "nature–nurture" controversies, where both organism and environment are construed in the most general terms, as illustrated in Figure 7.1.

Figure 7.1
Organism-Based versus Environment-Based Theorizing in Simplistic Form

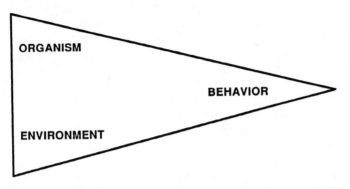

ORGANISM

BEHAVIOR

ENVIRONMENT

Of course, it was recognized long ago that the controversy of "heredity or environment" arose substantially from a badly posed question: A more valid and productive form of the question would address the nature of interaction between phylogenic and ontogenic contributions to behavior. Even though we presumably understand this, questions of "nature versus nurture" occasionally reappear in simple form; and when they do, they are argued with vehemence—as in some of the controversies surrounding sociobiology or the origins of linguistic functioning.

A constructive consideration of the two modes of theorizing requires that each be presented in greater detail. A first step is illustrated in Figure 7.2, which shows that both organism-based and environment-based accounts acknowledge

Figure 7.2
The Place of "Present Situation" in Two Types of Theorizing

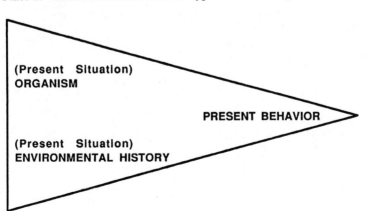

(Present Situation)
ORGANISM

PRESENT BEHAVIOR

(Present Situation)
ENVIRONMENTAL HISTORY

a current environmental context as relevant to behavior. Organism-based accounts attribute behavior to the characteristics of (or processes within) the organism acting in the context of that situation. An environment-based account, such as that introduced by Skinner, gives a more salient role to immediately eliciting or occasioning stimuli; however, the primary environments of environment-based theory are *past environments*, for the roles of the present stimuli are seen as dependent upon the organism's prior history. Even an *insensitivity* of behavior to immediately attendant stimuli is attributed to past history. Some organism-based theorists have either ignored or misunderstood this fact in asserting that behavior lacking immediate environmental causes constitutes an embarrassment to environment-based accounts (Hineline & Wanchisen, 1989; Lacey & Rachlin, 1978; Marr, 1983; Morris, Higgins, & Bickel, 1982).

Still, Figure 7.2 does not give sufficient detail to enable much comparison of the two viewpoints. Figure 7.3 indicates the types of elaboration that would be needed to handle specific cases. As shown, organism-based theory posits inferred processes within, or characteristics of, the organism–typically in the form of representations, expectations, physiological states, or personality characteristics. Perhaps less obviously, the "environmental history" of an environmental-based account is not simply a history of past environment but, rather, a history of behavior–environment interactions and stimulus–stimulus relations with respect to behavior. A history of behavior–environment interactions is what is meant by Skinner's often-used phrase "contingencies of reinforcement," although it should be emphasized that the environment-based account invokes additional principles besides reinforcement.

Figure 7.3
Elaboration of Organism-Based and Environment-Based Interpretation

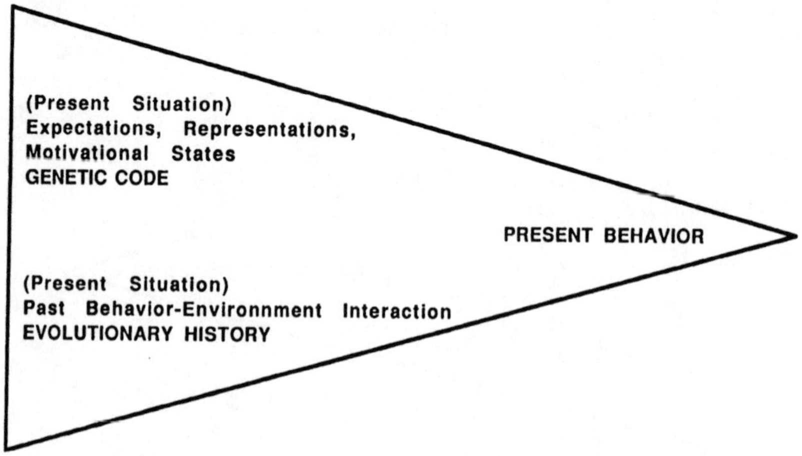

(Present Situation)
Expectations, Representations,
Motivational States
GENETIC CODE

PRESENT BEHAVIOR

(Present Situation)
Past Behavior-Environnment Interaction
EVOLUTIONARY HISTORY

Presenting the two viewpoints as complementary may obscure their potential for inducing the vehement interpretive disagreements that we experience. Nevertheless, the differing directionalities, while simple or subtle in themselves, play out in drastically differing research styles and strategies, accompanied by different assumptions regarding what constitutes a sound experiment or a legitimate explanation. First, and not to be underestimated when theorists of the two traditions evaluate each other's work, is the virtual inevitability of each slighting the other's favored causes; that is, in an environment-based account, the organism is treated as locus where environment and behavior interact. To the extent that particular characteristics of the organism are acknowledged, they have the status of background parameters.[1] Particular environment-behavior relations may hold for particular species, or within species for individuals of particular gender or age. In contrast, organism-based theory acknowledges past environments only indirectly, as the implicit sources of encoded representations or as the origins of expectations that are said to produce the immediate behavior. Thus, to an environment-based theorist, the expectations and representations of an organism-based account are merely redescriptions of history. Other environmental variables also are converted to components of the organism, as in deprivations or other more enduring conditions typically characterized as motivational states. While each type of account also includes an evolutionary component, one construes it as a genetic code, the other as environments on a vastly expanded time scale.

Second, the two types of interpretation are bound to disagree regarding the status of behavior. For an organism-based theorist, behavior is primarily an index of processes within the organism, whether those processes are understood as inferred physiological events or as metaphorical mental processes. In contrast, for environment-based theory, behavior is the main focus rather than index of something else: Descriptions of behavior–environment interactions comprise the theory. This is the meaning of Skinner's phrase, "a science of behavior." It follows that the two types of theory also disagree regarding what constitutes process. For organism-based theorists, processes are said to underlie behavior and to be located within the organism. For environmental-based theorists, processes consist in and of the interplay between behavior and environmental events. A behavioral process, then, is extended over time; by implication, there is no instantaneous "psychological now" within which the causation of behavior must occur.

This last point identifies a third characteristic difference—although it may not be a logically necessary one—between the two types of interpretation. Organism-based theorists tend to assume that contiguity is a necessary feature of causal relationships—specifically, that the causes of an action must be immediately attendant to that action. Environment-based theorists accept functional relations as sufficient to an explanatory account even though the functionally related events are separated in time.

Last, some organism-based accounts differ from environment-based accounts in their appeals to underlying physiology. In this context, it should be noted that from *The Behavior of Organisms* onward, Skinner consistently allowed for a physiological and thus a reductionistic and mechanistic account of behavior. However, he points out that the reductionistic sequence does not stop with physiology:

I am not overlooking the advance that is made in the unification of knowledge when terms at one level of analysis are defined ("explained") at a lower level. Eventually a synthesis of the laws of behavior and of the nervous system may be achieved, although the reduction to lower terms will not, of course, stop at the level of neurology. The final description will be in terms of whatever quasi-ultimate physical units are then in fashion. (Skinner, 1938, p. 428)

To be sure, in Skinner's view, the neurological, organism-based account is a distinct explanatory domain properly construed more as part of biology than of psychology. In addition, in the chapter that addresses physiology and behavior, Skinner explicitly denies any primacy of physiological accounts and, by implication, of organism-based theory:

What is generally not understood by those interested in establishing neurological bases is that a rigorous description at the level of behavior is necessary for the demonstration of a neurological correlate. The discovery of neurological facts may proceed independently of a science of behavior if the facts are directly observed as structural and functional changes in tissue, but before such a fact may be shown to account for a fact of behavior, both must be quantitatively described and shown to correspond in all their properties. (Skinner, 1938, p. 422)

Several contemporary theorists (e.g., see Rosnow & Georgoudi, 1986; Sarbin, 1977) have found it useful to characterize psychological viewpoints in terms of their "root metaphors," as delineated by Pepper (1942). According to that rubric, organism-based theories are either mechanistic or organismic in nature, whereas environment-based theories may be mechanistic or contextualistic. The interpretive tradition that originated in Skinner's work is well characterized as a thoroughgoing contextualist account (Hayes, 1986; Hayes, Hayes, & Reese, 1988; Morris, 1988). Indeed, in its purest form, behavior-analytic theory is contextualistic to the extent of virtually excluding mechanistic metaphors. Hence, while one can identify complementarities between the concepts of behavior analysis and those of competing theories (e.g., see Catania, 1973; Segal, 1977), any attempt at rigorous integrative theory based upon these complementarities risks foundering on the incompatibility of fundamentally conflicting metaphors. As pointed out by Hayes, Hayes, & Reese (1988), Pepper's analysis implies that eclectic combinations of elements from distinct root metaphors will be inherently confusing. Hence, the two interpretive modes will be treated as distinct in this chapter.

INTERPRETIVE DIRECTIONALITY IN ORDINARY LANGUAGE

The above characterizations have described two interpretive modes as applying to formal psychological theories. However, most psychological theorizing involves ordinary as well as special language. Consequently, identifying similar interpretive differences as they occur in everyday language may be important to our understanding a major component of the clash between behavior analysis and other viewpoints. The crucial characteristic is still directionality of interpretive talk, and a most important fact is that in ordinary conversation we all speak comfortably in both directionalities. Furthermore, each directionality seems usually to occur without apparent prejudice to the other, apparently because distinct occasions are conventional for each. Delineating those occasions may reveal some likely origins of the thoroughgoing environment-based account that originated in the laboratory research described in *The Behavior of Organisms*. That delineation may also enable a new understanding of the controversies that arose when that account was addressed to issues beyond the "operant laboratory."

Social psychologists have taken note of the two interpretive modes in ordinary language, under the rubric of "attribution theory." For example, Heider (1958) identified the two modes as persons using either "situational factors" or "dispositional factors" in accounting for human actions. Kelley (1967) formalized and elaborated the sets of factors contributing to the two modes, in terms of a "covariance model," asserting that a person executes a sort of intuitive analysis of variance in adopting one or the other type of account. Thus, for example, observers of a behavior that seems at odds with the situational demands of its immediate context tend to attribute that behavior to internal or dispositional characteristics of the actor (Jones & Davis, 1965). More important for our present concerns are factors that Kelley identified as contributing to external attributions. Prominent among these were (1) *distinctness of entities*, which denotes the strength of correlation between particular environmental events and the action; (2) *consistency over time*, referring to changes in those entities over time, and to whether their presence versus absence corresponds to the occurrence versus non-occurrence of the behavior in questions; (3) *consistency over modality*, which addresses the degree to which the entity's correlation with behavior is robust over a range of variations in the entity; and (4) *consensus*, whether other people make similar attributions regarding an external entity. In Kelley's model, which seems representative of attribution theory, positive relations of these four types should result in external attributions, that is, in environment-based interpretations of behavior.

Ironically, attribution theory itself is usually stated as a predominately organism-based account, whose central points are couched in terms of dispositional factors (properties of an intuitive analysis of variance). (For a clear illustration of this point, which will be of special interest later, as well as for a clear and systematic introduction to that theory, see Ross, 1977.)

The strategy of experimentation portrayed in *The Behavior of Organisms* is strikingly well described by the first three factors identified above. Thus, according to attribution theory, Skinner's style or research—systematically manipulating "entities" through repeated presentations and removals of experimental conditions, evaluating results over time by means of the cumulative record, and replicating results in detail with several individual subject—should lead inexorably to an environment-based account. Furthermore, Skinner's own description of the formative phases of that work (Skinner, 1956) indicates that his research strategies evolved through interplay between data, apparatus, and experimenter's behavior; they did not begin with an ideological stance. If Kelley had been in a position to observe Skinner at work, he would have described Skinner's research and its interpretation as entirely consistent with the predictions of attribution theory.

BEHAVIOR-ANALYTIC THEORY FROM THE VIEWPOINT OF ATTRIBUTION THEORY

If these aspects of attribution theory are correct, virtually anyone who closely followed such experiments from beginning to end should, as a member of the vernacular culture, give an environment-based interpretation. How, then, is Skinner's approach so controversial? Can this question still be answered in terms of attribution theory and the directionality of interpretive prose? There are several bases whereby it can indeed; for while Skinner's interpretations appear to be culturally typical in the context of the experimentation where they emerged, they are not culturally typical as applied to other situations.

First, Skinner's experiments were not like the statistically based group designs that have typified most of psychology. While a co-worker or even a naive observer who was given extended exposure to the same sequences of observation would give causal status to the environmental manipulations of the experiment (thus appealing to situational factors when explaining the subject's behavior), most psychologists were (and are) accustomed to interpreting data in very different circumstances. Typical experiments in psychology are based upon brief observations of many subjects—circumstances that favor internal or dispositional (organism-based) interpretations. Most readers of Skinner's type of interpretation have not been exposed to the types of circumstances that occasioned his interpretations. Furthermore, a psychologist thoroughly immersed in a strongly differing tradition of research and interpretation may even have difficulty in understanding Skinner's type of experiment.[2] Thus, the directionality of Skinner's interpretations is unconventional when offered separate from the extended context of his experiments. In addition, the unconventionality of the experiments themselves probably exacerbates the problem.

A closely related point: Attribution theory is presented as an attempt to characterize the intuitive psychologizing of "the person on the street" (or the equally naive college sophomore), rather than that of the psychologist trained in scientific method. The present thesis is that attribution theory applies to formal psychological theorizing as well, but of course there are major differences between the specific occasions of the professional and of the "intuitive" psychologist's interpretive activity. In the interpretations that attribution theory typically addresses, experimental subjects are asked to account for acts in particular, isolated sets of circumstances. A coherent, general interpretation, independent of particular situations, is neither solicited nor examined. In contrast, Skinner's consistent program of experimental manipulations led to a systematic set of interpretive principles, which were then applied to other subjects' actions in other situations. Of course, this is the standard way for a scholarly psychologist to proceed. In Skinner's case, however, this meant that his type of interpretation, although "culturally normal" in the context of the scientific experiments that occasioned it, was offered on occasions when that type of interpretation was not culturally normal.

Thus, perhaps the interpretations of individual experiments were not what was controversial; instead, the generalizing of those interpretive principles beyond the experiments was the main provocation. This, too, can be understood in terms of attribution theory, as addressed to additional determinants of the directionality in ordinary interpretive language.

A second major factor identified by attribution theorists identifies behavior-analytic interpretation as more distinctly countercultural. In a widely cited essay, Jones and Nisbett (1971) assert that attribution is strongly affected by the relation of the interpreter to the action in question; that is, if one is interpreting one's own action, one tends to speak or write in environment-based locutions. In contrast, if one is observing someone else's action, one tends to interpret it in terms of characteristics of the actor. Even though the tendency of an observer of an action to give disproportional credence to dispositional factors has been characterized as "the fundamental attribution error" (Ross, 1977), attribution theorists themselves conform to this cultural convention. For example, Kelley's analysis of variance model is construed not as identifying the variables that control directionality of interpretive talk but, rather, as characterizing the interpreter's intuitive process of inferring causation. Ironically, and fundamental error or not, the cultural convention that Jones and Nisbett expose in their article is illustrated by their own exposition; they describe that convention in terms of *biases* on the part of the actor and upon the part of the observer.

To be sure, any serious theorist states the interpretations of action from the viewpoint of the observer: Objective psychology is the "science of the other one." As attempts at such, most psychologies conform to the cultural norm that Jones and Nisbett identify, of observers giving organism-based interpretation. Skinner's interpretive stance also conforms to the standard, "other one" convention of serious psychological theory. In so doing, Skinner offers, from the viewpoint of the observer, an account whose directionality would be culturally conventional only if it were offered from the viewpoint of the actor. That may explain why behavior analysis has always been outside the mainstream of psychology.[3]

Last, the factor of "consistency," identified in Kelley's (1967) covariance model, seems to have a pervasive but mostly unnoticed role in controversies surrounding Skinnerian interpretations. Its subtle but determining role in directionality is well illustrated by the following two statements:

1. I have carried out an extensive set of observations, with myself as subject, and have discovered that wine is stronger than beer.
2. Based on a comparable set of observations, I have discovered that I am more allergic to tulips than to roses.

Logically, the choice of an environmental-based description in the first case and of an organism-based description in the second is arbitrary: The potency of a beverage is one's susceptibility to it, and one's allergy to a flower is its potency to induce sneezing and related behavior. Furthermore, while each potency or susceptibility has a recognized underlying physiological mechanism (one involves neurotransmitters and the other involves the immune system), it is unlikely that these are the bases of the differing directionality; the verbal patterns surely antedated the understanding of those mechanisms. Even today most people could not identify the difference of mechanism, but virtually all would engage in the same attributional patterns.

The basis for the differing attributions and for the interpretive directionality that flows with them is more evident if we convert each statement to culturally atypical form:

1. I have carried out an extensive set of observations, with myself as subject, and have discovered that I am more easily intoxicated by wine than by beer.
2. Based on a similar set of observations, I have discovered that tulips are more allergenic than roses.

Both the intuitive and the professional psychologist are likely to find something odd here, reacting to the first by remarking, "This is news?" and to the second: "Speak for yourself!" (Note that the evident sarcasm of these reactions might constitute mild punishment of the culturally atypical attributions if the reactions were overt.) Kelley's "intuitive analysis of variance" version of attribution theory identifies the key dimension here; that is, one-half liter of wine is more potent than the same quantity of beer for virtually everyone. In contrast, tulips produce sneezing in some people but not in others. Within the culture, then, occasions where everyone is affected similarly are occasions for one directionality of causal descriptions—from environment to behavior. In contrast, occasions where individuals are affected differently are occasions for the other directionality—from dispositions to behavior. Applied to Skinnerian theory, this identifies an irony: Even though Skinnerian experimentation focuses upon the behavior of individuals rather than upon groups of individuals, and even though Skinnerian prescriptions for educational or therapeutic practice are necessarily tailored to the particular needs of the individual, and even though Skinnerian interpretation explicitly declines to blame the individual when addressing antisocial behavior or failures to learn—these are all stated with a directionality that, in the verbal practices of the culture, is occasioned by situations in which everyone is alike. This, then, may be a key factor in reactions to Skinner's theory as "dehumanizing" in its more popularized versions, and as nonmainstream in the domain of learning theory.

Both the social psychologist and the nonpsychologist, then, are likely to react to behavior-analytic interpretation as insensitive to a very important dimension in the texture of social discourse. In its own technical terms, behavior-analytic interpretation risks being reacted to as a failure of stimulus control. Just as a person may react with defensive apprehension to the "word salad" of schizophrenic speech while unable to specify what is strange or threatening about that speech, that person may also act as if threatened by Skinnerian interpretation.

CONVENTIONAL AND UNCONVENTIONAL ATTRIBUTION IN *THE BEHAVIOR OF ORGANISMS*

Summarizing this behavior-analytic rendition of attribution theory's account of behavior analysis: Both organism-based and environment-based interpretations of behavior are standard vernacular repertoires, but they normally occur in different types of situations. Skinner's thoroughgoing environment-based interpretations of his early experiments were culturally conventional in the context of the type of experiments that he did. Also, it was scientifically conventional to develop individual experiments into an integrated body of work, with the resulting interrelated concepts then extrapolated to account for behavior outside as well as within experimental settings. However, many of Skinner's extrapolations, and those of behavior-analytic theory more generally, offer environment-based interpretations of behavior for situations in which organism-based interpretations are the firmly entrenched cultural pattern. Arguments supporting those interpretations have focused on claims of "objectivity" or on the pragmatic superiority of environmental variables over hypothetical constructs. However, the cultural resistance to Skinnerian explanations and, in turn, to behavior-analytic approaches to problems in the world at large, may arise from this other operative but largely unnoticed dimension that is not addressed by those arguments. That is, the source of resistance to a behavior-analytic approach may be the largely unnoticed but unconventional directionality of attributions that are characteristic of that approach.

Sometimes this unconventionality may be reacted to simply as explanation insensitive to its occasioning context, as in the observer's directionality of interpretation that, according to Jones and Nisbett (1971), is culturally appropriate only from the stance of the actor. In other cases, the unconventional directionality would be reacted to as implicitly asserting that all people are alike when vernacular explanations would appeal to distinct inferred characteristics of each person. Thus, from the viewpoint of attribution theory, it is remarkable that the resulting approach could ascend to prominence and endure within a culture whose interpretive patterns are so thoroughly at odds with it. Given the massive inertia of cultural conventions, the manner in which behavior analysis was introduced may have been crucial to its gaining a foothold; thus, its early introduction, as well as the circumstances of its development, bear examining in terms of the relationships that have been identified here.

With the publication of *The Behavior of Organisms*, the distinctive characteristics of Skinner's empirical approach were substantially developed and in place. Close examination of that book reveals, however, that Skinner's initial theorizing was not entirely pure in its environment-based stance. In addition, a joint focusing of attribution theory and some principles of behavior analysis—both of these addressed to the expository sequencing in that book—provides sidelights that may illuminate the manner in which that environment-based theory occurred to its progenitor, as well as the manner in which it was introduced to others.

The book opens with several prefatory paragraphs, the first one stating Skinner's criticism of mentalistic concepts as being granted preferential explanatory status simply because they are internal to the behaving organism and thus inaccessible to disproof. The forgoing discussion suggested that the differences between organism-based and environment-based interpretation can be framed more generally. The second paragraph, however, fits hand in glove with the present account in addressing the status of behavior with respect to interpretation: Organism-based theories treat behavior as a mere index of process rather than as a psychological phenomenon in and of itself. Next, Skinner explicitly rejects vernacular terms "that imply conceptual schemes," while he otherwise favors ordinary rather than technical language. One can infer from his examples that such schemes appeal to an organism's agency, or to intentionality, as initiating or guiding its actions. For Skinner, the basic role of acceptable language is characterized as narration ("a running account of a sample of behavior as it unfolds itself in some frame of reference" [p. 8]). His is to be a "descriptive theory," beginning with the identification of analytical units rather than theoretical constructs. The reflex is offered as an example, and he is on his way.

Conceptually, the unconditional reflex is an obvious starting point as a likely simplest unit of behavior. Furthermore, Skinner's seminal papers during the early 1930s can be seen as attempts to extend a basic reflexology that already had ample precedent in the recognized physiology of behavior and in Watson's behaviorism (Coleman, 1984). We shall see that the flavor of classic reflexology lingers in many pages of the 1938 book. However, even in a treatise whose main thrust is to depart from pure reflexology, the reflex also may be an effective starting point for a purely expository reason: By definition, unconditional reflexes are features that all members of a species have in common, and so it is culturally conventional to give an environment-based account of them. A puff of air or a bit of dust in the eye is said to produce an eyeblink; one is not tempted to appeal to the organism for initiation of such behavior. Thus, Skinner's pattern of interpretation is culturally conventional as he enumerates the "static laws of the reflex"—threshold, latency, magnitudes, after-discharge, and temporal summation. These are described as general principles rather than as specific empirical results; it is uncontroversial that they give salience to environmental determinants, for it is well established that they are essentially uniform across individuals. Next come the dynamic laws, which include two—facilitation and inhibition (of the kind that Pavlovians would call *external* inhibition)—that give as much salience to stimuli as to responses. Other dynamic laws—refractory phase and reflex fatigue—give greater emphasis to responses than to their eliciting stimuli and might induce one to appeal to fluctuations within the organism, but these are still characteristic of all individuals, so most any reader will find environment-based interpretation to be appropriate. Those initial pages of exposition build upon the fact that all readers have repertoires of environment-based interpretation, by describing situations that are normal occasions for those repertoires. With the environment-based pattern of interpretation established through varied but conventional repetitions, the reader is prepared for the subsequent process of "fading" by successive steps, maintaining environment-based locutions while gradually introducing features that normally would occasion organism-based ones.

Continuing with dynamic laws of the reflex, Skinner briefly describes Pavlovian conditioning (denoted as "Type S") which introduces hints of differences between individuals. Even here, in the conditional reflex, the form of response would not differ between individuals, for only the particular eliciting stimuli that produce it would be individualized. Furthermore, conditioned as well as unconditioned reflexes inherently involve immediately attendant stimuli that qualify as "entities" in an attributional account, and these support that continuing environment-based interpretation. Then, operant conditioning and extinction are added to the set of dynamic laws, but these phenomena are introduced in a way that minimizes the fact that they might induce different individuals to act differently. Skinner construes the defining feature of operant behavior as the absence of eliciting stimuli, so it is important that the continuing environment-based interpretation is supported by a language of "everyone is similar," even though the similarities are now based on *absence* of environment events proximal to the behavior at issue.

With that much in place, and more than twenty pages into his account, Skinner interrupts the gradual succession, venturing to deal with relationships for which organism-based theorizing would be far more conventional:

The operations characterizing drive and emotion differ from the others listed in that they effect concurrent changes in *groups* of reflexes. The operation of feeding, for example, brings about changes in all the operants that have been reinforced with food and in all the conditioned and unconditioned respondents concerned with ingestion. Moreover, a single operation is not unique in its effect. There is more than one way of changing the strength of the group of reflexes varying with ingestion or with an emotional stimulus. In addition to the formulation of the effect upon a single reflex, we must deal also with *the* drive or *the* emotion as the "state" of a group of reflexes. This is done by introducing a hypothetical middle term between the operation and the resulting observed change. "Hunger," "fear" and so on, are terms of this sort. (Skinner, 1938, p. 24)

In defending his inclusion of these terms, which seem inconsistent with the main thrust of his approach, Skinner acknowledges the need for meticulous parsimony in their use:

In the present system hypothetical middle terms ("states") will be used in the cases of drive and emotion, but no other properties will be assigned to them. A dynamic law always refers to the change in strength of a single reflex as a function of a single operation, and the intermediate term is actually unnecessary in its expression. (Skinner, 1938, p. 24)

He is arguing, then, for confining the status of such intervening terms to that of intervening variables—summary terms for environmental contributors—rather than the status of hypothetical constructs, which would be imputed mediating events within the organism. This distinction was clarified a few years later by MacCorquodale and Meehl (1948).

However, the next term that is introduced in *The Behavior of Organisms*—the reflex reserve—has the distinct flavor of hypothetical construct. The term is initially defined as a property of the behavior itself or of the environmental operations that affect behavior:

. . . we may speak of a certain amount of *available activity*, which is exhausted during the process of repeated elicitation and of which the strength of the reflex is at any moment a function. . . . In one sense the reserve is a hypothetical entity. It is a convenient way of representing the particular relation that obtains between the activity of a reflex and its subsequent strength. . . . The notion applies to all operations that involve the elicitation of the reflex and to both operant and respondent behavior, whether conditioned or unconditioned. (Skinner, 1938, pp. 26–27)

But there immediately follows the suggestion of underlying process that is distinct from the behavior to be accounted for:

One distinction between an unconditioned and a conditioned reflex is that the reserve of the former is constantly being restored spontaneously, when it is not already at a maximum. In the particular case of reflex fatigue, a spontaneous flow into the reserve is evident in the complete recovery from fatigue that takes place during rest. . . . In conditioned reflexes the reserve is built up by the act of reinforcement, and extinction is essentially a process of exhaustion comparable with fatigue. The conception applies to both types of conditioning and leads to a much more comprehensive formulation of the process than is available in terms of mere change in strength. (Skinner, 1938, p. 27)

This is more than a momentary lapse, for in the continuing discussion of reflex reserve, we find that behavior has been displaced from primary focus to the role of the barely mentioned index of underlying process:

In a phasic respondent the refractory phase suggests a smaller subsidiary reserve which is either completely or nearly completely exhausted with each elicitation. This subsidiary reserve is restored from the whole reserve, but the rate of restoration depends upon the size of the latter. Thus, during the fatigue of such a respondent the refractory phase is progressively prolonged. (Skinner, 1938, p. 28)

Thus, we see a dramatic departure from purely environment-based theory and an illustration of changes that attend such a shift. Even in Skinner's own prose, inclusion of intervening "states" results in behavior being described mainly as the index of underlying process.

Immediately after introducing and briefly discussing the reflex reserve, the introductory chapter of *The Behavior of Organisms* returns to its gradual progression that maintains the pattern of environment-based interpretations. Now the progression is to a few situations of greater complexity, where there might be greater variability over time or between individuals. These are handled by describing principles of interaction between reflexes when more than one is simultaneously operative, either in combination or in competition. No new initiating principles are required for generating the more complex or variable behavior; purely combinatorial principles appear to suffice, and so the environment-based pattern is maintained in situations that have still greater tendency to induce the organism-based one.

The final section of the first chapter and the first part of the second is a more complex expository sequence that might be better characterized in terms of conventional logic than the simple dimension of interpretive directionality. The exposition of basic principles is punctuated by asides that address a variety of tangential but crucial issues, anticipating criticisms of Skinner's position that have persisted over the decades since *The Behavior of Organisms* was written. Among these are (1) accounting for novel behavior by showing how it is accommodated in specifications of even the most basic behavior-environment relations,[4] (2) acknowledging biologically based separations ("natural lines of fracture") between functional units of behavior, (3) acknowledging and justifying his emphasis upon operant rather than respondent behavior, (4) pointing out limitations and distortions that result from adopting vernacular concepts into scientific language, (5) taking a position on the issue of molar-versus-molecular scales of analysis, (6) explicitly including the interpreter's behavior in his interpretive system, and (7) providing a definition of verbal behavior that anticipates by nearly two decades his book-length work on that topic. Meta-theory is explicitly addressed, characterizing the approach as a descriptive rather than explanatory system but asserting the need for structure in interpretive systems of whatever kind.

The second chapter, "Scope and Method," includes a detailed description of Skinner's basic experimental arrangement. This introduction to specific, innovative features of method prepares the way for descriptions of experiments and results that, as I noted earlier, provide an entirely different basis for supporting environment-based interpretation: Unlike the between-group studies that are more typical of experimentation in psychology—whose brief observations of each subject and emphasis on differences between groups of individuals plays into the cultural bias toward organism-based interpretation—Skinner's experiments follow each individual's behavior as it tracks the changes of experimental procedure. Since the individual is a constant during these sequential changes of procedure and behavior, it is culturally conventional to appeal to the environment context of action rather than to characteristics of the actor when accounting for what the individual does.

In this new mode, the expository sequence alternates between respondent and operant behavior, emphasizing similarities more than differences between them while basic conditioning and extinction are described. Skinner's own data are presented with ample attention given to individual subjects' differing behavior patterns; still, these are handled with minimal appeal to dispositional characteristics of the individuals. For example, in characterizing the original conditioning of each of seventy-eight rats' lever pressing, nine individual cumulative records are presented as representing the range of effects. The few atypical cases are discussed in terms of four types of likely interplay between environmental events and behavior; a fifth, one-sentence alternative, might be viewed as suggesting organism-based difference—that of emotional reactivity to novel stimulation. Even there, it is a specific environmental stimulus that is said to produce the atypical reaction.

With basic demonstrations of conditioning in place, the sequence again builds from simple to complex, but now the development occurs over the course of several chapters. Delayed reinforcement, conditioned reinforcement, intermittent reinforcement, discrimination, and generalization all are mainly characterized as behavior-environment interaction; that is, they are described in the terms of environment-based theory. While there are occasional discussions of the implications of data for the reflex reserve, these have the character of asides or of afterthoughts, appended to accounts of data that appeal directly to procedural determinants. When individual differences are salient—as when periodic reconditioning generates highly individualized and complex performances in particular experimental subjects—the observed differences are accounted for in terms of ancillary environment-based processes such as discrimination, generalization, and specific spatial relationships in the conditioning situations, rather than appealing to differences between the subjects' capacities for establishing a reserve, or the like.

THE TRANSITION FROM CLASSIC REFLEXOLOGY TO THE LANGUAGE OF OPERANT THEORY

In beginning *The Behavior of Organisms* with reflex relations, Skinner established an environment-based interpretive directionality that he then maintained through transitions to domains in which that directionality is less conventional. These latter are especially the domains of operant behavior, where one encounters separations of time between behavior and its relevant environmental events, as well as widely ranging differences between individuals' actions and capabilities. That transition to a focus mainly on operant behavior is accomplished quite early in the book. However, the book begins not only with descriptions of reflexive behavior but also with descriptions and discussions couched in the language of classic reflexology, whose frequent references to elicitation continually suggest immediate environmental precursors of behavior even when no specific elicitors are identified. The book's expository shift away from this language of reflexology lags behind the topical progression from reflexes to operant language that we now identify with behavior analysis. This more modern language draws a clean distinction between elicited reflexes and emitted environmental precursors. It also differs from the vernacular and mainstream psychology in various other ways, to the extent that it might be considered a distinct dialect (Hineline, 1980). Besides its expository function, the shift may be reflecting the ontogenesis of environment-based interpretive patterns in Skinner's own behavior.

To be specific, the early parts of the book characterize all behavior—even operant behavior—in the language of elicitation. For example, Skinner initially construes the conditioning of a lever press response as dealing with a "chain of reflexes involved in pressing the lever and obtaining food." (Skinner, 1938, p. 66). Later on, rates of responding are described rather than rates of elicitation, with "elicitation" occurring only once or twice in the course of several pages. Within that general trend, however, are some striking transitions between the two modes of description that provide convenient illustrations of both types. For example, consider first a description of operant behavior in the language of classic reflexology:

. . . When an organism comes accidentally (that is to say, as the result of weak investigatory reflexes) upon a new kind of food, which it seizes and eats, both kinds of conditioning presumably occur. When the visible radiation from the food next stimulates

the organism, salivation is evoked according to Type S. This secretion remains use-
less until the food is actually seized and eaten. But seizing and eating will depend
upon the same accidental factors as before unless conditioning of Type R has also
occurred—that is, unless the strength of $sS^D : food . R : seizing$ has increased. Thus,
while a reflex of Type S prepares the organism, a reflex of Type R obtains the food
for which the preparation is made. And this is in general a fair characterization of the
relative importance of the two types. (Skinner, 1938, p. 111)

A few pages later, we find a mixture of modern behavior-analytic and classic
reflexive language:

An operant may be strengthened or weakened through reinforcement or the lack of it,
but the phenomena of acquisition and loss of strength are only part of the field defined by reinforcement as an operation. (Skinner, 1938, p. 116)

In general the states of strength of the conditioned reflexes of an organism are
submaximal with respect to the operation of reinforcement. . . . Special properties of
conditioned reflexes arise under periodic reconditioning which have no counterpart
in the original conditioning and extinction of a reflex. They are properties of the reflex reserve and of the relation of the reserve to the rate of elicitation. We may approach the subject by examining the effect of periodic reconditioning upon the state
of our representative operant. (Skinner, 1938, p. 117)

Then, with descriptions of extended response patterns on fixed-interval
schedules, individuals' extended histories and the resulting performances are
portrayed mainly in the details of cumulative records while "rate of elicitation" still appears in the accompanying prose. This descriptive phrase gradually becomes less frequent in the course of pages 117–139.

Somewhat later, Skinner's interpretive statements begin to catch up with
these evolving descriptions of data, as when he defines "Discrimination of
Type R":

Although the response is free to come out in a very large number of stimulating
situations, it will be effective in producing a reinforcement only in a small part of
them. The favorable situation is usually marked in some way, and the organism makes
a discrimination of a kind now to be taken up. It comes to respond whenever a stimulus is present which has been present upon the occasion of a previous reinforcement
and not to respond otherwise. The prior stimulus does not elicit the response; it merely
sets the *occasion* upon which the response will be reinforced. . . . Three terms must
therefore be considered: a prior discriminative stimulus (S^D), the response (R^O), and
the reinforcing stimulus (S^1). (Skinner, 1938, p. 178)

Then, as Skinner proceeds to describe various experiments on discrimination,
there is only brief mention of the reflex reserve and only occasional mention of
"rates of elicitation." Many descriptions are in terms of "rates" with no modifiers,
but vestiges of reflexology are still evident through description in terms of the
relative strengths of a reflex (lever pressing) in the presence of different stimuli.

Still later, Skinner refers to "the reinforcement of an operant" rather than of a reflex; and shortly thereafter, he explicitly distances the operant from the reflex concept:

The lack of an eliciting stimulus in operant behavior together with the law of the operant reserve throws considerable weight upon the response alone, and this may seem to weaken any attempt to group operants under the general heading of reflexes. . . . it should be understood that the operant reserve is a reserve of *responses*, not of stimulus–response units. Whether the same can be said for respondents is not clear. (Skinner, 1938, p. 230)

Continuing on, we find some modern, nonreflexive language of operant behavior:

The discriminative stimulus [defined with respect to operant behavior] has a very different status from that of the eliciting stimulus [defined with respect to respondent behavior]. It is less likely to be regarded as a spur or goad and is perhaps best described as "setting the occasion" for a response. Whether or not the response is to occur does not depend upon the discriminative stimulus, once it is present, but upon other factors. . . . Strictly speaking we should refer to a   discriminated operant as "occurring in the presence of" rather than "elicited as a response to" S^D. (Skinner, 1938, p. 241)

At long last, the formal conception has caught up with the changes that could be discerned earlier in the descriptions of experiments and data (Skinner, 1938, p. 243):

The various functions of stimuli may be summarized in this way: a stimulus may:

(1) elicit a response ("elicitation"),

(2) set the occasion for a response ("discrimination"),

(3) modify the reserve ("reinforcement"), or

(4) modify the proportionality of reserve and strength ("emotion," "facilitation," and "inhibition").

Later in the book are chapters addressing the concepts of drive, emotion, and reflex reserve, whose initial characterizations constituted lapses into organism-based theory that I have already described. This time, Skinner introduces the concept of drive with an observation that anticipated by several decades the account in terms of attribution theory:

The problem of drive arises because much of the behavior of an organism shows an apparent variability. A rat does not always respond to food placed before it, and a factor called its "hunger" is invoked by way of explanation. . . . It is because eating is not inevitable that we are led to hypothesize an internal state to which we may assign the variability. Where there is no variability, no state is needed. Since the rat usually responds to a shock to its foot by flexing its leg, no "flexing drive" comparable to hunger is felt to be required. (Skinner, 1938, p. 341)

The ensuing treatment of his research under the heading of "drive" remains, for the most part, consistent with Skinner's initial environment-based characterization, quoted earlier as having initially occurred on page 24: Drives are identified in terms of *classes* of operant or of reflexes that collectively are affected by particular variables. When we identify drives, we are identifying classes of operations having similar effects on a given unit of behavior, or classes of units of behavior affected by a single operation: "Whether or not a given reflex belongs to a given drive must be answered by considering covariation rather than any essential property of the behavior itself" (Skinner, 1938, p. 371). Then, treating emotion in a manner analogous to that of drive:

In both cases [drive and emotion] we must describe the covariation of the strengths of a number of reflexes as functions of a particular operation. Drive and emotion are separate fields only because the appropriate operations can be separated into different classes. In many cases, this distinction is thin. . . . It is not essential to this formulation that drive and emotion constitute two different classes. The important thing is the recognition of a change in strength as a primary datum and the determination of the functional relationship between the strength and some operation. (Skinner, 1938, pp. 408–409)

Both discussions, however, hint at a departure from pure environment-based interpretation: "An emotion is a dynamic process rather than a static relation of stimulus and response" (p. 409). "It is a poor substitute to measure the operation responsible for the state of a drive until the relation between the state and the operation is accurately known" (p. 402). In the general comments of his concluding chapter, the problematic status of some of these concepts is acknowledged:

The concepts of "drive," "emotion," "conditioning," "reflex strength," "reserve," and so on, have the same status as "will" and "cognition," but they differ in the rigor of the analysis with which they are derived and in the immediacy of their reference to actual observations. (Skinner, 1938, p. 441)

BEYOND *THE BEHAVIOR OF ORGANISMS*

After the publication of *The Behavior of Organisms* in 1938, Skinner's theorizing continued to evolve in some respects, while being addressed to an ever-increasing range of topics. In a 1940 convention paper, he reported findings that were not readily accommodated by the concept of reflex reserve (for Abstract, see Skinner, 1940), and soon after, the reflex reserve faded from Skinner's prose. Similarly, the locutions of reflexology are seldom found in his later works. Skinner's own confidence in the consistency of his position is evident in a recent exchange: In a commentary on Skinner's work, Blanchard, Blanchard, and Flannelly (1984) sketch a distinction between "organismic" and environment-based interpretation that is very similar to the one

I have presented here; and they suggest that organism-based concepts are essential to an adequate science of behavior. Skinner replies as follows:

I would point out that in my thesis, published in 1931 [which was substantially incorporated into *The Behavior of Organisms*], I hazarded a guess that there were three kinds of variables of which behavior would prove to be a function. I referred to them with the terms conditioning, drive, and emotion. Blanchard et al. would call the last two organismic. Over the years I have spent a good deal of time on them, but simply as different sets of variables of which the probability of response is a function. (Skinner, 1984, p. 702)

This claim to have maintained a purely environment-based stance (with its parsimonious superiority implied by his use of the term "simply" in the above quotation) is a plausible one, and it does describe most work of Skinner's extensive career. Whether he has entirely eliminated emotion as an organism-based locution could be assessed through detailed examination of his subsequent writings.

While the origins and initial introduction of behavior-analytic concepts may be substantially portrayed in *The Behavior of Organisms*, that book may not reveal the most effective bases of those concepts' movement into the psychological community. Indeed, Knapp (this volume) asserts that *The Behavior of Organisms* in itself was not a particularly successful book ("Only Edward C. Tolman, one of the intellectual progenitors of cognitive psychology, offered unqualified praise.") and that, in fact, it was saved from near intellectual oblivion by Keller and Schoenfeld's program at Columbia University. A key feature of that program was the introduction of behavioral principles through a laboratory course in which each student conditioned the behavior of a laboratory rat. Such laboratory procedures provide shaping and fading procedures that may well be more effective than any textbook can provide: The major components for interpreting operant behavior are systematically introduced as they are built into the animals' repertoires of consistently expanding complexity. Hence, the infusion of theory from *The Behavior of Organisms* into the culture may be better examined via the details of the behavioral tradition as it radiated out from Columbia, aided by Keller and Schoenfeld's own textbook *Principles of Psychology* (1950). Nevertheless, Skinner's many other publications surely have been continuing, and the most prominent component of the continuing presence of behavior analysis as a distinct viewpoint.

Last, it must be acknowledged that interpretive directionality is not the only unconventional feature of Skinner's approach. Its construing of process extended over time, for example, is another; and his well-recognized assertions of strong determinism and rejections of mentalistic terms surely have contributed to the Skinnerian controversies as well. At the time of its genesis, as well as over the ensuing years, the merits of Skinner's approach were and have continued to be argued and evaluated in terms of issues such as determinism versus autonomy of persons on the one hand (e.g., see Coleman, 1984), as well as in terms of theoretical coherence on the other (e.g., see Verplanck, 1954). Surely both the conventional logic of the latter and the prescientific value commitments of the former have been operative in the controversies surrounding this approach. Nevertheless, even within the arguments stated in those terms, it may be that the simple but subtle feature of interpretive direction, and its relationship to conventional interpretive patterns within the broader culture in which we all participate, has had much to do with those controversies.

AUTHOR'S NOTE

Special thanks are owed to two of my colleagues who are expert in social psychology—to Louise H. Kidder, for introducing me to attribution theory, and to Marianne E. Jaeger, for helpful comments on a draft of this manuscript.

Chapter 8

Quantum Physics and Radical Behaviorism: Some Issues in Scientific Verbal Behavior

M. Jackson Marr

Among the products of intellectual ferment in the twentieth century, one—quantum physics—fundamentally changed the picture of nature; another—behaviorism—changed the picture of ourselves. Although these endeavors ostensibly deal with very different domains, I would like to discuss certain common influences and correspondences and, in particular, to consider possible contributions of Skinner's treatment of scientific verbal behavior to some issues raised by interpretations of quantum formalism.

Scientific behavior may be ultimately expressed by nonverbal behavior maintained by nonverbal consequences; but such behavior is largely verbal, emerging from the descriptions of relatively stable environmental contingencies. Attempts at analysis of the verbal behavior of scientists in any field might prove valuable, but a consideration of modern theoretical physics offers special challenges and fascinations.

First, psychology bears the heavy imprint of classical physics, both historically and philosophically. That legacy is worth exploration in itself (see, e.g., Marr, 1989, 1992), but it is of special interest to consider correspondences between psychology and *modern physics*. In an address to the American Psychological Association nearly forty years ago, Oppenheimer (1956)warned that if psychology desired to model itself after physics, it had better be aware of the significant differences between classical and modern physics.

Second, some of those differences between classical and modern physics involve issues that are of major concern to psychology as a science (e.g., how one talks about unobservable phenomena). This problem is just as acute in modern physics as it is in psychology. Although the mathematical formalism of quantum mechanics is enormously successful, it has engendered disturbing questions about what this formalism actually describes and how it is possible to predict features of nature by talking about it, particularly when there appears to be no "experiential referents" for the mathematical language. Kline (1980) has called this "the greatest paradox in mathematics" (p. 340).

Third, while the nonphysicist typically considers physics to be the zenith of objective science, reaching ever upward toward absolute truth, the fact is that very few theoretical physicists would agree with this assessment. In the view of many, modern physics must dispense with classical causality, objective reality, and even common logic, and it becomes necessary then to ask just what physics is about (see, e.g., Herbert, 1985).

The reader of Skinner's works will recognize the issues mentioned above as reflecting various aspects of his treatment of verbal behavior. What follows is a discussion of some of these issues, largely from the perspective of radical behaviorism. My intent is not to resolve the issues but, rather, to indicate to physicists that a science of behavior not only shares certain problems with it but may, in fact, contribute something toward understanding their behavior as scientists and to indicate to psychologists that modern physics offers a rich and waiting field for analysis of verbal behavior.

STRUCTURE AND FUNCTION

Experimental psychology—in its history, its philosophical foundations, its theoretical formulations, and its practice—has deep roots in the soil of classical physics. Many of those whom we recognize as founders of experimental psychology were physicists, for instance, Weber, Fechner, and Helmholtz. It is hardly an accident that psychophysics represented the first truly quantitative analysis of behavior. Others, like Wundt and his pupil Titchener explicitly related their structuralist positions to atomistic concepts in physics. Further influences are reflected in Freud's thermodynamic model, Gestalt field theory, models of man as the latest machine, and the metaphors of cognitive psychology.

Perhaps the most important source of joint influence on modern physics and modern experimental psychology was Ernst Mach (1838–1916). In his book *The Science of Mechanics* (1893/1960), Mach emphasized what he termed "economy of thought" and provided a critical analysis of certain concepts in classical physics, rejecting them on the basis that they were either tautological or hypothetical. By the latter, he meant without reference to sensory experience: What was without direct empirical foundation was metaphysical and did not belong in a scientific account. Sensations were his primitives: "Nature is composed of sensations as its elements" (p. 579). This view has remained dominant to this day. Compare the psychologists Kendler and Spence, writing in 1971, "Sensory experience of the observing scientist is the basic datum of psychology" (p. 12). The goal of science for Mach was to relate sensory experiences in the most economical way, namely, as *functional relationships*. Thus, he says,

Faithful adherence to the method that led the greatest investigators of nature, Galileo, Newton, Sadi Carnot, Faraday and J. R. Mayer, to their greatest results, restricts physics to the expression of *actual facts*, and forbids the construction of hypotheses behind the facts, where nothing tangible and verifiable is found. If this is done, only the simple connection of the motions of masses, of changes in temperature, of changes in the value of the potential function, of chemical changes, and so forth is to be ascertained, and nothing is to be imagined along with these elements except the physical attributes or characteristics directly or indirectly given by observation. (Mach, 1893/1960, p. 597)

Mach's phenomenalist or positivistic position was reflected in nineteenth-century physics in at least two principal ways relevant to issues to be considered in a science of behavior. The first was the development of classical thermodynamics by such people as Carnot (1791–1832), Clausius (1822–1888), and especially Gibbs (1839–1903) (d'Abro, 1951). Classical thermodynamics restricted its attention to macroscopic (i.e., observable) properties of matter. As Nash (1970) says, "Calling on only a minimal array of axiomatic postulates, it cunningly contrives to discuss material phenomena without making any assumption whatever about the constitution (atomic or otherwise) of matter" (p. 1). Thermodynamics embodies functional relationships between such variables as temperature, pressure, and volume, which, in turn, define *states* of systems (see, e.g., Marr, 1985, 1993b; Smith, this volume, for further discussion of Mach and behavior analysis).

The approach embodied in classical thermodynamics characterizes much of Skinner's experimental analysis of behavior, and indeed he describes the maintaining conditions for his own scientific behavior as follows: "It is reinforcing to find variables which change in an orderly fashion and which permit one to formulate behavior as a scientific system in the sense in which that term is used, for example, by Willard Gibbs" (Skinner, 1969, p. 93).

The "economy" of dispensing with any notion of the ultimate constitution of matter, characteristic of classical thermodynamics, was an expression of what Mach called the "principle of continuity"; and its implications were to be evident in psychology as well as physics. Mach (1893/1960) states the principle this way:

Once we have reached a theory that applies to a particular case, we proceed gradually to modify in thought the conditions of that case, as far as it is at all possible, and endeavor in so doing to adhere throughout as closely as we can to the conception originally reached. There is no method of procedure more surely calculated to lead to that comprehension of all natural phenomena which is the *simplest* and also attainable with the least expenditure of mentality and feeling. (p. 168)

An application of this principle led Mach to eschew atomic theory. Indeed, until the first decade of this century, most physicists did not believe in atoms. It is true that throughout the history of thought the discreteness of matter had been hypothesized, beginning with the Milesian school in sixth-century-b.c. Greece (Heisenberg, 1962), and formed a heuristic approach to significant problems of physics and chemistry in the nineteenth century. Mach (1893/ 1960, pp. 588–589) commented, however, on the heuristic aspect of atomic theory by arguing that the theory had not been formed by the principle of continuity but was devised simply to resolve the problems immediately facing the nineteenth-century physical sciences. True Newtonians, he suggested, would regard atomic theory as a "provisional" remedy and eventually produce a superior substitute.

Despite the apparent success of the atomic hypothesis, skepticism remained, supported not only by findings at variance with the hypothesis but also by the difficulties in explaining observable phenomena in terms of the unobservable. Ostwald, the founder of physical chemistry, warned against "hypothetical conjectures that lead to no verifiable conclusions"; and Gibbs wrote, "He builds on an insecure foundation who bases his conclusions on ideas concerning the ultimate structure of matter" (Guillemin, 1968, pp. 21–22).

Concurrent with the debate in physics about the atomic hypothesis, German psychology was searching for the irreducible elements of mental life. As Heidbreder (1933) points out:

In a sense, the scientific psychology of Germany was patterned on physics. Growing in large measure from the attempt to understand the sense organs as mechanical models, and influenced by this fact in its mode of attack upon psychic life, it undertook the task of discovering into what elemental parts mental states can be analyzed and of determining the ways in which these parts are combined. (p. 106)

This structuralist approach was first associated with Wundt, but its most influential form was the product of Titchener. Titchener repudiated many of Wundt's explanatory concepts of memory, perception, and consciousness as "unnecessary, overspeculative and even unscientific" (Leahey, 1981, p. 275). Titchener was, in fact, a disciple of Mach and emphasized the descriptive and observable. For him, introspection was a form of observation, no different in principle from the observation of the outside world. Titchener's elements were *dynamic processes* whose combination engendered the forms of conscious experience. The concept of unit as process has its counterpart in modern physics, as I will discuss shortly.

In 1905, Albert Einstein applied kinetic theory to the analysis of Brownian motion and thereby provided the most direct and convincing demonstration of the discreteness of matter. Einstein argued in the same year that electromagnetic radiation as well could be considered as composed of discrete units or "photons." Although this idea was given some vague plausibility by Planck's earlier work with black-body radiation, it was an extraordinarily radical suggestion. The vast power of Maxwell's field equations made the idea of photons seem ridiculous. Even Niels Bohr did not believe in photons until 1923, a decade after he proposed a very successful atomic model based on the notion of discrete energy states. Maxwell's theory was viewed as sacred despite that fact that it raised some difficult issues about the relationship of matter to radiation and represented processes not successfully analyzable by the laws of Newtonian mechanics. The electromagnetic field was a continuum, and its properties (e.g., energy) must of necessity be described by continuous variables. Einstein's heuristic concept of the photon could not negate the overwhelming evidence for the wave properties of light, nor indeed was that his intention. In a 1909 paper by Einstein, a remarkable equation appears suggesting that light may possess both particle and wave properties (Klein, 1979). This wave–particle duality was to become of enormous epistemological and ontological significance.

Einstein is, of course, best known for his theory of relativity. Its *special* form, presented in 1905, is basically an operational analysis of what can be meant by motion and time—and, beyond this, communication itself. Once again, a profoundly important influence was Ernst Mach, including his critique of the concepts of absolute space and time. It is ironic that Mach never accepted the theory of relativity. He wrote, "I do not consider Newton's principles as completed and perfect, yet, in my old age I can accept the theory of relativity as little as I can accept the existence of atoms and other such dogma" (1893/1960, p. xiv). Mach died in 1916 apparently untouched by the extraordinary developments in physics occurring in the last years of his life.

Beginning in the second decade of this century, the sweeping tide of Watsonian classical behaviorism, a view ostensibly imbued with the Machian principles of observability and "economy of thought," carried with it as well doctrines of structure. The mental processes of the structuralists were to be replaced in the new doctrines of methodological behaviorism by inferred conditioned reflex units, S-R bonds and chains, S-S associations, reaction potentials, r_g's, etc. In other words, one set of unobservables was replaced by another, but with the inherent prestige of being "operationally defined" (Moore, 1975, 1980).

There has been a tendency among a number of those calling themselves radical behaviorists to look suspiciously, if not disparagingly, upon issues of structure, both because structure smacks of internal mechanisms and because many of those in psychology who exhibit a particular interest in the structure of behavior are often antagonistic in word or deed toward an experimental analysis approach or radical behaviorist theory. Catania (1973) has pointed out, however, that functional and structural analyses are complementary approaches to providing an adequate descriptive account of behavior. Radical behaviorism, as practiced in the experimental analysis of behavior, has paid special attention to the notion of "units" of behavior. The concept plays a significant role in Skinner's *Verbal Behavior* (1957). There is a certain irony in all this. One of the advantages of the study of the so-called "free operant" is that behavior is emitted without undue interruption, allowing us to view the "behavioral stream" (Schoenfeld & Cole, 1972) as exemplified, for example, by patterns of responding engendered under various schedules of reinforcement. Although behavior is often considered as a continuous variable, little attention has been given to a "hydrodynamics" of the behavioral stream; instead, following a long and successful history in physics and chemistry and a tradition in earlier psychologies, attempts have been made to quantize behavior. The problem has been a difficult one (see, e.g., Marr, 1979; Shimp, 1979; Thompson & Zeiler, 1986; Zeiler, 1977); and the issues will not be dealt with here except to emphasize that the experimental analysis of behavior has, in the spirit of Mach, treated the problem of units in terms of functional relationships. Branch (1977), for example, states: "Units can be defined as such, only by demonstration of functional relations between the supposed units and certain environmental events or arrangements, and the functional relations must bear a resemblance to those described for other proposed units" (p. 176). Shimp (1979), applying Mach's principle of continuity, states his criterion for a unit as follows:

The present writer's criterion places heavy emphasis on *invariance* in empirical functional relations; if a set of functional relations is more nearly *invariant*, is simpler, and is more coherent when expressed in terms of one behavior than in terms of another, then the first behavior better qualifies as a behavioral unit. (p. 203)

The conception of behavioral units in terms of functional relationships finds its counterpart in particle physics. The word *particle* does not refer to some tiny billiard ball but is, at the least, an extended tact[1] under the control of certain functional relationships in a mathematical account. Beyond that, in the words of Zukav (1980), "Subatomic particles are 'tendencies to exist', and 'correlations between macroscopic observables'" (p. 197). Similarly, Skinner (1931) defined the reflex in terms of a relationship between two events—stimulus and response—and while the operant is defined with less consistency (compare Schick, 1971), it can be considered in terms of relationships among responses, stimulus arrangements, and reinforcement contingencies.

THE PROBLEM OF OBSERVABILITY

In 1913, J. B. Watson proclaimed the behaviorist manifesto in his paper "Psychology as the Behaviorist Views It" and set forth a movement which, in its several guises, was to provide the most influential methodological and theoretical frame for experimental psychology in this century. Sadly, Watson had no real data to explain and, if he had, no way to explain it. His goal of prediction and control of behavior seems in retrospect an extraordinarily empty promise. His positive contribution lay in unshackling psychology from mentalism by defining the appropriate subject matter as observable behavior.

In that same year, a young physicist, Niels Bohr, published a long article in the *Philosophical Magazine* entitled "On the Constitution of Atoms and Molecules" that represented the most significant break from concepts of classical physics yet espoused and led ultimately to the formation of quantum mechanics. Bohr combined features of Rutherford's "planetary" atom with Planck's quantum of action and, with the addition of a pair of bold assumptions, produced an atomic model capable of explaining an enormous quantity of data, including the enigmatic Balmer formula for hydrogen spectra.

Bohr's (1913) article suggested a clear and profound repudiation of classical electrodynamics in the advocacy of stationary, nonradiating states of moving electrons. Radiation was emitted or absorbed only through transitions between these stationary states. In common with Watson, Bohr eschewed certain unobservables by declaring that these transitions were nonclassical and, therefore, it was not possible to talk about what happened to electrons between stationary states. Bohr's treatment of the concept of observability may seem odd, since one could ask whether electrons *within* stationary states are observable. What is actually observed are the various frequencies and intensities of radiations emitted by hydrogen, so, at most, the stationary states are operationally defined. What about the electron or, indeed, the atom itself? As I discussed earlier, data from various sources indicated the existence of discrete substructures of matter. Those data were treated in a classical frame; in other words, the behavior of these hypothesized objects was analyzed as if they obeyed the same laws as observable, ponderable bodies. For example, statistical mechanics represents an application of the principles of classical mechanics to aggregates of interacting elastic particles. Contrary to what Mach may have thought about atoms, in the early days of developing the atomic hypothesis the mode of analysis closely followed his principle of continuity. As more data were gathered, the theoretical developments, of necessity, strayed further away from the classical formulations.

As successful as Bohr's theory was, he recognized its provisional nature and its limitations. The next major step was taken by Heisenberg who established what came to be known as matrix mechanics (van der Werden, 1967). He was guided in this extraordinary work by the principle that "physicists must consider none but observable magnitudes when trying to solve the atomic puzzle" (Heisenberg, 1971, p. 60). Matrix mechanics was the first theory able to treat atomic problems in any general way. The irony is that, considering the approach was founded on the basis of treating only observables, the observables appear as elements in an infinite matrix. As d'Abro (1951) points out, "The procedure of the matrix method is entirely mathematical; it makes no appeal to familiar modes of representation" (p. 811). In other words, the measurable properties of nature are predicted by what appear to be purely abstract operations.

Heisenberg seems initially to have adopted a Machian view, but in actual fact, his theory included a number of nonobservables (e.g., the phases of emitted radiation). Aside from this, however, he softened his position after a lengthy discussion with Einstein (Heisenberg, 1971), who asked: "But you don't seriously believe . . . that none but observable magnitudes go into a physical theory?" Heisenberg countered that Einstein had done precisely the same thing with relativity—dispensing with absolute motion and time because in principle they were unobservable. Einstein replied:

Possibly I did use this kind of reasoning . . . but it is nonsense all the same . . . in principle, it is quite wrong to try founding a theory on observable magnitudes alone. In reality, the very opposite happens. It is the theory that decides what we can observe. (p. 63)

Returning to the context of psychological theory, Titchener believed that introspection was a form of observation, a view many modern psychologists would not hold, although Skinner's radical behaviorism is not greatly at variance with it (Day, 1969b). Skinner treats observation and its more subtle form, attention, as a controlling relation between a stimulus and a response. The response of observing or attending is "an act which makes a stimulus more effective" (Skinner, 1974, p. 104). He notes, for example, that "the production of additional stimuli favoring a discriminative response is a familiar part of science" (p. 105). The essence of observation, then, is discrimination, a product—at least in part—of reinforcement contingencies. Schnaitter (1980), in his discussion of science and verbal behavior, provides a behavior-analytic perspective on the Einstein–Heisenberg exchange by making the following point:

The past history of the scientist includes prolonged interaction with scientific knowledge—the corpus of rules, principles and concepts leading to effective action of the scientist. Such a history results in the scientist making discriminations regarding his environment consistent with the concepts and relations in the abstract and constructed verbal behavior that characterizes his scientific knowledge. (p. 158)

The viewpoint described by Schnaitter is further exemplified by Skinner's treatment of private events. Methodological behaviorism, in an attempt to free itself from the nagging problems of introspection, passionately embraced Bridgman's operationism and the tenets of the logical positivists. Moore (1975) states it well:

Inasmuch as the sensations, mental states, etc., of the observing scientists are not amenable to public observation, and, inasmuch as science is restricted only to public observations, the sensations constituting the concepts of science must be "operationalized," that is, the concepts must be instantiated through symbolic reference to operations and resulting data products. Accordingly, operationalism was interpreted as a technique for reducing the two dimensions [mental vs. physical] inherent in both the perceiver and the perceived so that the mental phenomena may be dealt with scientifically. (p. 126)

Skinner (1945; 1972c) has discussed the public–private distinction inherent in methodological behaviorism and, in an application of Mach's principle of continuity, asserts that control of our behavior by private events reflects the same processes descriptive of our behavior with respect to public events. This control, manifested for example, by the term *consciousness*, is achieved through interaction with the verbal community which "teaches the individual to know himself" (Skinner, 1953, p. 260). One can say that we observe private events in the same way we observe public events. As for sensations comprising the basic datum of a science, Skinner, using the response "red" as an example, says:

The response "red" is imparted and maintained . . . by reinforcements which are contingent upon a certain property of stimuli. . . . The older psychological view, however, was that the speaker was reporting not a property of the stimulus, but a certain kind of private event, the sensation of red. . . . This seems like a gratuitous distinction. (1945, pp. 275–276; 1972c, p. 378)

Skinner's views on the observability of private events are counter to the generally accepted definition of an observable in terms of intersubjective agreement. Yet the philosophy of truth by agreement is not as "arid" as Skinner claimed it was in the "Operational Analysis of Psychological Terms" (see 1945, p. 293; 1972c, p. 363)—by his own analysis. First, control via private events is a function of our interaction with the verbal community. Second, while I might take effective action by observing my private events, it will be less likely that anyone else could do so. The implication is that we are not in a position to develop a *science* based upon private events. As Skinner notes, "In a rigorous scientific vocabulary private effects are practically eliminated" (1945, p. 275; 1972c, p. 377), and "The scientific community encourages the precise stimulus control under which an object or a property of an object is identified or characterized in such a way that practical action will be most effective" (1957, p. 419).

The public–private distinction of psychology lies at the heart of the revolution that is quantum physics, both in terms of the meaning of observability and the attendant issues of subjectivism and ontology. Quantum mechanics has had to adopt an extremely complex approach to the problem of observables, and only a brief sketch can be presented to provide some flavor and focus of analysis. Nontechnical presentations of some of the issues considered here can be found in Herbert (1985), Jauch (1989), and Zukav (1980). For the more mathematically inclined, an excellent introduction to quantum formalism is Gillespie (1973).

Shortly after Heisenberg published his paper on matrix mechanics, which, as mentioned earlier, was cast in an abstract formalism wherein measurable properties of atomic processes appeared as elements in infinite matrices, Erwin Schrödinger (1928) presented an alternative approach called *wave mechanics*. Wave mechanics was founded upon a differential equation that came to play the same fundamental role in quantum mechanics as Newton's equations of motion play in classical mechanics. Just as in the case of Newton's second law—force equals mass time acceleration—Schrödinger's equation was not so much derived but intuitively constructed by considering matter in the guise of both wave and particle. The mathematical structure of wave mechanics was more conventional than matrix mechanics and was far easier to apply. Within a couple of years, physicists, whose bread and butter is gotten from deriving and solving differential equations, had solved a plethora of major problems. The solution to the Schrödinger equation is known as a wave function. Under proper mathematical treatment, the wave function will yield measurable properties of atomic systems (e.g., energy states of the electron). However, the exact physical interpretation of the wave function remains elusive. Schrödinger and others searched in vain for a more or less classical "picture" of the world of the wave function. It was quickly recognized by Schrödinger himself that matrix mechanics and wave mechanics were mathematically equivalent. Matrix mechanics was built to avoid pictures and yet yield measurable (observable) variables; wave mechanics, as it turned out, was no less abstract.

Quantum mechanics, as the whole theoretical effort is termed, was ultimately developed into a formal axiomatic system where solutions of Schrödinger's equation are represented by complex vector functions, called state vectors, in an infinite-dimensional, Hilbert space (Gillespie, 1973; Persico, 1950; von Neumann, 1955). Under appropriate mathematical operations, such solutions yield probability density functions. Thus, although everything that can be known is specified by the state vectors, they can only yield *probabilities* of measurement outcomes. In a classical, causal account, specifications of the state of a system provide the initial or boundary conditions which, coupled with appropriate functional relationships (e.g., a differential equation), would allow, in principle, prediction of both future and past states to an arbitrary degree of precision. This principle of causality is based upon the assumption that the observation—in other words, measurement—of the state contributes nothing to the state so that the results of an operation of measurement, the "observable," and the state are indistinguishable.

However, state functions in quantum mechanics are not in themselves observables. As mentioned earlier, they are complex vector functions in Hilbert space. Measurement involves mathematical operations on these functions to yield discrete, real "eigenvalues"—the observable properties of the state. As Gillespie (1973) puts it, "In classical mechanics no real distinction is made between the mathematical representation of an observable and the value of the observable; however, in quantum mechanics such a distinction is of fundamental importance" (p. 43). Emerging from the formalism is Heisenberg's principle of uncertainty which states in essence that certain "canonically conjugate variables" (e.g., position and momentum, energy and time) can be simultaneously measured with a precision that is limited by Planck's constant:

$$h = 6.625 \times 10^{-34} \text{ joule-sec.}$$

Such indeterminacy places a limit *in principle* on what can be observed.

Atoms and their constituents are nature's ultimate private events. These events, which appear to obey very different functional relationships from the public world described by classical physics, significantly relate to the public world. They can be said to account for the stability of the universe as we experience it. This situation is in sharp contrast to the radical behaviorists' generally negative stance on reductionism and on the fundamental significance of private events accounting for public behaviors. Indeed, given that private events are "of such stuff" as public events, it would be difficult to understand how the latter could consistently originate in the former.

On the issue of a public–private distinction, radical behaviorism is much closer to classical physics where the constituents of matter, if hypothesized at all, were presumed to obey similar functional relationships to those of the observable world (e.g., gas molecules behaving as billiard balls). When one considers the issue of determinism, however, Skinner's views may be closer to the spirit of modern physics. A superficial consideration indicates a relatively traditional stance on the question of determinism (Vorsteg, 1974). Skinner says in *Science and Human Behavior*:

If we are to use the methods of science in the field of human affairs, we must assume behavior is lawful and determined. We must expect to discover what a man does is the result of specifiable conditions and that once these conditions have been discovered, we can anticipate and to some extent determine his actions. (1953, p. 6)

Begelman (1978) argues convincingly, however, that the radical behaviorist's stance on strict causality is ambiguous. Day (1969b) sees the position as follows:

The practice of looking for functional relationships is obviously similar in certain respects to the effort to find relations between cause and effect. Yet in attempting to discover functional relationships the radical behaviorist does not accept any *a priori* logical assumption of a universe that is orderly in a mechanical sense upon which he feels he must base his scientific work. (p. 318)

The concept of probability of a response is central to the theoretical framework of radical behaviorism. It is unclear whether this probabilistic approach is reflective *only* of a practical lack of specifiability in the initial conditions or reflects, at least in part, random processes controlling the emission of behavior. In a presentation of Skinnerian theory, Catania (1980) remarks: "Admitting the possibility that behavior could occur *spontaneously* was a critical conceptual step in operant theory" (p. 138). Skinner (1974) says it this way:

To distinguish an operant from an elicited reflex we say that the operant response is "emitted." (It might be better to say simply that it appears, since emission may imply behavior exists inside the organism and then comes out. But the word need not mean ejection; light is not in the hot filament before it is emitted). *The principal feature is that there seems to be no necessary prior causal event.* (p. 53, italics added)

Quantum physics provides numerous analogous processes. In radioactive decay, for example, individual processes occur at random; one can only assign measures (e.g., the half-life) to aggregates. Consider the process of beta decay. In its simplest form, a free neutron is converted into a proton, a neutrino, and an electron (the beta particle). Neutron is not made up of these three "products," however. These particles are not inside a bag that we call the neutron. They simply appear at random. So far as I know, there is no way physicists can exert practical *control* over processes like radioactive decay. They cannot, for example, change the half-life of strontium-90. It is a defining property of conditioning, however, that certain experimental arrangements can change the probability of behavior. In spite of their spontaneity, organisms, unlike atoms, have a "sense of history."

The fact remains, however, that the properties of the world as we experience it seem to emerge from a very different world. A measured wavelength of electromagnetic radiation equal to 7000 angstroms is not comprised of "red" photons, nor are mercury atoms silvery and slippery. Little would be gained from an atomic hypothesis if this were so. But how is the verbal behavior of the quantum physicist brought under control of this *Nebelheim*? In the language of Skinner's *Verbal Behavior* (1957), how can a physicist tact a stimulus or a property of a stimulus in the absence of any precise discriminative history with respect to that stimulus? This problem of conceptual structure has received some considerable attention by physicists (e.g., Bergstein, 1972; Bohr, 1958; 1963; Heisenberg, 1962), and there is no shortage of controversy. I wish to present briefly some of the different perspectives interspersed with comments from the standpoint of a behavioral analysis.

RETREAT TO THE CLASSICAL

From the beginning, some of the quantum physicists, for example, Schrödinger and de Broglie, attempted to provide conceptual models of the atomic processes which included such terms as "electron cloud," "matter wave," and "charge density." Quantum mechanics is often introduced to students this way—particularly by chemists who, although the major beneficiaries of the quantum theory of chemical bonding, are rarely comfortable with its formalism. On a deeper level, however, some physicists believe strongly that quantum mechanics is incomplete in the sense that underlying its probabilistic frame is a classical determinism describing interactions among physical objects. Einstein held to this notion, and such a theory has been developed by Bohm. (See Bohm, 1961, for a nontechnical presentation, and d'Espagnat, 1976; Jammer, 1974; and Jauch, 1989, for critical discussions.) There are certain analytical reasons to reject such a formulation, but, in addition, as Bergstein (1972) points out:

If the variables are really hidden, which means that they are fundamentally non-observable, they have, of course, no physical significance whatsoever. If, however, the variables are thought of as observable in principle, then this very idea is contradictory to quantum theory . . . the reasons why so much effort has been spent to retain classical objectivity in quantum physics is obviously the basic psychological condition that the conceptual scheme of ordinary language used when comprehending external phenomena is not easily dispensed with in natural science. Classical mechanics is a straightforward mathematical idealization of the part of ordinary language treating the external world, and the reality of this world is directly transmitted to classical physical objects. (p. 33)

In a largely trivial behavioral analysis, we could say that the long and *continuing* history of social, educational, and practical reinforcement, coupled with the powerful discriminative control exerted by effective interactions with the observable environment, represent conditions likely to maintain the verbal behavior comprising classical theoretical physics. However, there are broader issues lurking here.

First, psychologists have witnessed a similar effect in this century, manifested as responses to behaviorism as a philosophical doctrine. The set of rules, principles, or assertions we tact as "radical behaviorism" may control alternative and incompatible responses to the sets of rules and other verbal stimuli we tact variously as "mentalism," "dualism," or "cognitive psychology." The doctrine of dualism or, more generally, the attribution of public behaviors to private mental causes, has a very long history involving extensive social, educational, and pragmatic reinforcement. As a consequence, radical behaviorism seems "inconceivable" to some. It is certainly not a "straightforward idealization of ordinary language" (Dinsmoor, 1988; Hineline, 1980). Methodological behaviorism and cognitive psychology—steeped in the tradition of dualism—have, by means of operationalism and mechanical metaphors, attempted such a program (Moore, 1975, 1980; Roediger, 1980; Skinner, 1945/1972c). As Skinner (1945/1972c) comments on the early attempts:

The reinterpretation of an established set of explanatory fictions was not the way to secure the tools then needed for a scientific description of behavior. Historical prestige was beside the point. There was no more reason to make a permanent place for "consciousness," "will," "feeling" and so on, than for "phlogiston" or "*vis anima.*" (1945, p. 292; 1972b, p. 381)

Second, the qualifying autoclitic[2] "classical" as applied to physics, emerged only in the context of alternative responses such as "modern," "relativistic," or "quantum." Bergstein (1972) is extraordinarily glib in his assessment of classical mechanics as a "straightforward mathematical idealization" of ordinary language. Yet it took people like Galileo, Newton, Laplace, and Lagrange to accomplish the task.

Third, even assuming the stance of naive realism, control of effective verbal behavior might have ranged over different stimulus dimensions or even different "logical structures" if our ordinary language had been different. For an illuminating discussion of these possibilities, see Whorf's (1956) chapters "Science and Linguistics" and "Languages and Logic," Schoenfeld's (1969) review of Kantor's works on logic, and Hineline's (1980) article which discusses some implications of Whorf's comparative analysis of grammar to verbal behavior in psychology.

BOHR-ING FROM WITHOUT

The second general formulation of quantum mechanics is that of Niels Bohr, and it is known as the Copenhagen Interpretation. The linguistic aspects have been articulated in detail by Bergstein (1972). (See also French & Kennedy, 1985; Heisenberg, 1962, 1971). The position is best introduced by Bergstein:

The appropriateness of a specific terminology immediately presents itself when the object cannot be directly observed by the sensory apparatus. Because objects of this kind just do not belong to the experiences of daily life, it might be thought that they would be most adequately described in terms not involving ordinary language at all. But this is impossible for two fundamental reasons. First, logic cannot, of course, be dispensed with and logic is a basic structure of ordinary language. Second, scientific description must fulfill the requirement of unambiguity, which means that the experimental conditions must always be specified to the extent necessary for unrestricted reproduction of the observed phenomena, and because this specification is about macroscopic objects it cannot avoid the implication of ordinary language. (1972, p. 27)

Thus, the experimental apparatus and associated initial conditions (sometimes called the "region of preparation") and the recording instruments (sometimes called the "region of measurement") are necessarily and appropriately described by ordinary language or its derivatives. What happens in between the region of preparation and the region of measurement is described by the Schrödinger wave function, which is expressible as a superposition of all possible outcomes of the experimental arrangement, given the initial conditions. The properties of this function, however, cannot be described in classical terms; and, in general, the quantum phenomena of interest are not to be considered as possessing properties *independent of the experimental arrangement*. This view has a number of significant implications that are best approached by considering one of the best-known puzzles of quantum physics, namely the nature of light.

Early on, Newton had suggested that light was corpuscular, but the overwhelming evidence was on the side of waves. In the nineteenth century, when Maxwell provided the enormously successful theoretical structure for the wave nature of electromagnetic radiation, no alternative formulation was deemed necessary. As mentioned earlier, it was left to Einstein to demonstrate that, at least under some conditions (e.g., the photoelectric effect), light behaves as if it had particle properties. Almost no one believed in photons at the time, however. Indeed, not until 1923 did the notion gain acceptance when Compton showed that the increase in wavelength of scattered X rays could be explained as the transfer of some of the energy from X-ray photons to the electrons in the scattering medium. Now there existed a dilemma: What was light—wave or particle? While this was being pondered, de Broglie, displaying an imaginative trust in the symmetry of nature, suggested that such dualism was not only characteristic of radiation but of matter as well. This was quickly demonstrated in the laboratory by showing that electrons can produce diffraction patterns, an unambiguous wave characteristic.

This wave–particle duality is, in fact, but one manifestation of Heisenberg's principle of indeterminacy dealing with relationships between canonical variables. Just as knowledge of the position of a particle is incompatible with knowledge of its momentum, so experimental arrangements that yield the particle properties of light are operations that could not demonstrate the wave properties of light. A contradiction from a classical perspective was avoided by Bohr when he defined the word *phenomenon*:

Bohr proposed that in quantum physics the word *phenomenon* should refer not only to the registration marks directly observed, but also to the properties of the macroscopic instruments ultimately responsible for the space–time distribution of the registration marks. Further, he introduced the term *complementarity* to denote the condition of mutual exclusion between observations pertaining to the same object. (Bergstein, 1972, p. 24, italics added)

For Bohr, the fact that light (or matter) exhibited two incompatible forms did not represent a fundamental contradiction but, instead, was reflective of a complementary aspect of nature. Light was not to be interpreted as a "wavicle": Whether it was a wave or particle depended on how we chose to observe it. As Zukav puts it, the two forms "are not properties of light. They are properties of our interaction with light" (1980, p. 93). Quantum systems as such have no intrinsic properties, and the wave function cannot be considered objective in the sense of reflecting a set of independent characteristics of a system. That is, as Bergstein (1972) has summarized, all we see of quantal phenomena are the "registration marks" they produce on our instruments. The properties of such phenomena (i.e., atoms) can be described unambiguously only in terms of quantum theory; such phenomena are "conceptual constructions" and "can be regarded as a product of human intellect only" (p. 32). The idea that terms such as *electron* refer to objects in the classical sense is no longer tenable because it suggests that individual electrons might be isolated and identified, which is impossible under quantum theory.

The Copenhagen interpretation of quantum mechanics represents the orthodox position; its various guises dominate the standard texts, to the extent that philosophical issues are discussed at all. Unfortunately, for our purposes, the interpretation has a number of interpretations. As Jammer (1974) puts it:

The Copenhagen interpretation is not a single, clear cut, unambiguously defined set of ideas, but rather a common denominator for a variety of related viewpoints. Nor is it necessarily linked with a specific philosophical or ideological position. It can be, and has been, professed by adherents to most diverging philosophical views, ranging from strict subjectivism and pure idealism though neo-Kantianism, critical realism, to positivism, and dialectical materialism. (p. 87)

Somewhat like one of the blind men discerning the features of the elephant, I am emphasizing those aspects of the Copenhagen Interpretation which seem to me of particular interest from a behaviorist position. Bohr placed primary emphasis upon issues of epistemology, but more popular accounts have focused upon ontological questions. Another approach involves quantum logic, a behaviorally interesting topic that space does not allow me to detail (but see Birkhoff & von Neumann, 1936; Hughs, 1981; Jammer, 1974; Marr, 1986; Zukav, 1980).

At first glance, Bohr's position appears strongly positivistic and purely operational with quantum concepts being "synonymous with a corresponding set of operations." Bohr himself, however, was uncomfortable with some of the tenets of positivism. For example, he could not understand how such a thing as a quantum of action could possibly be an experience (von Weizsäcker, 1980). His feelings about positivism were expressed to Heisenberg and Pauli this way: "For my part, I can readily agree with the positivists about the things they want, but not about the things they reject" (Heisenberg, 1971, p. 207). His principal concern was that positivism did not allow the free expression he believed necessary to discuss quantum phenomena in ordinary language:

Positivist insistence on conceptual clarity is, of course, something I fully endorse, but their prohibition of any discussion of the wider issues, simply because we lack clear enough concepts in this realm, does not seem useful to me—this same ban would prevent our understanding of quantum theory. (p. 208)

Quantum theory . . . provides us with a striking illustration of the fact that we can fully understand a connection though we can only speak of it in images and parables. (p. 210)

For him "images" and "parables" are embodied in such terms as *wave* and *particle*.

Bohr apparently held that the "data" of scientific formulation did not constitute the subjective perceptions of an observer but, instead, the observer's *descriptions* of phenomena in classical terms, for example, the verbal behavior of the observer (Jammer, 1974). Feyerabend called this "positivism of a higher order" (1958, p. 82), but this seems an appropriate label only if one embraces the traditional view that verbal behavior emerges from "ideas" and "perceptions".

In contrast to the traditional view, a radical behaviorist position would require us to consider the conditions that control responses like "wave," "particle," "electron," and "spin." The inseparability between apparatus and the effects of applying that apparatus seems reflective of the role of contingencies in the expression of nature. The terms are, perhaps, more expressive of behavior of the joint system of experimenter and apparatus. Bridgman expressed it this way: "An electron is an aspect of the total situation, the major part of which is the rest of the apparatus. We should not talk about 'electron' as such, but rather say: 'Under such and such conditions the apparatus *electrons'*" (1959, p. 176). What is missing from Bridgman's account are the contingencies and rule-governed behaviors of the experimenter. From this point of view, terms like *electron* are reifications of *behaviors* emitted by experimenters (and, indeed, theoreticians). In a similar way, a psychologist may emit the response "memory" as a tact under the control of the behavior of an organism subject to certain contingencies related to prior events. Neither "memory" nor "electrons" can be considered as "objects." At best they are descriptive of "our interaction with objects."

Day (1969b) has commented upon the issue of object status in radical behaviorist philosophy:

The radical behaviorist is aware that we may attribute thing-ness to events largely because we are accustomed to speak of the world about us as composed of objects which are felt to possess an inherent constancy or stability. He is reluctant to take for granted that all useful knowledge must be conceptualized in terms of verbal patterns of thought derived simply from our experience with material objects. Consequently, he is led to a position which is peculiarly anti-ontological. (p. 319)

The principle of complementarity is an expression of the effects of contingencies. Rules may be given for "generating" properties of nature which in themselves seem contradictory, even though classically they "refer" to the same "object." Bohr (1958, 1963) extended the notion to describe a number of phenomena in psychology and biology. For example, one can view, in a complementary way, the notions such as instinct–reason, contemplation–volition, consciousness–unconsciousness, logos–mythos, and right brain–left brain. A common thread among most of these "polar" nouns is another complementary phenomenon, namely, contingency-shaped versus rule-governed behavior (Skinner, 1969).

The concept of nonseparability inherent in the Copenhagen interpretation clearly opened the door to subjectivism (d'Espagnat, 1976, 1979). Although Bohr himself tended to discourage this view, a number of his followers embraced it. The most radical expression is that of Jordan: Observations not only *disturb* what is to be measured, they *produce* it. As Jammer (1974) puts it, "It is an absolute renunciation of any realistic conception of nature" (p. 162). Modern writers like Capra (1977) and Zukav (1980), in their zeal to show correspondences of modern physics to aspects of Eastern philosophy, are sympathetic to the renunciation of a realist doctrine.

In discussing the issue of subjectivism, Zukav (1979) states provocatively, "According to quantum mechanics we cannot eliminate ourselves from the picture. We are part of nature, and when one studies nature there is no way around the fact that nature is studying itself. Physics has become a branch of psychology, or perhaps the other way around" (p. 31). Such a view seems not far from Harzem and Miles's (1978) definition of psychology as "the study of the interaction between organism and environment" (p. 47). Zukav goes on to suggest the possibility that "physics is the study of the structure of consciousness" (1980, p. 31). If we take Harzem and Miles's (1978) analytic-behavioristic approach and attempt to translate the foregoing comment about mental events into a sentence about behavior, we might consider the following: "Physics is the study of those variables which control our responses to our own behavior." According to the radical behaviorist view, those variables are to be found largely in the environmental history of the individual. Once again, we are led to a process of interaction between the individual and the environment. But what is the *environment*? Is it a separate reality, or is it only the product of our behavioral history? Skinner rejects the notion of a distinction between reality and experience, but this does not lead him to the radical subjectivism expressed by Zukav. In discussion of the relative "true value" of scientific observation, Skinner says, "There is no world as it 'appears to be', there are simply various ways of seeing it *as it is*" (Blanshard and Skinner, 1967 p. 33, italics added) and "the behaviors of both scientist and nonscientist are shaped by *what is really there*, but in different ways (Skinner 1974, p. 127, italics added). As Zuriff (1980) notes:

What emerges from this conception is an almost Kantian metaphysics. On the one hand is the world as it is, the nominal world, and on the other hand, human responses to that world. Human knowledge of the world consists of responses to that world, but humans cannot transcend their own behavior to step out of the causal stream. (p. 342)

There is a kind of dualism expressed here—there is a world as it is and a world that is the product of our interaction with the world as it is. Most physicists would, I believe, be sympathetic with this view. It expresses the difference between the domain of classical physics with its strict determinism and its clear separation of the observer from the observed—and quantum mechanics with its probabilistic interpretation and the blending of the observer with the observed. These, too, are but complementary aspects of nature, in the best spirit of Bohr's principle.

RETREAT TO ABSTRACTION

A third approach to the issue of description is perhaps best expressed by Dirac, (1947) a leading formalist in the development of quantum mechanics:

The main object of physical systems is not the provision of pictures, but the formulation of laws generating phenomena, and the application of these laws to the discovery of new phenomena. If a picture exists, so much the better; but whether a picture exists or not is a matter of only secondary importance. In the case of atomic phenomena no picture can be expected to exist in the usual sense of the word "picture," by which is meant a model functioning along classical lines. One may, however, extend the meaning of the word "picture" to include any way of looking at the fundamental laws which makes their self-consistency obvious. (p. 10)

In the early days, Heisenberg (1971) despaired of convincing "even leading physicists that they must abandon all attempts to construct perceptual models of atomic processes" (p. 76). In his view, the language of quantum process is mathematics; and what is more, "We have no . . . simple guide for correlating the mathematical symbols with concepts of ordinary language" (Heisenberg, 1962, p. 177). The mathematical formalism provides no pictures, not even metaphors; what it does provide is prediction. The formulation is the ultimate expression of the awesome fact that we may be led to new and even surprising features of nature by talking about it. How can this be? It is tempting for some, perhaps, to characterize atomic processes as "pure thought," implying a form of conceptual causation with its attendant subjectivism. Zukav (1980) describes the wave function as "a tool for our understanding of nature . . . something in our thoughts" (p. 80) and, after Stapp, espouses an explicit dualism in which "physical reality is both idea-like and matter-like" (p. 81).

A radical behaviorist approach to the effectiveness of mathematical formalism might begin with the principle that *materia mathematica* be treated as features of the environment, for example, discriminative stimuli, where manipulations can be maintained by effective verbal as well as nonverbal consequences. The latter are represented by the control over nature attained, in turn, through control by the verbal stimuli. The verbal behavior itself consists of manipulation of abstract tacts and intraverbals expressed as qualifying and quantifying autoclitics (Skinner, 1957). This is rule-governed behavior of enormous complexity; but as Skinner points out, "Rules . . . are physical objects and they can be manipulated to produce other . . . rules" (1969, p. 144).

A deeper issue to be considered, however, is how do the rules of quantum formalism relate to environmental contingencies so that the application of these rules has effective consequences? Moore (1981) comments that "for the radical behaviorist, a given verbal stimulus occasions effective prediction and description presumably *because the stimulus is derived from some factor in the observed situation*, not because of its subjective or logical–theoretical status" (p. 65, italics added). Such factors seem to be missing from an abstract formalism and, indeed, it is sometimes said to be the expressed goal of a mathematical scheme to achieve ultimate abstraction, in the sense that the source of control is purely verbal, and having no relationship to environmental contingencies. This does not seem possible. Verbal behavior is rooted in nature; it is acquired through interaction with a verbal community, itself subject to a long history of environmental contingencies. In a simplistic formulation, we might view a hierarchy of complexity that always leads back to its source:

Nature $\rightarrow$ Contingencies $\rightarrow$ Contingency-shaped verbal behavior

$\uparrow$ $\downarrow$

Logic $\leftarrow$ Rules as abstract tacts, $\leftarrow$ Rule-governed behavior
mathematics   autoclitic processes, etc.

One cannot overestimate the complexity of these relationships, however (See Marr, 1986, for more details). First, it should be emphasized that the processes described here do not imply an unfolding of "ultimate truth," for reasons brought out in the earlier discussion of the Copenhagen interpretation. Mathematics is presumably a limited expression of nature and, therefore, limited in "what it has to say" about nature.

Second, the relationship between environmental contingencies and mathematical analysis is often indeed remote, leading Kline (1980) to comment on the issue of why mathematics works: "One might answer that the mathematical concepts and axioms are suggested by experience . . . but such an explanation is far too simplistic . . . human beings have created mathematical concepts and techniques in algebra, the calculus, differential equations and other fields that are not suggested by experience" (p. 339). However, the history of mathematics reveals an extended shaping of abstraction. Consider the progression from simply counting to rational fractions, to irrational numbers, to complex numbers, to quaternions, and so on. This process took thousands of years; and because mathematics was originally much more closely linked to "experience," in other words, to environmental contingencies, there was often considerable controversy about the "meaning" of the abstractions. Kline (1980) notes that most European mathematicians in the sixteenth and seventeenth centuries did not accept negative numbers as numbers. Presumably, negative numbers occasioned a similar class of responses to those controlled by wave functions today, for example, "inconceivable."

Mathematics developed through effective consequences of its construction and exercise, occasioned by the solution of practical problems, but it subsequently became an endeavor substantially maintained by verbal reinforcement. Unambiguous specifications of this form of reinforcement are elusive, but achieving control over verbal stimuli can be as powerful a consequence as achieving control over a nonverbal domain, a testament to the "object" status of verbal stimuli. At any rate, as a result, mathematics has often outdistanced its applications; so when more elaborate specifications of nature's contingencies were ultimately constructed, appropriate verbal repertoires were already available, now to be further strengthened by nonverbal consequences—complex variables for electromagnetic theory and hydrodynamics, non-Euclidean geometry and tensor analysis for general relativity, and Hilbert space and group theory for quantum mechanics. This is in accord with Skinner's pragmatic theory of truth (Skinner, 1953, 1945, 1974), a view that is distinctly Machian. The ultimate test for the soundness of a mathematical development is in its application (Kline, 1980)—and, as the diagram on page 126 illustrates, we come full circle.

WHERE HAVE WE COME?

This chapter has explored some historical and philosophical interrelationships between physics and psychology, and has considered in a rather general way possible contributions of radical behaviorist philosophy to an analysis of the verbal behavior of the modern physicist. The radical behaviorist, holding to no particular foundationalist position and certainly uncommitted to a realist ontology, is in a unique position to look at the behavior of the physicist and scientists and examine scientific behavior in the light of contingencies controlling effective descriptions of nature. The most effective verbal behavior for this purpose is mathematics. Modern mathematics is the repository of all physical "pictures" of nature, yet this form of description is so abstract that it seems beyond any ordinary use of the term *description*. Yet, as we have seen, one can trace a shaping of abstractions from the most concrete and mundane to the deepest portrayals of nature.

An impressive theme is that physics, considered by many as the Platonic ideal of a science, had, and continues to have, deep epistemological concerns. Classical concepts of realism, observability, and determinism have all been compromised by quantum mechanics; and controversies still rage today more than seven decades after its founding. In many ways, as I have tried to indicate, there are parallels in psychology, as exemplified not only by the antagonism between behavior analysis and cognitive psychology but by arguments among behavior analysts themselves (see, e.g., Marr, 1993a; Morris, 1993a).

A profound issue remains as to the most effective verbal behavior to achieve control over a subject matter. As most readers of this volume know, this was a major concern of B. F. Skinner. This was also a life-long struggle for Niels Bohr. Heisenberg (1971), in his intellectual autobiography *Physics and Beyond*, gives the following account of a conversation with Bohr:

If the inner structure of the atom is as closed to descriptive accounts as you say, if we really lack a language for dealing with it, how can we ever hope to understand atoms? Bohr hesitated for a moment, and then said: "I think we may yet be able to do so. But in the process we may have to learn what the word 'understanding' really means." (p. 41)

Perhaps Skinner's "empirical epistemology" can provide an approach toward that goal.

AUTHOR'S NOTE

Portions of this chapter are based on the presentation "Behaviorism and Modern Physics: Parallels and Antiparallels" given at the Association for Behavior Analysis meeting in Milwaukee in May 1981 and a symposium presentation on "The Science of Behavior" given at the National Autonomous University of Mexico, Mexico City, in February 1982. This latter presentation was subsequently published in Spanish by Trillas Press in *Language and Behavior*, edited by Emilio Ribes and Peter Harzem (Marr, 1990). Additional sources include Marr, 1982, 1985, 1986, and 1989. The present chapter is a combination of ideas from all of the above sources. I want to express my deep appreciation to Peter Harzem, Emilio Ribes, Ed Morris, and Jim Todd for the opportunity to publish a reasonably complete version of ideas that have been spread across many outlets, languages, and years.

Chapter 9 _____

The Varied Usefulness of History, with Specific Reference to Behavior Analysis

Stephen R. Coleman

Few question the usefulness of tools, even though the household hammer, pliers, and jar of small nails are used infrequently and spend the bulk of their collective life in the tool drawer. It may be the case that historical tools, that is, History of Psychology (see Author's Note on p. 147) research and writings, are also of merely occasional and job-specific use. For instance, it is widely assumed that historical tools come in handy on only two occasions: first, when a discipline is in the process of firmly establishing itself—at which time historical exploration appears to serve the role of legitimating the new field by showing that it is the answer to pressing concerns and comes from an ancient and honorable lineage (e.g., Gardner, 1987); second, during times of particularly troubling difficulty (e.g., Koch, 1971; Sarason, 1981), when historical exploration of the so-called "roots" of the specialty may seem imperative. Whether the "intensity" or direction of ongoing historical research is affected by such service calls is an investigatable question, but it is not of present concern to us.

It may also be true that historical study and reading are of use to individual researchers only at certain points in their development. For instance, it is unusual to find well-developed historical interests among newly minted Ph.D.s, but historical concerns and sophistication are more common in elder statesmen of the specialty. A comparative study of age of investigators in the History of Psychology and in other specialties could show whether such an impression is correct, but that also is not of present concern. Instead, in this chapter, I will describe various kinds of usefulness in reading or doing history, of which some are task specific, while others may be of value across a longer segment of the life span of disciplines and individuals.

TERMINOLOGICAL PRELIMINARIES

Ontologically speaking, the historian does not literally examine the past but only presently existing records (Parrott & Hake, 1983). However, historical practices are typically described, not in such a "constructivist" manner of speaking but, rather, in a "realist" fashion which treats the past itself (rather than its presently existing documentary residue) as the object of curiosity. In this chapter, I will adopt the more typical realist assumption.

On the other hand, I affirm the pragmatist core within constructivism in acknowledging that how we regard our evidence for inferences about the past is partially dictated by *how we use the evidence*. A time-honored distinction has been made between "primary-source" and "secondary-source" literature. A first-step approximation of the primary secondary distinction is that primary sources are the objects we study—typically books, articles, and other printed matter. They include, very prominently, the so-called classic papers and books that have retained a presence in the "secondary sources"—that is, in the literature that describes, interprets, and discusses the primary sources. Another important category of primary sources is unpublished documents, such as notes, correspondence, manuscripts, and so on. Such materials are usually made available for study by an archive that has preserved and catalogued and now houses these materials.

However, the primary–secondary distinction is ultimately pragmatic: A discussion or critique (i.e., a secondary-source item), such as Koch's (1954) critical analysis of Hull's (1943) behavior theory, *is treated as a primary source* if one's project involves a study of favorable and critical reactions to *Principles of Behavior* (Hull, 1943). Correspondingly, a classic, such as E. C. Tolman's (1932) *Purposive Behavior in Animals and Men*—which is a primary source of information on Tolman's behavior theory—*could be treated as a secondary source* of information about J. B. Watson's behaviorism. Admittedly, few would use Tolman's book for such a purpose, but one could conceivably (and foolishly) use Tolman's discussion as one's only information about Watson's behaviorism.

Reading a secondary source may substitute for reading primary sources—the secondary source provides a plausible selection and organization of the materials of the field that one is studying—but it is obvious that the secondary source is fundamentally an opinion, a distillation, or an interpretation of primary sources. Consequently, the unexpectedly vague phrase, "reading history," can mean reading the classics *or* reading the secondary-source literature about the classics and about the historical development that a sequence of classic papers seems to exhibit. Because different benefits may be expected from reading in these two different literatures, the primary–secondary distinction is worth keeping in mind in discussing the usefulness of "reading or studying history."

IMPORTS AND EXPORTS IN THE HISTORY OF PSYCHOLOGY

As a scholarly specialty, the History of Psychology follows its own disciplinary agenda; the resulting products vary greatly in their relevance to the needs of nonhistorians; and the result is an uneven record of success in serving, being of interest to, and influencing other specialties.

Prior to the 1960s, the History of Psychology had no institutional status but existed as an avocation that was chosen by a few individuals who lacked formal training as historians but who wrote *as* psychologists and for the benefit of psychologists (e.g., Boring, 1929, 1950b; Flugel, 1933; Heidbreder, 1933; Murphy, 1932; Woodworth, 1931; see Watson, 1977, pp. 62–64). In the 1960s, amateurism lost its grip on the History of Psychology, as several institutional milestones were attained in that specialty. In 1965 alone, an archive for primary-source documents in psychology was created at the University of Akron, divisionalization in APA (Division 26) was accomplished, and a journal was established (*Journal of the History of the Behavioral Sciences*). A doctoral program in History of Psychology was begun at the University of New Hampshire in 1967, and a professional society (the Cheiron Society) was founded in 1968. As the discipline developed, old authorities were eventually questioned (O'Donnell, 1979; Weimer, 1974); unanticipated benefits of archival work were noted with approval (e.g., Balance, 1975; Cadwallader, 1975); reports of progress were published (e.g., Brozek, Watson, & Ross, 1970); and periodic stock-taking of efforts in the discipline was undertaken (e.g., Ash, 1983; Littman, 1981; Mackenzie & Mackenzie, 1974; Moore, 1987).

Institutional recognition as a specialty intensified self-consciousness in practitioners of the new History of Psychology. Furthermore, some practitioners had come through History of Science graduate programs and brought with them ideas and issues from that more mature specialty; even without such biographical accidents, the fledgling field of the History of Psychology would probably have heeded warnings—particularly if they concerned methodological issues, about which psychologists have long had serious concern— from those with more extensive or formal experience in the history of the exact and inexact sciences (e.g., Stocking, 1965; Young, 1966; see also Sokal, 1984). Much of the discussion concerned the contrast of "internalism" and "externalism." The internalist examines the development of a scientific discipline as seen from "inside" its technical boundaries; the externalist tries to locate the discipline within a "surrounding matrix" of cultural, institutional, and economic circumstances that affect disciplinary activity.

Concern with such "historiographic" issues (as they are called) is probably found only among historians; it is unlikely that behavior analysts would be very concerned with such historical options—unless they embark on serious historical projects and need to play the game by accepted rules, at which point these issues would probably become salient.

A second methodological contrast, that of "presentism" and "historicism," shows even more strongly the intradisciplinary direction of some History of Psychology concerns. A historicist approach aims at understanding past events and people in their own right and apart from any purported relevance or lessons that might be extracted in regard to present-day issues. A presentist approach involves the assumption that the present-day framework is essentially correct and that, therefore, the main lines of progress—as well as the dead ends and mistakes—can be clearly discerned in the historical record of the discipline (Hyman, 1982; Stocking, 1965; cf. D. L. Hull, 1979). Generally the historicist claims to describe *whatever* happened; the presentist is more selective, dispensing with material that appears to be "irrelevant" in the light of the present shape of the discipline, and is more evaluative, praising progress and cursing traditionalism, obscurantism, and "resistance to progress" (cf. Kuhn, 1962).

Yet another obstacle to the relevance of historical writings is the fact that the History of Psychology is subject to influence by its own particular kind of fads and fashions. The larger field of History is also no stranger to reorientations of outlook (Higham, 1965/1973), and the same holds true for the History of Psychology specialty. In addition, work in the History of Psychology is subject to intrinsic periodicities. For instance, the visibility of particular historical figures is strongly affected by anniversaries, which promote historical work that ordinarily reaches a peak about the time of the anniversary and then declines. The centennial celebration of Wundt's 1879 laboratory at Leipzig affords a good example, as Figure 9.1 shows.

Figure 9.1 displays the number of articles (culled from *Psychological Abstracts*) in a yearly pool of published papers that were concerned principally with Wundt, and a larger number that were concerned secondarily with Wundt.[1] The figure shows a well-defined peak in 1980, probably the result of a publication process in which conference papers delivered in 1979 at anniversary symposia appeared as journal articles the following year. Anniversary phenomena are not unusual in the history of the sciences: A similar productivity jump occurred in Darwin scholarship around the 1959 centennial of the publication of *On the Origin of Species* (Darwin, 1859/1966). Other examples of fashion could be provided (e.g., Geuter, 1983, pp. 192–193), but the implication is apparent: Specific subjects and historical figures may be either "hot" or "cold" and, therefore, ready or unready for export into adjacent specialties, depending on such extraneous factors as decimal-system coincidences.

A final impediment to the flow of exports from History of Psychology—and it is probably the most serious of those I discuss—is antiquarianism. In following the imperative of historicism by suspending present-day concerns, the historian of psychology may produce a historical account that strikes nonhistorian onlookers as precious and trivial. Onlookers are more likely to ask for its relevance to their own present-day concerns, a criterion that the historicist has suspended, merely neglected, or even avoided.[2]

Figure 9.1
Number of Articles per Year Concerning Wilhelm Wundt as Indicated by
Psychological Abstracts **(1975–1985)**

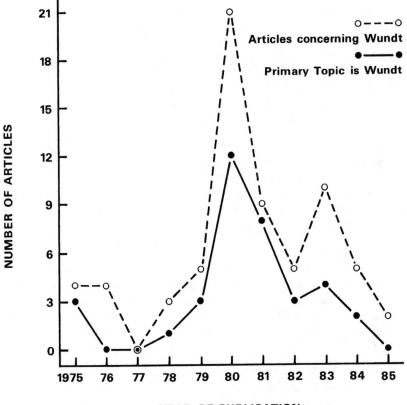

YEAR OF PUBLICATION

   Though other obstacles to the usefulness of history could be listed, by now it is apparent that work in the History of Psychology depends on aims, anxieties, seasonal imperatives, and assumptions that may diminish or qualify its usefulness to other specialties.

TRADITIONAL CLAIMS OF USEFULNESS

   Accusations of irrelevance are likely to be directed at thought systems whose validity is not simply a matter of practical demonstration. Therefore, historians of psychology have had to defend themselves against the serious complaint of irrelevance by describing presumptive benefits of historical research and reading, of which the following thirteen formulas—selected from Hearnshaw (1984), Henle (1976), Robinson (1976, pp. vii–ix), Wertheimer (1980), and other sources—are an illustrative sample.

Studying History Is a Type of Therapy

To be unaware of past influences allows them to have unchecked and unexamined influence on a present-day research program (e.g., Krantz, 1965; Watson, 1966). To be aware of the influences presumably allows one to decide whether to indulge or to resist and nullify them.

History Is a Series of Cautionary Tales

A closely related claim is made in the aphorism attributed to George Santayana, to the effect that those who are ignorant of the past are doomed to repeat its mistakes. Being aware of particular past mistakes presumably enables one (or one's specialty) to avoid similar mistakes in the present (Willis & Giles, 1978). The idea that history provides "lessons" is a related notion.

The Study of History Provides a More Perfect Understanding

This claim, advanced by Jaynes (1973), Stagner (1988, p. vii), and others, postulates understanding rather than error avoidance as the primary objective and holds that the only way to understand the present is to study the particular past history upon which the present situation of some specialty depends. Boring (1959) found this the only defensible rationale for learning about the past.

The History of Psychology Is a Basis for the Unification of Psychology

The History of Psychology supplies a "more generalized knowledge" that counterbalances specialization and facilitates appreciation of the unity of historically related subfields. Practical consequences for the profession, in terms of collaboration or borrowing from unexpectedly related areas, may follow. This type of usefulness is also acknowledged in the presence of a History and Systems course as a required senior-year vehicle for integrating knowledge based on other coursework in some undergraduate psychology curricula and as an available option in APA-approved doctoral programs in clinical psychology.

History Is a Form of Travel

Travel is fatal to prejudice, bigotry, and narrow-mindedness, as Mark Twain is said to have quipped. By providing vivid examples of particular opinions and arrangements that are almost unthinkable today, reading in the history of psychology enlarges one's horizon of possibilities. This experience may provide a liberating removal of the confinements of one's particular time, place, and specialty (Notterman, 1985).

History Provides the "Big Picture"

A related function of historical reading is to provide perspective upon the present by seeing it *sub specie aeternitatis*. Stephen Toulmin's engaging description of the succession of scientific generations is a good example of this function:

History brings its own revenges. Those who compete in the Sacred Groves of science should do so knowing that the Golden Bough will be in their keeping only for a limited time. Here as elsewhere, every transfer of authority helps to prepare the ground for the next. . . . Each new generation of apprentices, while developing its own intellectual perspectives, is also sharpening up the weapons for an eventual professional takeover. Five, ten, or twenty years hence, their word will carry weight in the profession, their authority will guide and reshape the discipline; and meanwhile, at their heels, still younger men are coming along, who will in due course form the generation of their own successors. (1972, p. 287)

Studying History Is Like Getting an Immunization

Knowledge of the major theoretical shifts and of the fads and orthodoxies that have come and gone in psychology can reduce the persuasive power of new fads by inculcating a healthy skepticism (e.g., Robinson, 1976, p. 6). Esper (1964) suggested that historical awareness affords protection against bandwagon effects that accompany the arrival of most new psychologies.

History Is a Lesson in Sobriety

According to Crutchfield and Krech, "Knowledge of the history of one's science teaches the scientist humility and tolerance for opposing views" (1962, pp. 5–6). Presumably we are to believe that science practiced under those conditions is more effective than science practiced under conditions of personal aggrandizement (e.g., J. D. Watson, 1968) and intolerance for other views.

History Is Like a Treasure Hunt

A number of scholars have claimed that the study of history occasionally results in "recovery of material [that is, a neglected idea or theory] relevant to the present" (R. I. Watson, 1966, p. 69; see also Benjamin & Perloff, 1982, pp. 341–342; Kessel & Bevan, 1985, p. 288; Marmor, 1977, p. xiii). Because this is the only claim that historical study has really tangible benefits (i.e., the recovery of lost resources), we will examine this claim further.

In speaking of an idea as being "rescued from oblivion," R. I. Watson (1966) seems to suggest that the historian (or other scholar) stumbles upon *completely forgotten* treasures. It is unlikely that such dramatic rediscovery is the typical case. More commonly, references to the older, and soon to be "rescued," theory or phenomenon are already circulating at low frequency in the literature. Unexpectedly, interest in the theory or phenomenon is sparked by a writer's description of various possibilities, for example, that the neglected theory or phenomenon may permit theoretical expansion or resolution of old anomalies. The theory (or phenomenon) then enjoys a period of greatly enhanced visibility.

An example may be useful. The factual corpus of visual perception is an untidy assortment of visual phenomena, many of which had been reported in the late nineteenth century. This arrangement affords numerous opportunities for new theories to explain old phenomena, for example, the use of lateral inhibition in the retina (Ratliff, 1965) to account for Mach bands, or the use of quantitative models (e.g., Grossberg & Mingolla, 1985) to explain subjective contours (e.g., Kanizsa, 1976). Occasionally an older theoretical model is vindicated, as in the revival of Hering's theory of color vision by Hurvich and Jamison (1957, 1974) and by DeValois and DeValois (1975). Rediscoveries happen occasionally in the behavior-theory field, too. Killeen's (1988) reexamination of Skinner's (1938) concept of reflex reserve provides a surprising contemporary example from Behavior Analysis. An interesting illustration of the solution of a persistent anomaly concerns the classic problem-box study of Guthrie and Horton (1946). Guthrie and Horton had demonstrated an impressive amount of stereotypy in the instrumental escape behavior of cats. Escape from their problem-box apparatus required the cat to push against a vertical pole near the middle of the cage; they regarded the stereotypy which they found in this behavior as evidence supporting Guthrie's molecularist theory of learning. Moore and Stuttard (1979) carried out a partial replication of the Guthrie–Horton study; systematic variations of the procedure showed that the stereotypic character of the pole pushing depended not on escape from confinement (or on provision of reward) but on the presence of humans. On the basis of these findings and of previously reported ethological observations of cat behavior, Moore and Studdard argued that the escape response was actually species-specific "greeting behavior" and that its stereotypy demonstrated its instinctual (rather than learned) character. Such striking reversals of interpretation, though dramatic, are probably rare in psychology.

History Is a Crystal Ball

Some writers (e.g., Esper, 1964; Reisman, 1976; Willis & Giles, 1978) propose that a knowledge of historical roots helps to predict, chart, or anticipate future developments. E. G. Boring's (1959) skepticism on this point coincided with culturally generalized doubt about predicting the future and may have contributed to making this one the least frequently voiced apology for researching and reading in the history of psychology.

History Is a Magic Bullet

Knowledge of how a present-day controversy began and how it gradually came to be formulated may assist in the resolution of that controversy (e.g., Bickhard, Cooper, & Mace, 1985; Coleman & Gormezano, 1979; Restle, 1957). More often than not, the controversy has already subsided or been resolved in other ways by the time the historian, resembling more the coroner than the physician, arrives to analyze the issues (e.g., Amundsen, 1985).

History Teaches Appreciation

The study of the history of psychology makes one aware of the cumulative nature of scientific work in psychology (e.g., Cartwright, 1979, p. 87; Posner, 1982). Having such an appreciation reduces the appeal of unjustifiably pessimistic appraisals of the field (cf. Finkelman, 1978, and Snoeyenbos & Putney, 1980; cf. Koch, 1974, and Farrell, 1978).

History Is a Mark of the Educated Person

A knowledge of history provides familiarity with events, concepts, and cultural landmarks that are common coin in the world of ideas beyond psychology and beyond the social sciences. The traditional ideal of the liberally educated person implies that even the specialist might find it useful to become better acquainted with the landmarks and vocabulary of humane letters.

ON REPRESENTING HISTORY

Having completed our brief and generally uncritical survey of traditional testimony to the beneficial results of reading primary and secondary historical literature, we move on to qualify claims for usefulness that we might otherwise profess. We do so in order to make more apparent the *contingent value* of history: Whether historical work and reading can serve Behavior Analysis depends on what jobs it can assist in that discipline. These considerations might be aided by Figure 9.2, which hazards a pictorial representation of how practitioners of a specialty stand in relation to the recent and to the more remote past of their specialty.

Figure 9.2 assumes that the concerns and interests of most workers in a specialty are confined largely to their specific current projects and the immediate background. These interests provide criteria that identify certain past events or materials as relevant, as "leading up to the present topic" in a metaphorically straight line, represented in Figure 9.2 by the arrows lying in and

Figure 9.2
Pictorial Representation of Some Features of the Relation of Present to the Past

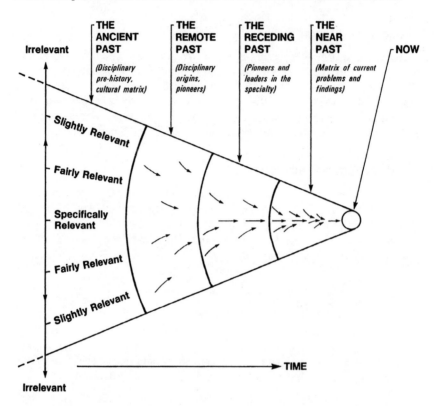

near the horizontal plane that passes through the middle of the cone; other materials are of decreasing relevance, which is represented by arrows located at increasing distance above and below the horizontal plane. However, as one moves further and further back in time, to ten and twenty and more years prior to the present, the range of relevance increases. This feature is represented by the progressive widening of the cone; and it is also reflected in the greater dispersal of the arrows, which represent use of chronologically distant materials that lie to the side of the well-marked path leading up to particular present-day research areas.

In part, the range of relevance widens with increasing age because circumstances that, at an earlier time, might have seemed accidental are found in hindsight to have had substantial influence on the present shape of the discipline; and in part, the widening reflects the fact that researchers can make more finely discriminative appraisals of the relevance of research and theoretical items in the present and immediate past than can be made among the items of the more remote past, with which researchers are less familiar. If we consider the left-to-right direction of movement, the past appears as a series of ever-narrowing constraints that have focused present concerns, activities, options, and awareness in the discipline.

Figure 9.2 provides a spatial representation of *a particular model* of the historical past, a model that makes use of the widely available geographical metaphor of rivers and their source waters. Other metaphors from the natural world are available. For example, as the specialty grows and as an ocean of forgetfulness (or irrelevance) submerges more and more of the once-relevant literature, a few items remain visible above the waters and serve as landmarks of the disciplinary terrain that is now ordinarily inaccessible—except, of course, to intrepid historians equipped with their scholarly scuba gear. Two skeptical observations are appropriate at this point. First, other pictorial models of history are possible; and they may be even more plausible in their application to particular historical developments: There is the metaphor of straight-line progress, of the circle and spiral of recurring process, and of the pendulum swinging from one extreme to its opposite (e.g., Gergen, 1985, p. 270). *General-level discussions* of historical process are plagued by an al-most-irresistible reliance upon spatial analogies and other simple models that have very dubious empirical status.

Because the worth[3] of the past varies, depending on how recently or remotely one searches, historical investigation can hardly be of uniform usefulness. There are different kinds of historical study, and they do not all deliver the same actual and potential benefits. Guided by these differentiations, we move on to consider the varied benefits of different kinds of historical study. This exposition might be regarded as an addendum to and correction of the traditional claims that I summarized above; and it will include more specific reference to Behavior Analysis.

SUPERFICIAL HISTORY

The most rudimentary, abbreviated, and pragmatic of historical exercises is the brief literature review in the first page or two of a scientific report. Although attention is seldom called to an actual historical development in the prior findings cited, the literature-review section does link the research report to particular items in the past, particularly those in the "straight line" of Figure 9.2. (The linkage is quite selective: for social-science disciplines, more than 40 percent of all references are to literature that is no more than about five years old [Price, 1970].) This most superficial form of history serves rather confined purposes, primarily to give the reader enough information to assess the reliability of the present findings by comparing them to results of prior, related investigations.

A slightly more intensive use of history is made in an article that surveys the literature on a research topic. The author may actually highlight a histori-cal development in order to make a point about progress in the specialty or about decisive shifts in the development of the specialty. (The standpoint for this exposition is usually "presentist," in the sense explained earlier.) However, deliberately historical exposition is rare in such surveys, and for good reason: It would be counterproductive for a literature review to organize its material historically because such an arrangement would highlight chronological changes that are of secondary interest to readers looking for evidence classified by topic; and it would scatter chronologically separate projects on the same topic, thus defeating the primary intent to summarize. Historical practices, therefore, serve quite subordinate roles in the scientific-report literature.

References to the more-distant past—the "receding past" and the "remote past" in Figure 9.2—frequently occur in textbooks and in literature surveys. B. F. Skinner's laboratory research (Ferster & Skinner, 1957; Skinner, 1938)—that is, material in the receding past—is more likely to be cited than the writings of such behaviorist pioneers as Watson, Lashley, and Hunter, in the more remote past of behaviorism. Such references serve the didactic purpose of familiarizing the newcomer with the major achievements that were responsible for the present state of this specialty. (The standpoint for this exposition is also typically presentist.) A second function of such references may be to foster attachment to the discipline in its present form. Every specialty has its lore, its list of heroes to be admired, and its story of landmark achievements with which everyone in the specialty appears to be conversant.[4] The sort of historical exposition that presents the story of disciplinary pioneers is typically uncritical and involves name dropping at least for a discipline, such as psychology, in which discussion typically is organized in terms of persons rather than classes of demonstrated phenomena. Some writers have branded this historical literature "hagiographical" because it provides accounts of disciplinary champions that resemble the "lives of the saints" in religious education. Hagiography supports discipleship and middle-of-the-road attitudes toward the specialty. These are, in themselves, wholesome things for the specialty because they foster its "articulation" (Kuhn, 1962, pp. 25–34).

A third function of textbook-history practices is to enforce standard reference points for advanced discussion of the specialty. When the history is done with insufficient care or is dominated by persuasive agenda, it may produce "origin myths" regarding that specialty (Samelson, 1974; see also Leahey, 1987b, p. 457). To make matters worse for the reader, it is hard to tell a myth from a true story about the specialty unless one carries out a detailed historical investigation to check the truth of the plausible story, a task for which the ordinary practitioner in the specialty has had little preparation.

Such problems are predictable. The Latin *historia* is the etymological root of the English words *history* and *story*. Historical writing often involves the telling of a story, and such an objective entails (1) that there is greater dependence on narrative strategy than in reports of research findings; (2) that the facts have been subject to a more intensive process of selection because they must fit the story; (3) that much historical research is closer in spirit to the creative objectives of the humanities than to the descriptive aims of social science; and (4) that, to a much greater extent than in the sciences, narrative integration in historical research "does not depend on any systematic methodology" (Higham, 1965/1973, pp. 68–69).

Reference to the "ancient past" of psychology (see Figure 9.2) is generally rather infrequent and cursory in the literature of the specialty. A passing reference to Dewey or James is occasionally seen; and very infrequently an article on the roots of the discipline, such as Marr's (1985) article on Mach (just to take a convenient, recent example), turns up in the literature of the specialty. Even in this case, the selectivity of the inspection of the roots is as salient as the fact that the inspection takes place at all: Marr's article shows *no historical development*, a typical feature of writings within the specialty. Generally, the more remote past is left to writers outside the Behavior-Analysis specialty to explore (e.g., Birnbaum, 1955; Burnham, 1968; O'Donnell, 1985; Pauly, 1987), a state of affairs that is certainly not particular to Behavior Analysis.

DEEPER HISTORY

Having examined the superficial historical expositions that adequately serve routine needs of workers in a given specialty, we turn to "deeper histories." These are generally longer, are typically written from outside the specialty, are based on historical skills and experience, and are infused with concerns that go beyond those of the specialty. A deeper history may be intended to persuade the reader of a problematic thesis (e.g., Samelson, 1975, 1981; L. D. Smith, 1986), or it may simply involve telling a detailed story without defending a thesis (e.g., Schneider & Morris, 1987). Deeper histories serve distinct roles for the specialty, and some of these roles are probably incompatible with mere discipleship. I will describe a sample of roles they may play.

First, although the reader may come to appreciate the great truths at the foundation of the specialty, he or she may come to realize the arbitrariness and accidental character of the foundations or the unnecessary limitations of the specialty as currently practiced (e.g., Altschule, 1976, pp. 1–14). The reader may even come to appreciate the validity of other options that are presently condemned or simply forgotten (e.g., Lieberman, 1979). Such results of a more discriminating awareness are unlikely to support conservative attitudes (Brush, 1974; Samelson, 1974). On the other hand, it is hard to predict whether a resulting elasticity of attitudes is beneficial or detrimental to a given specialty; it probably depends on whether the specialty "needs" to be "loosened up" or "firmed up," and such judgments are likely to depend on extrapolations and analogies based on the historical fates of other similar specialties (e.g., Willis & Giles, 1978).

Second, historical research may remove an albatross that has burdened a research tradition. Behaviorism has labored under many misconceptions as to its fundamental objectives and tenets, as one can easily verify by comparing the diverse properties attributed to behaviorism(s) by various writers (e.g., Boring, 1950b, pp. 620–659, especially pp. 641–653; Chaplin & Krawiek, 1979, pp. 14–15, 53–57, 343–345, 430–432, 559–567; Leahey, 1980, pp. 321–324; Marx & Hillix, 1963, pp. 139–152, 268–270; Robinson, 1976, pp. 399–407; Zuriff, 1985). Reminders that radical behaviorism is quite different from other less adequate forms of behaviorism (e.g., Day, 1983, 1987; Moore, 1981; Skinner, 1974, pp. 18–19) have not prevented misunderstandings, with the result that the radical behaviorist has occasionally been tarred with a brush that ought to have been applied only to intellectual bumpkins who happen to be distant relatives[5] and, regrettably, share the family name (e.g., Leahey, 1980; Powers, 1973).

L. D. Smith's (1986) fine study of the relationship of Hull, Tolman, and Skinner to logical positivism shows convincingly that, although logical positivism suffered so many liabilities that eventually it was no longer considered a viable philosophy of science, its downfall was independent of the fates of these three neobehaviorists because none of them was ever dependent upon or closely aligned with logical–positivist intellectual commitments. One suspects that some of the defects that have been counted against "behaviorism" (e.g., Breger & McGaugh, 1965; Koestler, 1964; Leahey, 1980; Suppe, 1984) have embodied historical assumptions that are questionable and possibly, or even probably, mistaken.

A third service of deeper historical study is to defend or legitimate a present-day practice by showing it to be consistent with the roots of one's specialty, as elucidated historically. After identifying the historical accidents that played roles in the formation of a research tradition, one can examine present options with a more discriminating awareness of which commitments are essential and which ones are more peripheral (e.g., Gray, 1980; Herrnstein, 1969a). Watson's motor theory of thinking is an extraneous and accidental feature of behaviorism, and so is the exaggerated environmentalism in Watson's famous "give me a dozen infants" claim (Watson, 1924a, p. 82; see, especially, Boakes, 1983). Discriminative appraisals of the centrality of other behavioristic tenets require historical and conceptual analysis (e.g., Zuriff, 1985).

Fourth, present-day practices may be criticized by showing that there existed more promising options in the historical background,which were neglected or rejected for the wrong reasons. Wolford and Bower's (1969) clarification of the continuity theory of discrimination learning is an example of this approach. Another is afforded by Rescorla's (1969) demonstration that the experimental study of conditioned inhibition had languished in American classical conditioning and in his claim that the neglect sprang from theoretical commitments. One might show that a present-day practice or theory is defective by virtue of its lack of fruitfulness as revealed in the historical record (e.g., Coleman & Gormezano, 1979; Herrnstein, 1969b).

Fifth, historical investigation can be used to evaluate recipes for success. Kendler's (1985) suggestion that behaviorism needs to lean more in a biological direction in order to actualize its potential can be assessed by either determining whether the strongly biobehavioral research projects of the last ten years or so have solved more problems than those which remained apart from biological concerns, or examining the circumstances under which different forms of behaviorism established independence from biological interests (cf. Skinner, 1938, Chap. 12). Both responses to Kendler's (1985) advice seek out evidence, in the recent and in the remote historical record, relevant to the proposition that a closer union with neurophysiology and other biological disciplines has actually shown itself a more successful strategy than behavioral-science independence.

Sixth, historical reading can also be useful in altering the present shape of the specialty. Recommendations that some present commitments should be discarded will almost necessarily trot out a historical exposition, which shows that such and such a commitment has always been a peripheral—perhaps even accidental—element in the tradition. For example, it is possible that the critical, polemical, confrontational style that has characterized the radical behaviorist position (e.g., Krantz, 1971, pp. 66–67; Krantz, 1972, pp. 97–99; Lasch, 1979b, p. 37; Skinner, 1950, 1978, 1985) reflects situational characteristics that were specific to establishment of a new and aggressively confident specialty (e.g., Wendt, 1949) or may reflect "personal" qualities of B. F. Skinner (e.g., Skinner, 1976b, pp. 254–256, 262–269; Skinner, 1979, pp. 60–64, 80, 92–93; cf. Coleman, 1985a, pp. 87–88) or features of the cultural surround that Skinner inhabited as a young man in the 1920s (e.g., Coleman, 1985a, pp. 82–84). Such argument blends with the nonhistorical enterprise of conceptual analysis of a discipline, but argument is more likely to include reference to historical evidence.

Some Personal Benefits of Historical Study

Some consequences of doing or reading history are of nonspecific benefit for the individual worker, in the sense that their value is not particular to the worker's specialty or may even be irrelevant to the concerns of the specialty. First, encountering opinions that are radically different from any that one has thus far tested brings home forcibly the fact that other options are imaginable. American psychologists, without historical or specific interest in William James, are so accustomed to hear his name spoken in reverent tones that a balanced assessment of James as a thinker is unlikely to be looked for. It is unexpectedly refreshing, therefore, to encounter one of Santayana's several appraisals of James:

His father was one of those somewhat obscure sages whom early America produced. . . . They were intense individualists, full of veneration for the free souls of their children, and convinced that every one should paddle his own canoe, especially on the high seas. William James accordingly enjoyed a stimulating if slightly irregular education: he never acquired that reposeful mastery of particular authors and those safe ways of feeling and judging which are fostered in great schools and universities. (1924/1967, p. 64)

Finding such opinions can be a liberating intellectual experience because it reminds one that "there are more things in heaven and earth . . . than are dreamt of in your philosophy" (*Hamlet*, Act I, Scene V). Unfortunately, unsettling one's habitual opinions is a mixed blessing. While it can have beneficial consequences for the specialty, it may be inimical to the function of mere discipleship, as Kuhn (1963) and others have observed.

There are safe uses of history, of course, and the history of a specialty probably need not be X-rated for consumption by its practitioners (Brush, 1974). An example is afforded by a second personal utility of historical study, which is to read classic papers in one's field in order to see what so-and-so *really said*. Typically, what so-and-so said is found to be more complex and even somewhat different from what the secondary-source summaries indicate (see, e.g., Blumenthal, 1975, 1980). For example, the reader will find that John Dewey's classic paper on the reflex arc has more to do with Hegelian dialectic than with reflexes (Dewey, 1896; Observer, 1975). Reading John B. Watson's papers allows one to determine what shortcomings are worth taking to heart in the blizzard of criticism that has fallen directly on whipping-boy Watson and, by extension and whether merited, on other forms of behaviorism.

Third, reading autobiographies and reminiscences—for example, those in the 1987 volume of the *Journal of the Experimental Analysis of Behavior* probably serves to "flesh out" abstract historical personae and events with subjectively vivid impressions that make the figures and events "more real" and, therefore, more relevant to present concerns. In addition, these materials may suggest generalizable principles of historical progress, rules and guides to success, and so on. Last, these materials lend themselves to unpredictable uses of the sort we lumped under categories of travel and perspective.

Fourth, many readers, especially younger researchers taking for granted that the specialty has progressed, are not well equipped to answer questions that involve a lengthy time frame or demand a comparative perspective, such as whether Behavior Analysis has shown *real* progress. Occasionally, a historical article addresses a very specific facet of such an issue (e.g., Wyatt, Hawkins, & Davis, 1986). More often one must rely on reading history, especially broader histories, for sophistication in addressing questions for which one has had no special training. To answer such questions, it may also be helpful to read widely in the history and philosophy of science. For example, Laudan's (1977, 1984) work on scientific progress provides plausible criteria of progress in a research program, which could serve as the basis for a balance sheet of achievements and failures in any research program, particularly in comparison with its competitors but also in terms of comparison with the early promise of that program. Historical study is the principal source of such balance sheets.

PLAUSIBLE QUESTIONS

I will close with a short list of questions that is certainly not exhaustive of what behavior analysts might ask of the background of their discipline and of closely related areas. The questions underrepresent the applied wing, but they may prompt further questions that are more germane to Behavior Analysis at this anniversary point.

1. In the disciplinary history of Behavior Analysis, what were the major landmarks, and which ones appear (or, even better, might be shown) to have fostered the development of the field? Has the insularity[6] of operant conditioning been an advantage or a disadvantage? In what demonstrable ways? What unique institutional features has Behavior Analysis acquired as a result of its particular historical development? Which of these features appear, in retrospect, to have been assets? Which are liabilities? Which are accidental (and, hence, easily modified) in the sense of being extraneous to the central concerns of the specialty?

2. What happened to *other* forms of behaviorism in the period of modern criticism beginning about the mid-1950s? Why did they succumb, or in what way did they succumb? Was there a cognitive revolution (in Kuhn's [1962] original sense)? What was the nature of the change in experimental psychology, how did radical behaviorism survive, and exactly in what form did it survive (cf. Leahey, 1987b, pp. 444, 446)? An excellent opportunity for comparative historical analysis is afforded by these related questions.

3. A related question: Recognizing that failure is a multiply determined phenomenon (e.g., Krantz & Wiggins, 1973; Tolman, 1959), what factors appeared to be most important in Tolman's failure, in comparison to the Hull–Spence system? What lesson is there in the decline of influence by the Hull–Spence system (e.g., Leahey, 1980, pp. 312–313; cf. Gormezano & Coleman, 1985). It is simplistic to assume that Hull's enterprise failed merely *because* it was a premature effort to develop an overarching theory of behavior, and that Skinner's (1938) behavior theory succeeded just *because* his descriptivism was the "correct" strategy for behavioral psychology. Not only would many disagree with such a claim regarding descriptivism; but in addition, such assumptions prematurely terminate efforts to determine what the factual record suggests about the strengths of the Skinnerian enterprise and how the balance sheet of assets and liabilities has been altered by changes in the enterprise (e.g., popularization, as in Skinner's *Science and Human Behavior*, or the turn to technology). Examination of these historical phenomena is likely to pro-

vide results that may serve as suggestions and guidelines, even if they cannot serve as prescriptions for avoiding failure.

4. Because one of the principal criticisms of behaviorism—now accepted widely as conventional wisdom—is that it has always had an *unhealthy* restrictive influence on theoretical and other forms of disciplinary development (e.g, Breger, 1969; Suppe, 1984, pp. 91–97; Toulmin & Leary, 1985; Weimer, 1974), how can this charge be evaluated or answered from specifics in the historical record? If the charge proves to be generally accurate, what implications follow?

5. Recent calls for a more latitudinarian stance on theorizing in radical behaviorism (e.g., Killeen, 1984; Shimp, 1976; Wessells, 1981; Williams, 1986) offer a relatively distinct new choice in the spectrum of options for radical behaviorists. The recommendations invite an impartial assessment of the track records of the latitudinarian and of the traditionally "restrictive" positions, with an eye to determining which recommendation has actually been, up to this point, more successful in Behavior Analysis. Comparative information from other specialties provide the opportunity to look for a generalizable evaluation.

6. Given the established separation of the Experimental Analysis of Behavior and physiological and biological enterprises—with the clear exception of Psychopharmacology—does Skinner's demarcation of the two (e.g., Skinner, 1938, Chap. 12) appear, in retrospect, to be a strategy that was merely right for that particular time (in the late 1930s); or was it an appropriate blueprint for disciplinary boundaries in the future? Given that other related fields (e.g., Animal Pavlovian Conditioning) have established close ties to biobehavioral and neuroscience programs, beginning about the late 1960s, how should the present situation of Behavior Analysis be appraised?

7. The entire history of the distinction between the Instrumental Conditioning field and the Experimental Analysis of Behavior (Williams, 1987; cf. Mackintosh, 1974) has practical implications regarding whether efforts to bridge the gap ought to be undertaken by individuals and promoted by journals and organizations. An accurate history of the division and of its identifiable consequences would be useful in making informed decisions.

CONCLUSION

The 1988 double anniversary focuses attention on the historical background of Behavior Analysis and invites exploration of that background. Given the past record of anniversary phenomena, I anticipate that the anniversary will have temporary effects on productivity in the study of the background of Behavior Analysis. Less explicit and countable effects of the anniversary are not as easily predicted. Whether historical investigation and reading can be of worth to Behavior Analysis depends on whether behavior analysts have any jobs that send them to the tool drawer.

AUTHOR'S NOTE

A shortened form of this chapter was presented at a symposium at the annual meeting of the Association of Behavior Analysts, May 28, 1988, in Philadelphia, PA. Mike Ludwig's helpful suggestions on the figures and Phil Cola's help in data collection are gratefully acknowledged. James Todd, Edward K. Morris, and Richard Rakos made helpful suggestions on an earlier draft. Throughout the chapter, I represent the discipline in capital letters (i.e., History of Psychology) and the object of study in lower case (i.e., history of psychology).

Chapter 10

The Behavior of Organisms at Fifty

B. F. Skinner

I have lived my professional life by decades. It was 60 years ago, in 1928, that I arrived at Harvard as a graduate student in psychology. Behaviorism was then only fifteen years old. Ten years later, in 1938, I published *The Behavior of Organisms;* and ten years after that, in 1948, *Walden Two.* Things were then taken out of my hands, but still by decades. Nineteen fifty-eight saw the first issue of *The Journal of the Experimental Analysis of Behavior,* the title reminiscent of the subtitle of *The Behavior of Organisms*; and ten years later the behavioral engineering of *Walden Two* moved from fiction to real life in the first issue of *The Journal of Applied Behavior Analysis.* Of all the anniversaries one is likely to celebrate in a lifetime, the fiftieth is the golden one, and that is why this chapter is about *The Behavior of Organisms* and how it looks to me after half a century.

First, however, a word about sources. The commitment to behaviorism that sent me from college to graduate study in psychology was at the time no better supported than my commitment in high school to the theory that Francis Bacon wrote the works of Shakespeare. I had taken my college degree in English Language and Literature with a minor in Romance Languages and was hoping to be a writer. An important book for writers at that time was *The Meaning of Meaning* by C. K. Ogden and I. A. Richards (1923). Bertrand Russell (1926) reviewed it for a literary magazine called *Dial,* to which I subscribed; and in a footnote, he acknowledged his indebtedness to "Dr. Watson," whose recent book *Behaviorism* (1924a) he found "massively impressive." I bought Watson's book and liked its campaigning style. Later, I bought Russell's *Philosophy* (1927), in which he treated a few mentalistic terms in behavioristic way. Although I had never had a course in psychology, I became an instant behaviorist. When a book called *The Religion Called Behaviorism*

(Berman, 1927) appeared, I wrote a critical review and sent it to *The Saturday Review of Literature*. (Fortunately, the review was never published.)

Philip Pauly's *Controlling Life* (1987) has reminded me of an earlier source of *The Behavior of Organisms*. I wanted to study the behavior of an organism quite apart from any reference to mental life, and that was Watson, but I also wanted to avoid references to the nervous system, and that was Jacques Loeb. Loeb was a German biologist who had come to America and, like Watson, had come into contact with the Functionalist School at the University of Chicago. (Later, at the Rockefeller Institute, he would become the model for Max Gottleib in Sinclair Lewis's *Arrowsmith*.) My biology professor at Hamilton College had shown me Loeb's *Comparative Physiology of the Brain and Comparative Psychology* (1900) and later his *The Organism as a Whole* (1916), and at Harvard I found myself in the biological laboratories of W. J. Crozier, Loeb's major disciple, who, as Loeb was said to have done, "resented the nervous system." I don't believe I coined the term *radical behaviorism*; but when asked what I mean by it, I have always said, "the philosophy of a science of behavior treated as a subject matter in its own right apart from internal explanations, mental *or physiological.*"

The chapter in *The Behavior of Organisms* on the relevance of the nervous system ends with a quotation from still another source. As Laurence Smith (1986) has shown, logical positivism came too late to influence Tolman, Hull, or me in any important way, but it was itself largely due to an earlier figure, Ernst Mach. My doctoral thesis acknowledged my indebtedness to Mach's *The Science of Mechanics* (1893/1960), and it is probably relevant that, although Loeb and Mach never met, they corresponded. (I owned a copy of Mach's *Erkenntris und Irrtum* [*Knowledge and Error;* 1905/1976], but it was in German, and I doubt that I got much out of it at the time.)

A friend, Cuthbert Daniel, who would become a distinguished statistician, put me on to another man in the same tradition. Daniel had come to Harvard to work with P. W. Bridgman, and he told me to read Bridgman's *The Logic of Modern Physics* (1927a). So far as I can now identify them, those were the sources of my theoretical position in *The Behavior of Organisms*.

Watson's famous manifesto (1913) begins; "Psychology as the behaviorist views it is a purely objective experimental branch of natural science. Its theoretical goal is the prediction and control of behavior." Those are carefully written sentences. Psychology is a branch of science. Behaviorism is the philosophy of that science, the way behaviorists view it.

There were not many examples of the prediction and control of behavior in psychology at that time. Indeed, as the expression of mental life, behavior was beyond control by definition. Biology offered something better. Loeb had preferred the tropism, and it was certainly a beautiful example of control, but very little of the behavior I was interested in could be described as a function of a field of force. Reflexes were closer. With a light shock to the foot of a decerebrate cat, Sir Charles Sherrington (1906) could make its leg flex, and with a bit of food or significantly, a stimulus frequently paired with food, Pavlov (1927) could make a dog salivate, and that was control. Reflexes, however, were the behavior of only parts of an organism. Like Loeb, I wanted to study the behavior of the "organism as a whole."

I built an apparatus in which a white rat ran along a delicately mounted pathway. The forces exerted on the pathway were recorded more or less as Sherrington had recorded the forces exerted by a single muscle on his "torsion-wire myograph." However, something else turned up in my experiment. The rat was hungry and got a bit of food at the end of each run. I noticed that after it had finished eating, it did not always start immediately on another run. The delays in starting seemed to vary in an orderly way, and that suggested another kind of control in the "organism as a whole." After a long series of steps, I found myself recording the rate at which the rat ate pellets of food or got them by pressing the lever.

I recorded the behavior in a cumulative curve, a form of graph not well understood for a long time. It had many advantages. The curve that resulted showed a steady decline in slope, suggesting an orderly process of satiation as the rat ate its daily ration. When I did not let the rat get pellets for a few minutes, it ate more rapidly when they were again available; and the cumulative record rose to meet a rough extrapolation of the earlier part. A rather subtle change in behavior was exposed to view. I doubt that I should have so quickly recognized the process of satiation as such if I had recorded the behavior in any other way.

Changes in the slope of a cumulative record showed chages in what I called the strength of behavior. Reflexes—conditioned and unconditioned—were also said to vary in strength. A flexion reflex was strong if the stimulus elicited a vigorous response. A salivary reflex was strong if the stimulus elicited a great deal of saliva. In other words, reflex strength was measured as the ratio of the magnitudes of stimulus and response. I could not see that such a measure was possible with pressing a lever. In some sense, the lever must be acting as a stimulus; but I could not turn it on or off or measure it. The rate at which the rat ate pellets of food or pressed a lever could serve as an alternative, however. Rate of responding has proved, in fact, to be a highly useful dependent variable. In a later paper, I could report that it varied usefully over a range of at least 600 to 1.

Rate of responding was also more useful as a measure because it could be said to show the probability that a response would be made at a given time. Nothing of the sort could be said of a reflex, where the stimulus determined whether or not a response was made. Probability simply did not fit the stimulus–response pattern. It was also not an issue in research with mazes, where the question was how an animal learned to find (and hence to know how to find) its way. But I was asking not whether my rat knew how to press a lever to get food, but how strongly it was inclined to press. Later, I would ask how that inclination was affected by the presence or absence of a discriminative stimulus.

Two Polish physiologists, Konorski and Miller, were doing experiments much like mine. They were adding a reinforcing consequence to a reflex. For example, they shocked the foot of a hungry dog and gave it food when its leg flexed. Eventually the leg flexed although the foot was not shocked. They went to Leningrad to tell Pavlov about their experiment, and they sent me a book (written in Polish, but with generous marginal notations added in French). Later, they published a paper in English (1935), to which I replied (Skinner,1937a). I argued that the shock to the foot in their experiment was unnecessary. They could have waited to give food when the dog flexed its leg for any reason whatsoever, and flexion would have been conditioned. The shock served merely to bring out the response so that it could be reinforced. As I would say later, it "primed" the behavior. It was in my reply to Konorski and Miller that I first used the word *operant*.

In 1935, I published a paper called "The Generic Nature of the Concepts of Stimulus and Response" (Skinner, 1935) in which I argued that a reflex was not something that could be observed on a given occasion. What was observed was a response, which might not be exactly like responses observed at other times, and it was elicited by a stimulus which might not be quite like other stimuli. (We could not always be sure precisely which of its properties the organism was responding to on a given occasion.) There were defining properties, however, and the orderliness of the observed data told us what they were and established their validity.

The paper was too strongly tied to the concept of the reflex. What I was really worrying about was operant behavior. For example, I was asking questions about a "reflex reserve" (of which more later). Did a single reinforcement always add the same number of responses to the reserve? Did a single unreinforced response always subtract the same number during extinction? A smooth extinction curve, of which I had some beautiful examples, seemed to justify speaking of a unit of behavior in spite of a considerable diversity in the properties of single instances. It was such a unit that I called an *operant*. What was *reinforced* was a response as an instance; what was *strengthened* was an operant—the probability that other responses would occur.

Instead of *operant*, Watson would have said *habit*; and there were, no doubt, similarities. Running through a maze was not a habit; it was something a rat did because it *had* a habit. That was close to the distinction between an operant as a kind of behavior and an operant response as an instance. Habits could also have been said to vary in strength, although a "strong habit" was not standard usage. A habit was usually nothing more than something an organism did. Precisely how likely it was to do it was seldom an issue.

The main difference between an operant and a habit seemed to be one of size. Pressing a lever could have been called a habit; but so could running through a complicated maze, which was composed of many operants, each with its own stimulus, response, and consequence. An operant was a kind of behavioral atom. True, I could take pressing a lever apart by extinguishing its parts separately (Skinner, 1938, p. 102); but even so, it was close to a minimal unit.

What remained to be done in science of behavior seemed clear. I should look for other independent variables and observe their effects. Here are a few of what seem to me to be important ways in which the research reported in *The Behavior of Organisms* differed from what was being done by others at the same time.

LEARNING

Contemporary work on animal behavior emphasized learning. Although I had reported satiation curves when rats were pressing a lever to get pellets of food, I had not watched them learn to press. When I turned to the so-called "learning process" directly, the result was surprising. Its significance is still not always recognized. An accident had led me to an important feature of the experiment. Pavlov had taught me the importance of controlling conditions, and I wanted my rats to be as free as possible of disturbances when they first pressed the lever and got food. To accustom them to the experimental box, I fed them their daily rations in it for several days. To reduce the distrubing effects of being put into the box, I put them first into a small compartment inside, from which I could silently release them when the experiment began. To prevent any disturbances from the sound of the food dispenser, I dispensed many pellets when the lever was in its lowest position and could not be pressed down. It would be years before I understood what I had thus done. I had unwittingly conditioned the sound of the dispenser as a reinforcer. When that was done, a *single reinforcement* was enough to condition pressing the lever as an operant. There was no learning curve and, hence, little to be attributed to a learning process.

Operant conditioning is an abrupt change in the way an organism behaves. The "learning process" supposedly revealed by a learning curve varies with the setting in which the organism is said to learn and with the repertoire the organism brings to the setting. The shape of the curve varies accordingly. I do not think the word *learn* has any useful referent. There is only one entry in the index of *The Behavior of Organisms* under learning, and the text to which it refers is in quotation marks.

Many textbooks in psychology continue to describe operant conditioning as trial-and-error learning. I think Thorndike's experiment on the Law of Effect, clearly an anticipation of operant conditioning, led to that misunderstanding. His cat was "trying" to get out of the puzzle box in the sense that its behavior was due to two kinds of earlier consequences. It was responding as members of its species had, for millions of years, responded to (and gained by escaping from) physical restraint. It was constraints with reinforcing consequences during its lifetime. But one may reinforce almost anything an organism is doing, and it will become an operant. The organism need not be trying to do anything. Many of the things Thorndike's cats did could also be called errors in the sense that reinforcing consequences did not follow, but my rats learned from their successes. There was neither trial nor error.

PUNISHMENT

Throughout the book, I misused the expression *negative conditioning*; but I think the experiments were productive. I did not want to shock my rats and built a device which, as I said, merely slapped their paws when they pressed the lever. When responses were followed by slaps, the rats responded more rapidly for a few moments and then stopped. When responses were "negatively reinforced" in this way for a few minutes at the start of extinction, the rats stopped responding, but once free of slapping they recovered; and by the end of two one-hour sessions, the extinction curve was essentially where it would have been if no responses had been slapped.

What I called negative conditioning should, of course, have been called punishment. *Reinforcement* (and its synonym *conditioning*) means to strengthen, but the behavior in my experiment grew weak. A negative reinforcer is properly defined as "a stimulus the *reduction or removal* of which strengthens behavior." If we define a positive reinforcer as a stimulus that strengthens behavior when presented and a negative reinforcer as one that strenghtens when removed, then punishment consists of presenting a negative reinforcer (as I had done) or removing a positive one.

The effect of punishment, however, seems reasonably well explained in the book. When a response is followed by, say, a shock, an emotional reaction to the shock is conditioned according to Type S (Pavlovian) conditioning. Approaching the lever elicits such a reaction, which reduces the strength of lever pressing. I could have added that incompatible behavior would also be strengthened by any reduction in such a conditioned aversive stimulus and would oppose the occurrence of the behavior punished.

THE DISCRIMINATIVE STIMULUS

In mentalistic or cognitive psychology, stimuli are things to be acted upon. We see or perceive them, and the question is how well we do so. A stimulus plays a different role, however, when as a "cue" it tells us *when* to do something (*cue* comes for the Latin *quando,* meaning "when") or as a "clue" *what* to do (etymologically the first clue was the thread that lead Theseus out of the Labyrinth). The role of the stimulus in operant behavior remained unclear for many years. In my 1935 paper about two types of conditioned reflex and a pseudo type (Skinner 1935b), the stimulus in the pseudo type had a special function, which had appeared in some experiments on discrimination. I had been reinforcing a response every five minutes in what I called "periodic reconditioning." I arranged a given reinforcement by dropping a pellet into a food dispenser, to be released when the rat next pressed. But the rat could hear the pellet drop, and it responded immediately afterward. To correct that fault, I built an electrical dispenser with which I could set up a reinforcement silently by closing a switch.

The response to the sound of the pellet was worth studying in its own right, however. In the place of the sound, I would use a light. I called it an "S-Dee" (S^D)—a discriminative stimulus. When a response was reinforced only in the presence of the light as an S^D, the rat responded slowly in its absence (which, unfortunately, I called "S-Delta" [S^Δ], hard to print) but responded immediately when the light came on. The light could have been called a cue or clue, of course; and cognitive psychologists, if there had been any, might have said that it conveyed information about when to press the lever. It was simpler, however, to say only that an operant was stronger in the presence of any stimulus in the presence of which it had been reinforced.

That avoided speculating about processes. It is often said, for example, that Pavlov's dog associated the bell with food; but, as I have often pointed out, it was Pavlov who associated them in the sense of putting them together, making a society of them. All we can say of the dog is that reinforcement changed it in such a way that it responded to the bell as it had responded to the food. The same mistake is made in speaking of an operant discrimination. When a pigeon pecks any picture in which a person appears but does not peck any in which there are no persons, it is said to have formed a concept; but it is the experimenter who had done so by arranging the contingencies. (For that matter, it is misleading to say that a pigeon "forms a discrimination." The pigeon is changed in such a way that it responds more often to settings which have certain properties.)

The rat's own behavior presumably generated discriminative stimuli, and they seemed to explain the performances appearing under "periodic reconditioning." When I first reinforced responses intermittently, a small extinction curve followed each reinforcement; but the curves soon fused, and for some time the rat responded at a steady rate. Stimuli from its own behavior, however (together with stimuli from other events occurring as time passed) soon began to have an effect. Eventually the rate dropped to a low value immediately after reinforcement and then steadily increased until another reinforcement occurred. The overall rate under "periodic reconditioning" became a useful dependent variable. In the experiments reported in *The Behavior of Organisms,* it varied with the period of reconditioning and with the level of deprivation. It has been widely used to study the effects of other "third variables."

When I began to reinforce the last of a fixed number of responses, stimulation generated by a given number proved to be more powerful than stimulation due to the passage of time, and the rat began to respond rapidly. A very large number of responses could be "added to the reserve" with a single occasional reinforcement.

DIFFERENTIATION AND SHAPING

Topographical features of operant behavior (e.g., the speed or energy with which a response was executed) were also presumably due to reinforcing consequences, and the contingencies needed to be studied. Suppose we want a rat to press a lever very hard. We cannot reinforce especially hard responses because they do not occur, but we can take advantage of spontaneous variations. We begin by reinforcing all responses and measuring, say, the force with which they are made. The measured forces will be distributed about a mean. If we select particularly forceful responses for further reinforcement, a new distribution will emerge in which some responses will be more forceful than any in the first distribution. We can then select a still harder response for reinforcement. Eventually, we reach a distribution about an extremely forceful mean. The origin of behavior is thus very much like the origin of species. When particular features of an operant are strengthened by differential reinforcement, new features come into existence as variations. It is in the nature of behavior, as it is in the nature of a genetic trait, that there are variations, and that new behavior and new genomes emerge when variations are selected by their consequences.

The Behavior of Organisms contains an example in which the topography of behavior is shaped in a rather similar way. A rat learned to release a marble from a rack, carry it to a slot, and drop it in. The necessary contingencies were programmed by changing the apparartus in small steps. (It was only later, on Project Pigeon [Skinner, 1960], that we discovered how much more expeditiously we could shape complex behavior by operating a food dispenser with a hand switch.)

THE NERVOUS SYSTEM

The chapter called "Behavior and the Nervous System" contains no new data. It is rather contentious. Sentences begin with expressions such as "What I am here contending . . . ," "I am asserting . . . ," or "What I am arguing . . . " That was probably my reaction to the open contempt for psychology shown by physiologists at the Harvard Medical School (except for that gentle man, Walter B. Cannon) and at Minnesota. A declaration of independence from physiology was essential to "radical behaviorism," however, and I argued the case strenuously.

In my thesis, I had pointed out that Sherrington never saw the action of the synapse about which he spoke so confidently, and I could convert its supposed properties into laws of behavior. Sherrington's book was not about the integrative action of the nervous system; it was about the behavior of part of a decerebrate cat. Nor had Pavlov seen "the physiological activity of the cerebral cortex" mentioned in the subtitle of his book. The book was about the control of salivation.

I am afraid my argument that behavior should be recognized as a subject matter in its own right has been misunderstood. I have never questioned the importance of physiology or, in particular, brain science or its relevance to behavior. What is happening inside the skin of an organism is part of its behavior, but it does not explain what the organism does in the space around it until it has been explained in turn. If the nervous system (or, better, the whole organism) is the product of the evolution of the species and of what has happened to the individual during its lifetime, and if what the organism does is the product of current processes in the nervous system (or, better, the whole organism), then what the organism does is the product of natural selection and of what has happened to the individual, and that is what ethology and the experimental analysis of behavior are all about.

We are likely to search the brain (or mind?) for explanations of behavior when no other explanation is available. The more we learn about the environmental variables of which behavior is a function, however, the less likely we are to search. We can predict and control behavior without knowing anything about what is happening inside. A complete account will nevertheless require the joint action of both sciences, each with its own instruments and methods.

The Behavior of Organisms had its critics (see Knapp, this volume), of course, but I thought I could answer most of their complaints. They said my title was wrong, for example. The book was not about organisms; it was about a particular strain of white rat. (But Sherrington's book was about the nervous system *of the cat* and Pavlov's about conditioned reflexes *in the dog*.) Other critics said that the cumulative record was nothing but a subtle way of smoothing data. The curves were indeed often smoother than "learning curves" obtained with mazes, even when scores for many subjects were averaged; but that was scarely a fault. Critics said that single-organism research left a great deal of "noise" in the data. The data were closer to what organisms actually did, however, and many of them were far from noisy.

The book had more serious faults, of course, which are easier to see from a distance of fifty years. In spite of my insistence that behavior should be studied as a function of external variables apart from any reference to mental or physiological states or processes, I was not yet wholly free of the traditional view. For example, I spoke as if behavior were inside the organism before it came out. A reflex was traditionally said to be "elicited" in the etymological sense of "drawn out." Operant behavior was different, and I tried to emphasize the difference by saying that it was "evoked," in the sense of "called out." (The ethologists would soon be saying "released.") I also said that operant behavior was "emitted," and later I tried to justify that usage by pointing out that the light emitted from a hot filament was not in the filament.

The "reflex reserve" carried the metaphor much further. Conditioning put responses into the reserve, and they came out during extinction. I designed experiments to find out how many responses a single reinforcement put in, and I argued that anything that changed the strength of an operant must change either the size of the reserve or the relation between it and rate of responding. Within a year after publication of the book, I abandoned the "reflex reserve," but I should have done so much sooner. Speculating about internal processes was a violation of a basic principle. An operant response was not emitted; it simply occurred.

Of course, I was also too strongly committed to the "reflex." The action of a stimulus in "eliciting" a response was a good example of control, and many behaviorists remained committed to some version of stimulus-and-response for many years, but according to my experiments, what happened *after* an organisms behaved played a much larger role than what happened before. Unfortunately, I decided to use *reflex* as the word for any unit of behavior. In doing so, I no doubt contributed to the fact that one will still find a behavioral analysis called *stimulus–response psychology.*

The Behavior of Organisms can, I think, be properly evaluated only by comparing it with the other work that was being done at the time. The issues of the *Journal of Comparative Psychology* for 1937 and 1938 may be a fair sample. Roughly 38 percent of the papers in them were about physiological variables—brain lesions, drugs, and so on. Roughly 11 percent would now be called ethological; they were studies of behavior in the field. Another 11 percent were on motivation or emotion. A few, perhaps 5 percent, were inspired by Gestalt psychology. The remaining 34 percent were in the field of my book. They dealt with Pavlovian conditioning and behavior mazes and discrimination boxes. Conditioning involved a certain amount of "prediction and control," but it was the behavior of an organ, not an organism. Glandular behavior, moreover, was of limited interest. Leg flexion was studied on the conditioned reflex pattern as an example of skeletal behavior; but it was again the behavior of a mere organ, and the experiments usually involved a mixture of respondent and operant contingencies. What organisms did in mazes and discrimination boxes was seldom, if ever, treated as a function of manipulable variables. In short, contemporary animal research was not moving very fast toward Watson's "theoretical goal" of prediction and control.

Perhaps a book can be said to contain the seeds of what grew out of it. Although I had said, "Let him extrapolate who will," I was soon extrapolating. Chronologically, Project Pigeon came first. Our pigeons never guided any real missiles, but I think they made a contribution to the discussion with which *The Behavior of Organisms* ends. In most of my experiments, I had used four rats; I am not quite sure why. They did not all behave in precisely the same way, and I was once criticized for calling a cumulative record "typical," although I believe I did so on only four of the roughly one hundred fifty curves in the book. Even when I reported an averaged curve, I almost always gave individual samples and argued that they were more valuable than the average.

Project Pigeon demonstrated my point about statistics beautifully. You cannot put the "average pigeon" into a missile. It must be one real pigeon, and it must behave precisely in a given way under many distracting circumstances. Our pigeons behaved exactly as we wanted them to; and so far as I am concerned, Project Pigeon should have been the end of the "average organism" in the study of behavior.

A second offshoot was theoretical. Near the end of the book I raised the question of whether human behavior had "properties . . . which will require a different kind of treatment [from that of nonhuman animals]?" I thought we could not answer that question so long as we knew so little about either kind, but "the only differences I expect to see . . . between the behavior of rat and man (aside from enormous differences of complexity) lie in the field of verbal behavior." I had begun writing a book on that subject before finishing *The Behavior of Organisms,* and I returned to it on a Guggenheim fellowship when the Manhattan Project made the precision bombing of Project Pigeon unnecessary. *Verbal Behavior* was not published until 1957; but in 1945 I was asked to contribute to a symposium on operationism, and I took some material from the manuscript. How do we learn to talk about private events? Most of the first paragraph of Watson's (1913) manifesto was an attack on introspection. Data obtained through introspection, said Watson, were not "objective" and could not be used in a natural science. That was an anticipation of logical positivism, but I disagreed with Watson's distinction between objective and subjective. It was not, I thought, a difference in nature, character, or quality of the data, or even of their accessibility. It was a difference in the way in which verbal behavior could be brought under the control of private events. What one felt or introspected was not a "feeling" or a "thought" but a state of one's body, and one came to talk about it only under certain verbal contingencies of reinforcement. Introspection would always be a problem because the contingencies were necessarily defective.

A third by-product of *The Behaviorism of Organisms* was still further from a laboratory science. Within a day after finishing my paper on the operational analysis of psychological terms, I started to write the book that became *Walden Two* (Skinner, 1948). The war was coming to an end; many people would be reconstructing a way of life. Why not make it a better way with the help of a science of behavior? Much of the book was a fictional anticipation of what was eventually known as applied behavior analysis. The book's protagonist called it "behavioral engineering." There were examples of respondent conditioning and, especially, the step-by-step shaping of operant behavior. *Walden Two* was a social environment or culture free of the negative reinforcers of governments and religions and the contrived positive reinforcers of capitalistic enterprises. It was free also of many annoyances of daily life that were due to accidental or careless planning. The result was the "good life."

The schools in *Walden Two* were not much of a contribution to the good life. They could have been designed by John Dewey. When my own children went to school, however, I became interested in education, and the special power of immediate conditioned reinforcers and the possibility of shaping complex behavior with a program of small, carefully arranged steps could simply not be overlooked. Good contingencies of instruction were beyond the reach of the classroom teacher who must teach twenty or thirty students at the same time. Like other professions, education must turn to instruments.

My first teaching machines were designed, like Sidney Pressey's, simply to reinforce behavior immediately; but the machine I demonstrated in 1954 used programmed material. IBM made an improved model of it three years later. It was a mechanical anticipation of the computer used as a teaching machine. Programmed instruction has become an important part of industrial and technical education; but the educational establishment is, unfortunately, still not aware of what it means to teach, and its burgeoning problems remain unsolved.

I have not yet mentioned the most important by-product of *The Behavior of Organisms*—the work done by others using the same procedures according to much the same analysis. The procedures have, in fact, been greatly improved; and experiments in laboratories throughout the world have yielded a vast corpus of facts beside which those reported in my book are minuscule. Not only are there many new facts, but, as in other fields of science, the facts hang together. They compose, it seems to me, the most consistent picture of what behavior really is.

That the majority of psychologists are not familiar with that picture is a fact with respect to which a fiftieth anniversary has another significance. Operant conditioners are said to be insular. They read each other's papers and books, but few of those written by other psychologists. That favor is reciprocated. The trouble may have its roots in history. In the early days of the experimental analysis of behavior, the editors of the standard journals would not publish reports of research on single organisms or with behavior recorded in cumulative curves. It was necessary to start a new journal, which has never been widely read outside the field. Similar difficulties in finding space for meetings led to the founding of Division 25 of the APA. Its meetings are attended almost exclusively by behavior analysts.

The insularity has been costly. A paper in *Science* by Roger Shepard (1987) shows the problem. It is called "Toward a Universal Law of Generalization for Psychological Science." It begins with the classic experiment by Guttman and Kalish (1956) on stimulus generalization, one of the most beautiful examples of a behavioral analysis. In an experiment with pigeons, Guttman and Kalish reinforced pecking a blue-green disk on a variable-interval schedule. During extinction they changed the color of the disk at random across the spectrum. The numbers of responses made to different colors yielded the curve in which Shepard is interested. He then cites presumably similar data from experiments by cognitive psychologists, in which errors made in memorizing invented names of colors seemed to show a similar effect. But what about all the other experiments that have been based on Guttman and Kalish? Instead of reinforcing responses to blue-green, begin with a discrimination. Reinforce responses to blue-green but not to blue. The peak of the generalization gradient will then shift toward yellow. Is the pigeon avoiding the color to which responses were extinguished? Not at all. A negative generalization gradient must be taken into account. It suppresses responses to blue-green more than to yellow, with the result that more responses are made to yellow, which is now at the peak of the curve. If the discrimination has been formed errorlessly, however, with the procedure designed by Herbert Terrace (1963) in which not responses are extinguished, there is no negative gradient and no peak shift. These facts are quite out of reach of any current cognitive procedure, and they tell us much about what should be covered by a "universal law of generalization."

More than forty years have passed since *Walden Two* was published, and the meaning of the good life has undergone drastic change. It is not enough to design a way of life in which everyone will be happy. We must design one that will make it possible for generations as yet unborn to live a happy life. That was the point of my book *Beyond Freedom and Dignity* (Skinner, 1971), which is, I believe, another by-product of *The Behavior of Organisms*. How are we to stop exhausting our resources, polluting the environment, and bearing too many children, and how are we to prevent nuclear holocaust? How, in short, are we to take the future of the world into account? Natural contingencies of reinforcement will not do it, nor will contingencies maintained by governments, religions, and capitalistic systems. We need surrogate contingencies of reinforcement under which people will behave as if the future were acting now. Can we design them and put them into effect? In a preface written for a new printing of *Beyond Freedom and Dignity*, I say that I am no longer sure, but I remain quite sure that if we ever do, it will be with the help of psychology that is, as Watson put it, "a purely objective experimental branch of natural science."

Part II

Comments on B. F. Skinner and Contemporary Behaviorism

Chapter 11 _____

Beyond Behavior and the Environment: The Contingency

Vicki L. Lee

Behavior analysis has been referred to as "contingency oriented" (e.g., Pierce & Epling, 1980, p. 2). Contingencies are at the heart of behavior analysis. They need to be understood if behavior analysis is to be understood. This chapter argues that contingencies are accurately characterized as causal relations between a change at an operandum (i.e., a thing that an organism can change) and a change mediated by an operandum. As this chapter shows, this characterization refines established characterizations of the contingency, which depend on the terms behavior and environment.

CONTINGENCIES AS CAUSAL RELATIONS

A contingency can be characterized in a preliminary way as follows: If a particular behavioral event occurs, then a particular consequential event will occur, but not otherwise. Examples of contingencies include the following: If a key is depressed, then a visual display will appear on the computer screen, but not otherwise; if the sum of two digits is entered into an edit field on the computer screen, then the next addition problem will appear, but not otherwise; if the light switch is depressed, then the room will be illuminated, but not otherwise; and so on. Stated generally, a contingency is a causal relation between two events, such that one event (i.e., the consequential event) will occur only if another event (i.e., the behavioral event) has occurred. The behavioral event is a requirement for the consequential event. The if–then–but-not-otherwise relation is the contingency.

Contingencies have to do with some facts about how organisms can change parts of both the world and themselves. First, to make a difference, or to produce or prevent changes, or to get results, no matter how small or momentary, an organism must expend effort. An organism must expend effort to bring about changes in its location; changes in the physical appearance of parts of its own body; changes in the location and function of objects; changes in what is available for it to see, hear, or otherwise detect; changes in its proximity to other organisms; and so on. Stated generally, without an expenditure of effort, no one can write a computer program (i.e., bring a completed computer program into existence), cross a road (i.e., change one's location from one side of the road to the other), prepare a meal (i.e., change the availability of food), or bring about any other such change.

Second, there is usually more than one good alternative way to bring about a particular change or to satisfy the requirements of a particular contingency. A person can illuminate a room by depressing a light switch or by prompting someone else to depress the light switch. A person can decrease the glare of the sun in his or her eyes by putting on a hat, putting on sunglasses, standing in the shade, going indoors, and so on. As a final example, a person can get a meal in various ways, including preparing a meal from raw ingredients, cooking a frozen meal, eating out, phoning to order a home-delivered meal, and so on. Stated colloquially, there are usually multiple alternative means to the same end or, put differently, more than one effective behavioral option for bringing about a particular consequential event. This plasticity, which is permitted by many, if not most, contingencies, has been referred to variously throughout the history of psychology. Relevant terms include response class, operant, equifinality, intersubstitutability, variation, and functional equivalence (e.g., Abelson, 1981; Glenn, Ellis, & Greenspoon, 1992; Lee, 1981; Lundh, 1981; McFall, 1982; McKearney, 1977; Moore & Lewis, 1953; Morgan, Morgan, & Toth, 1992; Salzinger, 1967; Tolman, 1959). The phenomenon is also captured in the ordinary expressions, "There is more than one way to skin a cat" and "There is more than one means to an end."

Third, in most, if not all, cases, behavioral events can bring about consequential events only under limited circumstances. For example, depression of a light switch will illuminate a room only if the house is supplied with electrical power, if the circuit is intact, and so on. As another example, breathing fills the lungs with air, but not if the breather's head is under water, unless the breather is wearing a snorkel. As a final example, dialing a particular phone number will result in the opportunity to speak to a particular person, but only if the phone is connected, if the person is available, and so on. These limiting or boundary conditions must be discriminated if all possible consequential events are to be obtained and if no unnecessary effort is to occur.

When behavior analysts speak of contingencies, they speak of the work requirements, causal relations, task demands, or practical realities that make it necessary for human beings and other animals to act in any one of a limited number of alternative ways under particular conditions if they are to bring about particular changes in the world and in themselves. The contingencies designed, implemented, and investigated in the closed microworld of the behavior-analytic laboratory (e.g., Haring, Breen, & Laitinen, 1989; Sigurdardottir, Green, & Saunders, 1990) are a subset of the universe of possible contingencies. The laboratory contingencies nonetheless have the essential properties of all contingencies: the work requirement, the multiple alternative means to an end, and the limiting conditions. Several discussions about contingencies can be consulted for further information (e.g., Davison, 1993; Findley, 1962; Hake & Vukelich, 1972; Moxley, 1982; Sidman, 1986, Skinner, 1958; Snapper, 1990).

INCONSISTENCIES

It is commonly implied that contingencies are environmental variables. This implication is evident in the expression "environmental contingencies," which has been widely used by behavior analysts and other psychologists (e.g., Lundh, 1981; Neuringer, 1991; Robertson, 1987; Schnaitter, 1975; Skinner, 1957, p. 31; Skinner, 1971, p. 186; Skinner, 1977b, p. 10). The meaning of "environment" is not unequivocal, but it is often used in the ordinary sense of a setting for behavior. This meaning is exemplified by Skinner's (1953) list of "a new car, a new friend, a new field of interest, a new job, a new location" (p. 66) as examples of a new environment.

Contingencies have also been characterized as relations of, or interactions between, behavior (or organism) and environment. For example, Skinner (1969) spoke of "the interactions between organism and environment represented by the concept of contingencies of reinforcement" (p. 97); Harzem and Williams (1983) spoke of the "contingent relations between our behavior and our environment" (pp. 565–566); and Parsons, Taylor, and Joyce (1981) said that the "interactions of an organism with the environment constitutes a contingency of reinforcement" (p. 253). Contingencies cannot be both environmental variables (i.e., variables outside the organism and external to its behavior) and interactions of behavior and environment. The two characterizations contradict each other. The causal relations referred to as "contingencies" are demonstrably powerful in their effects on the things that organisms do, but these relations need to be characterized in a consistent way.

The data collected by behavior analysts show that the things done by organisms are sensitive to contingencies, but like contingencies, these data need to be characterized in a consistent way. The data are often said to represent the behavior of the organism, where "behavior" is sometimes equated with "bodily activities." Exemplifying this interpretation of "behavior," Skinner said that "behavior is as much a part of the organism as are its anatomical features" (Skinner, 1953, p. 157) and that "the behavior of an organism is simply the physiology of its anatomy" (Skinner, 1969, p. 173). This interpretation of "behavior" as the activities of an organism's body contradicts assertions made elsewhere; for example, that "new forms of behavior have come into existence [during the last 25,000 years of human existence]" (Skinner, 1969, p. 179).

Human beings have done new things (e.g., written computer programs, sent people to the moon) in the sense of bringing about new changes in the world, but the motions of human body segments around human joints (e.g., flexion of the elbow) and the other activities of the parts of human bodies have not changed. The data collected by behavior analysts *as* behavior analysts do not represent the activities of the parts of a human or nonhuman body. The data represent the changes (e.g., depressions of a lever, contacts with a touch screen) that are brought about by a human being or other animal at an operandum (i.e., a thing an organism can change). Many of these changes cannot be observed if an observer watches only an organism in isolation from the things on which an organism acts. These events should be characterized properly as "changes brought about by an organism" rather than vaguely and contentiously as "the behavior of an organism."

PROPOSAL FOR RESOLVING THE INCONSISTENCIES

The contingencies designed, implemented, and investigated by behavior analysts can be characterized without using the terms *behavior* and *environment*. The items referred to as "contingencies" can be described generically as causal relations between a change brought about at an operandum and a change mediated by an operandum. This assertion relies on three terms or expressions (i.e., "operandum," "changes brought about at an operandum," and "changes mediated by an operandum"), which will now be explained.

An experimental operandum is an operandum used in experimental research, from which an experimenter can collect data automatically (Skinner, 1962). Experimental operanda include levers, buttons, keys, joysticks, and touch-sensitive screens. As already implied, the word *operandum* can be defined broadly to mean anything an organism can change. With the term defined this way, operanda include parts of an organism's own body (e.g., "brush one's own hair"), other organisms (e.g., "ask someone the time"), and objects outside a particular organism (e.g., "turn on the computer").

The data collected by behavior analysts represent changes brought about by one or more organisms. Behavior analysts usually refer to these events as "responses" or "behaviors." This usage reflects the historical influence of the reflex arc concept on Skinner's (1938) initial terminological practices. The traditional usage is not the most precise way of characterizing the events represented by the data. Characterized generically, the data collected from an experimental operandum represent changes brought about by an organism at an operandum—for example, a depression of a lever, a depression of a button, or a contact with a touch-sensitive computer screen. There is no reason, other than tradition, to use *response* or *behavior* to refer to these events. The events can be referred to more precisely, less ambiguously, and less contentiously as the "things done by an organism" or "the changes brought about by an organism." Neither *behavior* nor *response* conveys these latter meanings unambiguously, as made clear by several critiques of these words (e.g., Hamlyn, 1953; Kitchener, 1977; Purton, 1978).

Behavior analysts design their experiments so that a human being or other animal can bring about changes directly at one or more operanda (e.g., button, lever, touchscreen). Behavior analysts also design their experiments so that operanda can mediate other contingent changes (e.g., change in screen display, occurrence of sounds). For example, provided that specified numerical, temporal, serial, relational, or combined (e.g., temporal and numerical) requirements have been met, then a temporary change in the accessibility of food might follow a depression of a lever, the presentation of the next addition problem might follow completion of a correct answer, the presentation of a signal might follow a depression of a button, and so on. The mediated changes depend on (i.e., are contingent on) a prior change at the operandum that is brought about directly by an organism.

Contingencies are causal relations between the changes that can occur at an operandum and the changes that can be characterized without mentioning the actual changes at the operandum that are the sources of the dependent variables in behavior analytic research (e.g., the particular depressions of a particular lever brought about by a particular human being or other animal at particular times). In addition, this characterization includes contingencies in which both the direct change and the mediated change occur in the organism itself and not in the organism's environment. The term *environmental contingencies* tacitly excludes this possibility, although behavior analysts plainly want to include such subtle contingencies under the rubric of "contingencies" (e.g., Vaughan & Michael, 1982). As implied above, an organism can function as an operandum on which it can act. For example, a human being can act through the mediation of a toothbrush on its own teeth, thus removing plaque; a human being can brush his or her own hair, thereby increasing the silky appearance of the hair; a human being can count silently to ten, thus in some sense hearing his or her own counting; and so on.

Both contingencies and the events represented by behavior-analytic data can be discussed without using "the behavior of the organism," "environmental contingencies," "contingencies as interactions of behavior and environment," and other such phrases that rely on the terms *behavior* and *environment.*" For example, there is no reason, other than tradition, to use the expression "the behavior of the organism" to refer to the sources of the data collected by behavior analysts. These data, or at least the data collected by basic researchers, represent the changes brought about either by one organism acting alone or by two or more organisms who can combine their effects in bringing about particular changes at, and through the mediation of an operandum (e.g., Hake & Vukelich, 1972; Schmitt, 1984). Behavior analysts might better convey their science to other psychologists if they would stop asserting that their subject matter is the behavior of organisms. This assertion does not correspond precisely and unambiguously to the data collected by behavior analysts in their basic research, and it embroils behavior analysts in much unnecessary controversy. If the terminological legacy of the reflex arc concept (Dewey, 1896) is expunged, then behavior analysts could say that they design and implement causal relations between changes that can occur at an operandum (e.g., a thing that an organism can change) and changes that can be mediated by an operandum. Behavior analysts could say that they determine what happens when an organism acts on an operandum that enters into one or more such causal relations. Further, behavior analysts could say that they determine what an organism does when these causal relations change either gradually or abruptly through time and either conditional on or independent of what an organism does.

AUTHOR'S NOTE

The revision of this Chapter was supported by Australian Research Council Grant Number A79331585 for the project entitled "Act-Based Reformulation of Behavior Change Research."

Chapter 12 _____

Continuity over Change within the Experimental Analysis of Behavior

Gerald E. Zuriff

As several articles in this volume attest, behavior analysis, as a self-conscious school within psychology, traces its lineage to Skinner's work in the 1930s culminating with his *The Behavior of Organisms* published in 1938. Although Skinner's work clearly falls within the behaviorist tradition founded by John B. Watson in 1913, behavior analysts are quick to distance themselves from Watson and to complain that many attacks against behaviorism are really criticisms of the Watsonian form rather than their own. Whereas a sharp discontinuity is felt between modern behavior analysis and the behaviorisms of Watson, Tolman, Guthrie, and Hull, a direct link is felt with Skinner's version.

Indeed, the conventional wisdom is that contemporary behavior analysts are merely implementing the research program articulated by Skinner in his early theorizing. As in any normal science, behavior analysis is seen as elaborating the original theory by investigating new environmental variables, discovering new functional relations, and integrating these findings into an overall theory in a continuous and cumulative fashion. This picture is supported by Skinner's own view of scientific theory (Skinner, 1950), which holds that a theory is a formulation using a minimum number of terms to represent a large number of experimental facts. It evolves as additional empirical relationships are presented in a formal way, and as it develops, it integrates more facts in increasingly more economical formulations. For many behavior analysts, this is a fairly precise description of how their own research grows out of Skinner's initial formulation.

CONTINUITY

Yet it is clear that serious and substantive deviations from Skinner's approach have occurred both in method and theory. Among the most obvious changes is the current lack of interest in the analysis of moment-to-moment changes in behavior and in the cumulative record used to measure them (Skinner, 1976a). Most data presented today consist of "steady-state points" that may summarize many hours of behavior. This change represents not simply a change in method but, more fundamentally, a change in research strategy as Ferster (1978) notes.

Other changes, equally fundamental, are directed against Skinner's emphasis on the importance of studying the "free operant." Today we find discrete-trials procedures commonly used in experiments reported in the pages of the *Journal of the Experimental Analysis of Behavior.* In a related development, a dependent variable frequently used in basic operant research is the relative frequency of response rather than the absolute rate. Similarly, relative rate of reinforcement is a common independent variable. Ironically, the use of discrete-trials procedures, relative rate measures, probabilities, and choice experiments in operant "Skinnerian" research represents a partial victory for Tolman and Hull, who advocated the study of the "behavior ratio," over Skinner (1950), who opposed it.

On the theoretical side, the deviations from Skinner are even more serious. Although Skinner vigorously opposed the introduction of theoretical concepts, it is not uncommon today to see references to such cognitive concepts as "short-term memory" and to economic concepts such as "set-points" and signal-detection theory analyses, with their assumptions of hypothetical distributions, in the pages of the *Journal of the Experimental Analysis of Behavior.* Even within Skinner's own thinking, many changes have occurred since 1938 when pure intervening variables were evident. For example, his theory of motivation in 1938 included concepts such as "emotion," "drive," "reflex reserve." By 1950, all these were eliminated in favor of a leaner theory with virtually no intervening variables. Today the influence of ethological theories and studies of adjunctive behavior have further separated modern theories of motivation within behavior analysis from Skinner's theorizing (see Herrnstein, 1977).

Despite these deviations, criticisms, differences, and changes, the feeling of continuity over the past fifty years still persists. It is as if the discontinuities are treated like the anomalies within a scientific paradigm: They are ignored; or if not ignored, then acknowledged and quickly dismissed; or if not dismissed, then discussed but without impact on perceptions. Why?

Behavior analysis is not alone in asking this sort of question. The beginnings of psychoanalysis preceded those of behaviorism by about two decades, and psychoanalysis is still viewed as a coherent school of psychology, derived from the early clinical and theoretical work of Freud. Yet, it is far from clear what contemporary psychoanalytic theories, such as self psychology, object-relations theory, and ego psychology have in common with one another, much less with Freudian theory. Modern psychoanalysts have had to grapple with the question of how a clinical practice or theoretical hypothesis qualifies as "psychoanalytic" (Eagle, 1987).

Outside the field of psychology, we find Wittgenstein (1953) wondering what his work has in common with the work of earlier philosophers and why both are considered "philosophy." Similarly, when we look at the practices of contemporary Judaism—even its orthodox version—and compare them to the practices of biblical Judaism, we find so little overlap that we are puzzled as to why they are thought to be the same religion. In all these examples—behavior analysis, psychoanalysis, philosophy, and Judaism—we find a strongly held perception of continuity and coherence in the face of serious and, in many cases, radical change.

The resolution of this paradox cannot be found simply in historical facts. The mere fact of temporal continuity of development is insufficient to explain the paradox. For example, chemistry is not alchemy, although it may have developed from it; nor is astronomy astrology; nor is Christianity Judaism, although it may have developed from it. As noted above, behavior analysis is not Watsonian behaviorism, even though it developed from it. The basic question we are confronted with is this: When is a change viewed as a *break from* the past, and when is it seen as a *development within*? When is it perceived as a revolution and when as an evolution?

I have purposely emphasized the element of human judgment in this question by using words like *perceived, viewed,* and *seen* because I suspect that the difference between revolution and evolution is a matter of human perception as well as objective historical or scientific fact. A good example of the contribution of human judgment can be found in the early history of behaviorism. Today, we take it for granted that Watson and his behaviorism were a radical break away from the earlier introspective psychology. Indeed, we commonly speak of the "behaviorist revolution." However, listen to America's leading introspective psychologist as he reviews in 1914 Watson's behaviorist manifesto:

Logically, so far as I can see, behaviorism is irrelevant to introspective psychology. Materially, I believe that [introspective] psychology will be furthered by [behaviorism]. . . . Neither logically nor materially can behaviorism "replace" [introspective] psychology. (Titchener, 1914, p. 6)

"Logically," Titchener was correct. Behaviorism and introspectionism could have developed along parallel tracks, with each one supplementing the other. Indeed, for a while this "dual track" approach was tried (see, e.g., Smith & Guthrie, 1921). However, for reasons that are not fully clear, the attempt failed. Introspectionism in its original form disappeared, and behaviorism was seen as "overthrowing" introspectionism.

Because of this role of human judgment, the question of what distinguishes revolution from evolution or discontinuity from continuity is a psychological or perhaps sociological question about the human behavior we call "science." Although I do not have an answer to this question, I shall try to shed some light on the matter by considering two instances of perceived discontinuities within the development of behavior analysis. I shall suggest environment variables responsible for the discontinuity, point to evidence that supports my suggestion, and then show how my suggestion fits into the behaviorist conception of science.

STIMULUS AND RESPONSE

For decades after the beginnings of behaviorist research, controversies raged over the question of how behavior and the environment should be described in behavioral laws and theories. I have elsewhere (Zuriff, 1985, Chap. 3) described the issues involved. For present purposes, it will suffice to list some of the debates to give a flavor for the conceptual turmoil. On the stimulus side were disagreements over whether a stimulus should be defined relationally (e.g., "the larger square") or absolutely (e.g., "the three-inch square"), distally (energy at the stimulating object) or proximally (energy at the receptor), formally (the stimulating object) or effectively (aspects of the object which actually affect behavior). On the response side were disagreements over whether behavior should be described at the molar or the molecular level, whether a response should be defined in terms of physical movements, acts (e.g., "the cat turned the latch"), or achievements (e.g., "the latch was turned"), whether a response should be measured in functional or formal units, and whether learning is in terms of place or response.

Then, almost abruptly, the debates ceased. The received wisdom is split on the reason why. On the one hand, some scholars believe that the debates ended because Restle (1957) settled most of the issues. On the other hand, many behavior analysts hold that the controversies were relevant only to theorists interested in instrumental learning theories but not to Skinner's operant research. The latter is said to bypass the old problems as described in Skinner's (1935) influential paper "The Generic Nature of the Concepts of Stimulus and Response." As operant research methods eventually came to dominate, there was no need to be concerned with the old questions any longer.

In either case, the conventional explanations for the perception of a discontinuity are too facile. First, it is now clear that Restle's paper by no means "settled" the issue (Segal & Lachman, 1972; Zuriff, 1985, p. 286, footnote 82). Second, although Skinner's (1935) paper was a brilliant exposition of one set of positions on the range of issues, it in no way refuted the others or definitively established the truth in an unassailable way. In hindsight, the questions over response-and-stimulus definition were not "resolved" but merely faded away. Why?

I suggest that the critical factor in ending the debates and in creating the perceived discontinuity was the invention of the operant chamber, that is, the so-called "Skinner box." As an experimental method, the operant chamber initiated an extremely successful research program that, fifty years later, shows no signs of abating. At the same time, the box allowed researchers to ignore all the issues surrounding stimulus-and-response definition because it provided its own set of answers. First, the box narrowed the range of behavior to a simple response, switch closing, usually by key pecking or bar pressing, and the range of environmental factors to a similarly small number of simple stimuli. Second, within this narrow range of stimuli and responses, the original issues were no longer pressing. For example, in the box, the formally defined response is also the functionally defined response, or so it seemed for a long time anyway (discussed more fully below). Similarly, the act description ("the rat pressed the lever") is equivalent to the achievement description ("the lever was pressed"), and the distinction between molar and molecular description seemed irrelevant (until recently) for a simple repetitive response. Thus, the success of the box permitted behavior analysis to ignore a number of issues that had plagued earlier behaviorists and allowed it to create the perception of a sharp *break away* from the past.

To test the hypothesis that a particular variable is responsible for a change of behavior, one can remove the variable and see if the behavior returns to baseline. In the case of the suggestion that Skinner's experimental chamber was responsible for the discontinuity with earlier learning theory debates, we have a natural experiment to examine. In more recent years, behavior analysis has moved away from the box and into more complex human environments. If my suggestion is valid, we would expect to find the early debates re-emerging, and I think I see some evidence along that line. For example, Barrett (1987) examined all the articles published in the *Journal of Applied Behavior Analysis, Behavior Modification,* and *Behavioral Assessment* and has found problems in response specification. She shows that increasingly, behavior is no longer measured in basic behavioral units such as response rate but, rather, by rating scales, standardized tests, and psychometric subjective scales. Thus, as the behavior studied becomes more complex, the issues that were set aside by the box now re-emerge.

The second line of evidence comes from within the box itself. As operant research has become more sophisticated, assumptions about the simplicity of the operant response in the box have been questioned. Shimp (1979), for example, has shown that the question of molecular versus molar description cannot be ignored for even the simple lever press and has reopened the debate. Similarly, questions about the functional equivalence of all pecks has, in effect, reopened the question of functional versus formal units of behavior (Schwartz & Gamzu, 1977; for other examples of problems within the box over response definition, see Thompson & Zeiler, 1986). As behavior analysis expands into the area of human verbal behavior, the problems of response unit have proven nearly intractable. Ironically, their solution may require a reiteration of the debates within learning theory from the 1930s and 1940s.

PSYCHOANALYSIS

Throughout its history, behaviorism has criticized psychoanalysis for its unscientific methods and theorizing. Nonetheless, for most of this history, behaviorists have attributed some credence to psychoanalytic clinical findings and generalizations. For the most part, they have been concerned with interpreting psychoanalytic theory and principles in behavioral terms that could be scientifically tested and integrated within a learning theory of behavior. Many of the important behaviorists, including Watson (1930), Guthrie (1944), and Tolman (1942), attempted such interpretations and integrations. Perhaps one of the most influential of these attempts was by Dollard and Miller (1950) in the neo-Hullian tradition. For behavior analysis, the most important interpretation and integration was achieved by Skinner (1953) in Chapter 24 of *Science and Human Behavior.*

Abruptly in the 1960s, attempts at integrating psychodynamic theory and behaviorism were halted. Behavior therapy had recently been introduced as the application of scientific learning theory to behavior problems. The founders of behavior therapy, including Wolpe (1963), denounced psychoanalysis. They saw it as unsalvageable and argued that any attempt to learn something useful from it is not worth the effort required to winnow the wheat from the chaff. Every bit of psychoanalysis is so contaminated by unscientific thinking that nothing can be gained from it.

Again, we have a sharp discontinuity with the past. At the time, one of the reasons often given for the break was the increasing success of learning theory, which could finally serve as the scientific basis for psychotherapy. This reason is not convincing because today it is generally agreed that behavior therapy methods do not derive from learning theory.[1] Instead, behavior therapy has had to develop its own scientific underpinnings. Then why the break?

I suggest that a critical factor was that the founders of behavior therapy, in contrast with those who attempted to integrate psychoanalysis and behaviorism, actually had an effective method for curing a psychological disorder. Wolpe had developed systematic desensitization for successfully eliminating phobias. Although the connection between this therapeutic method and "learning theory" is dubious, systematic desensitization allowed behavior therapists to cure while setting aside the psychological complexities addressed, however poorly, by psychoanalysis. While earlier behaviorists could confront those complexities by parasitically borrowing from psychoanalysis, behavior therapists could focus on treatment and pretend that the complexities did not exist.

As behavior therapy has moved into areas in which the technique of systematic desensitization does not apply, these complexities are re-emerging.

More and more behavior therapists have found it necessary to combine the methods of traditional behavior therapy with those of cognitive therapy. The result is a "cognitive behavior therapy" that is strikingly similar, in theory if not in treatment practice, to certain psychoanalytic theories (cf. Weiss & Sampson, 1986).

Complexities are re-emerging even in the traditional behavior therapy methods. It has long been known that an enormous gap exists between the behavioral technique reported in the journal report and the complexity of what actually goes on in the social interaction between client and therapist. Why do clients comply with treatment instructions? Why do some drop out of treatment? Questions like these have compelled behavior therapists to look at client–therapist variables that were initially ignored but which have been examined by psychoanalysis since its inception. Although it is too early to say whether the result will be a return to the attempts to integrate behavior therapy and psychoanalysis, there are already several modern attempts (e.g., Marmor & Woods, 1980; Wachtel, 1977).

TECHNOLOGY AND EXEMPLAR

In these two case studies, we have examples of discontinuities, *breaks from* rather than *developments within*. Behavior therapy is seen as a revolution against psychoanalysis (despite earlier continuities), and behavior analysis is seen as discontinuous with earlier behaviorist questions about stimulus-and-response definition. An examination of what the two share is instructive.

In both cases, I have suggested that the introduction of a new technology was a decisive factor in the discontinuity: for behavior analysis, the invention of the Skinner box, and for behavior therapy, the development of systematic desensitization. In both cases, the technology represented an exemplar for a research program. Operant research was to be, in unspecified ways, "like" the study of a rat pressing a lever; and behavior therapy was to be, in unspecified ways, "like" systematic desensitization.

Both techniques set off new and successful research and applied programs that allowed their practitioners to set aside many of the issues addressed by their "pre-revolutionary" predecessors. The discarding of (rather than the resolution of) old issues and the establishment of a new direction in basic and applied research, both instigated by a new technology, seem to be the essence of the two revolutions. As the revolutionary approaches expand into new areas, the lines of similarity with the exemplars have become more difficult to construct; and some of the old discarded issues have re-emerged.

Why does the appearance of a new technology with its associated exemplar and research program redirect a science, creating a perceived discontinuity with the past? One explanation can be found in behavioral epistemology. Skinner (1957, p. 428; 1974, p. 235) long argued that scientific knowledge is a set of rules for effective action, effective for adaptation to the contingencies of reinforcement in the world. A technology that extends human control over the world, and over behavior in particular, increases effective action in this sense. The use of this technology will be reinforcing to the scientist, and it will therefore be adopted by the scientific community.

In the case of behavior analysis and behavior therapy, each had a technology that was highly effective in changing behavior. In those early reports of how a rat's behavior could be precisely controlled by contingencies of reinforcement or how life-long phobias could be eliminated in a dozen sessions, the authors' excitement is evident. Another way of putting this is that the use of those techniques highly reinforced the behavior of those scientists. This fact may help explain why behavior analysis and behavior therapy were so quickly and widely adopted. If so, then our two case studies illustrate a behavioral epistemology (Zuriff, 1985, Chap. 12) that sees the growth of knowledge and scientific activity as the development of effective action for adaptation to the world.

AUTHOR'S NOTE

This chapter is based, in part, on a presentation at the convention of the Association for Behavior Analysis, May 1988, Philadelphia, PA.

Chapter 13 _____

Things That Are Private and Things That Are Mental

Howard Rachlin

As Laurence Smith (this volume) points out, Skinner belongs "in the tradition of the descriptive, inductive *non*-logical positivism begun by Francis Bacon in the 17th century . . . Bacon . . . enjoined the scientists of his day to reject the authority of the past and turn to the study of nature rather than books." It might, therefore, be more consistent with Skinner's own work to develop and build on his methods than quote from his books. In this spirit, I would take issue with several of the chapters in Part I, particularly those of Moore (Chapter 5) and Day and Moore (Chapter 6).

The two figures in Moore's article representing the "received view" and an "alternative view" put the issue graphically. I agree with what Moore says about the received view, but I do not share his alternative view. I would reduce the angle of the branch representing Skinner's radical behaviorism to bring it much closer to cognitive psychology and add another higher branch on which would sit "teleological behaviorism" (Rachlin, 1992, 1993, 1994). What is teleological behaviorism? I have defined this form of behaviorism as an approach to the scientific study of the mind or as a way of using mental terms:

Teleological Behaviorism [is] the belief that mental terms refer to overt behavior of intact animals. Mental events are not supposed to occur inside the animal at all. Overt behavior does not just *reveal* the mind; it *is* the mind. Each mental term stands for a pattern of overt behavior. This includes such mental terms as "sensation," "pain," "love," "hunger," and "fear" (terms considered by the mentalist to be "raw feels"), as well as terms such as "belief" and "intelligence" that are sometimes said to refer to "complex mental states," sometimes "propositional attitudes" and sometimes to "intentional acts." (Rachlin, 1994, pp. 15–16)

Teleological behaviorism differs from "Skinnerian behaviorism," which I define as follows:

Skinnerian Behaviorism [is] the belief that all of the behavior of animals—including humans—may be explained in terms of prior stimulation (the cause of "involuntary" behavior) and contingencies of reinforcement (the cause of "voluntary" behavior). All behavior usually considered to be caused by the mind may be reinterpreted in terms of the animal's reinforcement history and natural selection of its species. Mental terms are therefore not properly a part of psychology. (Rachlin, 1994, p. 15)

The crucial issue between the two is whether mental terms belong in a scientific psychology. Teleological behaviorism claims they do; Skinnerian behaviorism claims they do not.

On this issue, Moore (this volume) says, "When Skinner argues for behavioral interpretations of mental terms, he is not arguing that the way to make mental terms meaningful is by referring to observable behavior." Day and Moore quote Day (1969b) regarding an exchange between Skinner and Scriven as follows: "Skinner is objecting . . . not to things that are private but to things that are mental." Skinner here explicitly rejects teleological behaviorism. Had he made just the opposite sort of objection—not to things that are mental but to things that are private—he would have been on the side of teleological behaviorism. Both Chapters 5 and 6 imply that Skinner was correct in objecting to the use of mental terms in psychology. Thus, both chapters implicitly reject teleological behaviorism.

Moore's argument rests on two logical steps. First, he correctly notes that cognitive psychology is a modern extension of the S-O-R, neobehavioristic mediational psychology of Hull, Tolman, and logical positivism. Second, however, he condemns neobehaviorism and cognitive psychology together because of their common use of mental terms. I agree with Moore's first step, but I believe that the common debility of neobehaviorism and cognitive psychology lies not in their use of mental terms but in their use of internal (private) mediators.

The cognitive psychologist John R. Anderson (1991, p. 513) says, "I have always felt that something was lost when the cognitive revolution abandoned behaviorism." Then he adds, "In doing this, however, I do not want to lose the cognitive insight that there is a mind between the environment and behavior." Here Anderson cites both characteristics that cognitive psychology shares with S-O-R behaviorism, the use of mental terms and internal mediation (private events). Skinnerian behaviorists (including Day and Moore) reject both cognitive psychology and S-O-R behaviorism because of the common reference to "things that are mental." Teleological behaviorists reject both because of their common reference to "things that are private."

When Hull and Spence internalized stimulus–response connections in the form of r_g's and s_g's, they were merely internalizing (and thereby trivializing) a perfectly valid concept. The concepts *stimulus* and *response,* as Skinner had pointed out in his thesis (Skinner, 1931) and reiterated in *The Behavior of Organisms* (1938), are classifications (categories) of correlated environmental and behavioral events, defined in relation to a whole organism—an intact organism. They have no meaning inside the organism. At the very threshold of American psychology, Dewey (1896) realized that an internal event (e.g., a neural discharge) cannot meaningfully be called a stimulus or a response because these terms are relevant only to the system being studied (the whole organism). To expect the internal mechanism of an animal to contain stimuli and responses is like expecting the internal mechanism of an automobile to consist of little automobiles. This is what Ryle (1949) was to call a "category mistake." All of this is clear enough and generally agreed upon. What then makes the status of internal operants, internal reinforcers and punishers, and internal discriminative stimuli (Zuriff, 1979b) any different? Cognitive psychologists may well argue that *their* view of the internal intrinsically private world as a computer mechanism is richer, more varied, more congruent with modern neurophysiology, and more applicable to human problems than is the internalization of operant concepts developed originally to explain the behavior of whole organisms.

Faced with complexity in behavior, teleological behaviorism continues to reject the internalization of behavioral concepts. To account for complexity, teleological behaviorism instead broadens those concepts. It defines mental terms, not as what a person says at the moment but as what a person says and does over an extended period of time.

The emotions portrayed by an actor on a stage are said to be imaginary rather than real, not because they do not go deeply enough into the actor's nervous system but because they do not extend broadly enough in time—they do not extend far enough into the past and future. We say the actor on the stage behaves "as though" the emotions actually existed because the actor did not behave that way before the curtain went up and will not behave that way after the curtain goes down. If, on the contrary, the behavior does persist (as when the actor must portray fear of a dental appointment on the stage just prior to an actual dental appointment, and the characteristics of the portrayal persist after the curtain comes down), we say that even though they were acted, the actor's emotions were nevertheless genuine.

The objections raised against behaviorism by philosophers—that it is limited to brief discrete responses such as a pigeon's pecks or a rat's lever presses—are not valid when behavior is viewed in molar terms over periods of time. Lacey and Rachlin (1978) argued that this view was at least as capable of accounting for complex human behavior including language, belief, and knowledge as the cognitive view. The key point is the extension of behavioral units from relatively brief events, such as microswitch closures, to patterns of events over extended temporal intervals.

Modern methods of analysis, such as melioration and maximization, have taken Skinner's original conception of the reflex as a correlation between stimulus and response and extended it to reinforcement as a correlation over time of behavior and consequences. The establishment of such a correlation is held to be both necessary and sufficient for behavioral change. For example, the establishment of a negative correlation between a rat's overall response rate and shock rate is necessary and sufficient for avoidance learning (Herrnstein, 1969b; Herrnstein & Hineline, 1966). The behavioral unit in such a conception is the molar characterization of responding in general rather than the individual response. The causal factor—the thing that makes reinforcement reinforcement—is the correlation between an abstract quality of the environment and an abstract quality of behavior rather than temporal contiguity between an individual reinforcer and an individual response. Thus, Churchland's "Argument X," cited by Day and Moore, that behaviorism cannot deal with interactions among abstract entities is directly contradicted by teleological behaviorism, which is concerned not with what an organism *would* do under certain circumstances but with what it actually *does* over time. Belief, boredom, and secretiveness are definable in terms of actual overt correlations over time.

The ultimate solution proposed by Day and Moore, consistent with Skinner's radical behaviorism (and with logical positivism), is to transfer mental states from the interior of the behaving organism to the interior of the observer: "Some of these interpretive behaviors [of the behavior analyst] are publicly observable, others only privately so." This will not do. Skinner's radical behaviorism, Day and Moore's interpretation, and my teleological behaviorism all consist of what we say, what we write, what we do—not what goes on inside us. It may seem a trivial point—the difference between speaking out loud and mumbling to oneself, the difference between actually writing on a piece of paper and twitching one's fingers—but that is exactly the difference between thinking as a measurable pattern of overt behavior with environmental feedback and thinking as an unmeasurable inherently private event, available only to introspection.

Thought belongs to the category of mental events that philosophers call "intentional acts." Intentional acts are believed by philosophers to be the domain of cognitive psychology (Dennett, 1978). However, teleological behaviorism can account for intentional acts at least as well as cognitive psychology can. The teleological approach to the thought of a writer, for example, would look for a writer's thought in the writer's writing, revising, and speaking (at the boundary between the whole organism and its environment) rather than inside the writer's head.

In addition to intentional acts, philosophers have claimed that behavior cannot account for "raw feels"—"pure sensations" like pains or what happens when a baby hears a sound. A definition of sensation as an instance of an *overt* discrimination within a larger *overt* discriminatory pattern (a definition that goes as far back as Aristotle) accounts very well for sensation as studied in the laboratory and also reflects common sense (unfettered by medieval scholasticism). Suppose, for example, a person normally discriminates between red lights and other stimuli. While driving, for instance, that person looks at a red light and stops. Then that person may be said (by definition) to sense the red light. If, in the context of the *same* normal discrimination of red lights and other stimuli, the person looks and stops, but in this specific instance a red light is not there, the person may be said to be imagining a red light. For a teleological behaviorist, however, neither sensation nor imagination has meaning without a normal discriminatory pattern, regardless of what may or may not be happening inside. Nothing about sensation or imagination in the laboratory or in everyday life contradicts such a definition or detracts from its usefulness. Application of teleological behavioral analysis to pain has enabled physicians to develop useful methods of treatments (Fordyce, 1976) and is immune to the sort of philosophical complaints advanced by Putnam (1980) and cited by Moore and Day (see Rachlin, 1985, for an extensive discussion of pain as behavior).

Teleological behaviorism tackles difficult problems on their own terms instead of internalizing them. It attempts to answer the question of *why* organisms behave the way they do rather than *how* they do it. It does not claim to offer an internal mechanism better than that of cognitive or physiological psychology. As Skinner originally envisioned, it provides the groundwork for the cognitive or physiological study of internal mechanisms. In short, things that are mental are more useful in psychology than things that are private.

Chapter 14

Selection in Biology and Behavior

A. Charles Catania

In both operant conditioning and the evolutionary selection of behavioral characteristics, consequences alter future probability. Reflexes and other innate patterns of
behavior evolve because they increase the chances of survival of the *species.* Operants grow strong because they are followed by important consequences in the life of
the *individual.* (Skinner, 1953, p. 90)

This opening quotation is one of B. F. Skinner's earliest references to the analogy between phylogenic and ontogenic selection. There is substantial continuity between the research that he brought together and presented in *The
Behavior of Organisms* (Skinner, 1938) and his later writings, but this citation is a significant marker of his transition from a treatment of behavior that
took physics as its reference science to one that emphasized behavior as fundamentally a part of the subject matter of biology. The learning theories of
the 1930s attempted to formulate laws and to derive principles from those
laws, and, like other learning theorists of the time, Skinner included such components in his early work (e.g., his Laws of the Reflex: Skinner, 1938, pp. 12–33).

In *Science and Human Behavior* (Skinner, 1953), however, the ties to biology became explicit in the many references to evolutionary contingencies,
and those ties were strengthened and expanded in later works (Skinner,
1966a, 1975, 1977a, 1984a, 1984b). For example, Skinner's discussion of
phylogenic selection shifted from the selection of species to the selection of
organs and organ systems (Skinner, 1988), and his treatment of the nature of the
units that were selected represented an integration of selection with some of his
earliest concerns about behavioral units (Skinner, 1935). He elaborated on the
nature of selection and its operation in the three realms of phylogeny, ontogeny,
and culture in a paper entitled "Selection by Consequences" (Skinner, 1981b).

Given the central role of selection in Skinner's work, this commentary briefly reviews some of its properties and implications. First, it provides an overview of Darwinian selection. Then it considers some parallels between Darwinian selection and the variety of selection by consequences during the lifetime of the individual organism that stands as one of Skinner's most important contributions to the science of behavior. In the course of this comparison, it examines some of the similar problems of acceptance faced by Darwinian and Skinnerian selection, using the contrast between natural and artificial selection as a primary example.

NATURAL SELECTION

Natural selection refers to Darwin's account of evolution in terms of the differential survival and reproduction of the members of a population; the environment selects the individuals who pass their characteristics on from one generation to the next and thereby shapes the characteristics of those in later populations (for a lucid and detailed account, see Dawkins, 1976, 1986). Evolution by natural selection requires variations within populations; these variations are the stuff upon which selection works.

Selection was well known even before Darwin, but it was the sort used by humans in horticulture and animal husbandry. People knew how to breed plants or livestock selectively for hardiness or yield or other characteristics. This selective breeding, artificial selection, created new varieties of vegetables and flowers and so on. Workhorses were selected for strength and racehorses for speed. One part of Darwin's insight was that a similar kind of selection occurred in nature, without human intervention. There was no argument with artificial selection in Darwin's day; natural selection was the problem.

Consider an example of natural selection. In a population of prey animals (e.g., zebras), the members vary in the speed at which they can run; the reasons might include differences in anatomy such as bone length or muscle size, sensory differences that allow some to get off to a quicker start than others, and other indirect factors that slow some down, such as susceptibility to disease. If these animals are preyed upon by predators, the ones most likely to be caught are the slowest ones, everything else being equal.

At any time during its history, this prey population has some mean or average speed. Some members are above that mean, and others are below it. The ones below are those most likely to be caught and so are less likely to pass their genes on to the next generation. The next generation will then include more descendants of those above the mean than of those below; in other words, it will include fewer of the previous slow and more of the previous fast runners. Thus, the mean speed will be higher in this generation than in the last one. However, the same kind of selection still operates on this generation: Again, the slowest are more likely to be caught than the fastest. Over many generations, the mean speed becomes faster and faster (a similar kind of selection operates on the speed of the predators, because the slowest of those are less likely to catch their prey than the fastest).

The evolution of the horse provides striking evidence for this kind of selection (Simpson, 1951). Over the 50 million years or so since *eohippus*, the so-called dawn horse, the individuals in the populations from which modern horses are descended gradually increased in size. These size changes were accompanied by other changes, such as bone length, anatomy of the foot, and presumably also behavior: *Eohippus* was the ancestor of modern horses, but compared to them it was undoubtedly slow.

Eohippus is extinct, and that fact is relevant to the story. Many descendants of *eohippus* must also have been the fastest of their kind in their time, but they are no longer around either. When selection operates on some relative property, such as speed relative to the mean for a population, the mean for the population changes. For example, after capture by predators has repeatedly selected faster escape in a population, few descendants of the originally slow runners will be left even if that slower running speed had provided a selective advantage at a much earlier time when it was very fast relative to the population mean. In other words, as *eohippus* demonstrates, examples of ancestral forms should not be expected within current populations. The mean running speed of horses has been moved so far by 50 million years of equine evolution that, in its prime, even the slowest of contemporary horses would be able to outrun the vast majority of its ancestors.

According to these arguments, the source of selection is in the environment (the environments of predators include their prey, and the environments of prey include their predators). Selection creates the features of organisms, but selection is necessary to maintain them as well as to create them. For example, the ancestors of whales were once land mammals. After they moved back into the sea, the environmental contingencies that made legs advantageous no longer maintained the selection of well-formed legs. Instead, selection began to favor limbs that were effective for movement through water. The legs of the ancestors of whales gradually disappeared; in a sense, it is appropriate to say that the legs had extinguished or become extinct (Skinner, 1988, p. 73). Selection operates on species, but it does so by acting on particular organs and systems and body parts.

Consider another example. Environments that include tall trees with edible leaves are environments in which long necks may be advantageous, especially if shorter trees are scarce or if their leaves are often depleted by competitors. Giraffes arose through the natural selection of relatively long necks; such selection could not occur in environments that lacked tall trees (the tall trees set the occasion for the selection of long necks: cf. Skinner, 1988, p. 73). But the selection also depended on what there was to start with. In one species variations among individuals might allow the selection of those with longer necks; but in another, they might allow the selection of those who climb trees more efficiently. The environment selects from populations of organisms, but that selection can only operate on the range of variations available within those populations (compare the behavioral principle that a response cannot be reinforced unless it is emitted). Topographical factors must be included among the constraints on possible variations. In the human species, for example, our four-limbed mammalian ancestry precludes the evolution of a pair of wings emerging from our shoulder blades.

Natural selection along a single dimension such as running speed seems straightforward enough, but evolution involves more than changes along single dimensions. It results in organized complexity, such as the intricate structure of the human eye. Is it reasonable to believe that natural selection could have produced such organized complexity? The eye could not have emerged full blown as a product of natural selection. What selective advantage could just part of an eye confer? The answer is that even 1 percent of an eye is a substantial advantage if all of one's contemporaries have even less. Any sensitivity to light is better than none; 2 percent is better than 1 percent, 3 percent is better than 2 percent, and so on (cf. Dawkins, 1986, p. 81).

Can such an account be extended to unusual cases such as animal mimicry? A stick insect may look so much like a stick that a bird that otherwise would have eaten it will pass it by. But how much good would it do to have merely a 5 percent resemblance to a stick? In response to this question, Dawkins (1986, pp. 83–84) points out that a 5 percent resemblance may be just enough to make a difference in twilight or in fog or if the bird is far away. Once individuals in the population vary in their resemblance to sticks, natural selection based even on small differences may drive the population to more and more convincing mimicry.

Resemblance to sticks is an unusual property and is, of course, only one of many possible directions of selection. Selection can operate on different features in different populations, and not every feature that seems adaptive is necessarily a product of natural selection. Darwin regarded natural selection as the most important mechanism of evolution but took pains to point out that natural selection was not the only possible one: "I am convinced that Natural Selection has been the main *but not exclusive* means of modification" (Darwin, 1859/1966, p. 6; italics added). Selectionist accounts of the features of a population demand more than just a plausible story about how those features might be advantageous. The same is true of selectionist accounts of the development of individual behavior (to say that a response has been reinforced, it is not enough to know that it occurs often).

Some phylogenic features might come about as incidental by-products of selection. The cathedral of San Marco in Venice provides an analogy (Gould & Lewontin, 1979). San Marco has a dome supported by arches. Where two arches come together at the top of a common pillar, the tapering triangular space above the pillar and between the two arches has been filled in and used as a surface for a mosaic. The space is called a *spandrel*, and the mosaics of San Marco fit harmoniously into the spandrels. However, the arches were constructed for the support of the dome and not for the artwork; the dome was not built in order to create the spandrels. The spandrels were an inevitable but incidental by-product of constructing a dome on rounded arches. Analogously, some features of contemporary populations may not be direct products of natural selection; instead, they may be incidental by-products of other unrelated features that have arisen through selection. When the source of an inherited feature is uncertain, the question is sometimes put in terms of the San Marco analogy: Is it a product of natural selection or is it a spandrel?

THE OPPOSITION TO NATURAL SELECTION

Darwin's main arguments were first published in his *On the Origin of Species* (1859/1966). They were warmly received in some quarters and strongly resisted in others. The resistance grew, and by the end of the nineteenth century the belief was widespread that Darwinism was dead. It did not recover until well into the twentieth century. The half century or so that preceded that recovery has been called the eclipse of Darwinism (Bowler, 1983; cf. Catania, 1987).

The reason for the eclipse was not that evolution itself had been discredited but rather that other theories than Darwin's had become dominant. Three prominent alternatives were Lamarckism, orthogenesis, and the combination of Mendelian genetics with mutation theory. In his time, Lamarck did much to make a case for the fact of evolution. His theory was that characteristics acquired during an organism's lifetime could be passed on to its offspring, through changes in the parent's genetic material or germ plasm (but one problem was in saying why advantageous acquired characteristics should be any more likely to be passed on than disadvantageous ones such as injuries).

According to the theory of orthogenesis, evolution was directed by forces within organisms, without reference to the demands of the environment; it could be likened to a developmental unfolding. One manifestation of this unfolding was supposed to be the recapitulation of phylogeny, the evolutionary history of an organism, by ontogeny, its individual development. During ontogeny, the embryo was thought to pass through stages corresponding to its phylogeny (this idea of recapitulation, however, has severe limitations and is no longer central to evolutionary theory; Gould, 1977).

The problem with Mendelian genetics was that by itself it provided no mechanism for variation. In strict Mendelian descent, dominant and recessive genes in one generation determined their proportions in the next. Without variation, there was nothing on which natural selection could work. To provide for the appearance of new forms, Mendelian accounts added mutation theory, which at that time held that evolution proceeded through spontaneous and usually very large genetic changes.

In the nineteenth century, genes were theoretical entities. The techniques of cell biology had not reached the point at which genes had been identified within actual cells. Nevertheless, all of these evolutionary theories assumed that hereditary material of some sort was passed on from one generation to the next and that evolution was determined by its properties. A major flaw in some theories was the assumption that the genetic material constituted a representation or copy of the organism. In the earliest versions of orthogenesis, called preformationism, the embryo was literally a homunculus—a tiny individual complete in all its parts. In later variations, it took on ancestral forms, as ontogeny was said to recapitulate phylogeny. As for Lamarckism, the transmission of acquired characteristics required that they be preserved in the germ plasm in some way, so the germ plasm had to contain some kind of plan of those parts of the organism that were to be altered in subsequent generations. In either case, the germ plasm could be regarded as a representation or copy of the organism.

A *recipe* is a sequence of procedures or instructions. It describes how to create a product, but it does not necessarily incorporate a description of the product (a recipe for a cake does not look like a cake). A recipe can be informative, but it is not likely to contain information about its origins, such as the number of tries it took to make it work. A *blueprint,* on the other hand, does not ordinarily say how to construct the structure that it shows. Like a recipe, it can be informative; but it, too, is likely to omit information about its origins, such as the order in which different parts were designed. A blueprint is a representation or copy but a recipe is not; Lamarckism and the preformationist orthogenetic accounts treated genetic materials as blueprints rather than recipes.

A major achievement in contemporary biology was the reinterpretation of genetic material not as a blueprint for the organism's structure but rather as a recipe for its development (see Dawkins, 1986, Chap. 11, for an elaboration of the metaphors of blueprint and recipe). The modern formulation demanded rethinking of the sense in which genetic material can be said to contain information, whether about evolutionary history or about the structure of the organism (cf. Dawkins, 1982, Chap. 9). Genetic materials provide limited information about the past environments in which they have been selected because they do not include the genetic materials of all those other organisms that did not survive. They also provide limited information about the eventual structure of an organism because they are recipes for the production of proteins rather than blueprints for body parts. The implications were profound. One is that Lamarckism and at least some varieties of orthogenesis became untenable alternatives to Darwinian selection because their implicit copy theories were inconsistent with what had been learned about how the genetic material worked.

This is the appropriate place for the ontogenic analogy. Skinner has often argued that organisms do not make copies of the world (e.g., "Organisms do not store the phylogenic or ontogenic contingencies to which they are exposed; they are changed by them" [Skinner, 1988, p. 302]). Here, too, the analogy of recipe versus blueprint is helpful. Once effective behavior has been selected in ontogeny, it is more appropriate to say that the organism has a recipe for behaving effectively in certain circumstances than that the organism has a blueprint for behavior. The advantage of the vocabulary of recipes is that it provides an alternative to that of representations and copies. (It may also be worthwhile to note that not all usages of the language of representations imply that representations are copies. For example, remembering a seen letter by its sound is sometimes called a representation, but rather than being a copy, it is a recipe for saying the letter later when it is recalled.)

It is time to return to the Darwinian part of the story. It is ironic that, along with Lamarckism and orthogenesis, Mendelian genetics had also been seen as a serious challenge to Darwinian selection. The integration of Mendelian genetics with Darwinian selection in the 1920s and 1930s, known as the modern synthesis, became the core of contemporary biology. Genetic experiments with *drosophila,* the fruit fly, not only elaborated on genetic mechanisms but also brought mutations into the laboratory. With *drosophila,* many generations could be studied within a relatively short time. The research gave evidence on natural rates of mutation and on the magnitude of mutation effects, which were relatively small in comparison to the changes that had been assumed in prior mutation theories. The combination of Mendelian genetics with the facts of mutation provided the variability needed for the workings of natural selection.

The Darwinian view had to face and overcome other problems besides the competing theories (cf. Mayr, 1982). For example, one problem was the incompleteness of the fossil record. What is known of prehistoric life depends on the accidental preservation of occasional members of earlier species, but the circumstances of their preservation and discovery inevitably leaves gaps. Furthermore, hard parts such as bones or shells are much more likely to be preserved than soft parts.

NATURAL AND ARTIFICIAL SELECTION

Each of the three varieties of selection described by Skinner (1981b) involves some kind of variation that provides the source materials upon which it operates, and each has some basis for selecting what survives. The first kind, phylogenic selection, has already been discussed. In ontogenic selection, responses are affected by their consequences within the lifetime of the individual organism. For the food-deprived organism, for example, responses that produce food continue to occur; other responses do not. Food is the consequence that selects some responses and not others. The responses that produce food survive, and the others extinguish. Such cases of selection are instances of reinforcement; reinforcement can also occur in particular environments or settings when a situation sets the occasion on which responses are reinforced. Parallels between natural selection and the ontogenic selection of behavior by its consequences have been explored elsewhere in considerable detail (e.g., Catania, 1978, 1987; Skinner, 1981b; T. L. Smith, 1986).

Thus, what follows elaborates on just one aspect of those parallels: the problems of acceptance that each has faced.

Like Galileo's displacement of the earth from the center of the universe to an orbit around the sun, these accounts overturned traditional ways of thinking about the place of our species in nature. Some of the substantive challenges have also been similar. For example, as noted earlier, artificial selection was familiar in Darwin's time; what was questioned was whether such selection could operate naturally. The operant parallel is provided by shaping, which is also an artificial selection procedure, as when an experimenter shapes a pigeon's figure-eight turns or as when a behavior therapist shapes the vocalizations of a nonverbal institutionalized child. The effectiveness of shaping is self-evident; what is questioned is whether it operates naturally to produce some of the varied patterns of behavior that are seen in everyday life.

It would be best to have documented cases in which the changes in contingencies have been identified early and tracked. Typically, however, only outcomes are available, after the natural contingencies have already done their work. For example, it can be assumed that ontogenic selection was involved in shaping the skill with which grizzly bears catch salmon in the rivers of the Pacific Northwest, but what is seen are the differences between the inefficient performances of the young novices and the well-coordinated actions of the experienced adults. The shaping itself is not seen because it continues over too long a time (the phylogenic analogy is in the incompleteness of the fossil record).

Furthermore, shaping can be hard to see if one does not know what to look for; someone who has actually done shaping is more apt to notice it in natural environments than someone who has only read about it. Thus, the parents who always wait awhile before attending to a crying child may not notice that they have gradually shaped louder and more annoying cries. The attention reinforces the crying, and annoying cries are, by definition, the ones most likely to get attention. If one watches what a parent does when a child throws tantrums, it is often easy to guess where the tantrums came from.

The contingencies that produce such problem behavior seldom occur in isolation, so other behavior or other reinforcers may eventually displace the problem behavior. The spontaneous disappearance of the problem behavior might be taken as evidence that the behavior had a source independent of shaping. Yet, it would be as inappropriate to draw such a conclusion in this ontogenic case as it would be to use evidence that the extinction of dinosaurs was a by-product of the impact of comets to support the conclusion that dinosaurs did not evolve as a result of natural selection.

Time is another factor in the acceptance of both types of selection. For Darwinian natural selection, the question was once whether the earth had existed long enough for such selection to have taken place. The estimate for the age of the earth in the nineteenth century was so short that it did not seem that there had been enough time for evolution to have come about through natural selection. That issue has been laid to rest because the age of the earth has been revised vastly upward during this century.

The comparable problem is easier to deal with for ontogenic selection. Shaping can be demonstrated over minutes rather than over days or years or millennia. If reinforcers can do so much to behavior when contingencies are deliberately arranged over relatively short periods of time, it is reasonable to assume that they will also affect behavior when natural contingencies operate over substantial periods throughout an organism's lifetime. The issue has been particularly controversial with respect to the acquisition of verbal behavior in children, and only limited data are available to demonstrate the role of contingencies (e.g., Moerk, 1983; Whitehurst & Valdez-Menchaca, 1988).

Many contingencies may take hold of behavior over the course of months or years in the life of a young child. Some may be subtle, especially given the very broad range of events that can serve as reinforcers. Some may produce behavior that is desirable; others may do the opposite. The self-injurious behavior of an institutionalized nine-year-old child may seem resistant to change, but nine years is a very long time over which contingencies can operate. This does not mean that all such behavior is solely a product of contingencies. In the face of such possibilities, however, it is certainly more appropriate to be alert for the effects of such contingencies than to assume that they do not exist. A new kind of behavioral ecology is needed: The time is ripe to document the operation of natural contingencies.

CULTURAL SELECTION

The third variety of selection occurs when behavior can be passed on from one organism to another, as in imitation or, more important, as in verbal behavior. For example, what someone has said or written can survive that person's death if it is passed on to and repeated by others. The verbal behavior that has survived within and been shared among the members of a group is part of the culture of that group. Behavior shared in this way need not be correlated with genetic relatedness (e.g., one need not be a member of an ethnic group to learn how to cook that kind of ethnic food). It remains to be seen whether the analysis of the selection of social and cultural practices requires an expansion of the existing taxonomy of behavioral processes (compare Catania, 1983; Dawkins, 1976; Harris, 1977; Skinner, 1957, 1981b).

Whatever else is involved in cultural selection, it is relevant to point out that the contents of this very volume illustrate some of its properties. Behavior analysis is a set of practices, and these practices are passed on from one generation of students to the next. A significant consequence of Skinner's analysis of the varieties of selection is that the science of behavior generated by these practices has been turned upon the practices themselves. Analyses of the contingencies that increase the effectiveness with which the practices of behavior analysis are taught are also likely to ensure the survival of those practices. The analysis of verbal behavior is central to that endeavor, and the properties of verbal behavior place it squarely in the realm of the third variety of selection. That is why Skinner's legacy, like Darwin's, will be an enduring one.

Chapter 15 ⎯⎯⎯⎯⎯⎯⎯⎯⎯⎯⎯⎯⎯⎯⎯⎯⎯⎯⎯⎯⎯⎯

Conclusion: Some Historiography of Behavior Analysis and Some Behavior Analysis of Historiography

Edward K. Morris, James T. Todd,
Bryan D. Midgley, Susan M. Schneider,
and Lisa M. Johnson

That behavior analysis had become an active basic research program by the middle of the twentieth century is evident in the founding of the *Journal of the Experimental Analysis of Behavior* (*JEAB*) (est. 1958; see Skinner, 1966c). That it soon thereafter established an active applied program of research is evident in the founding of the *Journal of Applied Behavior Analysis* (*JABA*) (est. 1968; see Baer, Wolf, & Risley, 1968). By the early 1970s, the field had matured sufficiently to warrant a journal devoted to the conceptual analysis of behavior—*Behaviorism* (est. 1972; now *Behavior and Philosophy*). Then, with the founding of the Association for Behavior Analysis (ABA) in 1975, and the publication of its house journal, *The Behavior Analyst* (est. 1978), these three subdisciplines—basic, applied, and conceptual—were integrated more formally as a discipline unto itself. Behavior analysis is, today, *contemporary behaviorism* (Day, 1980).

The discipline has continued to grow, and in one way especially: It has developed a concern with the collection, organization, and examination of historical materials about its past practices and products. This literature comprises (1) bibliographies of the work of particular scholars, most notably that of B. F. Skinner (e.g., Epstein, 1977, this volume); (2) graphs describing the growth of the discipline, for instance, growth in the number of behavioral journals (e.g., Wyatt, Hawkins, & Davis, 1986); (3) citation analyses of important features of the discipline, both present (e.g., women's contributions, see Meyers, 1993) and past (e.g., sales of *The Behavior of Organisms;* see Knapp, 1986a); and (4) indexes for unindexed texts of historical significance, such as Skinner's autobiographical volumes (e.g., Skinner, 1979; see Epstein & Olson, 1983, 1984).

Clearer evidence of the discipline's maturity, however, lies in the emergence of more serious historical research and writing, that is, in the emergence of historiography regarding the discipline's development, both as a whole (e.g., Day, 1980) and in each of its subdisciplines—basic (e.g., Boakes, 1984), applied (e.g., Kazdin, 1978), and conceptual (e.g., L. D. Smith, 1986). The present book volume constitutes a further case in point. Although the book is in no way definitive, it joins with other recent work as part of the emergence of the new history of behaviorism (cf. Furumoto, 1989; see Morris, Todd, Midgley, Schneider, & Johnson, 1990).

This concluding chapter offers an overview of behavior-analytic historiography and integrates the preceding chapters into that literature in the process. More specifically, this chapter (1) introduces the discipline of historiography as it pertains to behavior analysis; (2) it organizes the historical materials by source and by type and topic; (3) it offers reasons for the conduct of behavior-analytic historiography; and (4) it describes three methodological considerations pertinent to the conduct and evaluation of historical research and writing—internalist versus externalist, great person versus Zeitgeist, and presentist versus historicist—offering a behavior-analytic perspective on each. By way of introduction, let us turn first to the nature and purpose of historiography.

HISTORIOGRAPHY

Whereas "history" is largely a chronological rendering of events, sometimes with explanations regarding cause and effect, "historiography" (ca. 1535) is, broadly speaking, the writing of history; but it is more than that. It is

the writing of history; *esp*: the writing of history based on the critical examination of sources, the selection of particulars from the authentic materials, and the synthesis of particulars into a narrative that will stand the test of critical methods. (*Webster's Ninth New Collegiate Dictionary,* 1987, p. 573)

As such, historiography is both a discipline unto itself (ca. 1800) and a domain of scholarship within other academic disciplines. As a discipline unto itself, its methods are largely independent of any particular field of inquiry (see Beringer, 1978; Bloch, 1953; Cantor & Schneider, 1967). Indeed, from a behavior-analytic perspective, historiography could even approach the status of science itself (Parrott & Hake, 1983). Alternatively, as a domain of scholarship, historiography is manifestly about something, for instance, about the natural science (e.g., biology) and the social sciences (e.g., sociology) (see, e.g., Brozek & Pongratz, 1980), in which case it is part of the conceptual sub-discipline of these disciplines.

In either case, historiography entails the process and product of (1) methods for collecting and organizing historical materials for their authenticity, soundness, and significance; (2) the analysis and integration of these materials, often in the context of other historiography; and (3) the critical evaluation of texts based on these materials, the latter of which gives rise to the three methodological considerations mentioned earlier.

The Purposes of Historiography

The purposes of historiography and studying its products are legion (see Kantor, 1964; Wertheimer, 1980). Coleman (this volume) has described those most commonly cited: Historiography (1) helps resolve current dilemmas by examining their origins and development; (2) illustrates how a discipline may have gone astray and what its future may hold; (3) describes how various cultural, political, economic, intellectual, social, and personal factors affect a discipline's growth and how those factors influence its methodology, assumptions, and values, often in ways unknown to its practitioners; and (4) keeps us from repeating the errors of the past. In words attributed to George Santayana, "Those who cannot remember the past are condemned to repeat it." Farrington (1949b) nicely summarizes these and additional purposes:

History is the most fundamental science, for there is no human knowledge which cannot lose its scientific character when men forget the conditioning under which it originated, the questions which it answered, and the function it was created to serve. A great part of the mysticism and superstition of educated men consists of knowledge which has broken base from its historical moorings. (p. 311)

Although these are important purposes, justifying them all is beyond the purview of this chapter; readers are otherwise referred to Coleman (this volume). For the present, four more-circumscribed purposes of behavior-analytic historiography are offered—two here and two later.

Clarifying the Scientific Discipline. That behavior analysts are interested in the history of their discipline may seem odd, for John B. Watson's (1913) classical behaviorism was, in part, a counteraction to the history and traditions of psychology until his time, or to history and traditions that were not his own (see Heidbreder, 1933, pp. 234–286; Samelson, 1994). Watson's behaviorism was self-statedly a "fresh clean start" to the problems of psychology (Watson, 1924a, p. 4). It was modern, pragmatic, and forward looking, not overly concerned with the past because the causes of behavior are in the present—"History is more or less bunk," as Henry Ford once put it (1916; see Skinner, 1982, p. 196). Although Watson's vision of psychology remains fresh, it is neither new nor well understood, especially with respect to its contributions (or lack thereof) to behavior analysis today (see Logue, 1994) and culture at large (see Coon, 1994).

Herein lies an opportunity and one purpose for behavior-analytic historiography: Behavior analysis can be understood not only in terms of its current internal practices and the external contrasts those practices make with psychology as a whole, but also in terms of how those practices and contrasts evolved historically (see Baum, 1994; Salzinger, 1994). Just as the behavior of an organism is a function of its history, so too is the activity of a scientific discipline, that is, the history of the behavior of its scientists (see Hull, 1988).

Skinner's 1931 paper, "The Concept of the Reflex in the Description of Behavior," is suggestive about what benefits might accrue from this Machian approach to historical analysis (see Marr, 1985, pp. 130–131). Skinner (1931) wrote:

Certain historical facts are considered for two reasons: to discover the nature of the observations upon which the concept [of the reflex] has been based, and to indicate the source of the incidental interpretations with which we are concerned. (p. 427)

In considering these facts, Skinner was able to clear away irrelevant associations and assumptions and thereby elucidate the generic and molar character of his subject matter—the reflex as a correlation of stimuli and responses (Skinner, 1935). With that accomplished, a unit of analysis could be defined and a research program begun, both undeterred by prior irrelevancies. In a like manner, the historiography of behavior analysis may clarify the central features of the discipline such that its basic, applied, and conceptual programs may continue undeterred—or at least less deterred—by misguided associations and assumptions, both from within and from without. Such clarification seems forever a challenge (see Catania & Harnad, 1988; Zuriff, 1985).

Developing the Behavior-Analytic Philosophy. A second purpose of behavior-analytic historiography is to enhance the behavior-analytic conceptual system. Not only does the study of the history of a scientific discipline seem inevitably to clarify the philosophy of its science, such study also contributes to the development of its philosophy. Just as a theory of behavior emerges from ongoing basic and applied analyses of behavior (see Skinner, 1947, 1950, 1956), so too does the philosophy of the science of behavior emerge from ongoing conceptual analyses—conceptual analyses of which historiography is an integral part.

One point embedded in this purpose is that today's philosophy of the science of behavior will not be tomorrow's, nor should it be. Behavior-analytic philosophy will continue evolving as long as behavior analysts analyze the behavior of organisms, including their own behavior as scientists. In this context, Skinner's (1938) observation about empirical systems seems true as well for conceptual systems:

It would be an anomalous event in the history of science if *any* current system [read: philosophy of the science of behavior] should prove to be ultimately the most convenient (and hence, so far as science is concerned, correct). The collection of relevant data [read: conceptual analyses] has only just begun. (p. 438)

The historiography of behavior analysis can contribute to the collection of these "relevant data" as part of the ongoing conceptual analysis of behavior, as well as to the conceptual analysis of those conceptual analyses, and so on. As such, historiography will yield material for the continued evolution of behavior-analytic philosophy and epistemology (see, e.g., Hayes, Hayes, Reese, & Sarbin, 1993; Hineline, this volume; Lee, 1988; Morris, 1988, pp. 293–298). With this as background, we now turn to the nature of historiographic resources and the lineage of behavior analysis.

HISTORIOGRAPHIC SOURCES AND THE LINEAGE OF BEHAVIOR ANALYSIS

Preparing an overview of the extant materials on the history of behavior analysis presupposes some agreement about what behavior analysis uniquely constitutes, both previously and at present. That is not always so easy a task, though, as can be gleaned from some of the preceding chapters and commentaries (e.g., Rachlin, this volume). Even where agreement can be reached, we still face the problem that behavior analysis did not emerge preformed. Rather, it developed in part from Watson's behaviorism and the subsequent neobehaviorist versions, of which Tolman's, Hull's, and Skinner's largely dominated experimental psychology in the United States between the 1920s and the 1960s (see Hilgard, this volume). The history of behavior analysis thus reaches far back into the history of modern psychology and even farther back into antiquity (see Kantor, 1963). That broad a scope, however, is beyond what can be accomplished at present; thus, we have tried to find (or draw) and describe some lines of fracture so as to manage the diversity of the material.

Historiographic Sources

The first set of fractures is not definitional so much as organizational, but the material described is illustrative. These fractures are drawn along the lines of the three sources of historical material—primary, secondary, and tertiary. The differential inclusion of these materials in historical writing (e.g., the ratio of secondary to primary sources) produces consequences that affect the nature, quality, and usefulness of the resulting historiography. This is an important methodological consideration, perhaps fundamental to all the others.

Tertiary Sources. Tertiary material, which is drawn from primary, secondary, and other tertiary sources, encompasses general textbook and survey treatments of a discipline. Such work provides an overview of a discipline's history, along with references to pertinent secondary and primary sources.

As a whole, the history of behavior analysis has received no comprehensive textbook treatment, nor have any of its subdisciplines, except applied behavior analysis (i.e., Kazdin, 1978). The most widely available tertiary materials are chapters on the history of behaviorism written for textbooks on the history and systems of psychology. Some of these chapters are excellent in insight and exposition, for instance, Heidbreder's chapter on behaviorism in her *Seven Psychologies* (1933), while others are technically sound about certain aspects of behaviorism at the middle of the century (e.g., Marx & Cronan-Hillix, 1987, pp. 145–188, 313–379). As for the history of *behavior analysis* per se, this is usually described in whatever history of "radical behaviorism" subsections may be found in these chapters (e.g., Leahey, 1992a, pp. 387–397). Few of these chapters, though, stand out for special mention. They are often dated, incomplete, or relatively pro forma in scholarship. They may also misrepresent—not merely criticize—behavior analysis through error and innuendo (Todd & Morris, 1992).

One set of tertiary material that does not suffer these liabilities may be found in the historical treatments offered in behavior-analytic textbooks. Some of these texts intersperse "history of" material throughout, as in Catania's *Learning* (1992). Other texts devote full chapters to such material, as do Martin and Pear (1992, pp. 380–392) in "Giving It All Some Perspective: A Brief History" (see also Tawney & Gast, 1984, pp. 13–49).

Secondary Sources. In contrast to the survey treatments offered by the tertiary sources, secondary sources have more circumscribed-goals. As books, monographs, and articles, their scholarship is deeper and more closely focused on specific topics, for instance, on specific eras, individuals, places, controversies, publications, concepts, and terminology. The historical material on behavior analysis—like most of that in this volume—is composed largely of such secondary sources, material itself based on primary and other secondary sources. Among the topics addressed by the secondary sources are those covering important periods in the discipline's development, such as Watson's research career as a comparative psychologist and ethologist (e.g., Logue, 1978; Todd & Morris, 1986; see Boakes, 1994; Dewsbury, 1994) and as a public figure (Buckley, 1994; Burnham, 1994). Other secondary source material covers various episodes and interludes, for instance, Skinner's "dark year" (Coleman, 1985a); individuals, such as Pavlov (Skinner, 1981a); institutions, such as Harvard University (Keller, 1970); cultural contexts, such as Skinner and the American tradition (Bjork, in press); controversies, such as the continuity of species (Logue, 1978); concepts, such as the operant (Scharff, 1982); and terminology, such as "radical behaviorism" (Schneider & Morris, 1987).

One secondary source that does not fit neatly into the foregoing categories deserves special mention: Willard Day's (1980) chapter, "The Historical

Antecedents of Contemporary Behaviorism." Although Day's treatment of the history of behavior analysis, especially of its conceptual lineages, is as broad ranging as one might find in any tertiary source, his analysis is vastly more subtle, scholarly, and astute. To date, his chapter is the best available treatment of the broad historical–philosophical underpinnings of the discipline.

Although Day focused on conceptual material, he related it—albeit briefly—to the other two branches of the discipline, which brings us to a third purpose of behavior-analytic historiography: Historiography can clarify and strengthen the discipline's underlying unity by integrating its subdisciplines, especially when diversity among them leaves them isolated from one another in ways not conducive to the field's overall development (see Moxley, 1989). Just as various subdisciplines within physics and biology complement one another—for example, theoretical and quantum physics, or evolutionary biology and systematics—so too can the different subdisciplines of behavior analysis. Behavior analysis is not merely the sum of its basic, applied, and conceptual programs. It is their interrelationship, wherein each draws strength and integrity from the others. With the unity of behavior analysis clarified, the whole of the discipline emerges as, shall we say, greater than the sum of its parts.

Primary Sources. Primary sources are fundamental to the conduct of historiography, for they constitute the "raw data" from which the secondary sources draw. Primary sources encompass books, chapters, and manuscripts (published and unpublished), written by members of the discipline and by those who prefigured it (see Keller, this volume), as well as correspondence, notes, interviews, business records, catalogues, and scientific instruments. Primary sources are often described in manuscript notes (e.g., footnotes and endnotes) such that serious historiography often has a relatively high note-to-text ratio: These notes support the historiography with detail and data, just as do data appendixes in research reports.

Published primary-source materials are, of course, widely available in libraries, or accessible through microfilm and the electronic media (e.g., PsycLIT CD-ROM). As for unpublished materials, they are available in public and private archives, both in the United States and abroad. One step in locating these sources would be to consult Sokal and Rafail's (1982), *A Guide to Manuscript Collections in the History of Psychology and Related Areas* (see also Woodward, 1980). Not covered in this guide, however, are newer collections, for example, Skinner's materials at the Harvard University Archives.

The Smithsonian Institution also houses relevant primary sources, as does the Archives of the History of American Psychology.[1] The latter, for instance, is the repository for business records from the Society for the Experimental Analysis of Behavior, as well as "some records from the offices of various editors of its journals, *JEAB* and *JABA*" (James A. Dinsmoor, Report of the Ad Hoc Committee on the History of Behavior Analysis, December 3, 1987).

Two other sources of primary material are also available. First, obviously, are the autobiographical writings of behavior analysts and their predecessors.

These are available as books (e.g., Skinner, 1983), chapters (e.g., see Keller, 1994), and journal articles (e.g., Keller, 1989, 1992), primarily those written by Watson, Skinner, and Keller. A second source is historical publications reprinted in books and journals, for example, Skinner's (1944/1989b) review of Clark Hull's *Principles of Behavior* (1943). These reprints are sometimes accompanied by material that offers important scholarship of its own, for instance, Wood's (1986) commentary on Russell's (1927) review of Ogden and Richards's (1923) *The Meaning of Meaning*, in which Russell described some affinity with Watson's *Behaviorism* (1924a). As for sourcebooks, whose purpose is to organize and reprint historically pertinent primary source materials (e.g., Herrnstein & Boring, 1965), behavior analysis unfortunately has none.[2]

Having now drawn these organizational fractures with respect to the sources of material on the history of behavior analysis, and provided examples pertinent to behavior analysis, we return to the earlier problem of finding (or drawing) lines of fracture with respect to the lineage of behavior analysis.

The Lineage of Behavior Analysis

Defined *currently* as a discipline unto itself, behavior analysis is perhaps best equated with Day's (1980, pp. 204–205) description of contemporary behaviorism, for which Skinner's (1974) radical behaviorism and the experimental analysis of behavior (Skinner, 1966c) are definitional. Behavior analysis so construed is cogently presented in chapters by Michael (1985) and Reese (1986), who describe the central features of the discipline, distinguishing it from other philosophies, psychologies, and behaviorisms.

Defined *historically* by lineage, matters are less clear. To argue that behavior analysis did not exist until the term *behavior analysis* attained prominence in the 1970s is not workable because those who were behaviorists before then, and who later called themselves behavior analysts, conducted their science little differently before then than afterwards. Prior to the 1970s, *radical behaviorism* was often used to denote general behavior-analytic practices. Defined as the *philosophy* of the science of behavior (Skinner, 1974, p. 3), however, radical behaviorism does not encompass all that is, or was, behavior analysis. Even if we take radical behaviorism to be synonymous with behavior analysis, the term *radical behaviorism* was not used in published print by Skinner until 1945 (Skinner, 1945), and did not achieve widespread use for his views until the 1960s, when a good deal of behavior analysis had already been conducted. Moreover, Skinner did not even coin the term "radical behaviorism"—Mary Calkins (1921) did in her well-known *Psychological Review* article in which she compared and contrasted Watson's "*radical behaviorism*" with other behaviorisms of the day (see Schneider & Morris, 1987). The further back we go, the more difficult the lineage of behavior analysis is to define and describe.[3]

The historiography of behavior analysis, or of any discipline, should not, of course, overly concern itself with *terms* referring to specific practices but, rather, with the lineage of those *practices,* for it is those practices—basic, applied, and conceptual—that define the discipline. A proper history of behavior analysis, then, will have to trace practices, not terms. In preparing such a history, some compromise among these alternatives will be necessary—compromises that make historiography feasible without at the same time foregoing necessary breadth and depth of coverage. In other words, in describing the lineage of behavior analysis, the discipline will eventually need to approach its history in ways that neither overly constrain its purview through narrow operational definitions nor permit overly idiosyncratic, phenomenalistic definitions of behavior analysis as "I know it when I see it." Thus, in the next section, we begin with broader considerations of materials that describe the lineage of behavior analysis (e.g., books on behaviorism) before narrowing the focus more selectively (e.g., behavior-analytic newsletters and bibliographic material).

TYPES AND TOPICS OF HISTORICAL MATERIAL AND THE BEHAVIOR ANALYSIS OF HISTORIOGRAPHY

In describing the extant historical material, we force another set of fractures by organizing it into categories defined by publication type and topic. The first five categories refer to types—books, chapters, journal articles, reference works, and newsletters. The next seven comprise both publication type and topic—autobiographical material; book reviews; memoria; commentaries; professional trends and brief histories; bibliographies, indexes, and reference lists; and pedagogical materials. In what follows, we emphasize the first five; the subsequent seven are covered in a more cursory fashion.[4] We also take up the three historiographic considerations mentioned earlier.

Books

In considering the history of behavior analysis, the most inclusive category of materials might be the extant texts on the history of behaviorism. Here, behaviorism would refer to John B. Watson's (1913, 1919) classical behaviorism and to the behaviorisms arising thereafter. Behavior analysis is, of course, one of these behaviorisms, but not all behaviorisms are strictly behavior analysis (e.g., social or paradigmatic behaviorism, see Woodward, 1982). Hence, not every book would be included. Moreover, even where more general texts might seem appropriate, on close examination they might not be. For instance, Richards's (1987) *Darwin and the Emergence of Evolutionary Theories of Mind and Behavior* (see Ginsburg, 1990) is more about minds and morals than about behaviorism. It has but a single page citation to Skinner and includes no references to his work. This is not a fault with the book, of course, but given its apparent purview, perhaps surprising.

Behaviorism was, and is, not just a discipline but also an intellectual movement—part of the history of Western civilization and part of the social and
cultural history of the United States. As such, behaviorism arises in major
historical works (see, e.g., Lasch, 1979a; May, 1959; Wiebe, 1967), as well
as in literature contemporaneous with Watson, for instance, Berman's (1927)
The Religion Called Behaviorism and Wickham's (1931) *The Misbehaviorists*
(see also Dell, 1930; King, 1930). Although these books do not focus on the
history of behavior analysis per se, they warrant consideration if that history is to
be understood as anything but an "internalist trinity of reason, argument, and evidence" (Hull, 1988, p. 2). This raises the first methodological consideration with
respect to the conduct of historiography—the internalist–externalist dichotomy.

Internalist and Externalist History. Internalist histories of science are
largely self-contained accounts of a discipline's progression through time,
written from within the discipline, often independently of broader intellectual
and social contexts. They are usually written by knowledgeable, but not historically trained, senior members of a field. These histories describe a discipline—its theories, methods, and data—and how it progressed in solving
what are taken to be its well-defined problems through its well-accepted rational, scientific methods and logic (see Kuhn, 1962, on "normal science").
Internalist histories often justify and legitimize the field, its present practices,
and its "great persons." This is history as it has usually been written.

Contemporary historiography, in contrast, is increasingly externalist in nature. It is often written by professional historians outside of a scientific discipline, many of whom will question a discipline's fundamental assumptions,
practices, and principles (see Furumoto, 1989). Indeed, these historians may
not even be neutral in perspective but, rather, work from alternative theoretical orientations, for instance, social constructionism (e.g., Bohan, 1990) or
psychoanalysis (see, e.g., Elms, 1981, on Skinner's writing of *Walden Two*
[1948]). In any event, at the very least, externalist history begins with the
premise that science does not develop independently of the personal characteristics of a discipline's members or of its cultural, political, economic, intellectual, and social contexts. Excellent examples of such externalist
historiography pertinent to some of psychology's underlying social and
sexual biases have been chronicled in Scarborough and Furumoto's (1987)
Untold Lives: The First Generation of American Women Psychologists and in
Guthrie's (1976) *Even the Rat Was White.*

Within behaviorism, Boakes (1984), a well-respected researcher of animal
behavior, comes perhaps the closest to having written an internalist prehistory
of the experimental analysis of behavior, just as Kazdin (1978) has written an
internalist history of applied behavior analysis. Both describe the who, what,
when, where, why, and how of individuals and events that were part of the
early development of these two subdisciplines. In contrast, O'Donnell's
(1985) *The Origins of Behaviorism: American Psychology, 1870–1920* is
externalist. It focuses on the cultural and scientific milieu and the social and

economic pressures that affected the discipline's early development. To point out Boakes (1984), Kazdin (1978), and O'Donnell (1985), though, is not to suggest that their texts exemplify any necessary rights or wrongs. Rather, their work is differentially informed by internal and external considerations such that the strengths of their texts lie in different domains.

As a first attempt at a behavior analysis of historiography, we offer three observations about the internalist–externalist dichotomy, ranging from the penetratingly obvious to the more subtle. First, both internalist and externalist historiography—although not their conflicting theoretical orientations—seem necessary for understanding a scientific discipline. Internalist history provides the "figure" of a discipline's development, while externalist history provides its context or "ground." Neither alone may be sufficient for apprehending the gestalt; an overemphasis on one or the other may distort the historical account. Internalist historians, for example, may overemphasize "reason, argument, and evidence" and concomitantly overlook important external factors that contributed to or inhibited scientific progress (see Zuriff, this volume). In contrast, externalist historians may overgeneralize the external factors and, lacking scientific and technical expertise in the discipline, overlook important particulars when drawing together specific concepts and lineages (see Catania, this volume, on distinctions between S-R psychology and behavior analysis; Hineline, this volume, on the directionality of control).

Second, both internalist and externalist history are relative to one another. For instance, a methodological behaviorist's account of behavior analysis would be external to behavior analysis but internal to psychology as a whole. Internalist and externalist histories are not objectivist things with immutable defining properties. They can only be defined with respect to one another.

Third, all historiography is essentially internalist—it is internal to the cultural time and place in which it is written (see Kantor, 1963, pp. 3–31). Historiographers (and critics alike) cannot step outside the stream of their behavior to know the truth of the history (or criticism) they are writing because "knowing the truth" of that history is also behavior in context (Morris, 1988); that is, historiography is, in part, a social construction (or interpretation) that emerges from the interaction between historians and their materials (compare Nowell-Smith, 1977).

Turning back to the main line of discourse here—that is, books pertinent to the history of behavior analysis—we should not overlook biographies of behaviorism's pioneers and founders. These are central to the history of behaviorism and often relevant to the history of behavior analysis. Among the more notable of these are Pauly's (1987) biography of Loeb (see Logue, 1988), Gray's (1979) and Babkin's (1949) of Pavlov, Jonçich's (1984) of Thorndike, Buckley's (1989) of Watson (see Morris, 1991), and Bjork's (1993) of Skinner (see Wood, 1994).

The work of still other scientists also prefigured important aspects of behaviorism, for instance, Charles Darwin's contributions to evolutionary theory (Clark, 1984), Claude Bernard's contributions to experimental logic (Olmsted, 1938), and Ernst Mach's contributions to positivism (Blackmore, 1972). Biographies of these "great persons," though, rarely speak to specific lineages, parallels, and antiparallels with respect to behavior analysis and may, at this point, be better approached through such secondary sources as Catania (1987) on Darwin, Thompson (1984) on Bernard, and Marr (1985) on Mach (see also Smith, this volume, on Mach and Bacon).

Great Person and Zeitgeist History. This discussion of biographies raises a second methodological consideration affecting the conduct and evaluation of historiography—the dichotomy between the "great person" and the Zeitgeist. Great-person history emphasizes the contributions of particular individuals to the development of a discipline (see Boring, 1950a; Boring 1950b, pp. ix–xii). Although such historiography may be conducted as a straightforward descriptive exercise, it often presupposes more than that. It often presupposes a "personalistic" theory or explanation of scientific development—a theory that assumes great people are necessary for, and even the free and independent agents of, scientific progress. Such historiography, often internalist in nature, emphasizes the rationality and creativity of these individuals and their active, intentional success in advancing science and promoting their careers.

In contrast, Zeitgeist ("spirit of the times") history emphasizes the cultural, political, economic, intellectual, social, and personal conditions present during scientific development (see Boring, 1950a, 1955; R. I. Watson, 1971). It also often presupposes an explanatory theory of how these conditions account for scientific development—what is called a "naturalistic theory." In this view, the appearance that great persons are responsible for scientific advancement is illusory because other people would eventually have accomplished those ends, given the Zeitgeist.

On a behavior-analytic account, the great person–Zeitgeist dichotomy raises three points. First, great person and Zeitgeist historiography are not necessarily incompatible at a descriptive level. Both contribute to the conduct and richness of historiographic accounts. It is at the explanatory level that difficulties and incompatibilities arise.

Second, the Zeitgeist can be badly over generalized. If the history of science is the history of the behavior of scientists, then the unit of conceptual analysis must include the behavior of scientists and the contingencies that enter into their behavior. Individual scientists, however, are affected as much by a Zeitgeist as by specific, often idiosyncratic contingencies within it and their own lives (Hull, 1988). The concept of the Zeitgeist averages the effects of these contingencies across scientists, leaving considerable variability unexplained.

A third behavior-analytic point is that the great person and the Zeitgeist are, in a way, inseparable. The great person is the locus for a confluence of variables both internal and external to science (e.g., cultural, political, economic, intellectual, and social—the Zeitgeist). This person, though, is also a unique locus in that no two scientists ever have the same history, leading each to interact differently with the subject matter and thereby to make contributions to the science that no one else would have made (see Boring, 1955). Both the Zeitgeist and great persons have their effects but not independently of one another. They form a dialectic: Neither has a sole agency or any agency at all without the other.

Returning again to the extant books related to the history of behavior analysis, the criteria for what constitutes "historical" material are not entirely unambiguous. The primary difficulty in the present category of material (i.e., books) is in drawing distinctions in the following two cases. First, although not intended as historiography per se, conceptual–philosophical work often encompasses historical analysis, as in Zuriff's (1985) *Behaviorism: A Conceptual Reconstruction*, L. D. Smith's (1986) *Behaviorism and Logical Positivism: A Reassessment of the Alliance,* and Chiesa's (1994) *Radical Behaviorism: The Philosophy and the Science* (see Moore, this volume; Day and Moore, this volume). Although largely conceptual, these texts also speak substantively not just to the history of behaviorism broadly defined but also to the history of behavior analysis.[5] Thus, whether pristinely historical, conceptual material needs to be examined.

The second difficult case in defining "historical" material is that the books written by behaviorists and behavior analysts are not histories of the discipline per se but of psychology more generally, for instance, Keller's (1937, 1973) *The Definition of Psychology*. These works deserve consulting because of the uniquely behavioral perspective their authors bring to the history of psychology—especially Kantor (1963, 1969) in his two-volume *The Scientific Evolution of Psychology*—and hence to the history of behavior analysis. A similar problem arises closer to the behavior-analytic core in texts on theories of learning, many of which include material of historic interest (see, e.g., Bower & Hilgard, 1981). Authors with special expertise in behavior analysis, however, may have an advantage in placing the discipline within that literature (see, e.g., Malone, 1990).

Before closing this discussion on the available books, one valuable source of materials is often overlooked—dissertations. Indeed, many of the books on the history of behaviorism were originally dissertation projects, for instance, Buckley (1989), O'Donnell (1985), and L. D. Smith (1986). Not all dissertations are published or published quickly, or are easily accessible; thus, the *Dissertation Abstracts International* becomes a useful resource. Looking back far enough, for instance, we find Diehl's (1932) *An Historical and Critical Study of Radical Behaviorism as a Philosophical Doctrine*. More recent are Dean's (1981) *The Evolution of Experimental Operant Psychology*, Gudmundsson's (1983) *The Emergence of B. F. Skinner's Theory of Operant Behavior: A Case Study in the History and Philosophy of Science*, and Wiklander's (1989) *From Laboratory to Utopia: An Inquiry into the Early Psychology and Social Philosophy of B. F. Skinner*.

Chapters

Turning to material available in book chapters, a smaller proportion of these may need consulting with respect to the history of behavior analysis, at least at first. Material on Watson and classical behaviorism should be examined, of course, for instance, Logue's (1985a, 1985b) chapters on the origins and growth of behaviorism. Material on other behaviorists and behaviorisms may need perusal only where they address historical lineages, parallels, and antiparallels with respect to behavior analysis—not so much with respect to behaviorism broadly defined. Material on Watson warrants examination largely because Skinner (1976b, pp. 298–300) wrote that Watson's work prefigured his own. Keller (1982, p. 7; 1994), too, has remarked on Watson's priority in shaping his own views. Thus, although Watson's behaviorism, like those of Tolman and Hull, would not be behavior analysis today, it is the predecessor of the work of those who founded behavior analysis. This does not mean that behavior analysis draws only—or even primarily—from Watson's behaviorism, but rather, that Watson is, in a retrospective reconstruction, its most obvious predecessor. In many important ways, the experimental and conceptual practices of contemporary behaviorism are more broadly informed by traditions outside classical behaviorism than by contemporary behaviorism itself (Day, 1980; see, e.g., Catania, 1987; Skinner, this volume; Smith, this volume; Thompson, 1984).

Once we begin restricting material on these grounds, though, we begin to exclude material on social learning theory, both dynamic (as in Dollard and Miller) and cognitive (as in Bandura); on learning theories other than Skinner's, such as Guthrie's, Hull's, and Tolman's; on the analytic philosophy of Russell, Ryle, and Wittgenstein; on the early behaviorism of Hunter, Lashley, Meyer, Thorndike, and Weiss; on the functionalism and pragmatism of Angell, Carr, Dewey, and Mead; on the Russian reflexology of Bechterev and Pavlov; on the early physiological and comparative psychology of Bernard, Romanes, Morgan, Loeb, Crozier, and Kuo; and on Darwinian evolutionary theory. We can go back even further, for, as Kantor (1968) pointed out, the first behaviorist was probably Aristotle (see Kantor, 1963, pp. 116–151). To paraphrase Ebbinghaus (1910, p. 9), behavior analysis has a short history but a long past.

Presentist and Historicist History. These matters bring us to a third methodological consideration—that of "presentism" and "historicism." A search of the historical literature that is overly narrow and restricted in the definition of behavior analysis may yield a historical account that is not only more internalist than externalist, as discussed above, but also one that is more presentist than historicist (see Fischer, 1935; Samelson, 1974; Stocking, 1965).

Presentist history selects, interprets, and evaluates past discoveries, conceptual advances, and great persons as prescient of science as it has come to be, that is, of the "winning" tradition. On this view, the history of science is important for justifying the present, as though the march through time were simply an ever-increasingly true, almost teleological unfolding of today's "correct" view. It also serves the pedagogical functions of establishing tradition and attracting students (Kuhn, 1968; Samelson, 1974). Presentist history is comforting and feels right, for it is written largely in the context of currently accepted and fashionable views. It is also generally great person-ish. Equally important, not only do presentist histories justify and celebrate winning traditions, but they also celebrate what are taken to be losing traditions. In other words, histories that selectively interpret the past as the justification for the present fall from favor of a particular perspective are presentist as well and not uncommon in material on behaviorism (see, e.g., Mahoney, 1989; Catania, 1991; Morris, 1990).

In contrast, historicism views scientific discoveries, conceptual changes, and historical figures as events to be understood in the context of their own times and places, not in the context of the present (see Furumoto, 1989). On this view, historiography is concerned with the function (or meaning) of past events in their own time and place and less so with their possible function (or meaning) in explaining a discipline at present—an eminently behavior-analytic perspective. Historicist methodology is more exhaustive and less selective in its inclusion of material and historical contingencies. It does not dismiss previous work for not conforming to current fashion, and it makes fewer distinctions about what may and may not be relevant for present purposes. In this regard, historicists commonly regard presentists as naive about historical studies, as the following historicist joke-cum-story attests:

A tourist, recently returned from Greece, was boasting about the fabulous old coin he had purchased for a song on the Athenian black market for antiquities; he had cleverly smuggled it outside the country right in his pants pocket along with his other change. "It's priceless," he bragged, "pure gold, and coined in 469 B.C.!" "How could you tell when it was coined?" asked his skeptical friend. "Easy," came the quick reply, "the date was right on it." (see Marx & Cronan-Hillix, 1987, p. 5)

In 469 B.C., of course, no one could have known that Christ would be born 469 years thence.

Importantly, then historicist history can undermine normative views regarding the foundations and character of a discipline offered in well-accepted presentist accounts—a point made by Brush (1974) in "Should the History of Science Be Rated X?" L. D. Smith's (1986) work, for instance, illustrates the inaccuracy of what is largely believed to have been the alliance between behaviorism and logical positivism such that the demise of logical positivism brought an end to behaviorism (see Koch, 1964) or that the demise of behaviorism was evidence of the flawed methods of logical positivism (see Mackenzie, 1977). The neobehaviorisms, however, did not adhere to logical positivism, but rather to something more like philosophical pragmatism (see Zuriff, 1979a, 1985), at least for Skinner.

Historicist historiography may also identify and correct "origin myths" (Samelson, 1974) about certain features or events in the history of a discipline—features and events to which presentist history often contributes. Such scholarship has been conducted, for instance, by Harris (1979) on Watson and Rayner's (1920) "Little Albert" study (see also Buckley, 1994), by Verhave (1990) on Watson's theory of thinking as but subvocal movements of the larynx (see also Buckley, 1989), and by Costall (1993) on Lloyd Morgan's "canon."

The above notwithstanding—indeed, in light of it—historiography need not be conducted solely for historicist interests. Historiography may be conducted for the express purpose of correcting misunderstandings about presently held views (see Hull, 1979). This is a fourth purpose for behavior-analytic historiography: Contemporary behavior analysis is misunderstood in ways that historicist historiography can correct by describing actual lineages and alliances. Indeed, historicist histories of behavior analysis will often require the revision of currently-accepted and normative, but inaccurate, views about the discipline, both from within and without. From within, recent historicist accounts have shown that the term *radical behaviorism* does not have its roots in Skinner (1945) or its meaning in "thoroughgoing" as so often presumed (see Schneider & Morris, 1987). From without, behavior analysis is commonly depicted as adhering to certain philosophical "isms," such as associationism, objectivism, and certain versions of mechanism, and as overlooking phenomena such as biological and private events, all of which belies its actual views and scope (see Morris, 1988). These are misunderstandings that historiography of a presentist sort can correct. For instance, L. D. Smith's (1986) "demythification" of the behaviorists' alliance with logical positivism has already altered Leahey's (1992a) historical account of the discipline (see Leahey, 1988). Moreover, recent historiography reveals the affinity between poststructuralist linguistics and Skinner's (1957) analysis of verbal behavior (see Andresen, 1990).

Journal Articles

As for the substantive journal articles, reading them all would present obvious logistical difficulties, for that would entail something close to reading all the references cited in the pertinent books and chapters. Thus, any initial journal search might be confined to material published in the primary United States journals having "behavior-analytic" titles—*JEAB, JABA,* and *The Behavior Analyst*—drawing upon original and reprinted materials pertinent to the history of the discipline.

Although these criteria would focus a search of but a few, largely internalist publications, these three journals are arguably at the forefront of basic and applied research and conceptual analysis (Day, 1980). The sources that are eventually examined, though, would have to go beyond these and include, for instance, pertinent material from *Behavior and Philosophy* and the *Journal of the History of the Behavioral Sciences* (est. 1965), and the reference sections of the books and chapters mentioned previously (see also "Reflections on B. F. Skinner and Psychology" in *American Psychologist* [Lattal, 1992]; Chiesa, 1992; Moxley, 1992).

Also not to be overlooked is *The Psychological Record,* founded in 1937 by Kantor, and publication outlet for many behavioral articles, both at present, (e.g., Coleman, [1985b] and historically (e.g., Skinner, (1937a). After that, the other behavior modification and behavior therapy journals might be searched. Still additional resources are the sometimes-difficult-to-obtain or no-longer-published foreign journals, for example, *Behaviour Analysis Letters, Behaviour Change, Behavioural Processes,* the *Japanese Journal of Behavior Therapy,* and the *Mexican Journal of Behavior Analysis.*

Casting our search even wider, we might turn to journals pertinent to the history of science, such as *ISIS* (est. 1913), published by the History of Science Society, and especially its annual *Critical Biography.* Among other journals are the *History of Science* (est. 1962), the *Journal of the History of Ideas* (est. 1948), the *Journal of the History of Philosophy* (est. 1963), and *Studies in the History and Philosophy of Science* (est. 1970).

Although books, chapters, and journal articles comprise the bulk of serious historiographic sources, two other sources often provide useful ancillary material that historicist historiography should not overlook: reference works and newsletters.

Reference Works

Entries on behaviorism and its history found in reference works provide general, although not necessarily infallible, capsule summaries of the discipline at the time and in the intellectual context they were written. Among the works that might be consulted are the *Encyclopedia Britannica,* the *Encyclopedia of Philosophy,* the *Dictionary of the History of Ideas,* and the *Social Science Encyclopedia* (e.g., Bijou, 1985, 1986; Vaughan, 1987). Some of these, such as the *Encyclopedia of the Social Sciences* (see Kallen, 1930), have undergone revision through enough editions that a study of the changes in their coverage might prove a valuable exercise (K. Buckley, personal communication, December 8, 1988).

Reference works that focus more specifically on psychology are likewise a useful source of material. Corsini's *Concise Encyclopedia of Psychology* (1987), for example, contains well-informed entries on behaviorism by Leahey (1987a) and on its history by Krasner (1987). Gregory's (1987) *The Oxford Companion to the Mind* covers similar material and includes as well an entry by B. F. Skinner (1987a)—"Behaviorism, Skinner on." Although more selective, Popplestone and McPherson's *Dictionary of Concepts in General Psychology* (1988) and Pronko's *From AI to Zeitgeist* (1988) offer accurate and still deeper coverage.

Newsletters

Although not typically archival in nature, a search of the newsletters of behavioral organizations and their special interest groups, and of behavioral divisions of nonbehavioral organizations, also warrant a systematic search. Among these are the *ABA Newsletter;* the Association for the Advancement of Behavior Therapy's *The Behavior Therapist;* and APA Division 25's newsletter, *The Recorder. The Recorder* (1990, Vol. 24/25, Issue 3), for instance, published memoria in honor of Skinner written by the Division's past presidents. The *ABA Newsletter* has also offered brief pieces on the history of behavior analysis (see, e.g., Michael, 1991). More generally, Cheiron, the International Society for the History of the Behavioral and Social Sciences (est. 1968), publishes a newsletter and holds annual meetings, as does APA Division 26 for the History of Psychology (est. 1965), whose newsletter publishes occasional "bibliography updates."

Material by Type and Topic

In this final section, we turn briefly to the remaining categories of material: autobiographical; book reviews; commentaries; memoria; professional trends and brief histories; biographies, indexes, and reference lists; and pedagogical.

Autobiographical Material. Autobiographical materials will need to be searched, perhaps beginning with the series *A History of Psychology in Autobiography* (see Lindzey, 1989), which includes chapters by Watson (1936) and Skinner (1970). We would also want, of course, to read Keller's and Skinner's autobiographical volumes, chapters, and articles (e.g., Keller, 1982; Skinner, 1983).

Book Reviews. Reviews of books on behaviorism not only describe their content but often contribute to historiography through the scholarly interpretation and evaluation of texts. They allow us, for example, to approach the history of behavior analysis in a more informed fashion through reviews of books whose historical analyses are not accurate on all accounts. Zuriff's (1979a) review of Mackenzie's *Behaviorism and the Limits of Scientific Method* (1977), for instance, is helpful in this regard. Retrospective reviews of classic works are also important, for they offer still further historical analyses. Among these are Marr (1985) on Ernst Mach's *The Science of Mechanics* (1893/1960), Thompson (1984) on Claude Bernard's *An Introduction to the Study of Experimental Medicine* (1865/1957), and those in a special 1988 issue of *JEAB* in honor of the fiftieth anniversary of the publication of Skinner's (1938) *The Behavior of Organisms* (see, e.g., Dinsmoor, this volume; Galbicka, 1988; Thompson, 1988).

Commentaries. Commentaries consist largely of journal and newsletter publications that are briefer and more informal than the substantive journal articles described earlier. These are sometimes commissioned in celebration of historically significant events, for instance, the thirtieth anniversary of the first Conference on the Experimental Analysis of Behavior (Dinsmoor, 1987) but are more often submitted as comments on previously published articles (e.g., Mountjoy & Ruben, 1984) and book reviews (e.g., Samelson, 1981). The latter are especially valuable where they correct historiography that is poor or technically unsound, for instance, Harris's (1981) comment on Begelman's (1980) review of Cohen's (1979) biography of Watson.

Memoria. Memoria written in honor of behaviorists and behavior analysts might also be examined to good effect, for example, Skinner's (1981a) comments on Pavlov (see also *The Recorder* as mentioned above). These can serve as important adjuncts to biographical and autobiographical material.

Professional Trends and Brief Histories. Brief histories and materials on professional trends describe a discipline's development, often quantitatively conveyed through tables and figures. These are the "institutional" components of the history of a discipline typically overlooked in favor of the grand history of ideas. Material is available, for instance, on the founding of the ABA (e.g., Peterson, 1978), publication trends and demographics in *JEAB* (e.g., Williams & Buskist, 1983), citation analyses of such behavior-analytic texts as *Verbal Behavior* (Skinner, 1957; see McPherson, Bonem, Green, & Osborne, 1984), and the natural history of *The Behavior of Organisms* (see Knapp, this volume).

A distinction that might be drawn at this point is one between quantitative and qualitative historiography. Qualitative historiography is the more common form. It involves the analysis and integration of materials on a discipline's history—materials that range, for instance, from its conceptual basis (e.g., Zuriff, 1985), to its theories (e.g., Skinner, 1950), to its unit of analysis (e.g., Skinner, 1935), and to its scientific methods (e.g., Skinner, 1956). Quantitative historiography, in contrast, is just as it suggests: It describes and analyzes history via tables, graphs, and statistics in ways that words alone sometimes cannot convey (see Haskins & Jeffery, 1990; Simonton, 1990). For instance, Buskist and Miller (1982) have described the importance of particular research topics in the experimental analysis of behavior via citation analyses. Suffice it to say, however, that the standards for scholarship and logic are no less rigorous or refined in quantitative than in qualitative historiography, the "softness" or the "hardness" of the data notwithstanding (Young, 1966). Each approach informs the other.

Bibliographies, Indexes, and Reference Lists. Bibliographies of the work of important figures in behavior analysis are useful because they document those contributions and otherwise inform the historical record (see, e.g., R. I. Watson, 1976a, pp. 438–439; 1976b, pp. 1060–1066, for primary and secondary source references to J. B. Watson; cf. Todd, Dewsbury, Logue, & Dryden, 1994). Prepared subject indexes to texts containing important historical content, such as Epstein and Olson's (1983) indexes for Skinner's autobiographies or Knapp's (1974) for Skinner's *Beyond Freedom and Dignity* (1971), facilitate the location of historiographically significant material. The same is true, as well, for prepared reference lists for books lacking them (e.g., *Verbal Behavior*, see Morris & Schneider, 1986). These materials do not elucidate the history of behavior analysis so much as they are tools for historiographic research.

Pedagogical Material. Finally, a small but important literature exists for those interested in teaching the history of psychology and of behavior analysis within that history. For this, the special 1979 issue of the *Teaching of Psychology* (Vol. 6, Issue 1) might be consulted; it is published by APA's Division 2 for the Teaching of Psychology. Thoughtful articles were included on the content of such courses (e.g., Raphelson, 1979; Robinson, 1979; see also Woodward, 1980, pp. 46–51), as well as specific instructional strategies (e.g., Benjamin, 1979; Caudle, 1979; see also Berrenberg, 1990; Coffield, 1973). Additional material has also been published on how to involve students in preparing departmental histories (see Benjamin, 1990; see also Hilliz & Broyles, 1980; Weigel & Gottfurcht, 1972).

CONCLUSION

This chapter has introduced the discipline of historiography, offered an overview of the available material on the history of behavior analysis, presented several purposes for conducting behavior-analytic historiography and engaging its products, and presented three methodological considerations pertinent to historiographic inquiry.

The methodological considerations, in particular—like those in basic and applied research—are fundamental. Rigorous descriptive and analytic methods are required in the basic, applied, and conceptual (including historical) analyses of behavior, in both the process of analysis and the evaluation of the products of that process. Historiography can never be bias free, of course, because historiographers can never step out of their own historical and current contexts. By making methodological considerations and standards explicit, we improve our basis for producing and evaluating the products of such work.

Just as in other conceptual analyses, historiography allows us, as Skinner (1979, p. 282) might have put it, to discover uniformities, to order confusing data, and to resolve puzzlement about the diverse heritage and present practices of behavior analysis. In other words, just as the proper organization of our empirical data enhances our effectiveness in describing and predicting behavior, so too does proper historiography assist in establishing and clarifying the behavior-analytic world view, in enhancing our understanding of the discipline, in bringing unity to a discipline of seemingly independent subdisciplines, and in correcting misunderstandings about it. Having now introduced these historical materials and described some relevant methodological considerations, perhaps the use to which these are put will further these ends. This chapter can only be the beginning of more serious behavior-analytic historiography.

AUTHORS' NOTE

This chapter owes much to an introduction to a bibliography on the history of behavior analysis prepared for Division 25 of the APA under the auspices of the Division's Ad Hoc Committee on that topic—James A. Dinsmoor (chair), Alexandra W. Logue, Edward K. Morris, and W. Scott Wood (members)—and published in *The Behavior Analyst* (Morris, Todd, Midgley, Schneider, & Johnson, 1990; Copyright, Society for the Advancement of Behavior Analysis; see also Morris, 1993b). We thank Kerry W. Buckley, A. Charles Catania, S. R. Coleman, Deborah J. Coon, Alan Costall, Ernest R. Hilgard, Fred S. Keller, Terry Knapp, Victor G. Laties, Marion White McPherson, and B. F. Skinner for providing references, advice, and commentary on the original project and for taking time to lead us gently through historiography of which we were unaware.

Appendix

An Updated Bibliography of
B. F. Skinner's Works

Robert Epstein

At a professional meeting a few years ago, I gave a talk about my penchant for collecting and cataloging "Skinneria," called, "Running Just to Keep in the Same Place." Like the Red Queen in *Alice in Wonderland*, I had to run fast just to stay still because Skinner produced new works of all sorts at a high rate. Alas, now that he has died (in August 1990), I may finally catch up. I will miss the exercise dearly.

This is the third bibliography of Skinner's works I have published, and yet another has been in preparation for over a decade: Terry Knapp and I will soon complete a book entitled *B. F. Skinner: An Annotated Guide to Primary and Secondary References.*

Listed here are Skinner's major published papers and books. Many have been reprinted, sometimes under different titles. Without exception, I have listed only the first version of the work and omitted a great many lesser publications—abstracts, book reviews, prefaces and forewords, short comments, and letters to editors, for example—many of which are notable and all of which will be included in the *Annotated Guide*. Skinner's words are also preserved in films, audiotapes and videotapes, and scores of published interviews. Thousands of pages of unpublished writings remain for the historians—personal notes, correspondence, unpublished manuscripts, classroom materials, memoranda to colleagues, grant proposals and progress reports, patent materials, construction manuals, and even a script for a television show that was never produced. The Harvard archives currently holds more than 27 cubic feet of such materials in eighty-two boxes, and that is just the beginning.

I am grateful to Julie S. Vargas, Skinner's daughter and director of the B. F. Skinner Foundation, for allowing me to access to Foundation materials to complete this listing.

All of the information below has been verified in the original sources. Brackets next to the names of co-authors indicate the order in which the names appeared.

BIBLIOGRAPHY

On the conditions of elicitation of certain eating reflexes. *Proceedings of the National Academy of Sciences*, 1930, *16*, 433–38.

On the inheritance of maze behavior. *Journal of General Psychology*, 1930, *4*, 342–46.

The progressive increase in the geotropic response of the ant *Aphaenogaster. Journal of General Psychology*, 1930, *4*, 102–12. (with T. C. Barnes [1])

The concept of the reflex in the description of behavior. *Journal of General Psychology*, 1931, *5*, 427–58.

Drive and reflex strength. *Journal of General Psychology*, 1932, *6*, 22–37.

Drive and reflex strength: II. *Journal of General Psychology*, 1932, *6*, 38–48.

On the rate of formation of a conditioned reflex. *Journal of General Psychology*, 1932, *7*, 274–86.

A paradoxical color effect. *Journal of General Psychology*, 1932, *7*, 481–82.

The abolishment of a discrimination. *Proceedings of the National Academy of Sciences*, 1933, *19*, 825–28.

The measurement of "spontaneous activity." *Journal of General Psychology*, 1933, *9*, 3–23.

On the rate of extinction of a conditioned reflex. *Journal of General Psychology*, 1933, *8*, 114–29.

The rate of establishment of a discrimination. *Journal of General Psychology*, 1933, *9*, 302–50.

"Resistance to extinction" in the process of conditioning. *Journal of General Psychology*, 1933, *9*, 420–29.

Some conditions affecting intensity and duration thresholds in motor nerve, with reference to chronaxie of subordination. *American Journal of Physiology*, 1933, *106*, 721–37. (with E. F. Lambert [1] & A. Forbes [3])

A discrimination without previous conditioning. *Proceedings of the National Academy of Sciences*, 1934, *20*, 532–36.

The extinction of chained reflexes. *Proceedings of the National Academy of Sciences*, 1934, *20*, 234–37.

Has Gertrude Stein a secret? *Atlantic Monthly*, January 1934, pp. 50–57.

A discrimination based upon a change in the properties of a stimulus. *Journal of General Psychology*, 1935, *12*, 313–36.

The generic nature of the concepts of stimulus and response. *Journal of General Psychology*, 1935, *12*, 40–65.

Two types of conditioned reflex and pseudo type. *Journal of General Psychology*, 1935, *12*, 66–77.

Conditioning and extinction and their relation to drive. *Journal of General Psychology*, 1936, *14*, 296–317.

The effect on the amount of conditioning of an interval of time before reinforcement. *Journal of General Psychology*, 1936, *14*, 279–95.

A failure to obtain "disinhibition." *Journal of General Psychology*, 1936, *14*, 127–35.
The reinforcing effect of a differentiating stimulus. *Journal of General Psychology*, 1936, *14*, 263–78.
Thirst as an arbitrary drive. *Journal of General Psychology*, 1936, *15*, 205–10.
The verbal summator and a method for the study of latent speech. *Journal of General Psychology*, 1936, *2*, 71–107.
Changes in hunger during starvation. *Psychological Record*, 1937, *1*, 51–60. (with W. T. Heron [1])
The distribution of associated words. *Psychological Record*, 1937, *1*, 71–76.
Effects of caffeine and benzedrine upon conditioning and extinction. *Psychological Record*, 1937, *1*, 340–46. (with W. T. Heron [2])
Two types of conditioned reflex: A reply to Konorski and Miller. *Journal of General Psychology*, 1937, *16*, 272–79.
The behavior of organisms: An experimental analysis. New York: Appleton-Century, 1938.
The alliteration in Shakespeare's sonnets: A study in literary behavior. *Psychological Record*, 1939, *3*, 186–92.
An apparatus for the study of animal behavior. *Psychological Record*, 1939, *3*, 166–76. (with W. T. Heron [1])
Some factors influencing the distribution of associated words. *Psychological Record*, 1939, *3*, 178–84. (with S. W. Cook [1])
A method of maintaining an arbitrary degree of hunger. *Journal of Comparative Psychology*, 1940, *30*, 139–45.
The rate of extinction in maze-bright and maze-dull rats. *Psychological Record*, 1940, *4*, 11–18. (with W. T. Heron [1])
The psychology of design. In *Art education today*. New York: Bureau Publications, Teachers College, Columbia University, 1941, pp. 1–6.
A quantitative estimate of certain types of sound-patterning in poetry. *American Journal of Psychology*, 1941, *54*, 64–79.
Some quantitative properties of anxiety. *Journal of Experimental Psychology*, 1941, *29*, 390–400. (with W. K. Estes [1])
The processes involved in the repeated guessing of alternatives. *Journal of Experimental Psychology*, 1942, *30*, 495–503.
Reply to Dr. Yacorzynski. *Journal of Experimental Psychology*, 1943, *32*, 93–94.
Baby in a box. *Ladies' Home Journal*, October 1945, pp. 30–31, 135–36, 138.
The operational analysis of psychological terms. *Psychological Review*, 1945, *52*, 270–77, 291–94.
An automatic shocking-grid apparatus for continuous use. *Journal of Comparative and Physiological Psychology*, 1947, *40*, 305–307. (with S. L. Campbell [2])
Experimental psychology. In W. Dennis et al., *Current trends in psychology*. Pittsburgh: University of Pittsburgh Press, 1947, pp. 16–49.
Card-guessing experiments. *American Scientist*, 1948, *36*, 456, 458.
'Superstition' in the pigeon. *Journal of Experimental Psychology*, 1948, *38*, 168–72.
Walden two. New York: Macmillan, 1948.
Are theories of learning necessary? *Psychological Review*, 1950, *57*, 193–216.
How to teach animals. *Scientific American*, 1951, *185*(12), 26–29.

Science and human behavior. New York: Macmillan, 1953.

Some contributions of an experimental analysis of behavior to psychology as a whole. *American Psychologist,* 1953, *8,* 69–78.

A critique of psychoanalytic concepts and theories. *Scientific Monthly,* 1954, *79,* 300–305.

The science of learning and the art of teaching. *Harvard Educational Review,* 1954, *24,* 86–97.

The control of human behavior. *Transactions of the New York Academy of Sciences,* 1955, *17,* 547–51.

Freedom and the control of men. *American Scholar,* Winter 1955–56, *25,* 47–65.

A case history in scientific method. *American Psychologist,* 1956, *11,* 221–33.

Some issues concerning the control of human behavior: A symposium. *Science,* 1956, *124,* 1057–66. (with C. R. Rogers [1])

What is psychotic behavior? In *Theory and treatment of the psychoses: Some newer aspects.* St. Louis: Committee on Publications, Washington University, 1956, pp. 77–99.

Concurrent activity under fixed-interval reinforcement. *Journal of Comparative and Physiological Psychology,* 1957, *50,* 279–81. (with W. H. Morse [2])

The experimental analysis of behavior. *American Scientist,* 1957, *45,* 343–71.

The psychological point of view. In H. D. Kruse (Ed.), *Integrating the approaches to mental disease.* New York: Hoeber-Harper, 1957, pp. 130–33.

Schedules of reinforcement. New York: Appleton-Century-Crofts, 1957. (with C. B. Ferster [1])

A second type of superstition in the pigeon. *American Journal of Psychology,* 1957, *70,* 308–11. (with W. H. Morse [1])

Verbal behavior. New York: Appleton-Century-Crofts, 1957.

Diagramming schedules of reinforcement. *Journal of the Experimental Analysis of Behavior,* 1958, *1,* 67–68.

Fixed-interval reinforcement of running in a wheel. *Journal of the Experimental Analysis of Behavior,* 1958, *1,* 371–79. (with W. H. Morse [2])

Reinforcement today. *American Psychologist,* 1958, *13,* 94–99.

Some factors involved in the stimulus control of operant behavior. *Journal of the Experimental Analysis of Behavior,* 1958, *1,* 103–107. (with W. H. Morse [1])

Sustained performance during the very long experimental sessions. *Journal of the Experimental Analysis of Behavior,* 1958, *1,* 235–44. (with W. H. Morse [2])

Teaching machines. *Science,* 1958, *128,* 969–77.

Animal research in the pharmacotherapy of mental disease. In J. Cole & R. Gerard (Eds.), *Psychopharmacology: Problems in evaluation.* Washington, DC: National Academy of Sciences—National Research Council, 1959, pp. 224–28.

Cumulative record. New York: Appleton-Century-Crofts, 1959; Enlarged edition, 1961; Third edition, 1972.

The flight from the laboratory. In B. F. Skinner, *Cumulative record.* New York: Appleton-Century-Crofts, 1959, pp. 242–57.

John Broadus Watson, behaviorist. *Science,* 1959, *129,* 197–98.

The programming of verbal knowledge. In E. Galanter (Ed.), *Automatic teaching: The state of the art.* New York: John Wiley, 1959, pp. 63–68.

Concept formation in philosophy and psychology. In S. Hook (Ed.), *Dimensions of mind: A symposium*. New York: New York University Press, 1960, pp. 226–30.

Modern learning theory and some new approaches to teaching. In J. W. Gustad (Ed.), *Faculty utilization and retention*. Winchester, MA: New England Board of Higher Education, 1960, pp. 64–72.

Pigeons in a pelican. *American Psychologist*, 1960, *15*, 28–37.

Special problems in programming language instruction for teaching machines. In F. J. Oinas (Ed.), *Language teaching today*. Bloomington: Indiana University Research Center in Anthropology, Folklore, and Linguistics, 1960, pp. 167–74.

Teaching machines. *The Review of Economics and Statistics*, August 1960 (Supplement), *42*, 189–91.

The use of teaching machines in college instruction (Parts II–IV). In A. A. Lumsdaine & R. Glaser (Eds.), *Teaching machines and programmed learning: A source book*. Washington, DC: Department of Audio–Visual Instruction, National Education Association, 1960, pp. 159–72. (with J. G. Holland [2])

The analysis of behavior: A program for self-instruction. New York: McGraw Hill, 1961. (with J. G. Holland [1])

The design of cultures. *Daedalus*, 1961, *90*, 534–46.

Learning theory and future research. In J. Lysaught (Ed.), *Programmed learning: Evolving principles and industrial applications*. Ann Arbor: Foundation for Research on Human Behaviors, 1961, pp. 59–66.

Teaching machines. *Scientific American*, 1961, *205*(11), 90–102.

The theory behind teaching machines. *Journal of the American Society of Training Directors*, July 1961, *15*, 27–29.

Why we need teaching machines. *Harvard Educational Review*, 1961, *31*, 377–98.

Operandum. *Journal of the Experimental Analysis of Behavior*, 1962, *5*, 224.

Squirrel in the yard: Certain sciurine experiences of B. F. Skinner. *Harvard Alumni Bulletin*, 1962, *64*, 642–45.

Technique for reinforcing either of two organisms with a single food magazine. *Journal of the Experimental Analysis of Behavior*, 1962, *5*, 58. (with G. S. Reynolds [1])

Two "synthetic social relations." *Journal of the Experimental Analysis of Behavior*, 1962, *5*, 531–33.

Verbal behavior. *Encounter*, November 1962, pp. 42–44. (with I. A. Richards [1])

Behaviorism at fifty. *Science*, 1963, *140*, 951–58.

A Christmas caramel, or, a plum from the hasty pudding. *The Worm Runner's Digest*, 1963, *5*(2), 42–46.

Conditioned and unconditioned aggression in pigeons. *Journal of the Experimental Analysis of Behavior*, 1963, *6*, 73–74. (with G. S. Reynolds [1] & A. C. Catania [2])

L'avenir des machines à enseigner. *Psychologie Française*, 1963, *8*, 170–80.

Operant behavior. *American Psychologist*, 1963, *18*, 503–15.

Reflections on a decade of teaching machines. *Teachers College Record*, 1963, *65*, 168–77.

Reply to Thouless. *Australian Journal of Psychology*, 1963, *15*, 92–93.

"Man." *Proceedings of the American Philosophical Society*, 1964, *108*, 482–85.

New methods and new aims in teaching. *New Scientist*, 1964, *122*, 483–84.

On the relation between mathematical and statistical competence and significant scientific productivity. *The Worm Runner's Digest*, 1964, *6*(1), 15–17. (published under the pseudonym, F. Galtron Pennywhistle)

Stimulus generalization in an operant: A historical note. In D. I. Mostofsky (Ed.), *Stimulus generalization*. Stanford: Stanford University Press, 1965, pp. 193–209.

The technology of teaching. *Proceedings of the Royal Society, Series B*, 1965, *162*, 427–43.

Why teachers fail. *Saturday Review*, October 16, 1965, pp. 80–81, 98–102.

Conditioning responses by reward and punishment. *Proceedings of the Royal Institution of Great Britain*, 1966, *41*, 48–51.

Contingencies of reinforcement in the design of a culture. *Behavioral Science*, 1966, *11*, 159–66.

An operant analysis of problem solving. In B. Kleinmuntz (Ed.), *Problem solving: Research, method, and theory*. New York: John Wiley, 1966, pp. 225–57.

The phylogeny and ontogeny of behavior. *Science*, 1966, *153*, 1205–13.

Some responses to the stimulus "Pavlov." *Conditional Reflex*, 1966, *1*, 74–78.

What is the experimental analysis of behavior? *Journal of the Experimental Analysis of Behavior*, 1966, *9*, 213–18.

B. F. Skinner . . . An autobiography. In E. G. Boring & G. Lindzey (Eds.), *A history of psychology in autobiography* (Vol. 5). New York: Appleton-Century-Crofts, 1967, pp. 387–413.

The problem of consciousness—A debate. *Philosophy and Phenomenological Research*, 1967, *27*, 317–37. (with B. Blanshard [1])

Utopia through the control of human behavior. *The Listener*, January 12, 1967, pp. 55–56.

Visions of utopia. *The Listener*, January 5, 1967, pp. 22–23.

The design of experimental communities. In *International encyclopedia of the social sciences* (Vol. 16). New York: Macmillan, 1968, pp. 271–75.

Development of methods of preparing materials for teaching machines. Alexandria, VA: Human Resources Research Office, George Washington University, 1968. (edited by L. M. Zook)

Handwriting with write and see. Chicago: Lyons & Carnahan, 1968. (with S. Krakower [2]; a series of manuals for teachers and students, grades 1 to 6)

The science of human behavior. In *Twenty-five years at RCA laboratories 1942–1967*. Princeton, NJ: RCA Laboratories, 1968, pp. 92–102.

Teaching science in high school—What is wrong? *Science*, 1968, *159*, 704–10.

The technology of teaching. New York: Appleton-Century-Crofts, 1968.

Contingencies of reinforcement: A theoretical analysis. New York: Appleton-Century-Crofts, 1969.

Contingency management in the classroom. *Education*, 1969, *90*, 93–100.

Edwin Garrigues Boring. In *The American Philosophical Society: Yearbook 1968*. Philadelphia: The American Philosophical Society, 1969, pp. 111–15.

The machine that is man. *Psychology Today*, April 1969, pp. 20–25, 60–63.

Creating the creative artist. In A. J. Toynbee et al., *On the future of art*. New York: Viking Press, 1970, pp. 61–75.

Autoshaping. *Science*, 1971, *173*, 752.

A behavioral analysis of value judgments. In E. Tobach, L. R. Aronson, & E. Shaw (Eds.), *The biopsychology of development*. New York: Academic Press, 1971, pp. 543–51.

Beyond freedom and dignity. New York: Knopf, 1971.

B. F. Skinner says what's wrong with the social sciences. *The Listener*, September 30, 1971, pp. 429–31.

Humanistic behaviorism. *The Humanist*, May/June 1971, *31*, 35.

Operant conditioning. In *The encyclopedia of education, Vol. 7*. New York: Macmillan and Free Press, 1971, pp. 29–33.

Compassion and ethics in the care of the retardate. In B. F. Skinner, *Cumulative record* (3rd ed). New York: Appleton-Century-Crofts, 1972, pp. 283–91.

Freedom and dignity revisited. *New York Times*, August 11, 1972, p. 29.

Humanism and behaviorism. *The Humanist*, July/August 1972, *32*, 18–20.

A lecture on "having a poem." In B. F. Skinner, *Cumulative record* (3rd ed.). New York: Appleton-Century-Crofts, 1972, pp. 345–55.

Some relations between behavior modification and basic research. In B. F. Skinner, *Cumulative record* (3rd ed.). New York: Appleton-Century-Crofts, 1972, pp. 276–82.

Answers for my critics. In H. Wheeler (Ed.), *Beyond the punitive society*. San Francisco: W. H. Freeman, 1973, pp. 256–66.

Are we free to have a future? *Impact*, 1973, *3*(1), 5–12.

The free and happy student. *New York University Education Quarterly*, 1973, *4*(2), 2–6.

Reflections on meaning and structure. In R. Brower, H. Vendler, & J. Hollander (Eds.), *I. A. Richards: Essays in his honor*. New York: Oxford University Press, 1973, pp. 199–209.

Some implications of making education more efficient. In C. E. Thoresen (Ed.), *Behavior modification in education*. Chicago: National Society for the Study of Education, 1973, pp. 446–56.

Walden (one) and *Walden Two. The Thoreau Society Bulletin*, Winter 1973, pp. 1–3.

About behaviorism. New York: Knopf, 1974.

Designing higher education. *Daedalus*, 1974, *103*, 196–202.

Comments on Watt's "B. F. Skinner and the technological control of social behavior." *The American Political Science Review*, 1975, *69*, 228–29.

The ethics of helping people. *Criminal Law Bulletin*, 1975, *11*, 623–36.

The shaping of phylogenic behavior. *Acta Neurobiologiae Experimentalis*, 1975, *35*, 409–15.

The steep and thorny way to a science of behaviour. In R. Harré (Ed.), *Problems of scientific revolution: Progress and obstacles to progress in the sciences*. Oxford: Clarendon Press, 1975, pp. 58–71.

Farewell, my LOVELY! *Journal of the Experimental Analysis of Behavior*, 1976, *25*, 218.

Particulars of my life. New York: Knopf, 1976.

Between freedom and despotism. *Psychology Today*, September 1977, pp. 80–82, 84, 86, 90–91.

The experimental analysis of operant behavior. In R. W. Rieber & K. Salzinger (Eds.), *The roots of American psychology: Historical influences and implications for the future* (Annals of the New York Academy of Sciences, Vol. 291). New York: New York Academy of Sciences, 1977, pp. 374–85.

The force of coincidence. In B. C. Etzel, J. M. LeBlanc, & D. M. Baer (Eds.), *New developments in behavioral psychology: Theory, method, and application.* Hillsdale, NJ: Lawrence Erlbaum Associates, 1977, pp. 3–6.

Freedom, at last, from the burden of taxation. *New York Times*, July 26, 1977, p. 29.

Herrnstein and the evolution of behaviorism. *American Psychologist*, 1977, *32*, 1006–12.

Why I am not a cognitive psychologist. *Behaviorism*, 1977, *5*, 1–10.

Reflections on behaviorism and society. Englewood Cliffs, NJ: Prentice-Hall, 1978.

Why don't we use the behavioral sciences? *Human Nature*, March 1978, *1*, 86–92.

A happening at the annual dinner of the Association for Behavioral Analysis, Chicago, May 15, 1978. *The Behavior Analyst*, 1979, *2*(1), 30–33. (published anonymously)

Le renforçateur arrangé. *Revue de modification du comportement*, 1979, *9*, 59–69. (translated into French by Raymond Beausoleil)

My experience with the baby-tender. *Psychology Today*, March 1979, pp. 28–31, 34, 37–38, 40. (an expanded excerpt from *The Shaping of a Behaviorist* [1979])

The shaping of a behaviorist: Part two of an autobiography. New York: Knopf, 1979.

Notebooks. Englewood Cliffs, NJ: Prentice-Hall, 1980. (edited by R. Epstein)

Resurgence of responding after the cessation of response-independent reinforcement. *Proceedings of the National Academy of Sciences*, 1980, *77*, 6251–53. (with R. Epstein [1])

The species-specific behavior of ethologists. *The Behavior Analyst*, 1980, *3*(1), 51.

Symbolic communication between two pigeons. *(Columba livia domestica). Science*, 1980, *207*, 543–45. (with R. Epstein [1] & R. P. Lanza [2])

Charles B. Ferster—A personal memoir. *Journal of the Experimental Analysis of Behavior*, 1981, *35*, 259–61.

How to discover what you have to say—A talk to students. *The Behavior Analyst*, 1981, *4*(1), 1–7.

Pavlov's influence on psychology in America. *Journal of the History of the Behavioral Sciences*, 1981, *17*, 242–45.

Selection by consequences. *Science*, 1981, *213*, 501–504.

"Self-awareness" in the pigeon. *Science*, 1981, *212*, 695–96. (with R. Epstein [1] & R. P. Lanza [2])

The spontaneous use of memoranda by pigeons. *Behaviour Analysis Letters*, 1981, *1*, 241–46. (with R. Epstein [1])

Contrived reinforcement. *The Behavior Analyst*, 1982, *5*, 3–8.

"I am most concerned. . . ." *Psychology Today*, May 1982, pp. 48–49. (part of "Understanding Psychological Man: A State-of-the-Science Report," pp. 40–59)

"Lying" in the pigeon. *Journal of the Experimental Analysis of Behavior*, 1982, *38*, 201–203. (with R. P. Lanza [1] & J. Starr [2])

Skinner for the classroom. Champaign, IL: Research Press, 1982. (edited by R. Epstein)

A better way to deal with selection. *The Behavioral and Brain Sciences*, 1983, *3*, 377–78.

Can the experimental analysis of behavior rescue psychology? *The Behavior Analyst*, 1983, *6*, 9–17.

Enjoy old age: A program of self management. New York: W. W. Norton, 1983. (with M. E. Vaughan [2])

Intellectual self-management in old age. *American Psychologist*, 1983, *38*, 239–44.

A matter of consequences. New York: Knopf, 1983.

Canonical papers of B. F. Skinner. *The Behavioral and Brain Sciences*, 1984, *7*, 473–724. (edited by A. C. Catania & S. Harnad, with numerous commentators; reprinted in book form under the title, *The selection of consequences: The operant behaviorism of B. F. Skinner: Comments and consequences* [New York: Cambridge University Press, 1988])

The evolution of behavior. *Journal of the Experimental Analysis of Behavior*, 1984, *41*, 217–21.

The shame of American education. *American Psychologist*, 1984, *39*, 947–54.

Cognitive science and behaviourism. *British Journal of Psychology*, 1985, *76*, 291–301.

News from nowhere, 1984. *The Behavior Analyst*, 1985, *8*, 5–14.

Reply to Place: "Three senses of the word 'tact.'" *Behaviorism*, 1985, *13*, 75–76.

Toward the cause of peace: What can psychology contribute? In S. Oskamp (Ed.), *International conflict and national public policy issues (Applied Social Psychology Annual 6)*. Beverly Hills: Sage Publications, 1985, pp. 21–25.

B. F. Skinner ["The books that have been most important . . ."]. In C. M. Devine, C. M. Dissel, & K. D. Parrish (Eds.), *The Harvard guide to influential books: 113 distinguished Harvard professors discuss the books that have helped to shape their thinking*. New York: Harper & Row, 1986, pp. 233–34.

The evolution of verbal behavior. *Journal of the Experimental Analysis of Behavior*, 1986, *45*, 115–22.

Programmed instruction revisited. *Phi Delta Kappan*, 1986, *68*, 103–10.

Sleeping in peace. *Free Inquiry*, Summer 1986, *6*, 57.

Some thoughts about the future. *Journal of the Experimented Analysis of Behavior*, 1986, *45*, 229–35.

What is wrong with daily life in the western world? *American Psychologist*, 1986, *41*, 568–74.

A humanist alternative to A.A.'s Twelve Steps. *The Humanist*, July/August 1987, *47*, 5.

Outlining a science of feeling. *The Times Literary Supplement*, May 8, 1987, pp. 490, 501–502.

A thinking aid. *Journal of Applied Behavior Analysis*, 1987, *20*, 379–80.

Upon further reflection. Englewood Cliffs, NJ: Prentice-Hall, 1987.

What religion means to me. *Free Inquiry*, Spring 1987, *7*, 12–13.

Whatever happened to psychology as the science of behavior? *American Psychologist*, 1987, *42*, 780–86.

A fable. *The Analysis of Verbal Behavior*, 1988, *6*, 1–2.

Genes and behavior. In G. Greenberg & E. Tobach (Eds.), *Evolution of social behavior and integrative levels*. Hillsdale, NJ: Lawrence Erlbaum Associates, 1988, pp. 77–83.

The operant side of behavior therapy. *Journal of Behavior Therapy and Experimental Psychiatry*, 1988, *19*, 171–79.

Signs and countersigns. *The Behavioral and Brain Sciences*, 1988, *11*, 466–67.

A statement on punishment. *APA Monitor*, June 1988, p. 22.

War, peace, and behavior analysis: Some comments. *Behavior Analysis and Social Action*, 1988, *6*, 57–58.

The behavior of organisms at fifty. In B. F. Skinner, *Recent issues in the analysis of behavior*. Columbus, OH: Merrill, 1989, pp. 121–35.

The behavior of the listener. In S. C. Hayes (Ed.), *Rule-governed behavior: Cognition, contingencies, and instructional control*. New York: Plenum Press, 1989, pp. 85–96.

The initiating self. In B. F. Skinner, *Recent issues in the analysis of behavior*. Columbus, OH: Merrill, 1989, pp. 27–33.

The origins of cognitive thought. *American Psychologist*, 1989, *44*, 13–18.

Recent issues in the analysis of behavior. Columbus, OH: Merrill, 1989.

The school of the future. In B. F. Skinner, *Recent issues in the analysis of behavior*. Columbus, OH: Merrill, 1989, pp. 85–96.

Can psychology be a science of mind? *American Psychologist*, 1990, *45*, 1206–10.

The non-punitive society. *Japanese Journal of Behavior Analysis*, 1990, *5*, 98–106.

To know the future. *The Behavior Analyst*, 1990, *13*, 103–106. (published concurrently in C. Fadiman [Ed.], *Living philosophies: The reflections of some eminent men and women of our time*. New York: Doubleday, 1990, pp. 193–99)

A world of our own. *Behaviorology*, 1993, *1*, 3–5.

Notes

CHAPTER 2

1. Original copies of the letters cited in this chapter may be found in the Richard M. Elliott Archives, Walter Library, University of Minnesota, Minneapolis, Minnesota.

2. Skinner's other Century Series books are *Verbal Behavior* (1957), *Schedules of Reinforcement* (Ferster & Skinner, 1957), *Technology of Teaching* (1967), *Contingencies of Reinforcement: A Theoretical Analysis* (1969), the third edition (but neither the first nor the enlarged) of *Cumulative Record* (1972a), *Reflection on Behaviorism and Society* (1978), and *Upon Further Reflection* (1987).

3. The first entry appeared in 1940 under "conditioning operant"; beginning in 1973 entries were changed to "operant conditioning."

CHAPTER 4

1. Strictly speaking, the attribution of positivism to Bacon is an anachronism, given that the term *positivism* was not coined until nearly two centuries after Bacon's death. However, Bacon's emphasis on basing knowledge only on well-grounded direct observations (what were later called "positive" facts), his advocacy of experimental method, his opposition to speculative metaphysics, and his attention to potentially misleading use of language would otherwise qualify him as a positivist. Indeed, it is by virtue of these characteristics of his thought that he is often cited, along with David Hume, as one of the chief historical sources of positivism. No such chronological reservations surround the attribution of positivism to Mach, whose works were written after positivism had become a full-fledged philosophical movement. For a concise history of positivism, see Abbagnano (1967).

2. Skinner's concept of the reflex reserve has met with an uneven reception in the fifty years since it was introduced. Its exact status has never been clear (for discussions, see Ellson, 1939; Killeen, 1988; Verplanck, 1954; Zuriff, 1985), and Skinner himself abandoned the concept as fruitless and unnecessary not long after proposing it (see Skinner, 1956). Most members of the operant tradition have been content to follow Skinner in rejecting the concept, though one (Killeen, 1988) has resurrected

the construct in the form of an explicit physical model and advocated its adoption as a central concept of behavior theory. For present purposes, the important point is that Skinner's own treatment of the reserve was a minimalist one that befitted his roots in a relatively strict branch of the positivist tradition.

3. The movement toward philosophy of science in America during the 1930s and 1940s was broader than logical positivism proper, incorporating strands of neopragmatism and operationism. However, as noted by Koch (1964), logical positivism provided the "dominant contours" of the resulting amalgam (p. 10); and Skinner's advocacy of operationism should not be interpreted as an endorsement of logical positivism. Skinner's unorthodox version of operationism and the deep differences between it and logical positivism's version are discussed by Day (1969a), Flanagan (1980), and L. D. Smith (1986, pp. 284–287).

4. In terms of their philosophical standing, the reputations of both Bacon and Mach have undergone considerable fluctuations through the years. Criticisms of Bacon's philosophy may be found in Popper (1965); for a more recent sympathetic exposition, see Urbach (1987); scholarly, balanced assessments that place Bacon's thought in its historical context may be found in Jardine (1974), Perez-Ramos (1988), and Rossi (1968). A good, but in some respects atypical, treatment of Bacon—and one that Skinner himself read (1983, p. 406)—is that given by Farrington (1949). For a recent critique of Bacon's conflation of science with technology (and its implications for the assessment of Skinner), see Smith (1992, 1993). In regard to Mach's philosophy, sharp criticisms are provided by Mach's contemporary Max Planck (1910/1970); sympathetic treatments are given by Bradley (1971) and Hiebert (1970); a balanced account of Mach's life and his intellectual contributions is provided by Blackmore (1972); and various aspects of Mach's wide-ranging thought are discussed in Hintikka (1968) and Cohen and Seeger (1970). Although both Bacon and Mach have sometimes been depicted as having presented simplistic philosophies of science, it is now reasonably clear that both of their philosophies are more complex and subtle than often alleged.

CHAPTER 7

1. This also takes the form of omitting agency of person and thus is interpreted as denying personal responsibility and the like. For an example of an interpreter applying this to himself with respect to his own behavior, see Skinner (1972b). At the same time, when we speak of responsibility, we usually are concerned with appropriate consequences for action, which is a primary focus of environment-based accounts.

2. Brady (1987) recounts a clear instance of this, regarding the perplexity of a distinguished researcher in animal behavior (and President of the APA) when visiting a laboratory that used Skinner's research strategies and techniques.

3. For evidence of the nonmainstream status of behavior analysis even during its presumed heyday, see reminiscences of the founding of a behavioral journal (Hineline & Laties, 1987).

4. For elaboration of this aspect of "The Generic Nature of the Concept of Stimulus and Response," see Coleman (1984) and Hineline and Wanchisen (1989).

Chapter 8

1. A *tact* is "a verbal operant in which a response of a given form is evoked (or at least strengthened) by a particular object or property of an object or event" (Skinner, 1957, pp. 81–82). It is incorrect to regard the tact as being a description of or reference to a stimulus. According to Skinner (1957), in a tact, "the only useful functional relation is expressed in the statement that the presence of a given stimulus raises the probability of occurrence of a given form of the response" (p. 82).

2. An *autoclitic* is verbal behavior "which is based upon or depends on other verbal behavior" (Skinner, 1957, p. 315). Autoclitics modify the effects of associated verbal responses on listeners.

CHAPTER 9

1. Abstracts to articles published from 1975 through 1985 were gathered from *Psychological Abstracts* under the Index-volume heading "History of Psychology" and its associated categories (Associationism, Behaviorism, Structuralism, etc.). Dissertation abstracts were excluded. The 1610 abstracts were read, and those that mentioned Wundt were sorted into two categories: articles whose principal figure was Wundt considered either alone or in relation to some other historical figure or school; articles that included Wundt in the abstract but were clearly about a different topic, as indicated by the title and abstract.

2. The avoidance of relevance is not implausible because compelling demonstrations of relevance to a present-day concern require that the researcher has competence in the present-day literature of some specialty as well as in a wide range of historical sources that are in the background and in the surroundings of the specialty. That is, the "fully relevant" historican must master *two* literatures, the recent (contemporary) and the old (historical). If specialists tend to limit their activities to the domain of their specialty, then historians of psychology will *tend* to become antiquarian (in the particular historical topics of the older literature within their History of Psychology specialties) and to suffer a loss of capacity to be relevant to present-day fields.

3. *Worth* covers a multitude of evaluative terms, ranging from "directly relevant" to "stimulating." The thirteen rationales described include highly specific value (e.g., recovery of a forgotten theory) and highly general value (e.g., the benefits of travel). The question whether history is useful starts from an unreasonable presumption of a simple answer, whereas the utilities of history appear to be several in number and of diverse kinds.

4. A subclass of historical literature has the objective of enlarging readers' historical awareness by describing the contributions or even just the life of an individual who has been forgotten (e.g., Benjamin & Wallers, 1984). Other publications aim to question existing reputations (e.g., Grossman, 1976).

5. Todd (1994b) has shown that J. B. Watson's polemical claims, such as the "dozen healthy infants," have been used as representative behavioristic tenets that justify dismissive or critical appraisals of variants of behaviorism that are quite different from Watson's (1924a, 1924b).

6. The institutional separateness of the Experimental Analysis of Behavior (e.g., Coleman & Mehlman, 1992; Krantz, 1971, 1972) and of Behavior Analysis is so obvious that it hardly needs documentation. However, it does need a history of the phases, circumstances, and identifiable consequences of the process.

CHAPTER 12

1. Behavior therapy, in the present context, refers to the therapeutic work of Wolpe and others based primarily on classical conditioning methods. It is to be distinguished from "applied behavior analysis" (sometimes "behavior modification"), which developed from the operant tradition of B. F. Skinner.

CHAPTER 15

1. The Archives of the History of American Psychology are located at the University of Akron, Akron, OH. Its director and associate director are John A. Popplestone and Marion White McPherson, respectively.

2. Various guides to primary and secondary sources in the history of psychology are also available (e.g., Viney, Wertheimer, & Wertheimer, 1979; see Woodward, 1980, pp. 46–48). For a guide to serial publications, see Osier and Wozniak (1984). For a guide to the history of American psychology in "notes and news" columns of journals, see Benjamin et al. (1989).

3. Among the alternatives to such historicist treatments of specific practices would be to define behavior analysis beginning with Skinner and his *successors* rather than with Skinner and his predecessors (Deborah J. Coon, personal communication, February 10, 1989). Skinner's work would then mark the beginning of a lineage rather than the end. A related approach would be to date the discipline not from the work of Skinner himself but from the date at which a sufficient number of scholars had amassed to warrant calling their work "disciplinary," the beginnings of which might be the founding of a conference, society, journal, organization, or organizational division. For example, behavior analysis might be dated from 1957 when the Society for the Experimental Analysis of Behavior was incorporated; from 1958 when *JEAB* was first published; from 1964 when APA Division 25 was established; or from 1974 when the Midwest Association for Behavior Analysis, later the Association for Behavior Analysis, was founded.

4. Because behavior analysis was originally, and remains largely, based in the United States, we have restricted our considerations to English-language publications. Proper historiography, though, would search non-English books as well (e.g., Sanders, 1978; Scheerer, 1983; see Woodward, 1985). Other organizations of this literature are possible, the most useful of which might be to categorize it by substantive topic (S. R. Coleman, personal communication, December 3, 1988). Such an organization might parse the history of behavior analysis in many ways, for example, by its subdisciplines, and then by subsections within each branch. The latter might yield such topics as "Skinner and the Philosophical Pragmatists," which would contain such papers as "Mead and Skinner: Agency and Determinism" (Baldwin, 1988;

see also Blackman, 1991); or "The Institutionalization of Applied Behavior Analysis," which would contain such articles as "Shapers at Work" (Goodall, 1972); or "Radical Behaviorism and Logical Positivism," which would contain papers like "Some Historical and Conceptual Relations among Logical Positivism, Operationism, and Behaviorism" (Moore, 1985). Such an organization, though, would yield so great a diversity of headings that some of them would contain only one or two items, although that itself might be illuminating. This problem might be alleviated by restricting the categories to topics having a minimum number of entries, but a potpourri of material would still remain. In general, the literature on the history of behavior analysis may not be large enough for an inclusive topical treatment to be especially useful for the literature as a whole.

5. The extent of the historical material in other texts—for example, in Lee's (1988) *Beyond Behaviorism* (see Morris, 1989)—is, however, insufficient to consider them historical, albeit at the same time excluding some valuable resources on the conceptual underpinnings of the discipline.

References

Abbagnano, N. (1967). Positivism. In P. Edwards (Ed.), *The encyclopedia of philosophy*. New York: Macmillan.

Abelson, R. P. (1981). Psychological status of the script concept. *American Psychologist, 36,* 715–29.

Altschule, M. D. (1976). *The development of traditional psychopathology: A sourcebook*. Washington, DC: Hemisphere.

Amundson, R. (1985). Psychology and epistemology: The place versus response controversy. *Cognition, 20,* 127–53.

Anderson, J. R. (1991). More on rational analysis. *Behavioral and Brain Sciences, 14,* 508–13.

Andresen, J. T. (1990). Skinner and Chomsky thirty years later. *Historiographia Linguistica, 17,* 145–65.

Appleton-Century-Crofts observes its 125th anniversary. (1950, July 8). *Publisher's Weekly,* 120–27.

Ash, M. G. (1983). The self-presentation of a discipline: History of psychology in the United States between pedagogy and scholarship. In L. Graham, W. Lepenies, & P. Weingart (Eds.), *Functions and uses of disciplinary histories* (pp. 143–89). Dordrecht, Holland: Reidel.

Attneave, F. (1974). How do you know? *American Psychologist, 9,* 493–99.

Baars, B. J. (1986). *The cognitive revolution in psychology*. New York: Guilford.

Babkin, B. P. (1949). *Pavlov: A biography*. Chicago: University of Chicago Press.

Bacon, F. (1937). De dignitate et augmentis scientiarum. In R. F. Jones (Ed. and Trans.), *Essays, Advancement of Learning, New Atlantis, and other pieces* (pp. 377–438). Garden City, NY: Doubleday, Doran. (Original work published 1623.)

Bacon, F. (1942). New Atlantis. In G. S. Haight, (Ed.), *Essays and New Atlantis* (pp. 243–302). New York: Walter J. Black. (Original work published 1624.)

Bacon, F. (1960). *The new organon* (F. H. Anderson, Ed.). Indianapolis: Bobbs-Merrill. (Original work published 1620.)

Baer, D. M., Wolf, M., & Risley, T. R. (1968). Some current dimensions of applied behavior analysis. *Journal of Applied Behavior Analysis, 1,* 91–97.

Balance, W. D. G. (1975). Frustrations and joys of archival research. *Journal of the History of the Behavioral Sciences, 11*, 37–40.

Baldwin, J. D. (1988). Mead and Skinner: Agency and determinism. *Behaviorism, 16*, 109–27.

Barrett, B. (1987, December). *Trends in behavioral assessment.* Paper presented at the meeting of the New England Society for Behavioral Analysis and Therapy, Chestnut Hill, MA.

Baum, W. M. (1994). John B. Watson and behavior analysis: Past, present, and future. In J. T. Todd & E. K. Morris (Eds.), *Modern perspectives on John B. Watson and classical behaviorism* (pp. 133–40). Westport, CT: Greenwood.

Begelman, D. A. (1978). Skinner's determinism. *Behaviorism, 6*, 13–25.

Begelman, D. A. (1980). [Review of *J. B. Watson: The founder of behaviorism.*] *Contemporary Psychology, 25*, 363–64.

Bekhterev, V. M. (1913). *La psychologie objective.* Paris: Alcan.

Benjamin, L. T. (1979). Instructional strategies in the history of psychology. *Teaching of Psychology, 6*, 15–17.

Benjamin, L. T. (1990). Involving students and faculty in preparing a departmental history. *Teaching of Psychology, 17*, 97–100.

Benjamin, L. T., & Perloff, R. (1982). A case of delayed recognition: Frederick Winslow Taylor and the immediacy of reinforcement. *American Psychologist, 37*, 340–42.

Benjamin, L. T., Pratt, R., Watlington, D., Aaron, L., Bonar, T., Fitzgerald, S., Franklin, M., Jimenez, B., & Lester, R. (1989). *A history of American psychology in notes and news, 1883–1945: An index of journal sources.* Millwood, NY: Kraus International.

Benjamin, L. T., & Wallers, K. (1984). Henry Rutgers Marshall—The forgotten American Psychological Association president. *Revista de Historia de la Psicologia, 5*, 63–67.

Bergmann, G., & Spence, K. W. (1941). Operationism and theory in psychology. *Psychological Review, 48*, 1–14.

Bergstein, T. (1972). *Quantum physics and ordinary language.* London: Macmillian.

Beringer, L. (1978). *Historical analysis: Contemporary approaches to Clio's craft.* New York: Wiley.

Berlyne, D. E. (1975). Behaviourism? Cognitive theory? Humanistic psychology?—To Hull with them all! *Canadian Psychological Review, 16*, 69–80.

Berman, L. (1927). *The religion called behaviorism.* New York: Boni & Liveright.

Bernard, C. (1957). *An introduction to the study of experimental medicine* (H. C. Green, Trans.). New York: Dover Press. (Original work published 1865.)

Berrenberg, J. L. (1990). Integrative and goal-relevant essay questions for history and systems courses. *Teaching of Psychology, 17*, 113–15.

Bethlehem, D. (1987). Scolding the carpenter. In S. Modgil & C. Modgil (Eds.), *B. F. Skinner: Consensus and Controversy* (pp. 89–97). London: Falmer.

Bickhard, M. H., Cooper, R. G., & Mace, P. E. (1985). Vestiges of logical positivism: Critiques of stage explanations. *Human Development, 28*, 240–58.

Bijou, S. W. (1985). Behaviorism: History and educational applications. In T. Husen & T. N. Postlewaite (Eds.), *The international encyclopedia of education* (pp. 444–51). New York: Pergamon.

Bijou, S. W. (1986). Behaviorism. *Funk and Wagnall's New Encyclopedia* (pp. 391–93). New York: Funk and Wagnall's.

Bijou, S. W., & Baer, D. M. (1961). *Child development: Vol. 1. A systematic and empirical theory.* New York: Appleton-Century-Crofts.

Bijou, S. W., & Baer, D. M. (1965). *Child development: Vol. 2. Universal stage of infancy.* New York: Appleton-Century-Crofts.

Birkhoff, G., & von Neumann, J. (1936). The logic of quantum mechanics. *Annals of Mathematics, 37,* 823–43.

Birnbaum, L. C. (1955). Behaviorism in the 1920's. *American Quarterly, 7,* 15–30.

Bjork, D. W. (1993). *B. F. Skinner: A life.* New York: Basic Books.

Bjork, D. W. (in press). B. F. Skinner and the American tradition. In W. R. Woodward & L. D. Smith (Eds.), *B. F. Skinner and behaviorism in American culture.* Lehigh, PA: Lehigh University Press.

Blackman, D. E. (1991). B. F. Skinner and G. H. Mead: On biological science and social science. *Journal of the Experimental Analysis of Behavior, 55,* 251–65.

Blackmore, J. T. (1972). *Ernst Mach: His work, life, and influence.* Berkeley: University of California Press.

Blanchard, D. C., Blanchard, R. J., & Flannelly, K. J. (1984). A new experimental analysis of behavior—One for *all* behavior. *The Behavioral and Brain Sciences, 7,* 681–82.

Blanshard, B., & Skinner, B. F. (1967). The problem of consciousness—A debate. *Philosophical and Phenomenological Research, 27,* 317–37.

Bloch, M. (1953). *The historian's craft.* New York: Knopf.

Block, N. (Ed.). (1980). *Readings in philosophy of psychology* (Vol. 1). Cambridge: Harvard University Press.

Blumenthal, A. (1975). A reappraisal of Wilhelm Wundt. *American Psychologist, 30,* 1081–88.

Blumenthal, A. (1980). Wilhelm Wundt and the early American psychology: A clash of cultures. In R. W. Rieber (Ed.), *Wilhelm Wundt and the making of a scientific psychology* (pp. 117–35). New York: Plenum.

Boakes, R. A. (1983). Behaviorism and the nature–nurture controversy. In G. C. L. Davey (Ed.), *Animal models of human behavior* (pp. 15–35). New York: Wiley.

Boakes, R. (1984). *From Darwin to behaviorism: Psychology and the minds of animals.* Cambridge: Cambridge University Press.

Boakes, R. (1994). John B. Watson's early scientific career: 1903–13. In J. T. Todd & E. K. Morris (Eds.), *Modern perspectives on John B. Watson and Classical Behaviorism* (pp. 145–50). Westport, CT: Greenwood.

Bohan, J. S. (1990). Social constuctionism and contextual history: An expanded approach to the history of psychology. *Teaching of Psychology, 17,* 82–89.

Bohm, D. (1961). *Causality and chance in modern physics.* New York: Harper.

Bohr, N. (1913). On the constitution of atoms and molecules. *Philosophical Magazine, 26,* 132–59.

Bohr, N. (1958). *Atomic physics and human knowledge.* New York: John Wiley & Sons.

Bohr, N. (1963). *Essays 1958–1962 on atomic physics and human knowledge.* New York: Interscience Publishers.

Boring, E. G. (1929). *A history of experimental psychology.* New York: Century.

Boring, E. G. (1950a). Great men and scientific progress. *Proceedings of the American Philosophical Society, 94*, 339–51.

Boring, E. G. (1950b). *A history of experimental psychology* (2nd ed.). New York: Appleton-Century-Crofts.

Boring, E. G. (1955). Dual role of the Zeitgeist in scientific creativity. *Scientific Monthly, 80*, 101–106.

Boring, E. G. (1959). Science and the meaning of its history. *Key Reporter, 20*, 2–3.

Bower, G. H., & Hilgard, E. R. (1981). *Theories of learning* (5th ed.). Englewood Cliffs, NJ: Prentice-Hall.

Bowler, P. J. (1983). *The eclipse of Darwinism.* Baltimore: Johns Hopkins University Press.

Bradley, J. (1971). *Mach's philosophy of science.* London: Athlone Press.

Brady, J. V. (1987). Back to baseline. *Journal of the Experimental Analysis of Behavior, 48*, 458–59.

Branch, M. (1977). On the role of memory in the analysis of behavior. *Journal of the Experimental Analysis of Behavior, 28*, 171–79.

Brand, C. R. (1989). Review of B. F. Skinner's *Upon further reflection. Behaviour Research and Therapy, 27*, 311–12.

Breger, L. (1969). The ideology of behaviorism. In L. Breger (Ed.), *Clinical-cognitive psychology: Models and integrations* (pp. 25–55). Englewood Cliffs, NJ: Prentice-Hall.

Breger, L., & McGaugh, J. L. (1965). Critique and reformulation of "learning-theory" approaches to psychotherapy and neurosis. *Psychological Bulletin, 63*, 338–58.

Bridgman, P. W. (1927). *The logic of modern physics.* New York: Macmillan.

Bridgman, P. W. (1959). *The way things are.* Cambridge: Harvard University Press.

Brinker, R. P., & Jaynes, J. (1988). Waiting for the world to make me talk and tell me what I meant. In A. C. Catania & S. Harnad. (Eds.), *The selection of behavior. The operant behaviorism of B. F. Skinner: Comments and consequences* (pp. 169–71). Cambridge: Cambridge University Press.

Brozek, J., & Pongratz, L. J. (Eds.). (1980). *Historiography of modern psychology.* Toronto: Hogrefe.

Brozek, J., Watson, R. I., & Ross, B. (1970). A summer institute on the history of psychology: Part II. *Journal of the History of the Behavioral Sciences, 6*, 25–35.

Brush, S. G. (1974). Should the history of science be rated X? *Science, 183*, 1164–72.

Buckley, K. W. (1989). *Mechanical man: John Broadus Watson and the beginnings of behaviorism.* New York: Guilford.

Buckley, K. W. (1994). Misbehaviorism: The case of John B. Watson's dismissal from Johns Hopkins University. In J. T. Todd & E. K. Morris (Eds.), *Modern perspectives on John B. Watson and classical behaviorism* (pp. 19–36). Westport, CT: Greenwood.

Burnham, J. C. (1968). On the origins of behaviorism. *Journal of the History of the Behavioral Sciences, 4*, 143–51.

Burnham, J. C. (1994). John B. Watson: Interviewee, professional figure, symbol. In J. T. Todd & E. K. Morris (Eds.), *Modern perspectives on John B. Watson and classical behaviorism* (pp. 65–73). Westport, CT: Greenwood.

Buskist, W. F., & Miller, H. L. (1982). The study of human operant behavior, 1958-1981: A topical bibliography. *The Psychological Record, 32*, 249–68.

Cadwallader, T. C. (1975). Unique values of archival research. *Journal of the History of the Behavioral Sciences, 11*, 27–33.

Calkins, M. W. (1921). The truly psychological behaviorism. *Psychological Review, 28*, 1–18.

Cantor, N. F., & Schneider, R. I. (1967). *How to study history*. New York: Crowell.

Capra, F. (1977). *The tao of physics*. New York: Bantam Books.

Carnap, R. (1928). *Der logische aufbau der welt*. Berlin: Welkreis Verlag.

Carnap, R. (1935). *Philosophy and logical syntax*. London: Kegan Paul, Trench & Trubner.

Carnap, R. (1936). Testability and meaning. *Philosophy of Science, 3*, 419–71.

Carnap, R. (1937). Testability and meaning—continued. *Philosophy of Science, 4*, 1–40.

Cartwright, D. (1979). Contemporary social psychology in historical perspective. *Social Psychology Quarterly, 42*, 82–93.

Catania, A. C. (1973). The psychologies of structure, function, and development. *The American Psychologist, 28*, 434–43.

Catania, A. C. (1978). The psychology of learning: Some lessons from the Darwinian revolution. *Annals of the New York Academy of Sciences, 309*, 18–28.

Catania, A. C. (1980). Skinner. In G. M. Gazda & R. J. Corsini (Eds.), *Theories of learning: A comparative approach*. Itasca, IL: F. E. Peacock Publishers.

Catania, A. C. (1983). Behavior analysis and behavior synthesis in the extrapolation from animal to human behavior. In G. C. L. Davey (Ed.), *Animal models of human behavior* (pp. 51–69). New York: Wiley.

Catania, A. C. (1987). Some Darwinian lessons for behavior analysis. A review of Peter J. Bowler's *The eclipse of Darwinism. Journal of the Experimental Analysis of Behavior, 47*, 249–57.

Catania, A. C. (1988a). *The behavior of organisms* as work in progress. *Journal of the Experimental Analysis of Behavior, 50*, 277–81.

Catania, A. C. (Ed.). (1988b). A celebration of *The behavior of organisms* at fifty [Special issue]. *Journal of the Experimental Analysis of Behavior, 50*(2).

Catania, A. C. (1991). The gifts of culture and eloquence: An open letter to Michael J. Mahoney in reply to his article "Scientific psychology and radical behaviorism." *The Behavior Analyst, 14*, 61–72.

Catania, A. C. (1992). *Learning* (2nd ed.). Englewood Cliffs, NJ: Prentice-Hall.

Catania, A. C., & Harnad, S. (1988). *The selection of behavior. The operant behaviorism of B. F. Skinner: Comments and consequences*. Cambridge: Cambridge University Press.

Caudle, F. M. (1979). Using "demonstrations, class experiments and the projection latern" in the history of psychology course. *Teaching of Psychology, 6*, 7–11.

Chandler, A. R. (1934). *Beauty and human nature*. New York: Appleton-Century.

Chaplin, J. P., & Krawiec, T. S. (1979). *Systems and theories of psychology* (4th ed.). New York: Holt, Rinehart & Winston.

Chiesa, M. (1992). Radical behaviorism and scientific frameworks: From mechanistic to relational accounts. *American Psychologist, 47*, 1287–99.

Chiesa, M. (1994). *Radical behaviorism: The philosophy and the science*. Boston: Authors' Cooperative.

Chomsky, N. (1959). *Verbal behavior*, by B. F. Skinner. *Language, 35*, 26–58.

Churchland, P. M. (1984). *Matter and consciousness*. Cambridge: MIT Press.

Clark, R. W. (1984). *The survival of Charles Darwin: The biography of a man and an idea*. New York: Random House.

Coffield, K. E. (1973). Additional stimulation for students in history and systems. *American Psychologist, 28*, 624–25.

Cohen, D. (1979). *J. B. Watson: The founder of behaviorism*. London: Routledge & Kegan Paul.

Cohen, R. S., & Seeger, R. J. (Eds.). (1970). *Ernst Mach: Physicist and philosopher* (Boston Studies in the Philosophy of Science, Vol. 6). Dordrecht, The Netherlands: Reidel.

Coleman, S. R. (1981). Historical context and systematic functions of the concept of the operant. *Behaviorism, 9*, 207–26.

Coleman, S. R. (1984). Background and change in B. F. Skinner's metatheory from 1930 to 1938. *The Journal of Mind and Behavior, 5*, 471-500.

Coleman, S. R. (1985a). B. F. Skinner, 1926–1928: From literature to psychology. *The Behavior Analyst, 8*, 77–92.

Coleman, S. R. (1985b). When historians disagree: B. F. Skinner and E. G. Boring, 1930. *The Psychological Record, 35*, 301–304.

Coleman, S. R. (1987). Quantitative order in B. F. Skinner's early research program, 1928–1931. *The Behavior Analyst, 10*, 47–65.

Coleman, S. R., & Gormezano, I. (1979). Classical conditioning and the "law of effect": Historical and empirical assessment. *Behaviorism, 7*(2), 1–33.

Coleman, S. R., & Mehlman, S. E. (1992). An empirical update (1969–1989) of D. L. Krantz's thesis that the experimental analysis of behavior is isolated. *The Behavior Analyst, 15*, 43–49.

Collins, A. (1987). *The nature of mental things*. Notre Dame, IN: University of Notre Dame Press.

Coon, D. J. (1994). "Not a creature of reason:" The alleged impact of Watsonian behaviorism on advertising in the 1920s. In J. T. Todd & E. K. Morris (Eds.), *Modern perspectives on John B. Watson and classical behaviorism* (pp. 37–63). Westport, CT: Greenwood.

Corsini, R. J. (Ed.). (1987). *Concise encyclopedia of psychology*. New York: Wiley.

Costall, A. (1993). How Lloyd Morgan's canon backfired. *Journal of the History of the Behavioral Sciences, 29*, 113–22.

Crutchfield, R. S., & Krech, D. (1962). Some guides to the understanding of the history of psychology. In L. Postman (Ed.), *Psychology in the making: Histories of selected research problems* (pp. 3–27). New York: Knopf.

d'Abro, A. (1951). *The rise of the new physics*. (2 vols.) New York: Dover Publications.

Darwin, C. (1966). *On the origin of species*. Cambridge: Harvard University Press. (Original work published 1859.)

Davison, M. (1993). Concomitants, categories, and constraints. *The Behavior Analyst, 16*, 129–30.

Dawkins, R. (1976). *The selfish gene*. New York: Oxford University Press.

Dawkins, R. (1982). *The extended phenotype*. San Francisco: Freeman.

Dawkins, R. (1986). *The blind watchmaker*. New York: Norton.

Day, W. F., Jr. (1969a). On certain similarities between the *Philosophical investigations* of Ludwig Wittgenstein and the operationism of B. F. Skinner. *Journal of the Experimental Analysis of Behavior, 12*, 489–506.

Day, W. F., Jr. (1969b). Radical behaviorism in reconciliation with phenomenology. *Journal of the Experimental Analysis of Behavior, 12,* 315–28.

Day, W. F., Jr. (1976). Contemporary behaviorism and the concept of intention. In J. K. Cole & W. J. Arnold (Eds.), *Nebraska symposium on motivation, 1975* (pp. 65-131). Lincoln: University of Nebraska Press.

Day, W. F., Jr. (1980). The historical antecedents of contemporary behaviorism. In R. W. Rieber & K. Salzinger (Eds.), *Psychology: Theoretical–historical perspectives* (pp. 203–62). New York: Academic Press.

Day, W. F., Jr. (1983). On the difference between radical and methodological behaviorism. *Behaviorism, 11,* 89–102.

Day, W. F., Jr. (1986). What is radical behaviorism? In S. Modgil & C. Modgil (Eds.), *B. F. Skinner. Consensus and controversy* (pp. 13-39). Philadelphia: Falmer.

Dean, M. C. (1981). *The evolution of experimental operant psychology.* Unpublished doctoral dissertation. Syracuse University, Syracuse, NY.

Dell, F. (1930). *Love in the machine age: A psychological study of the transition from patriarchal society.* New York: Farrar & Rinehart.

Dennett, D. (1978). *Brainstorms.* Montgomery, VT: Bradford Books.

d'Espagnat, B. (1976). *Conceptual foundations of quantum mechanics* (2nd ed.). Reading, MA: W. H. Benjamin.

d'Espagnat, B. (1979). Quantum theory and reality. *Scientific American, 241,* 158–81.

DeValois, R. L., & DeValois, K. K. (1975). Neural coding of color. In E. C. Carterette & M. P. Friedman (Eds.), *Handbook of perception: Vol. 5. Seeing* (pp. 117–68). New York: Academic Press.

Dewey, J. (1896). The reflex arc concept in psychology. *Psychological Review, 3,* 357–70.

Dewsbury, D. A. (1994). John B. Watson: Profile of a comparative psychologist and proto-ethologist. In J. T. Todd & E. K. Morris (Eds.), *Modern perspectives on John B. Watson and classical behaviorism* (pp. 141–44). Westport, CT: Greenwood.

Diehl, F. (1932). *An historical and critical study of radical behaviorism as a philosophical doctrine.* Unpublished doctoral dissertation. Johns Hopkins University, Baltimore, MD.

Dinsmoor, J. A. (1987). A visit to Bloomington: The first conference on the experimental analysis of behavior. *Journal of the Experimental Analysis of Behavior, 48,* 441–45.

Dinsmoor, J. A. (1988). In the beginning. . . . *Journal of the Experimental Analysis of Behavior, 50,* 287-96.

Dinsmoor, J. A. (1992). Setting the record straight: The social views of B. F. Skinner. *American Psychologist, 47,* 1454–63.

Dirac, P. A. M. (1947). *The principles of quantum mechanics.* Oxford: Clarendon Press.

Dollard, J., & Miller, N. E. (1950). *Personality and psychotherapy: An analysis in terms of learning, thinking, and culture.* New York: McGraw Hill.

Donahoe, J. W., & Palmer, D. C. (1988). Inhibition: A cautionary tale. *Journal of the Experimental Analysis of Behavior, 50,* 333–41.

Eagle, M. N. (1987). *Recent developments in psychoanalysis.* Cambridge: Harvard University Press.

Ebbinghaus, H. (1910). *Abriss der psychologie.* Leipzig: Veit.

Ellson, D. G. (1939). The concept of reflex reserve. *Psychological Review, 46,* 566–75.

Elms, A. C. (1981). Skinner's dark year and *Walden two. American Psychologist, 36,* 470–79.

Epstein, R. (1977). A history of published works of B. F. Skinner, with notes and comments. *Behaviorism, 5,* 99–110.

Epstein, R., & Olson, J. K. (1983). An index to B. F. Skinner's *Particulars of my life. The Behavior Analyst, 6,* 167–80.

Epstein, R., & Olson, J. K. (1984). An index to B. F. Skinner's *The shaping of a behaviorist. The Behavior Analyst, 7,* 47–63.

Esper, E. (1964). *A history of psychology.* Philadelphia: Saunders.

Estes, W. K., Koch, S., MacCorquodale, K., Meehl, P., Mueller, C. G., Jr., Schoenfeld, W. N., & Verplanck, W. S. (Eds.). (1954). *Modern learning theory.* New York: Appleton-Century-Crofts.

Eysenck, H. J. (Ed.). (1960). *Behaviour therapy and the neuroses.* Oxford: Pergamon Press.

Farrell, B. A. (1978). The progress of psychology. *British Journal of Psychology, 69,* 1–8.

Farrington, B. (1949a). *Francis Bacon: Philosopher of industrial science.* New York: Henry Schuman.

Farrington, B. (1949b). *Greek science, Its meaning for us.* New York: Penguin.

Feigl, H. (1963). Physicalism, unity of science, and the foundation of psychology. In P. A. Schilpp (Ed.), *The philosophy of Rudolf Carnap* (pp. 227–67). La Salle, IL: Open Court.

Feigl, H. (1981). *Inquiries and provocations: Selected writings 1929–1974* (R. S. Cohen, Ed.). Dordrecht, The Netherlands: Reidel.

Ferster, C. B. (1978). Is operant conditioning getting bored with behavior? *Journal of the Experimental Analysis of Behavior, 29,* 347–49.

Ferster, C. B., & Skinner, B. F. (1957). *Schedules of reinforcement.* New York: Appleton-Century-Crofts.

Feyerabend, P. K. (1958). Complementarity. *Supplementary Volume 32 of the Proceedings of the Aristotelian Society,* 75–104.

Finan, J. L. (1939). [Review of *The behavior of organisms*]. *Journal of General Psychology, 22,* 441–47.

Findley, J. D. (1962). An experimental outline for building and exploring multi-operant behavior repertoires. *Journal of the Experimental Analysis of Behavior, 5,* 113–66.

Finkelman, D. (1978). Science and psychology. *American Journal of Psychology, 91,* 179–99.

Fischer, D. (1935). *Historian's fallacies: Toward a logic of historical thought.* New York: Harper & Row.

Flanagan, O. J. (1980). Skinnerian metaphysics and the problem of operationism. *Behaviorism, 8,* 1–13.

Flanagan, O. J. (1984). *The science of mind.* Cambridge, MA: Bradford.

Flugel, J. C. (1933). *A hundred years of psychology. 1833–1933.* London: Duckworth.

Fodor, J. A. (1968). *Psychological explanation.* New York: Random House.

Fodor, J. (1975). *The language of thought.* New York: Crowell.

Fodor, J. A. (1980). Methodological solipsism considered as a research strategy in cognitive psychology. *Behavioral and Brain Sciences, 3,* 63–110.

Ford, H. (1916, May 25). Interview. *The Chicago Tribune.*

Fordyce, W. E. (1976). *Behavioral methods for chronic pain and illness.* St. Louis: C. V. Mosby.

French, A. P., & Kennedy, P. J. (Eds.). (1985). *Niels Bohr: A centenary volume.* Cambridge: Harvard University Press.

Furumoto, L. (1989). The new history of psychology. In I. Cohen (Ed.), *The G. Stanley Hall lecture series* (Vol. 9, pp. 9–34). Washington, DC: American Psychological Association.

Galbicka, G. (1988). Differentiating *The behavior of organisms. Journal of the Experimental Analysis of Behavior, 50,* 343–54.

Gardner, H. (1985). *The mind's new science. A history of the cognitive revolution.* New York: Basic.

Gardner, R. A., & Gardner, B. T. (1984). A vocabulary test for chimpanzees (Pan Troglodytes). *Journal of Comparative Psychology, 98,* 381–404.

Garrett, H. E. (1930). *Great experiments in psychology.* New York: Century.

Gergen, K. J. (1985). The social constructionist movement in modern psychology. *American Psychologist, 40,* 266–75.

Geuter, U. (1983). The uses of history for the shaping of a field: Observations on German psychology. In L. Graham, W. Lepenies, & P. Weingart (Eds.), *Functions and uses of disciplinary histories* (pp. 191–228). Dordrecht, Holland: Reidel.

Gilgen, A. R. (1982). *American psychology since World War II: A profile of the discipline.* Westport, CT: Greenwood.

Gillespie, D. L. (1973). *A quantum mechanics primer.* London: International Textbook Company.

Ginsburg, B. E. (1990). Darwin, mind, and behavior [Review of *Darwin and the emergence of evolutionary theories of mind and behavior*]. *Contemporary Psychology, 35,* 228–31.

Glenn, S. S., Ellis, J., & Greenspoon, J. (1992). On the revolutionary nature of the operant as a unit of behavioral selection. *American Psychologist, 47,* 1329–36.

Goodall, K. (1972). Shapers at work. *Psychology Today, 6*(6), 53–62, 132–38.

Gormezano, I., & Coleman, S. R. (1985). An essay review of *Mechanisms of adaptive behavior: Clark L. Hull's theoretical papers, with commentary,* edited by A. Amsel and M. E. Rashotte. Columbia University Press: New York. 1984. *Behaviorism, 13,* 171–82.

Gould, J. L. (1982). *Ethology: The mechanisms and evolution of behavior.* New York: Norton.

Gould, J. L. & Marler, P. (1987). [Letter to the editor in response to Todd]. *Scientific American, 265*(4), 4.

Gould, S. J. (1977). *Ontogeny and phylogeny.* Cambridge: Harvard University Press.

Gould, S. J., & Lewontin, R. C. (1979). The spandrels of San Marco and the Panglossian paradigm: A critique of the adaptationist programme. *Proceedings of the Royal Society of London, 205,* 581–98.

Gray, J. A. (1979). *Ivan Pavlov.* New York: Viking.

Gray, P. H. (1980). Behaviorism: Some truths that need telling, some errors that need correcting. *Bulletin of the Psychonomic Society, 15,* 357–60.

Gregory, R. L. (Ed.). (1987). *The Oxford companion to the mind.* New York: Oxford University Press.

Grossberg, S., & Mingolla, E. (1985). Neural dynamics of form perception: Boundary completion, illusory figures, and neon color spreading. *Psychological Review, 92,* 173–211.

Grossman, W. I. (1976). Knightmare in armor: Reflections on Wilhelm Reich's contributions to psychoanalysis. *Psychiatry, 39,* 376–85.

Guillemin, V. (1968). *The story of quantum mechanics*. New York: Charles Scribner's Sons.

Gudmundsson, K. (1983). *The emergence of B. F. Skinner's theory of operant behavior: A case study in the history and philosophy of science*. Unpublished doctoral dissertation, University of Western Ontario, London, Ontario, Canada.

Guthrie, E. R. (1935). *The psychology of learning*. New York: Harper.

Guthrie, E. R. (1944). Personality in terms of associative learning. In J. M. Hunt (Ed.), *Personality and the behavior disorders* (pp. 49–68). New York: Ronald.

Guthrie, E. R., & Horton, G. P. (1946). *Cats in a puzzle box*. New York: Rinehart.

Guthrie, R. V. (1976). *Even the rat was white: A historical overview of psychology*. New York: Harper & Row.

Guttman, N., & Kalish, H. I. (1956). Discriminability and stimulus generalization. *Journal of Experimental Psychology, 51*, 79–88.

Hake, D. F., & Vukelich, R. (1972). A classification and review of cooperation procedures. *Journal of the Experimental Analysis of Behavior, 18*, 333–43.

Hamlyn, D. W. (1953). Behavior. *Philosophy, 28*, 132–45.

Hanfmann, E., & Kasanin, J. (1937). A method for the study of concept formation. *Journal of Psychology, 3*, 521–40.

Haring, T. G., Breen, C. G., & Laitinen, R. E. (1989). Stimulus class formation and concept learning: Establishment of within- and between-set generalization and transitive relationships via conditional discrimination procedures. *Journal of the Experimental Analysis of Behavior, 52*, 13–25.

Harris, B. (1979). Whatever happened to Little Albert? *American Psychologist, 34*, 151–60.

Harris, B. (1981). A non-historical biography of John B. Watson. *Contemporary Psychology, 26*, 62–63.

Harris, M. (1977). *Cannibals and kings*. New York: Random House.

Harzem, P., & Miles, T. R. (1978). *Conceptual issues in operant psychology*. New York: John Wiley & Sons.

Harzem, P., & Williams, R. A. (1983). On searching for a science of human behavior. *The Psychological Record, 33*, 565–74.

Haskins, L., & Jeffery, K. (1990). *Understanding quantitative history*. Cambridge: MIT Press.

Hayes, S. C. (1986). Behavioral philosophy in the late 1980's. *Theoretical and Philosophical Psychology, 6*, 39–43.

Hayes, S. C., Hayes, L. J., & Reese, H. W. (1988). Finding the philosophical core: A review of Stephen C. Pepper's *World hypotheses: A study in evidence. Journal of the Experimental Analysis of Behavior, 50*, 97–111.

Hayes, S. C., Hayes, L. J., Reese, H. W., & Sarbin, T. R. (Eds.). (1993). *Varieties of scientific contextualism*. Reno, NV: Context Press.

Hearnshaw, L. S. (1984). The two ingredients of history. *Revista de Historia de la Psicologia, 5*, 145–51.

Heidbreder, E. (1933). *Seven psychologies*. New York: Appleton-Century.

Heider, F. (1958). *The psychology of interpersonal relations*. New York: John Wiley & Sons.

Heisenberg, W. (1962). *Physics and philosophy*. New York: Harper & Row.

Heisenberg, W. (1971). *Physics and beyond*. New York: Harper & Row.

Hempel, C. (1949). The logical analysis of psychology. In H. Feigl & W. Sellars

(Eds.), *Readings in philosophical analysis* (pp. 393–407). New York: Appleton-Century-Crofts. (Reprinted from *Revue de Synthèse*, 1935, *10*, 27–42.)

Hempel, C. (1958). The theoretician's dilemma. In H. Feigl, M. Scriven, & G. Maxwell (Eds.), *Minnesota studies in the philosophy of science, Vol. 2: Concepts, theories, and the mind–body problem* (pp. 37–98). Minneapolis: University of Minnesota Press.

Henle, M. (1976). Why study the history of psychology? *Annals of the New York Academy of Sciences, 270*, 14–20.

Herbert, N. (1985). *Quantum reality*. Garden City, NY: Anchor Press.

Herrnstein, R. J. (1969a). Behaviorism. In D. L. Krantz (Ed.), *Schools of psychology: A symposium* (pp. 51–68). New York: Appleton-Century-Crofts.

Herrnstein, R. J. (1969b). Method and theory in the study of avoidance. *Psychological Review, 76*, 49–69.

Herrnstein, R. J. (1977). The evolution of behaviorism. *American Psychologist, 32*, 593–603.

Herrnstein, R. J., & Boring, E. G. (Eds.). (1965). *A sourcebook in the history of psychology*. Cambridge: Harvard University Press.

Herrnstein, R. J., & Hineline, P. N. (1966). Negative reinforcement as shock frequency reduction. *Journal of the Experimental Analysis of Behavior, 9*, 421–31.

Herrnstein, R. J., & Loveland, D. H. (1964). Complex visual concept in the pigeon. *Science, 146*, 549–51.

Hiebert, E. N. (1970). Mach's philosophical use of the history of science. In R. H. Stuewer (Ed.), *Historical and philosophical perspectives of science* (pp. 184–203). Minneapolis: University of Minnesota Press.

Higham, J. (1973). *History: Professional scholarship in America* (paperback ed.). New York: Harper & Row. (Original work published 1965.)

Hilgard, E. R. (1939). [Review of B. F. Skinner's *The behavior of organisms*]. *Psychological Bulletin, 36*, 121–25. (Reprinted in *Journal of the Experimental Analysis of Behavior, 50*, 283–86.)

Hilgard, E. R. (1948). *Theories of learning*. Appleton-Century-Crofts.

Hilgard, E. R. (1987). *Psychology in America: A historical survey*. New York: Harcourt Brace Jovanovich.

Hilgard, E. R., & Bower, G. (1975). *Theories of learning* (4th ed.). New York: Appleton-Century-Crofts.

Hilgard, E. R., Leary, D. E., & McGuire, G. R. (1991). The history of psychology: A survey and critical analysis. *Annual Review of Psychology, 42*, 79–107.

Hilliz, W. A., & Broyles, J. W. (1980). The family trees of American psychologists. In W. G. Bringmann & R. D. Tweney (Eds.), *Wundt studies* (pp. 422–34). Toronto: Hogrefe & Huber.

Hineline, P. N. (1980). The language of behavior analysis: Its community, its function, and its limitations. *Behaviorism, 8*, 67–86.

Hineline, P. N., & Laties, V. G. (Eds.). (1987). Anniversaries in behavior analysis. *Journal of the Experimental Analysis of Behavior, 48*, 439–514.

Hineline, P. N., & Wanchisen, B. A. (1989). Correlated hypothesizing and the distinction between contingency-shaped and rule-governed behavior. In S. C. Hayes (Ed.), *Rule-governed behavior: Cognition, contingencies, and instructional control* (pp. 221–68). New York: Plenum.

Hintikka, J. (Ed.). (1968). A symposium on Ernst Mach. *Synthèse, 18*, 132–301.

Hocutt, M. (1985). Spartans, strawmen, and symptoms. *Behaviorism, 15*, 87–97.

Hughs, R. I. G. (1981). Quantum logic. *Scientific American, 245*, 202–13.

Hull, C. L. (1920). Quantitative aspects of the evolution of concepts. *Psychological Monographs, 28* (1, Whole No. 123).

Hull, C. L. (1933). *Suggestion and hypnosis.* New York: Appleton-Century.

Hull, C. L. (1943). *Principles of behavior: An introduction to behavior theory.* New York: Appleton-Century.

Hull, D. L. (1979). In defense of presentism. *History and Theory: Studies in the Philosophy of History, 18*, 1–15.

Hull, D. L. (1988). *Science as a process.* Chicago: University of Chicago Press.

Hurvich, L. M., & Jamison, D. (1957). An opponent-process theory of color vision. *Psychological Review, 64*, 384–404.

Hurvich, L. M., & Jamison, D. (1974). Opponent processes as a model of neural organization. *American Psychologist, 29*, 88–102.

Hyman, B. (1982). Reconstructing accounts of psychology's past. *Journal of Mind and Behavior, 3*, 55–66.

Jammer, M. (1974). *The philosophy of quantum mechanics.* New York: John Wiley & Sons.

Jardine, L. (1974). *Francis Bacon: Discovery and the art of discourse.* Cambridge: Cambridge University Press.

Jauch, J. M. (1989). *Are quanta real?* Bloomington: Indiana University Press.

Jaynes, J. (1973). Introduction: The study of the history of psychology. In M. Henle, J. Jaynes, & J. J. Sullivan (Eds.), *Historical conceptions of psychology* (pp. ix–xii). New York: Springer.

Jonçich, G. (1984). *Edward Thorndike: The sane positivist.* Middletown, CT: Wesleyan University Press.

Jones E. E., & Davis, K. E. (1965). From acts to dispositions: The attribution process in person perceptions. In L. Berkowitz (Ed.), *Advances in Experimental Social Psychology* (Vol. 2, pp. 219–66). New York: Academic Press.

Jones, E. E., & Nisbett, R. E. (1971). The actor and observer: Divergent perceptions of the causes of behavior. In E. E. Jones, D. E. Kanouse, H. H. Kelley, R. E. Nisbett, S. Valins, & B. Weiner (Eds.), *Attribution: Perceiving the causes of behavior* (pp. 1–16). Morristown, NJ: General Learning Press.

Jones, F. N. (1939). [Review of *The behavior of organisms*]. *American Journal of Psychology, 52*, 659–60.

Kallen, H. M. (1930). Behaviorism. In E. R. A. Seligman & A. Johnson (Eds.), *The encyclopaedia of the social sciences* (Vol. 2, pp. 495–98). New York: Macmillan.

Kanizsa, G. (1976). Subjective contours. *Scientific American, 234*, 48–52.

Kantor, J. R. (1924). *Principles of psychology.* Chicago: Principia Press.

Kantor, J. R. (1942). Preface to interbehavioral psychology. *Psychological Record, 5*, 173–93.

Kantor, J. R. (1963). *The scientific evolution of psychology* (Vol. 1). Chicago: Principia Press.

Kantor, J. R. (1964). History of psychology: What benefits? *The Psychological Record, 14*, 433–43.

Kantor, J. R. (1968). Behaviorism in the history of psychology. *The Psychological Record, 18*, 151–65.

Kantor, J. R. (1969). *The scientific evolution of psychology* (Vol. 2). Chicago: Principia Press.

Kattsoff, L. O. (1939). Philosophy, psychology, and postulational technique. *Psychological Review, 46,* 62–74.

Kaufman, A. S. (1968). The aims of scientific activity. *Monist, 52,* 374–89.

Kazdin, A. E. (1978). *History of behavior modification: Experimental foundations of contemporary research.* Baltimore: University Park Press.

Kehoe, E. J. (1989). Connectionist models of conditioning: A tutorial. *Journal of the Experimental Analysis of Behavior, 52,* 427–40.

Kelleher, R. T. (1958). Concept formation in chimpanzees. *Science, 128,* 777–78.

Keller, F. S. (1937). *The definition of psychology.* New York: Appleton-Century.

Keller, F. S. (1970). Psychology at Harvard (1926–1931): A reminiscence. In P. B. Dews (Ed.), *Festschrift for B. F. Skinner* (pp. 29–36). New York: Appleton-Century-Crofts.

Keller, F. S. (1973). *The definition of psychology* (2nd ed.). Englewood Cliffs, NJ: Prentice-Hall.

Keller, F. S. (1982). *Pedagogue's progress.* Lawrence, KS: TRI.

Keller, F. S. (1989). A lost art. *The Behavior Analyst, 12,* 115–19.

Keller, F. S. (1992). Memories of psychology in the twenties. *The Behavior Analyst, 15,* 101–107.

Keller, F. S. (1994). A debt acknowledged. In J. T. Todd & E. K. Morris (Eds.), *Modern perspectives on John B. Watson and classical behaviorism* (pp. 125–30). Westport, CT: Greenwood.

Keller, F. S. & Schoenfeld, W. N. (1949). The psychology curriculum at Columbia College. *American Psychologist, 4,* 165–72.

Keller, F., & Schoenfeld, W. N. (1950). *Principles of psychology: A systematic text in the science of psychology.* New York: Appleton-Century-Crofts.

Kelley, H. H. (1967). Attribution theory in social psychology. In D. Levine (Ed.), *Nebraska symposium on motivation* (Vol. 15, pp. 192–238). Lincoln: University of Nebraska Press.

Kendler, H. H. (1985). Behaviorism and psychology. An uneasy alliance. In S. Koch & D. E. Leary (Eds.), *A century of psychology as science* (pp. 121–34). New York: McGraw Hill.

Kendler, H. H., & Spence, J. T. (1971). Tenets of neo-behaviorism. In H. H. Kendler and J. T. Spence (Eds.), *Essays in neo-behaviorism: A memorial volume to Kenneth W. Spence* (pp. 11–40). New York: Appleton-Century-Crofts.

Kessel, F. S., & Bevan, W. (1985). Notes toward a history of cognitive psychology. In C. E. Buxton (Ed.), *Points of view in the modern history of psychology* (pp. 259–94). New York: Academic Press.

Killeen, P. R. (1984). Emergent behaviorism. *Behaviorism, 12,* 25–39.

Killeen, P. R. (1988). The reflex reserve. *Journal of the Experimental Analysis of Behavior, 50,* 319–31.

King, W. P. (Ed.). (1930). *Behaviorism: A battle line.* Nashville: Cokesbury Press.

Kitchener, R. F. (1977). Behavior and behaviorism. *Behaviorism, 5,* 11–71.

Klein, M. J. (1979). Einstein and the development of quantum physics. In A. P. French (Ed.), *Einstein: A centenary volume* (pp. 133–51). Cambridge: Harvard University Press.

Kline, M. (1980). *Mathematics: The loss of certainty.* New York: Oxford University Press.

Knapp, T. J. (1974). An index to B. F. Skinner's *Beyond freedom and dignity. Behaviorism, 2,* 180–89.

Knapp, T. J. (1985). Who's who in American psychology. *Teaching of Psychology, 12,* 15–17.

Knapp, T. J. (1986a). Contributions to psychohistory: XI. *The behavior of organisms* and the *Principles of behavior:* Note on a technique of historical analysis. *Psychological Reports, 59,* 1293–94.

Knapp, T. J. (1986b). The emergence of cognitive psychology in the latter half of the twentieth century. In T. J. Knapp & L. C. Robertson (Eds.), *Approaches to cognition: Contrasts and controversies* (pp. 13–35). Hillsdale, NJ: Lawrence Erlbaum Associates.

Knapp, T. J. (in press). The verbal legacy of B. F. Skinner: An essay on the secondary literature. In W. R. Woodward & L. D. Smith (Eds.), *B. F. Skinner and behaviorism in American culture.* Lehigh, PA: Lehigh University Press.

Knapp, T. J., & Robertson, L. C. (Eds.). (1986). *Approaches to cognition: Contrasts and controversies.* Hillsdale, NJ: Lawrence Erlbaum Associates.

Koch, S. (1941). The logical character of the motivation concept. I. *Psychological Review, 48,* 15–38.

Koch, S. (1954). Clark L. Hull. In W. K. Estes, S. Koch, K. MacCorquodale, P. E. Meehl, C. G. Mueller, Jr., W. N. Schoenfeld, & W. S. Verplanck (Eds.), *Modern learning theory* (pp. 1–176). New York: Appleton-Century-Crofts.

Koch, S. (1964). Psychology and emerging conceptions of knowledge as unitary. In T. W. Wann (Ed.), *Behaviorism and phenomenology: Contrasting bases for modern psychology* (pp. 1–41). Chicago: University of Chicago Press.

Koch, S. (1971). Reflections on the state of psychology. *Social Research, 38,* 669–709.

Koch, S. (1974). Psychology as a science. In S. C. Brown (Ed.), *Philosophy of psychology* (pp. 3–40). London: Macmillan.

Koestler, A. (1964). *The act of creation.* New York: Macmillan.

Konorski, J., & Miller, S. (1935). On two types of conditioned reflex. *Journal of General Psychology, 12,* 66–67.

Krantz, D. L. (1965). Toward a role for historical analysis: The case of psychology and physiology. *Journal of the History of the Behavioral Sciences, 1,* 278–83.

Krantz, D. L. (1971). The separate worlds of operant and nonoperant psychology. *Journal of Applied Behavior Analysis, 4,* 61–70.

Krantz, D. L. (1972). Schools and systems: The mutual isolation of operant and nonoperant psychology as a case study. *Journal of the History of the Behavioral Sciences, 8,* 86–102.

Krantz, D. L., & Wiggins, L. (1973). Personal and impersonal channels of recruitment in the growth of theory. *Human Development, 16,* 133–56.

Krasner, L. (1987). Behaviorism: History. In R. J. Corsini (Ed.), *Concise encyclopedia of psychology* (pp. 125–27). New York: Wiley.

Krechevsky, I. (1939). [Review of *The behavior of organisms*]. *Journal of Abnormal and Social Psychology, 34,* 404–407.

Kuhn, T. S. (1962). *The structure of scientific revolutions.* Chicago: University of Chicago Press.

Kuhn, T. S. (1963). The function of dogma in scientific research. In A. C. Crombie (Ed.), *Scientific change* (pp. 347–69). New York: Basic Books.

Kuhn, T. S. (1968). Science: I. The history of science. In D. L. Sills (Ed.), *International encyclopedia of the social science* (Vol. 14, pp. 74–83). New York: Macmillan.

Kuo, Z. Y. (1923). A behavioristic experiment on inductive inference. *Journal of Experimental Psychology, 6*, 247–93.

Lacey, H. M., & Rachlin, H. (1978). Behavior, cognition and theories of choice. *Behaviorism, 6*, 177–202.

Lasch, C. (1979a). *Culture of narcissism: American life in an age of diminishing expectations*. New York: Norton.

Lasch, C. (1979b, August 4 & 11). [Review of *The shaping of a behaviorist* by B. F. Skinner]. *New Republic, 181*(5 & 6), 36–38.

Laties, V. G. (1987). Society for the experimental analysis of behavior: The first thirty years (1957–1987). *Journal of the Experimental Analysis of Behavior, 48*, 495–512.

Lattal, K. A. (Ed.). (1992). Reflections of B. F. Skinner and psychology [Special issue]. *American Psychologist, 47*.

Laudan, L. (1977). *Progress and its problems*. Berkeley: University of California Press.

Laudan, L. (1984). *Science and values. An essay on the aims of science and their role in scientific debate*. Berkeley: University of California Press.

Leahey, T. H. (1980). *A history of psychology: Main currents in psychological thought*. Englewood Cliffs, NJ: Prentice-Hall.

Leahey, T. H. (1981). The mistaken mirror: On Wundt's and Titchener's psychologies. *Journal of the History of the Behavioral Sciences, 17*, 273–82.

Leahey, T. H. (1987a). Behaviorism. In R. J. Corsini (Ed.), *Concise encyclopedia of psychology* (pp. 124–25). New York: Wiley.

Leahey, T. H. (1987b). *A history of psychology: Main currents in psychological thought* (2nd ed.). Englewood Cliffs, NJ: Prentice-Hall.

Leahey, T. H. (1988). More mythinformation corrected. *Behaviorism, 16*, 163–66.

Leahey, T. H. (1992a). *A history of psychology* (3rd ed.). Englewood Cliffs, NJ: Prentice-Hall.

Leahey, T. H. (1992b). The mythical revolutions of American psychology. *American Psychologist, 47*, 308–18.

Lee, V. L. (1981). The operant as a class of responses. *Scandinavian Journal of Psychology, 22*, 215–21.

Lee, V. L. (1988). *Beyond behaviorism*. Hillsdale, NJ: Lawrence Erlbaum Associates.

Lieberman, D. A. (1979). Behaviorism and the mind. A (limited) call for a return to introspection. *American Psychologist, 34*, 319–33.

Lindzey, G. (Ed.). (1989). *A history of psychology in autobiography* (Vol. 8). Englewood Cliffs: Prentice-Hall.

Littman, R. A. (1981). Psychology's histories: Some new ones and a bit about their predecessors—An essay review. *Journal of the History of the Behavioral Sciences, 17*, 516–32.

Loeb, J. (1900). *Comparative physiology of the brain and comparative psychology*. New York: Putnam.

Loeb, J. (1916). *The organism as a whole*. New York: Putnam.

Logue, A. W. (1978). Behaviorist John B. Watson and the continuity of species. *Behaviorism, 6*, 71–79.

Logue, A. W. (1985a). The growth of behaviorism. In C. Buxton (Ed.), *Points of view in the modern history of psychology* (pp. 169–96). New York: Academic Press.

Logue, A. W. (1985b). The origins of behaviorism. In C. Buxton (Ed.), *Points of view in the modern history of psychology* (pp. 141–67). New York: Academic Press.

Logue, A. W. (1988). A behaviorist's biologist. *The Behavior Analyst, 11*, 205–207.

Logue, A. W. (1994). Watson's behaviorist manifesto: Past positive and present negative consequences. In J. T. Todd & E. K. Morris (Eds.), *Modern perspectives on John B. Watson and classical behaviorism* (pp. 109–23). Westport, CT: Greenwood.

Loucks, R. B. (1941). The contribution of physiological psychology. *Psychological Review, 48*, 404–407.

Lundh, L. (1981). The mind considered as a system of meaning structures: Elementary meaning structures. *Scandinavian Journal of Psychology, 22*, 145–60.

Lundin, R. W. (1974). *Personality: A behavioral analysis* (2nd ed.). New York: Macmillan.

Lycan, W. (1984). Skinner and the mind–body problem. *The Behavioral and Brain Sciences, 7*, 634–35.

MacCorquodale, K., & Meehl, P. (1948). On a distinction between hypothetical constructs and intervening variables. *Psychological Review, 55*, 95–107.

Mach, E. (1942). *The science of mechanics* (5th ed., T. J. McCormack, Trans.). La Salle, IL: Open Court. (Original work published 1883.)

Mach, E. (1943). *Popular scientific lectures* (5th ed., T. J. McCormack, Trans.). La Salle, IL: Open Court. (Original work published 1894.)

Mach, E. (1959). *The analysis of sensations.* New York: Dover. (Original work published 1886.)

Mach, E. (1960). *The science of mechanics* (6th ed. T. J. McCormack, Trans.). La Salle, IL: Open Court. (Original work, first English ed., published 1893.)

Mach, E. (1976). *Knowledge and error: Sketches on the psychology of inquiry* (5th ed., T. J. McCormack & P. Foulkes, Trans.). Dordrecht, The Netherlands: Reidel. (Original work published 1905.)

Mackenzie, B. D. (1977). *Behaviorism and the limits of scientific method.* Atlantic Highlands, NJ: Humanities Press.

Mackenzie, B. D., & Mackenzie, L. (1974). The case for a revised systematic approach to the history of psychology. *Journal of the History of the Behavioral Sciences, 10*, 324–47.

Mackintosh, N. J. (1974). *The psychology of animal learning.* New York: Academic Press.

Mahoney, M. J. (1989). Scientific psychology and radical behaviorism: Important distinctions based on scientism and objectivism. *American Psychologist, 44*, 1372–77.

Malone, J. C. (1990). *Theories of learning: A historical approach.* Belmont, CA: Wadsworth.

Marmor, J. (1977). Foreword. In D. B. Klein, *The unconscious: Invention or discovery? A historico-critical inquiry.* Santa Monica, CA: Goodyear.

Marmor, J., & Woods, S. M. (1980). *The interface between psychodynamic and behavioral therapies.* New York: Plenum.

Marr, M. J. (1979). Second-order schedules and the generation of unitary response sequences. In M. Zeiler & P. Harzem (Eds.), *Reinforcement and the organization of behaviour* (Vol. 1, pp. 223–60). New York: John Wiley & Sons.

Marr, M. J. (1982). Determinism. *The Behavior Analyst, 5*, 205–207.

Marr, M. J. (1983). Memory: Models and metaphors. *Psychological Record, 33*, 12–19.

Marr, M. J. (1985). 'Tis the gift to be simple: A retrospective appreciation of Mach's *The science of mechanics. Journal of the Experimental Analysis of Behavior, 44*, 129–38.

Marr, M. J. (1986). Mathematics and verbal behavior. In T. Thompson & M. Zeiler (Eds.), *Analysis and integration of behavioral units* (pp. 161–83). Hillsdale, NJ: Lawrence Erlbaum Associates.

Marr, M. J. (1989). Some remarks on the quantitative analysis of behavior. *The Behavior Analyst, 12*, 143–51.

Marr, M. J. (1990). El lenguaje y la mechanica cuántica. In E. Ribes & P. Harzem (Eds.), *Lenguaje y conducta* (pp. 267–97). Mexico, DF: Trillas.

Marr, M. J. (1992). Behavioral dynamics—One perspective. *Journal of the Experimental Analysis of Behavior, 57*, 249–66.

Marr, M. J. (1993a). Contextualistic mechanism or mechanistic contextualism: The straw machine as tar baby. *The Behavior Analyst, 16*, 59–65.

Marr, M. J. (1993b). Macht's nicht? . . . A commentary on Staddon's "The conventional wisdom of behavior analysis." *Journal of the Experimental Analysis of Behavior, 60*, 473–76.

Martin, G., & Pear, J. (1992). *Behavior modification: What it is and how to do it* (4th ed.). Englewood Cliffs, NJ: Prentice-Hall.

Marx, M. H., & Cronan-Hillix, W. A. (1987). *Systems and theories of psychology* (4th ed.). New York: McGraw Hill.

Marx, M. H., & Hillix, W. A. (1963). *Systems and theories in psychology.* New York: McGraw Hill.

May, H. (1959). *The end of American innocence: A study of the first years of our time, 1912–1917.* New York: Oxford University Press.

Mayr, E. (1982). *The growth of biological thought.* Cambridge: Harvard University Press.

McDowell, J. J. (1988). Behavior analysis: The third branch of Aristotle's physics. *Journal of the Experimental Analysis of Behavior, 50*, 297–304.

McFall, R. M. (1982). A review and reformulation of the concept of social skills. *Behavioral Assessment, 4*, 1–33.

McKearney, J. W. (1977). Asking questions about behavior. *Perspectives in Biology and Medicine, 21*, 109–19.

McPherson, A., Bonem, M., Green, G., & Osborne, J. G. (1984). A citation analysis of the influence of research on Skinner's *Verbal behavior. The Behavior Analyst, 7*, 157–67.

Meyers, D. L. (1993). Participation of women in behavior analysis. *The Behavior Analyst, 16*, 75–86.

Michael, J. (1985). Behavior analysis: A radical perspective. In B. L.Hammonds (Ed.), *Psychology and learning* (pp. 99–121). Washington, DC: American Psychological Association.

Michael, J. (1991). Historical antecedents of behavior analysis. *The ABA Newsletter, 14*(2), 7–12.

Michael, J. (1993). *Concepts and principles of behavior analysis.* Kalamazoo, MI: Society for the Advancement of Behavior Analysis.

Miller, G. A., Galanter, E., & Pribram, K. (1960). *Plans and the stucture of behavior.* New York: Holt, Rinehart & Winston.

Miller, L. K. (1975). *Principles of everyday behavior analysis*. Monterey, CA: Brooks/Cole.

Moerk, E. L. (1983). A behavioral analysis of controversial topics in first language acquisition: Reinforcements, corrections, modeling, input frequencies, and the three-term contingency pattern. *Journal of Psycholinguistic Research, 12,* 129–55.

Moore, B. R., & Stuttard, S. (1979). Dr. Guthrie and *Felis domesticus* or: Tripping over the cat. *Science, 205,* 1031–33.

Moore, J. (1975). On the principle of operationism in a science of behavior. *Behaviorism, 3,* 120–38.

Moore, J. (1980). Behaviorism and private events. *The Psychological Record, 30,* 459–75.

Moore, J. (1981). On mentalism, methodological behaviorism, and radical behaviorism. *Behaviorism, 9,* 55–77.

Moore, J. (1984a). On behaviorism, knowledge, and causal explanation. *The Psychological Record, 34,* 73–97.

Moore, J. (1984b). On Skinner's radical operationism. *The Behavioral and Brain Sciences, 7,* 564–65.

Moore, J. (1985). Some historical and conceptual relations among logical positivism, operationism, and behaviorism. *The Behavior Analyst, 8,* 53–63.

Moore, J. (1987). The roots of the family tree: A review of four books on the history and nature of behaviorism. *The Psychological Record, 37,* 449–70.

Moore, O. K., & Lewis, D. J. (1953). Purpose and learning theory. *Psychological Review, 60,* 149–56.

Moore, T. V. (1939). *Cognitive psychology*. Philadelphia: Lippincott.

Morgan, D. L., Morgan, R. K., & Toth, J. M. (1992). Variation and selection: The evolutionary analogy and the convergence of cognitive and behavioral psychology. *The Behavior Analyst, 15,* 129–38.

Morris, E. K. (1988). Contextualism: The world view of behavior analysis. *Journal of Experimental Child Psychology, 46,* 289–323.

Morris, E. K. (1989). Roads less traveled: A review of Lee's *Beyond behaviorism. The Behavior Analyst, 12,* 233–37.

Morris, E. K. (1990). What Mahoney "knows." *American Psychologist, 45,* 1178–79.

Morris, E. K. (1991). [Review of *Mechanical man: John Broadus Watson and the beginnings of behaviorism.*] *Philosophical Psychology, 4,* 294–96.

Morris, E. K. (1993a). Behavior analysis and mechanism: One is not the other. *The Behavior Analyst, 16,* 25–43.

Morris, E. K. (1993b). Contextualism, historiography, and the history of behavior analysis. In S. C. Hayes, L. J. Hayes, H. W. Reese, & T. R. Sarbin (Eds.), *Varieties of scientific contextualism* (pp. 137–65). Reno, NV: Context Press.

Morris, E. K., Higgins, S. T., & Bickel, W. K. (1982). Comments on cognitive science in the experimental analysis of behavior. *The Behavior Analyst, 5,* 109–25.

Morris, E. K., & Larsen, S. E. (1986, May). *All causes have contexts: A historical note on contextual conditions in the experimental analysis of behavior*. Paper presented at the convention of the Association for Behavior Analysis, Milwaukee, WI.

Morris, E. K., & Schneider, S. M. (1986). Reference citations in B. F. Skinner's *Verbal behavior. The Analysis of Verbal Behavior, 4,* 39–43.

Morris, E. K., Todd, J. T., Midgley, B. D., Schneider, S. M., & Johnson, L. M. (1990). The history of behavior analysis: Some historiography and a bibliography. *The Behavior Analyst, 7,* 131–58.

Mountjoy, P. T., & Ruben, D. H. (1984). A science of history. *The Behavior Analyst,* *7,* 75–76.

Mowrer, O. H. (1950). *Learning theory and personality dynamics.* New York: Ronald Press.

Moxley, R. A. (1982). Graphics for three-term contingencies. *The Behavior Analyst,* *5,* 45–51.

Moxley, R. A. (1989). Some historical relationships between science and technology with implications for behavior analysis. *The Behavior Analyst, 12,* 45–57.

Moxley, R. A. (1992). From mechanistic to functional behaviorism. *American Psychologist, 47,* 1300–11.

Murphy, G. (1932). *Historical introduction to modern psychology.* New York: Harcourt Brace.

Nash, L. K. (1970). *Elements of classical and statistical thermodynamics.* Reading, MA: Addison-Wesley.

Neisser, U. (1967). *Cognitive psychology.* New York: Appleton-Century-Crofts.

Neuringer, A. (1991). Humble behaviorism. *The Behavior Analyst, 14,* 1–13.

Norcross, J. C., & Tomcho, T. J. (1994). Great books in psychology: Three studies in search of consensus. *Teaching of Psychology, 21,* 86–90.

Notterman, J. M. (1985). *Forms of psychological inquiry.* New York: Columbia University Press.

Nowell-Smith, P. H. (1977). The constructionist theory of history. *History and Theory, Studies in the Philosophy of History, 16,* 1–28.

Observer. (1975). Comments and queries: On reviewing psychological classics. *Psychological Record, 25,* 293–98.

O'Donnell, J. M. (1979). The crisis of experimentalism in the 1920s: E. G. Boring and his uses of history. *American Psychologist, 34,* 289–95.

O'Donnell, J. M. (1985). *The origins of behaviorism. American psychology, 1870–1920.* New York: New York University Press.

Ogden, C. K., & Richards, I. A. (1923). *The meaning of meaning.* New York: Harcourt Brace.

Olmsted, J. M. D. (1938). *Claude Bernard, physiologist.* New York: Harper.

Oppenheimer, R. (1956). Analogy in science. *American Psychologist, 11,* 127–36.

Osier, D. V., & Wozniak, R. H. (1984). *A century of serial publications in psychology, 1850–1950: An international bibliography.* Milwood, NY: Kraus International.

Palmer, S., & Kimchi, R. (1986). The information processing approach to cognition. In T. L. Knapp & L. C. Robertson (Eds.), *Approaches to cognition: Contrasts and controversies* (pp. 37–79). Hillsdale, NJ: Lawrence Erlbaum Associates.

Parrott, L. J., & Hake, D. F. (1983). Toward a science of history. *The Behavior Analyst, 6,* 121–32.

Parsons, J. A., Taylor, D. C., & Joyce, T. M. (1981). Precurrent self-prompting operants in children: "Remembering." *Journal of the Experimental Analysis of Behavior, 36,* 253–66.

Passmore, J. (1967). Logical positivism. In P. Edwards (Ed.), *Encyclopedia of philosophy* (Vol. 5, pp. 52–57). New York: Macmillan.

Pauly, P. J. (1987). *Controlling life: Jacques Loeb and the engineering idea in biology.* New York: Oxford University Press.

Pavlov, I. P. (1927). *Conditioned reflexes: An investigation of the physiological activity of the cerebral cortex.* London: Oxford University Press.

Pepper, S. C. (1942). *World hypotheses: A study in evidence.* Berkeley: University of California Press.

Perez-Ramos, A. (1988). *Francis Bacon's idea of science and the maker's knowledge tradition.* Oxford: Oxford University Press.

Persico, E. (1950). *Fundamentals of quantum mechanics.* New York: Prentice-Hall.

Peterson, M. E. (1978). The Midwestern Association of Behavior Analysis: Past, present, future. *The Behavior Analyst, 1,* 3–15.

Pierce, W. D., & Epling, W. F. (1980). What happened to analysis in applied behavior analysis. *The Behavior Analyst, 3,* 1–9.

Planck, M. (1970). On Mach's theory of physical knowledge: A reply. In S. Toulmin (Ed.), *Physical reality: Philosophical essays on twentieth-century physics* (pp. 44–52). New York: Harper & Row. (Original work published 1910.)

Popper, K. (1965). *Conjectures and refutations: The growth of scientific knowledge.* New York: Harper & Row.

Popplestone, J. A., & McPherson, M. W. (1988). *Dictionary of concepts in general psychology.* Westport, CT: Greenwood.

Posner, M. I. (1982). Cumulative development of attentional theory. *American Psychologist, 37,* 168–79.

Powers, W. T. (1973). Feedback: Beyond behaviorism. *Science, 179,* 351–56.

Price, D. (1970). Citation measures of hard science, soft science, technology, and nonscience. In C. E. Nelson & D. K. Pollock (Eds.), *Communication among scientists and engineers* (pp. 3–22). Lexington, MA: Heath.

Pronko, N. H. (1988). *From AI to zeitgeist: A philosophical guide for the skeptical psychologist.* Westport, CT: Greenwood.

Purton, A. C. (1978). Ethological categories of behaviour and some consequences of their conflation. *Animal Behavior, 26,* 653–70.

Putnam, H. (1980). Brains and behavior. In N. Block (Ed.), *Readings in philosophy of psychology* (Vol. 1). Cambridge: Harvard University Press.

Rachlin, H. (1985). Pain and behavior. *The Behavioral and Brain Sciences, 8,* 43–83.

Rachlin, H. (1989). *Judgment, decision and choice* (3rd ed.). New York: W. H. Freeman.

Rachlin, H. (1992). Teleological behaviorism. *American Psychologist, 47,* 1371–82.

Rachlin, H. (1993). The context of pigeon and human choice. *Behavior and Philosophy, 21,* 1–18.

Rachlin, H. (1994). *Behavior and mind: The roots of modern psychology.* New York: Oxford University Press.

Raphelson, A. C. (1979). The unique role of the history of psychology in undergraduate education. *Teaching of Psychology, 6,* 12–14.

Ratliff, F. (1965). *Mach bands: Quantitative studies on neural networks in the retina.* San Francisco: Holden-Day.

Reese, E. P. (1986). Learning about teaching about learning: Presenting behavior analysis in an introductory survey course. In W. P. Makosky (Ed.), *The G. Stanley Hall lecture series* (Vol. 6, pp. 69–127). Washington, DC: American Psychological Association.

Reichenbach, H. (1938). *Experience and prediction.* Chicago: University of Chicago Press.

Reisman, J. M. (1976). *A history of clinical psychology.* New York: Irvington.

Rescorla, R. A. (1969). Pavlovian conditioned inhibition. *Psychological Bulletin, 72,* 77–94.

Restle, F. (1957). Discrimination of cues in mazes: A resolution of the "place-vs.-response" question. *Psychological Review, 64*, 217–28.

Richards, R. J. (1987). *Darwin and the emergence of evolutionary theories of mind and behavior*. Chicago: University of Chicago Press.

Richelle, M. (1993). *B. F. Skinner: A reappraisal*. Hillsdale, NJ: Lawrence Erlbaum Associates.

Ringen, J. D. (1976). Explanation, teleology, and operant behaviorism. *Philosophy of Science, 43*, 223–53.

Robertson, L. C. (1987). A cognitive approach to behavior. In S. Modgil & C. Modgil (Eds.), *B. F. Skinner: Consensus and controversy*. London: Falmer.

Robinson, D. N. (1976). *An intellectual history of psychology*. New York: Macmillan.

Robinson, D. N. (1979). The history of psychology and the ends of instruction. *Teaching of Psychology, 6*, 4–6.

Robinson, D. N. (1994). How the *American Psychologist* saw B. F. Skinner. *Theory & Psychology, 4*, 372–73.

Roediger, H. L. (1980). Memory metaphors in cognitive psychology. *Memory and Cognition, 8*, 231–46.

Rosnow, R. L., & Georgoudi, M. (Eds.). (1986). *Contextualism and understanding in behavioral science: Implications for research and theory*. New York: Praeger.

Ross, L. (1977). The intuitive psychologist and his shortcomings: Distortions in the attribution process. In L. Berkowitz (Ed.), *Advances in experimental social psychology* (Vol. 10, pp. 173–220). New York: Academic Press.

Rossi, P. (1968). *Francis Bacon: From magic to science* (S. Rabinovitch, Trans.). Chicago: University of Chicago Press.

Russell, B. (1926, August). [Review of *The meaning of meaning*.] *Dial, 81*, 114–21.

Russell, B. (1927). *Philosophy*. New York: Norton.

Ryle, G. (1949). *The concept of mind*. London: Hutchinson House.

Salzinger, K. (1967). The problem of response class in verbal behavior. In K. Salzinger & S. Salzinger (Eds.), *Research in verbal behavior and some neuropsychological implications* (pp. 35–56). New York: Academic Press.

Salzinger, K. (1994). On Watson. In J. T. Todd & E. K. Morris (Eds.), *Modern perspectives on John B. Watson and classical behaviorism* (pp. 151–58). Westport, CT: Greenwood.

Samelson, F. (1974). History, origin myth, and ideology: Comte's "discovery" of social psychology. *Journal for the Theory of Social Behaviour, 4*, 217–31.

Samelson, F. (1975). On the science and politics of the IQ. *Social Research, 42*, 466–88.

Samelson, F. (1980). J. B. Watson's Little Albert, Cyril Burt's twins, and the need for a critical science. *American Psychologist, 35*, 619–25.

Samelson, F. (1981). Struggle for scientific authority: The reception of Watson's behaviorism, 1913–1920. *Journal of the History of the Behavioral Sciences, 17*, 399–425.

Samelson, F. (1994). John B. Watson in 1913: Rhetoric and practice. In J. T. Todd & E. K. Morris (Eds.), *Modern perspectives on John B. Watson and classical behaviorism* (pp. 3–18). Westport, CT: Greenwood.

Sanders, C. (1978). *Die behavioristische revolution in der psychologie*. Salzberg: Otto Muller Verlag.

Santayana, G. (1967). *Character and opinion in the United States*. New York: Norton. (Original work published 1924.)

Sarason, S. B. (1981). *Psychology misdirected.* New York: Free Press.

Sarbin, T. R. (1977). Contextualism: A world view from modern psychology. In A. W. Landfield (Ed.), *Nebraska symposium on motivation* (Vol. 24, pp. 1–41). Lincoln: University of Nebraska Press.

Scarborough, E., & Furumoto, L. (1987). *Untold lives: The first generation of American women psychologists.* New York: Columbia University Press.

Scharff, J. L. (1982). Skinner's concept of the operant: From necessitarian to probabilistic causality. *Behaviorism, 10,* 45–54.

Scheerer, E. (1983). *Die verhaltensanalyse.* Berlin: Springer-Verlag.

Schick, K. (1971). Operants. *Journal of the Experimental Analysis of Behavior, 15,* 413–23.

Schmitt, D. R. (1984). Interpersonal relations: Cooperation and competition. *Journal of the Experimental Analysis of Behavior, 42,* 377–83.

Schnaitter, R. (1975). Between organism and environment. A review of B. F. Skinner's *About behaviorism. Journal of the Experimental Analysis of Behavior, 23,* 297–307.

Schnaitter, R. (1980). Science and verbal behavior. *Behaviorism, 8,* 153–60.

Schnaitter, R. (1984). Skinner on the "mental" and the "physical." *Behaviorism, 12,* 1–14.

Schnaitter, R. (1985). The haunted clockwork: Reflections on Gilbert Ryle's *The concept of mind. Journal of the Experimental Analysis of Behavior, 43,* 145–53.

Schnaitter, R. (1986). Behavior as a function of inner states and outer circumstances. In T. Thompson & M. Zeiler (Eds.), *Analysis and integration of behavioral units* (pp. 247–74). Hillsdale, NJ: Lawrence Erlbaum Associates.

Schnaitter, R. (1987). Behaviorism is not cognitive and cognitivism is not behavioral. *Behaviorism, 15,* 1–11.

Schneider, S. M., & Morris, E. K. (1987). A history of the term *radical behaviorism*: From Watson to Skinner. *The Behavior Analyst, 10,* 27–39.

Schneider, S. M., & Morris, E. K. (1988, May). *On Verplanck (1954) on Skinner (1938): A retrospective analysis.* Paper presented at the Annual meeting of the Association for Behavior Analysis, Philadelphia, PA.

Schoenfeld, W. N. (1969). J. R. Kantor's *Objective psychology of grammar and psychology and logic*: A retrospective appreciation. *Journal of the Experimental Analysis of Beavior, 12,* 329–47.

Schoenfeld, W. N., & Cole, B. K. (1972). *Stimulus schedules.* New York: Harper & Row.

Schrödinger, E. (1928). *Collected papers on wave mechanics.* London: Blackie & Son.

Schwartz, B., & Gamzu, E. (1977). Pavlovian control of operant behavior. In W. K. Honig & J. E. R. Staddon (Eds.), *Handbook of operant behavior* (pp. 53–97). Englewood Cliffs, NJ: Prentice-Hall.

Segal, E. (1977). Toward a coherent psychology of language. In W. K. Honig & J. E. R. Staddon (Eds.), *Handbook of operant behavior* (pp. 628–53). Englewood Cliffs, NJ: Prentice-Hall.

Segal, E., & Lachman, R. (1972). Complex behavior or higher mental process. *American Psychologist, 27,* 46–55.

Shepard, R. N. (1987). Toward a universal law of generalization for psychological science. *Science, 237,* 1317–23.

Sherrington, C. S. (1906). *The integrative action of the nervous system.* New Haven: Yale University Press.

Shimp, C. P. (1976). Organization in memory and behavior. *Journal of the Experimental Analysis of Behavior, 26*, 113–30.

Shimp, C. (1979). The local organization of behaviour: Method and theory. In M. Zeiler & P. Harzem (Eds.), *Reinforcement and the organization of behaviour* (Vol. 1, pp. 261–95). New York: John Wiley & Sons.

Sidman, M. (1986). Functional analysis of emergent verbal classes. In T. Thompson & M. D. Zeiler (Eds.), *Analysis and integration of behavioral units* (pp. 213–45). Hillsdale, NJ: Lawrence Erlbaum Associates.

Sigurdardottir, Z. G., Green, G., & Saunders, R. R. (1990). Equivalence classes generated by sequence training. *Journal of the Experimental Analysis of Behavior, 53*, 47–63.

Simonton, D. K. (1990). *Psychology, science, and history: An introduction to historiometry.* New Haven: Yale University Press.

Simpson, G. G. (1951). *Horses.* New York: Oxford University Press.

Skinner, B. F. (1931). The concept of the reflex in the description of behavior. *Journal of General Psychology, 5*, 427–58.

Skinner, B. F. (1935). The generic nature of the concepts of stimulus and response. *Journal of General Psychology, 12*, 40–65.

Skinner, B. F. (1937a). The distribution of associated words. *The Psychological Record, 1*, 71–76.

Skinner, B. F. (1937b). Two types of conditioned reflex: A reply to Konorski and Miller. *Journal of General Psychology, 16*, 272–79.

Skinner, B. F. (1938). *The behavior of organisms: An experimental analysis.* New York: Appleton-Century.

Skinner, B. F. (1940). The nature of the operant reserve. *Psychological Bulletin, 37*, 423.

Skinner, B. F. (1945). The operational analysis of psychological terms. *Psychological Review, 52*, 270–77, 291–94.

Skinner, B. F. (1947). Experimental psychology. In W. Dennis, B. F. Skinner, R. R. Sears, E. L. Kelly, C. Rogers, J. C. Flanagan, C. T. Morgan, & R. Likert (Eds.), *Current trends in psychology* (pp. 16–49). Pittsburgh: University of Pittsburgh Press.

Skinner, B. F. (1948). *Walden two.* New York: Macmillan.

Skinner, B. F. (1950). Are theories of learning necessary? *Psychological Review, 57*, 193–216.

Skinner, B. F. (1953). *Science and human behavior.* New York: Macmillan.

Skinner, B. F. (1956). A case history in scientific method. *American Psychologist, 11*, 221–33.

Skinner, B. F. (1957). *Verbal behavior.* New York: Appleton-Century-Crofts.

Skinner, B. F. (1958). Diagramming schedules of reinforcement. *Journal of the Experimental Analysis of Behavior, 1*, 67–68.

Skinner, B. F. (1960). Pigeons in a pelican. *American Psychologist, 15*, 28–37.

Skinner, B. F. (1961a). *Cumulative record* (enl. ed.). New York: Appleton-Century-Crofts.

Skinner, B. F. (1961b). Current trends in experimental psychology. In *Cumulative record* (enl. ed., pp. 223–41). New York: Appleton-Century-Crofts. (Original work published 1947.)

Skinner, B. F. (1962). Operandum. *Journal of the Experimental Analysis of Behavior, 5*, 224.

Skinner, B. F. (1966a). The phylogeny and ontogeny of behavior. *Science, 153,* 1204–13.
Skinner, B. F. (1966b). Preface to the seventh printing. In *The behavior of organisms: An experimental analysis* (pp. ix–xiv). New York: Appleton-Century-Crofts.
Skinner, B. F. (1966c). What is the experimental analysis of behavior? *Journal of the Experimental Analysis of Behavior, 9,* 213–18.
Skinner, B. F. (1967). *The technology of teaching.* New York: Appleton-Century-Crofts.
Skinner, B. F. (1969). *Contingencies of reinforcement: A theoretical analysis.* New York: Appleton-Century-Crofts.
Skinner, B. F. (1970). B. F. Skinner. In G. Lindzey (Ed.), *History of psychology in autobiography* (Vol. 5, pp. 387–413). Chicago: University of Chicago Press.
Skinner, B. F. (1971). *Beyond freedom and dignity.* New York: Knopf.
Skinner, B. F. (1972a). *Cumulative record* (3rd ed.). New York: Appleton-Century-Crofts.
Skinner, B. F. (1972b). A lecture on "having" a poem. In B. F. Skinner, *Cumulative record* (3rd ed.) (pp. 345–55). New York: Appleton-Century-Crofts.
Skinner, B. F. (1972c). The operational analysis of psychological terms. In B. F. Skinner, *Cumulative record* (3rd ed.) (pp. 370–84). New York: Appleton-Century-Crofts. (Original work published 1945.)
Skinner, B. F. (1973). Answers for my critics. In H. Wheeler (Ed.), *Beyond the punitive society* (pp. 256–66). London: Wildwood House.
Skinner, B. F. (1974). *About behaviorism.* New York: Knopf.
Skinner, B. F. (1975). The shaping of phylogenic behavior. *Journal of the Experimental Analysis of Behavior, 24,* 117–20.
Skinner, B. F. (1976a). Farewell, my LOVELY. *Journal of the Experimental Analysis of Behavior, 25,* 218.
Skinner, B. F. (1976b). *Particulars of my life.* New York: Knopf.
Skinner, B. F. (1977a). Herrnstein and the evolution of behaviorism. *American Psychologist, 32,* 1006–12.
Skinner, B. F. (1977b). Why I am not a cognitive psychologist. *Behaviorism, 5,* 1–10.
Skinner, B. F. (1978). *Reflections on behaviorism and society.* Englewood Cliffs, NJ: Prentice-Hall.
Skinner, B. F. (1979). *The shaping of a behaviorist: Part two of an autobiography.* New York: Knopf.
Skinner, B. F. (1981a). Pavlov's influence on psychology in America. *Journal of the History of the Behavioral Sciences, 17,* 242–45.
Skinner, B. F. (1981b). Selection by consequences. *Science, 213,* 501–504.
Skinner, B. F. (1982). A lecture on "having" a poem. In R. Epstein (Ed.), *Skinner for the classroom: Selected papers* (pp. 191–203). Champaign, IL: Research Press. (Original work published 1972.)
Skinner, B. F. (1983). *A matter of consequences: Part three of an autobiography.* New York: Knopf.
Skinner, B. F. (1984a). The evolution of behavior. *Journal of the Experimental Analysis of Behavior, 41,* 217–21.
Skinner, B. F. (1984b). Phylogenic and ontogenic environments. *The Behavioral and Brain Sciences, 7,* 701–707.
Skinner, B. F. (1985). Cognitive science and behaviourism. *British Journal of Psychology, 76,* 291–301.

Skinner, B. F. (1987a). Behaviorism, Skinner on. In R. L. Gregory (Ed.), *The Oxford companion to the mind* (pp. 74–75). New York: Oxford University Press.

Skinner, B. F. (1987b). *Upon further reflection*. Englewood Cliffs, NJ: Prentice-Hall.

Skinner, B. F. (1988). Replies to commentators. In A. C. Catania & S. Harnad (Eds.), *The selection of behavior*. New York: Cambridge University Press.

Skinner, B. F. (1989a). The origins of cognitive thought. *American Psychologist, 44,* 13–18.

Skinner, B. F. (1989b). [Review of C. L. Hull's *Principles of behavior.*] *Journal of the Experimental Analysis of Behavior, 51,* 287–90. (Original work published in 1944.)

Skinner, B. F., & Vaughan, M. E. (1983). *Enjoy old age.* New York: Norton.

Smith, L. D. (1986). *Behaviorism and logical positivism: A reassessment of the alliance.* Stanford: Stanford University Press.

Smith, L. D. (1992). On prediction and control: B. F. Skinner and the technological ideal of science. *American Psychologist, 47,* 216–23.

Smith, L. D. (1993). Natural science and unnatural technology. *American Psychologist, 48,* 588–89.

Smith, S., & Guthrie, E. R. (1921). *General psychology in terms of behavior.* New York: Century.

Smith, T. L. (1986). Biology as allegory: A review of Elliott Sober's *The nature of selection. Journal of the Experimental Analysis of Behavior, 46,* 105–12.

Smoke, K. L. (1932). An objective study of concept formation. *Psychological Monographs, 42* (4, Whole No. 191).

Snapper, A. G. (1990). Control of contingencies of reinforcement in the laboratory. *The Behavior Analyst, 13,* 61–66.

Snoeyenbos, M. H., & Putney, R. T. (1980). Psychology and science. *American Journal of Psychology, 93,* 579–92.

Sober, E. (1983). Mentalism and behaviorism in comparative psychology. In D. W. Rajecki (Ed.), *Comparing behavior: Studying man studying animals* (pp. 113–42). Hillsdale, NJ: Lawrence Erlbaum Associates.

Sokal, M. M. (1984). History of psychology and history of science: Reflections on two subdisciplines, their relationship, and their convergence. *Revista de Historia de la Psicologia, 5,* 337–47.

Sokal, M. M., & Rafail, P. A. (1982). *A guide to manuscript collections in the history of psychology and related areas.* Milwood, NY: Kraus International.

Spence, K. W. (1948). The postulates and methods of behaviorism. *Psychological Review, 55,* 67–78.

Spence, K. (1966). Foreword to the seventh printing. In C. L. Hull, *Principles of behavior: An introduction to behavior theory* (pp. vii–xvii). New York: Appleton-Century-Crofts.

Stagner, R. (1988). *A history of psychological theories.* New York: Macmillan.

Stevens, S. S. (1939). Psychology and the science of science. *Psychological Bulletin, 36,* 221–63.

Stocking, G. W., Jr. (1965). On the limits of "presentism" and "historicism" in the historiography of the behavioral sciences. *Journal of the History of the Behavioral Sciences, 1,* 211–17.

Suppe, F. (1977). *The structure of scientific theories* (2nd ed.). Urbana: University of Illinois Press.

Suppe, F. (1984). Beyond Skinner and Kuhn. *New Ideas in Psychology, 2,* 89–104.

Sutherland, S. (1993). [Review of D. W. Bjork's *B. F. Skinner: A life.*] *Nature, 364,* 767.

Tawney, J. W., & Gast, D. L. (1984). *Single subject research in special education.* Columbus, OH: Merrill.

Terrace, H. S. (1963). Discrimination learning with and without errors. *Journal of the Experimental Analysis of Behavior, 6,* 1–27.

Thompson, T. (1984). The examining magistrate for nature. *Journal of the Experimental Analysis of Behavior, 41,* 211–21.

Thompson, T. (1988). *Benedictus* behavior analysis: B. F. Skinner's magnum opus at fifty. *Contemporary Psychology, 33,* 397–402.

Thompson, T., & Zeiler, M. D. (Eds.). (1986). *Analysis and integration of behavioral units.* Hillsdale, NJ: Lawrence Erlbaum Associates.

Timberlake, W. (1988). *The behavior of organisms:* Purposive behavior as a type of reflex. *Journal of the Experimental Analysis of Behavior, 50,* 305–17.

Titchener, E. B. (1914). On "Psychology as the behaviorist views it." *Proceedings of the American Philosophical Society, 53,* 1–17.

Todd, J. T. (1987). The great power of steady misrepresentation: Behaviorism's presumed denial of instinct. *The Behavior Analyst, 10,* 117–18.

Todd, J. T. (1994a). Conclusion: Watson now. In J. T. Todd & E. K. Morris (Eds.), *Modern perspectives on John B. Watson and classical behaviorism* (pp. 159-168). Westport, CT: Greenwood.

Todd, J. T. (1994b). What psychology has to say about John B. Watson: Classical behaviorism in psychology textbooks, 1920–1989. In J. T. Todd & E. K. Morris (Eds.), *Modern perspectives on John B. Watson and classical behaviorism* (pp. 75–107). Westport, CT: Greenwood.

Todd, J. T., Dewsbury, D. A., Logue, A. W., & Dryden, N. A. (1994). John B. Watson: A bibliography of published works. In J. T. Todd & E. K. Morris (Eds.), *Modern perspectives on John B. Watson and classical behaviorism* (pp. 169–78). Westport, CT: Greenwood.

Todd, J. T., & Morris, E. K. (1983). Misconception and miseducation: Presentations of radical behaviorism in psychology textbooks. *The Behavior Analyst, 6,* 153–60.

Todd, J. T., & Morris, E. K. (1986). The early research of John B. Watson: Before the behaviorist revolution. *The Behavior Analyst, 9,* 71–86.

Todd, J. T., & Morris, E. K. (1988, May). *The behavior of organisms* at fifty. Symposium conducted at the meeting of the Association for Behavior Analysis, Philadelphia, PA.

Todd, J. T., & Morris, E. K. (1992). Case histories in the great power of steady misrepresentation. *American Psychologist, 47,* 1441–53.

Todd, J. T., & Morris, E. K. (1993). Change and be ready to change again. *American Psychologist, 48,* 1158–59.

Todd, J. T., & Morris, E. K. (Eds.). (1994). *Modern perspectives on John B. Watson and classical behaviorism.* Westpost, CT: Greenwood.

Tolman, E. C. (1932). *Purposive behavior in animals and men.* New York: Century.

Tolman, E. C. (1942). *Drives toward war.* New York: Appleton-Century.

Tolman, E. C. (1949). Discussion [from Interrelationships between perception and personality: A symposium]. *Journal of Personality, 18,* 48–50.

Tolman, E. C. (1959). Principles of purposive behavior. In S. Koch (Ed.), *Psychology: A study of a science. Vol. 2. General systematic formulations, learning, and special processes* (pp. 92–157). New York: McGraw Hill.

Toulmin, S. (1972). *Human understanding*. Princeton: Princeton University Press.

Toulmin, S., & Leary, D. E. (1985). The cult of empiricism in psychology, and beyond. In S. Koch & D. E. Leary (Eds.), *A century of psychology as science* (pp. 594–617). New York: McGraw Hill.

Ullmann, L. P., & Krasner, L. (Eds.). (1965). *Case studies in behavior modification*. New York: Holt, Rinehart & Winston.

Ulrich, R., Stachnik, T., & Mabry, J. (Eds.). (1966). *Control of human behavior*. Glenview, IL: Scott, Foresman.

Urbach, P. (1987). *Francis Bacon's philosophy of science*. La Salle, IL: Open Court.

van der Werden, B. L. (1967). *Sources of quantum mechanics*. New York: Dover Publications.

Vaughan, M. E., & Michael, J. L. (1982). Automatic reinforcement: An important but ignored concept. *Behaviorism, 10,* 217–27.

Vaughan, W. (1987). Behaviorism. In G. Adelman (Ed.), *Encyclopedia of neuroscience* (Vol. 1, pp. 124–26). Boston: Birkhauser.

Verhave, T. (1990). Reflections on the impact of K & S as a systematic textbook. *The Behavior Analyst, 13,* 51–60.

Verplanck, W. S. (1954). Burrhus F. Skinner. In W. K. Estes, S. Koch, K. MacCorquodale, P. Meehl, C. G. Mueller, Jr., W. N. Schoenfeld, & W. S. Verplanck (Eds.), *Modern learning theories: A critical analysis of five examples* (pp. 267–316). New York: Appleton-Century-Crofts.

Viney, W., Wertheimer, M., & Wertheimer, M. (1979). *History of psychology: A guide to information sources*. Detroit: Gale.

von Neumann, J. (1955). *Mathematical foundations of quantum mechanics*. Princeton: Princeton University Press.

von Weizsäcker, C. F. (1980). *The unity of nature*. New York: Farrar Straus Giroux.

Vorsteg, R. H. (1974). Operant reinforcement theory and determinism. *Behaviorism, 2,* 108–19.

Wachtel, P. L. (1977). *Psychoanalysis and behavior therapy*. New York: Basic.

Watkins, M. J. (1990). Mediationism and the obfuscation of memory. *American Psychologist, 45,* 328–35.

Watson, J. B. (1913). Psychology as the behaviorist views it. *Psychological Review, 20,* 158–77.

Watson, J. B. (1919). *Psychology from the standpoint of a behaviorist*. Philadelphia: Lippincott.

Watson, J. B. (1924a). *Behaviorism*. New York: People's Institute.

Watson, J. B. (1924b). *Psychology from the standpoint of a behaviorist* (2nd ed.). Philadelphia: Lippincott.

Watson, J. B. (1930). *Behaviorism* (rev. ed.). Chicago: University of Chicago Press.

Watson, J. B. (1936). John B. Watson. In C. Murchison (Ed.), *A history of psychology in autobiography* (Vol. 3, pp. 271–81). Worcester, MA: Clark University Press.

Watson, J. B., & Rayner, R. (1920). Conditioned emotional reactions. *Journal of Experimental Psychology, 3,* 1–14.

Watson, J. D. (1968). *The double helix: A personal account of the discovery of the structure of DNA.* New York: Atheneum.

Watson, R. I. (1966). The role and use of history in the psychology curriculum. *Journal of the History of the Behavioral Sciences, 2,* 66–69.

Watson, R. I. (1971). Prescriptions as operative in the history of psychology. *Journal of the History of Psychology, 7,* 311–22.

Watson, R. I. (1976a). *Eminent contributors to psychology, Vol. 1. A bibliography of primary sources* (pp. 438–39). New York: Springer.

Watson, R. I. (1976b). *Eminent contributors to psychology, Vol. 2. A bibliography of secondary sources* (pp. 1060–66). New York: Springer.

Watson, R. I. (1977). The history of psychology as a specialty: A personal view of its first fifteen years. In J. Brozek & R. B. Evans (Eds.), *R. I. Watson's selected papers on the history of psychology* (pp. 61–73). Hanover, NH: University of New Hampshire Press.

Webster's ninth new collegiate dictionary. (1987). Springfield, MA: Merriam-Webster.

Weigel, R. G., & Gottfurcht, J. W. (1972). Faculty geneologies: A stimulus for student involvement in history and systems. *American Psychologist, 27,* 981–83.

Weimer, W. B. (1974). The history of psychology and its retrieval from historiography: I. The problematic nature of history. *Science Studies, 4,* 235–58.

Weiss, A. P. (1925). *A theoretical basis of human behavior.* Columbus, OH: Adams.

Weiss, J., & Sampson, H. (1986). *The psychoanalytic process.* New York: Guilford.

Wendt, G. R. (1949). The development of a psychological cult [Letter to the journal editor]. *American Psychologist, 4,* 426.

Wertheimer, M. (1980). Historical research—Why? In J. Brozek & L. J. Pongratz (Eds.), *Historiography of modern psychology* (pp. 3–23). Toronto: Hogrefe.

Wessells, M. G. (1981). A critique of Skinner's views on the explanatory inadequacy of cognitive theories. *Behaviorism, 9,* 153–70.

Wessells, M. G. (1982). A critique of Skinner's views on the obstructive nature of cognitive theories. *Behaviorism, 10,* 65–84.

Whitehurst, G. J., & Valdez-Menchaca, M. C. (1988). What is the role of reinforcement in early language acquisition? *Child Development, 59,* 430–40.

Whitney, C. (1986). *Francis Bacon and modernity.* New Haven: Yale University Press.

Whorf, B. L. (1956). *Language, thought and reading.* Cambridge: MIT Press.

Wickham, H. (1931). *The misbehaviorists: Pseudo-science and modern times.* New York: The Dial Press.

Wiebe, R. (1967). *The search for order, 1870–1920.* Westport, CT: Greenwood Press.

Wiklander, N. (1989). *From laboratory to utopia: An inquiry into the early psychology and social philosophy of B. F. Skinner.* Unpublished doctoral dissertation, Grotenborg, Norway.

Williams, B. A. (1986). On the role of theory in behavior analysis. *Behaviorism, 14,* 111–24.

Williams, B. A. (1987). The other psychology of animal learning: A review of Mackintosh's *Conditioning and associative learning. Journal of the Experimental Analysis of Behavior, 48,* 175–86.

Williams, R. A., & Buskist, W. F. (1983). Twenty-five years of *JEAB*: A survey of selected demographic characteristics related to publication trends. *The Behavior Analyst, 6,* 161–65.

Willis, J., & Giles, D. (1978). Behaviorism in the twentieth century: What we have here is a failure to communicate. *Behavior Therapy, 9*, 15–27.

Wittgenstein, L. (1922). *Tractatus logico-philosophicus* (C. K. Ogden, Trans.). New York: Harcourt Brace.

Wittgenstein, L. (1953). *Philosophical investigations.* New York: Macmillan.

Wolf, E. (1939). [Review of *The behavior of organisms.*] *Journal of Genetic Psychology, 54*, 475–79.

Wolford, G., & Bower, G. H. (1969). Continuity theory revisited: Rejected for the wrong reasons? *Psychological Review, 76*, 515–18.

Wolman, B. B. (1968). *Historical roots of contemporary psychology.* New York: Harper & Row.

Wolpe, J. (1963). *The practice of behavior therapy.* New York: Pergamon.

Wood, W. S. (1986). Bertrand Russell's review of *The meaning of meaning* (reprinted), with introductory comments. *Journal of the Experimental Analysis of Behavior, 45*, 107–13.

Wood, W. S. (1994). An American classic: A review of *B. F. Skinner: A life* by D. W. Bjork. *The Behavior Analyst, 17*, 177–81.

Woodward, W. R. (1980). Toward a critical historiography of psychology. In J. Brozek & L. J. Pongratz (Eds.), *Historiography of modern psychology* (pp. 29–67). Toronto: Hogrefe.

Woodward, W. R. (1982). The "discovery" of social behaviorism and social learning theory, 1870–1980. *American Psychologist, 37*, 396–410.

Woodward, W. R. (1985). [Review of *Die verhaltensanalyse.*] *Journal of the History of the Behavioral Sciences, 21*, 395–98.

Woodworth, R. S. (1931). *Contemporary schools of psychology.* New York: Ronald.

Wright, J. (1987). The illusion of a critique [Response to Bethlehem]. In S. Modgil & C. Modgil (Eds.). *B. F. Skinner: Consensus and controversy* (pp. 98–100). London: Falmer.

Wyatt, W. J., Hawkins, R. P., & Davis, P. (1986). Behaviorism: Are reports of its death exaggerated? *The Behavior Analyst, 9*, 101–105.

Young, R. M. (1966). Scholarship and the history of the behavioural sciences. *History of Science, 5*, 1–51.

Zeiler, M. D. (1977). Schedules of reinforcement: The controlling variables. In W. K. Honig & J. E. R. Staddon (Eds.), *Handbook of operant behavior* (pp. 201–232). Englewood Cliffs, NJ: Prentice-Hall.

Zempel, E. N., & Verkler, L. A. (Eds.). (1984). *First editions: A guide to identification.* Peoria, IL: Spoon Reviewer Press.

Zukav, G. (1980). *The dancing wu li masters.* New York: Bantam Books.

Zuriff, G. E. (1979a). The demise of behaviorism—An exaggerated rumor? A review of Mackenzie's *Behaviorism and the limits of scientific method. Journal of the Experimental Analysis of Behavior, 32*, 129–36.

Zuriff, G. E. (1979b). Ten inner causes. *Behaviorism, 7*, 1–8.

Zuriff, G. E. (1980). Radical behaviorist epistemology. *Psychological Bulletin, 87*, 337–50.

Zuriff, G. E. (1985). *Behaviorism: A conceptual reconstruction.* New York: Columbia University Press.

Index

Absolute rate, 172
Absolute truth, 108
Ad Hoc Committee on the History of Behavior Analysis, 201
Adjunctive behavior, 172
Advancement of Learning (Bacon), 43
Akron, University of, 131
American Journal of Psychology, 19
American Psychological Association (APA), 7, 28, 107, 160
American Psychologist, 211
Analysis (term), 33
Analysis of Sensations (Mach), 22, 44
Anderson, John R., 180
Angell, James R., 208
Anticipations of nature, 43
Antiformalism, 50
Antimentalism, 54. *See also* Mentalism
Antiquarianism (in history), 132–133
Appleton-Century (Appleton-Century-Crofts), 4–6, 7–11, 16–17
Applied psychology, 33
Archival collections, 201
Archives for the History of Psychology in America (University of Akron), 131, 201
"Are Theories of Learning Necessary" (Skinner), 28
Argument X, 80, 82, 182
Aristotle, 74, 208
Arizona State University, 15
Arrowsmith (Lewis), 150

Artificial intelligence, 79
Artificial selection, 186, 191–193
Association for Behavior Analysis (ABA), 19, 28; founding of, 213
Association for Behavior Analysis Newsletter, 212
Associationism, 210
Attention, 114
Attneave, Fred, 66
Attribution theory, 91–97, 103
Autobiographical material, 212
Autoclitic, 120
Autonomy (automomous initiating agent), 106
Autoshaping, 26
Averaging (of data), 157

B. F. Skinner Foundation, 18
Baars, Bernard J., 57
Babkin, Boris P., 205
Bacon, Francis (Baconian), 40, 149, 179; on description, 42; on experimentation, 40–42
Balmer, Johann J. (Balmer formula), 113
Bandura, Albert, 208
Beauty and Human Nature (Chandler), 9
Begelman, D. A., 117, 213
Behavior: contingency-shaped, 123; emitted, 118; functional definition of, 35–38; of individual organisms, 7; as lawful and orderly, 7, 10, 14, 19, 29,

About the Editors and Contributors

A. CHARLES CATANIA is Professor of Psychology at the University of Maryland, Baltimore County. He holds a Ph.D. in Psychology from Harvard University and has wide-ranging interests in the experimental, applied, and theoretical branches of behavior analysis. He has served as Editor of the *Journal of the Experimental Analysis of Behavior* (1967–1969) and is currently Associate Editor of *Behavioral and Brain Sciences*. He has also served as President of the Association for Behavior Analysis (1983) and Division 25 (Experimental Analysis of Behavior) of the American Psychological Association (1976–1979). His books include *Contemporary Research in Operant Behavior, The Selection of Behavior: The Operant Behaviorism of B. F. Skinner* (edited with S. Harnad), and *Learning* (3rd ed.).

STEPHEN R. COLEMAN is Professor of Psychology at Cleveland State University. His interests include history at several levels: the history of behaviorism and behavior (conditioning theory), the history and sociology of research specialties, historical methodology, and related topics. He has published on these subjects in a variety of behavior-oriented journals.

WILLARD F. DAY, JR. (1926–1989) was Professor of Psychology at the University of Nevada, Reno. His work on the history and philosophy of radical behaviorism was seminal in establishing this area of scholarship. He contributed early papers on the relationship between radical behaviorism and phenomenology and between Skinner's operationism and Wittgenstein's analytic philosophy. In 1972, he founded the journal, *Behaviorism*, and served as its editor until 1984. His achievements were honored by his election as a Fellow in the APA divisions for theoretical and philosophical psychology, the history of psychology, and the experimental analysis of behavior.

JAMES A. DINSMOOR is Professor Emeritus of Psychology at Indiana University. His major research interests include conditioned reinforcement, stimulus control, and the aversive control of behavior. He has served as President of the Society for the Experimental Analysis of Behavior, the Midwestern Psychological Association, and Division 25 (Experimental Analysis of Behavior) of the American Psychological Association.

ROBERT EPSTEIN is Founder and Director Emeritus of the Cambridge Center for Behavioral Studies in Cambridge, Massachusetts. He has served as Professor and Chair of the Department of Psychology at National University in San Diego and was recently appointed that university's first Research Professor. He earned his Ph.D. in Psychology from Harvard University, where he worked with B. F. Skinner. He has conducted research on creativity, problem solving, self-control, imitation, humor, and other topics.

ERNEST R. HILGARD is Professor Emeritus of Psychology at Stanford University. He has written on learning theory, the history of psychology, hypnosis, and other topics. He is author of "Review of B. F. Skinner, *The Behavior of Organisms*," *Conditioning and Learning* (with Donald G. Marquis), and *Psychology in America: A Historical Survey*.

PHILIP N. HINELINE is Professor of Psychology at Temple University. He recently completed a four-year term as Editor of the *Journal of the Experimental Analysis of Behavior* (*JEAB*) and as President of the Association for Behavior Analysis. He is currently Review Editor for *JEAB* and President of Division 25 (Experimental Analysis of Behavior) of the American Psychological Association. His initial research was in the domain of avoidance theory, which led to a focus on actions with respect to short-term versus long-term consequences. The current context for that work is an examination of relationships between biological foraging theory and phenomena of conditioning. An additional interest concerns the nature and language of explanation, which is the topic of his contribution to this book.

LISA M. JOHNSON is a Research Associate at the Greater Kansas City Mental Health Foundation. She has published, presented, and conducted research in the experimental analysis of behavior and on the relationship between violence and mental illness.

FRED S. KELLER is Professor Emeritus of Psychology at Columbia University. He received his B.S. degree at Tufts in 1926 and went on to Harvard University for his M.A. (1928) and Ph.D. (1931). He has held positions at Colgate University (7 years), Columbia University (26 years), Arizona State (3 years), and Western Michigan University (5 years). He was a Fulbright Professor at the University of Sao Paulo in 1961 and Professor at the University of Brasilia in 1964. He occupied the Cecil H. and Ida Green Chair at Texas Christian University in 1973 and was at Georgetown University in 1974 and 1975. Professor Keller is author of several textbooks and numerous articles on animal behavior, human skill, and teaching. Most notably, he is co-author (with W. N. Schoenfeld) of *Principles of Psychology*, which served as the introduction to behaviorism for many of the behavior analysts practicing today. Among his many honors, he received a Certificate of Merit from President Truman in 1948 for his work on radio-operator training in World War II, a Distinguished Teaching Award from the American Psychological Association in 1970, a Wundt Centennial Medal from the Brazilian Government in 1976, the Distinguished Contribution for Applications in Psychology Award from the APA in 1976, and a Lifetime Achievement Award in 1994 from the Association for Behavior Analysis.

TERRY J. KNAPP is Professor of Psychology at the University of Nevada, Las Vegas. His interests include the history of psychology, psychotherapy, and psychopathology. He co-edited (with Lynn Robertson) *Approaches to Cognition: Contrasts and Controversies*, and co-authored *Westphal's "Die Agoraphobie": The Beginnings of Agoraphobia*.

VICKI L. LEE is Senior Lecturer in the School of Graduate Studies at Monash University in Victoria, Australia. Dr. Lee has served on the editorial boards of several behavioral journals and has written in a variety of areas, particularly on conceptual issues in behavior analysis. She is the author of the recently published *Beyond Behaviorism*.

M. JACKSON MARR is Professor of Psychology at Georgia Institute of Technology, Atlanta. He has served as Associate Editor of the *Journal of the Experimental Analysis of Behavior* and on the editorial board of *The Behavior Analyst*. His present research interests include mathematical models of behavior dynamics; behavioral pharmacology; behavior analysis in zoo environments; and conceptual issues in radical behaviorism, with particular focus on relations to theory in physics.

BRYAN D. MIDGLEY is a doctoral student in the Department of Human Development at the University of Kansas. He has published and presented papers on behavior analysis and its relation to other approaches in the life sciences. He is author (with Edward K. Morris) of "Nature = f(Nurture): A Review of Oyama's *The Ontogeny of Information: Developmental Systems and Evolution*," published in the *Journal of the Experimental Analysis of Behavior*.

JAY MOORE is Professor of Psychology at the University of Wisconsin, Milwaukee. His interests include the laboratory study of operant behavior in nonhumans, particularly choice and conditioned reinforcement, as well as philosophical, historical, and conceptual issues in radical behaviorism. He is a former editor of *The Behavior Analyst* and has served on the editorial boards of several journals, including *The Psychological Record*, *Behaviorism*, and the *Journal of the Experimental Analysis of Behavior*.

EDWARD K. MORRIS is Professor in the Department of Human Development and Family Life at the University of Kansas. His research interests include topics in the experimental and conceptual analyses of behavior and in the history and philosophy of psychology. He is a past president of the Association for Behavior Analysis and a fellow in the American Psychological Association. Among his publications is *Modern Perspectives on John B. Watson and Classical Behaviorism* (co-edited with James T. Todd).

HOWARD RACHLIN is Professor of Psychology at the State University of New York at Stony Brook. He is interested in human and nonhuman discounting of probabilistic and delayed rewards, gambling, and choice. Two of his recent books are *Judgment, Decision and Choice* and *Behavior and Mind: The Roots of Modern Psychology*.

SUSAN M. SCHNEIDER is Assistant Professor of Psychology at St. Mary's College of Maryland. Her research interests include the quantitative analysis of behavior and the history and philosophy of the behavioral sciences.

B. F. SKINNER (1904–1990) was Edgar Pierce Professor of Psychology Emeritus at Harvard University. He was author of numerous books, including *The Behavior of Organisms*, *Walden Two*, *Verbal Behavior*, *Beyond Freedom and Dignity*, and *Enjoy Old Age* (with M. E. Vaughan). His awards and distinctions include the Distinguished Scientific Contribution Award of the American Psychological Association (1958), the National Medal of Science (1968), and Humanist of the Year Award of the American Humanist Society (1972).

LAURENCE D. SMITH is Associate Professor at the University of Maine and holds Master's degrees in Experimental Psychology and Philosophy of Science and a doctorate in the History of Psychology. He is author of *Behaviorism and Logical Positivism: A Reassessment of the Alliance*. He currently pursues experimental research on the psychology of science and historical research on pragmatism, behaviorism, and epistemology.

JAMES T. TODD is Associate Professor of Psychology at Eastern Michigan University. He holds a Ph.D. in Developmental and Child Psychology from the University of Kansas, is on the editorial board of *The Behavior Analyst*, and is the President of the Behavior Analysis Association of Michigan. He is co-editor (with Edward K. Morris) of *Modern Perspectives on John B. Watson and Classical Behaviorism*.

GERALD E. ZURIFF is Professor of Psychology at Wheaton College and Clinical Psychologist at the Massachusetts Institute of Technology. Parts of his chapter were written while he was Clinical Fellow at the Massachusetts General Hospital, Harvard Medical School. His speciality is conceptual issues in psychology, and he is author of *Behaviorism: A Conceptual Reconstruction.*